Good
Luck

# TRAINING YOUR RETRIEVER

# TRAINING
# YOUR
# RETRIEVER

## James Lamb Free

*With Special Reports by*
*S. Alan and Joan Williams*
*and*
*Perry E. and Zola R. Pound*

G. P. PUTNAM'S SONS    NEW YORK

FOR JULIE

I merely wrote it.
She had to read it—
again and again and again.

---

G. P. Putnam's Sons
*Publishers Since 1838*
200 Madison Avenue
New York, NY 10016

First G. P. Putnam's Sons Edition 1991

Library of Congress Cataloging-in-Publication Data

Free, James Lamb.
Training your retriever / by James Lamb Free; with special
reports by S. Alan and Joan Williams and Perry E. and Zola R. Pound.
p. cm.
Reprint. Originally published: 7th ed. New York: Coward, McCann & Geoghegan, c1980.
Includes bibliographical references and index.
ISBN 0-399-13620-7
1. Retrievers—Training. I. Title.
SF429.R4F7 1991 90-22789 CIP
636.7'52—dc20

*Printed in the United States of America*
5 6 7 8 9 10

This book is printed on acid-free paper.
∞

# CONTENTS

# PART III

*Illustrations follow page 80.*

# Acknowledgments

I AM DEEPLY INDEBTED TO:

Dr. William B. Wenner, who took all but five of the original photos for this book. He worked skillfully and patiently with the black dogs and me, every day for nearly a month. He took more than a thousand pictures in order to get the 120 which were snapped at just the right split second to illustrate clearly each step of training that we wanted to show.

Miss Evelyn M. Shafer, of New York, the famous field-trial photographer, for three pictures: 11, 119, and 122.

Miss Frances Sterry, for the picture of the litter of Labrador pups, Illustration 13.

The late Percy T. Jones, for the picture of Freehaven Jay used as Illustration 12.

Mrs. Thomas C. Marshall, for the picture of Ch. Bog's Jiggs, C.D., used as Illustration 129.

Mr. Ed Bruske, for the picture of the Curly-Coat used as Illustration 130.

Mr. Corey Winge, for the picture of the American Water Spaniel used as Illustration 131.

Mr. Jim Floyd and the Florida Game & Fresh Water Fish Commission for the picture of the Flat-Coat used as Illustration 132.

Mrs. George Murnane, owner, and Mr. Joseph M. Riser, trainer, for the picture of Double National Champion, Whygin Cork's Coot, used as front cover illustration.

Mrs. Walter Heller and Mr. Harold Mack, Jr., for the picture of the Chesapeake "Tule Tiger" used as illustration on the back cover.

The many members of the Labrador Retriever Club for their assistance and for their kind permission to use material from the

Club Year Books. The late J. Gould Remick, then the secretary, was most helpful in preparation of the first edition. His successor, William K. Laughlin, was equally cooperative. Thomas W. Merritt, Sr., has been generous with his assistance in the preparation of all three editions, both in his capacity as a Labrador Club officer and as editor-in-chief of *Retriever Field Trial News.*

The Chesapeake Club of America, for permission to use the records contained in its fine breed books, and for authority to quote the breed standard.

The Golden Retriever Club of America and the Irish Water Spaniel Club of America for permission to publish their breed standards.

The National Retriever Field Trial Club, Inc., which through its secretary-treasurer, George H. Gardner, M.D., graciously made extensive and accurate records available.

In equal measure, the National Amateur Retriever Club, which, through its president, Dr. John C. Lundy, made additional records available. These records were chiefly compiled by Richard H. Hecker and John W. McAssey, both great amateur handlers, who devoted many hours to checking and rechecking elusive facts.

In the greatest possible measure, *Field Trial News* and its successor, *Retriever Field Trial News.* That great gentleman, the late John Fraser, Jr., the founder and editor of *Field Trial News,* assisted with the second edition almost to the very end. His assistant then, and carrying on now as editor of the reorganized and renamed *Retriever Field Trial News,* Mrs. Toni Reynolds, made the third and fourth editions possible. Especially in the compilation of the list of winners in Appendix II, she has been an invaluable contributor.

S. Alan and Joan Williams and Perry E. and Zola R. Pound. The special chapters they wrote on, respectively, the National Amateur and the National [Open] Championships offer an intimate and colorful insight into the ultimate in retriever performance.

H. D. Bixby, John C. Neff, and Albert Dick. Through four editions these successive chief executives of the American Kennel Club have been very cooperative in interpreting rules, researching facts available only in the AKC's records, granting permission to quote from breed standards and AKC rules and regulations, and in making available the facilities of the AKC's splendid cynological library. Especially helpful with third and fourth edition research has been the AKC's secretary, Roy Carlberg.

and his associate, Thomas S. Adams. These men, who have done so much to encourage the retriever boom in Canada, combed their extensive records in order that a complete listing of all Canadian Retriever Field Trial Champions—National, Open, and Amateur— might be included in Appendix II.

Wayne H. Riser, D.V.M., M.S., director of the Orthopedic Foundation for Animals, Inc., who extended the weight of his researches and studies to the explanation of hip dysplasia—and Ralph A. Reilly, M.D., F.A.C.S., for his assistance with this subject.

Dr. Clarence Little, Director Emeritus of the Jackson Memorial Laboratory, Bar Harbor, Maine, who kindly examined and criticized the passages relating to canine color genetics.

James Hare, M.D., ophthalmologist and a great campaigner of bird dogs, who counseled on the care of eyes.

These busy veterinarians who were so generous with their time and their advice: Drs. D. R. Bartels, Robert D. Daniels, James Robertson, and R. W. Stockstill.

Mrs. Eloise Heller, who kindly permitted use of and reproduction from her excellent *Retriever Trial Handbook*.

Floyd Crowe of the Irish Water Spaniel Club of America, and Homer Downing of the Flat-Coated Retriever Society of America. Both extended patient help.

Ray Thomas. Because he is such a fine person and because he enjoys such a challenge, Ray devoted many hours to second- and third-edition research and checking.

Miss Beatrice E. Peterson, librarian of the American Kennel Club, for her assistance in compiling the bibliography.

And—to these retriever stalwarts who contributed materially to the second and third editions: August and Louise Belmont, Guthrie Bicknell, Mrs. W. R. Boston, Ted and Patty Fajen, Bob Files, Mike and Bonnie Flannery, Mrs. George H. Flinn, Jr., Harold Mack, Jr., and John and Barbara Nash.

Those professional trainers who enthusiastically responded to requests for assistance: Orin Benson, Cal Barry, Joe Riser, and Billy Wunderlich.

John Olin: this owner of many great campaigners has earned the gratitude of all retrieverdom—indeed all of dogdom—for his leadership in encouraging vital research in such areas as canine orthopedics.

Herm David, who has his tongue in his cheek when he calls himself a cynologist, but who has earned wide respect as a dedicated student of dogs and dogdom. Herm did all of the legwork, and wrote most of the revised copy, for the second, third and fourth editions. He succeeded in bringing my facts up to date without altering my concepts, my basic content, or my style. Thanks to his efforts, this is a more useful book than it has ever been.

All of my many friends in the retriever sport, without whose help and encouragement I never would have tackled and finished this chore.

My imposed-upon secretary, Miss Aileen Morgan, who not only typed several pounds of manuscript, but also did much of the necessary research work.

My durable wife Julie, who wore out her eyes reading and rereading every draft of every chapter. She edited and blue-penciled ruthlessly, but with such magnificent tact that I rarely even sulked.

—J.L.F.

# Author's Preface

According to my beloved and long-suffering wife, I am "retriever happy."

This I admit. And here is another thing I will admit: no matter what you have heard or read to the contrary, there isn't so much to training a good retriever. There's nothing to it that a fairly bright moron couldn't figure out for himself, if he had the time. Well, I *took* the time.

If you don't believe it is easy for practically anyone to train these dogs, I will again refer you to my wife. She is a bit weary of retrievers, possibly because at times we've owned a few too many of them, and she claims she was not cut out to be a kennel boy. But she will answer you honestly. She will tell you that for the past ten years I've been training my own dogs, shooting over them, and handling them myself in big-time field-trial competition. Then she'll add, loyally suppressing any hint of surprise in her voice, that I've done all right with them. She will let you draw your own conclusions about my IQ rating, as a good wife should.

Actually, it is so easy to get and make a well-trained retriever that I feel anybody who likes to shoot waterfowl or upland game is a sucker if he doesn't have one of these superior animals for a hunting companion. I won't go into a song and dance about all the game these dogs conserve. That has been covered thoroughly in everything ever written about retrievers.

I'll just say this: shooting feathered game is twice as much *fun* with a good retrieving dog—today, I wouldn't go out without one, and I've loved to shoot all my life, but that good dog work is even more fun than the shooting.

And another thing. Probably this isn't tactful, for it is rarely mentioned out loud in talk about retrievers, but these dogs fill your game bag. I often hear "sportsmen" making sneering cracks about "meat hunters." Well, I'm a meat hunter. I like game on my table. And I have mighty little respect for a "sportsman" who kills anything he doesn't care to eat, or who kills and cripples birds and leaves them to rot in field or marsh.

My retrievers put a lot of extra meat on my table. They run down many a crippled pheasant that nothing on two legs could catch. They find my ducks in the heaviest marsh cover. Day after day, they bring me in with limits I'd never get without them. That alone is reason enough for me to hunt with a retriever.

Now in this book I'm going to tell you what I've learned about these dogs. Where and how to find yourself a good one to start with —a dog worth training. I'm going to name names and give addresses.

Then I'm going to tell you how to train your own dog, quickly and easily. How to avoid all the confusion common to the amateur trainer, and all the fumbling mistakes I've made.

I didn't discover for myself all of the training tricks in this book, by any means. During the first few years, while this hobby was rapidly becoming a disease with me, I cribbed many of these shortcuts from the Hogans. For it was my good luck to stumble onto these wonderful dogs and the Hogan family simultaneously. The late Martin Hogan, dean of American retriever trainers, his daughter Mary, and his famous sons Frank and Jim. First they trained my dogs, and then they generously tried to train me to train and handle my own dogs. For quite a while they had rough sledding on the latter endeavor. I was unbelievably dumb.

I know now that my approach, like that of most beginning amateurs, was all wrong. I didn't understand the fundamentals of dog training, or try to. I was like an amateur doctor, trying to treat symptoms with patent medicines, and it didn't even occur to me to wonder about the causes. I struggled with many useless dogs. I struggled with, and ruined, some good youngsters because I tried to put them in college at kindergarten age. I spent too much time on my dogs. I wasted a lot of time.

I imposed on the Hogans, and leaned on them too heavily. I would ask them how to get a dog to do so-and-so, and they would show me. I was learning a lot of unrelated tricks, but I wasn't really learning the easy way to train a dog. I was going at it backwards.

In this book I'm going to try to tell you how to start right, and do it the easy way.

Part I will give simple and specific answers to such questions as: Where and how can I get a good one—a dog worth training—an easy-to-train dog? What is the best retriever breed for my purpose? Should I get a pup, or an older dog? What are my chances of buying a trained dog, and what would it cost? How important is the pedigree and what can you tell from it? What special care does a retriever require?

Part II will give, as simply as possible, quick and easy training methods for amateurs, for impatient amateurs who have very little spare time to waste.

Part III deals with retriever field trials, discusses typical tests to expect, trial procedure, and how the judges evaluate and compare the work of the dogs. Even though you have no interest in going into field-trial competition, the stuff in Part III will help you to understand what you should and should not fairly expect of your gun dog. *There is no difference whatever between getting a dog ready for hunting or for retriever-trial competition.* And don't let any uninformed smart aleck tell you there is.

Through the years, recognized retriever trials have evolved into practical hunting tests for the finest working retrievers. I've never yet seen a retriever field-trial champion that I wouldn't give my remaining natural teeth to have with me in a duck blind, or on a pheasant drive.

There are many retriever-trial clubs scattered through the East, the Middle West, and the Far Western states—with new ones being constantly organized. Most of them have fairly frequent informal practice trials, to which newcomers are cordially welcomed. There is no better way to give your dog a little extra experience on retrieving shot birds, and to sharpen him up for the hunting season, than to run him in some of these friendly competitions among gun-dog owners in your vicinity. It's fun. And who knows? Your dog might even win a ribbon!

Now then, while this book is aimed squarely at the impatient hunting man who yearns for a trained retriever, I hope it will also be worth the money to the man or woman who simply wants a well-mannered pet or companion dog of any breed. At cocktail parties people are always asking me, "Do Labradors [Goldens, Chesa-peakes] make good pets? Are they good with children? Are they good watchdogs? Could my husband use one for hunting, and let the children make a house pet of him at the same time?"

Or, "We have a Collie [Airedale, Dachshund, Scottie, Cocker, Wirehair, or whatnot] and I certainly wish it would behave like your retrievers. How could I teach him to sit, walk at heel, stop jumping up on people, barking at cars, and tipping over the neighbor's garbage can? How could I housebreak him?"

These questions and many more are answered in this book for people interested in dogs of any breed for any purpose. For anyone wanting to *buy* a companion dog or pet, the same principles apply as for the man in search of a good retriever.

And there are no quicker and easier methods of obedience training for any dog than those given in Part II. For a retriever must first be a perfectly behaved dog, before he can be anything more. He must be under absolute and quiet control.

Otherwise he is worse than useless—he is a nuisance in the field.

But he has so much more to learn about his work that a retriever trainer can't waste too much time on the obedience lessons. These have to be learned fast. And it is amazing how fast they *are* learned, by a *good* dog.

# Reviser's Preface
## To The Third Edition

Every author wants to create a book so strong and so full of truth that it will endure beyond his own time. Jim Free's *Training Your Retriever* is such a book. It helped to propel the boom in retrievers and in retriever trials and has been a starting point for most of America's successful amateur retriever trainers.

Because neither dogs nor people really change, none of the basic material has needed changing. In essence, the problems of selection and training are the same as they have always been—and the Free philosophy and Free-taught techniques remain the best approaches to their solutions. This edition has been updated and enlarged so that *Training Your Retriever* may have a continuing and maximum usefulness.

In readying the book for a new generation, I have been especially careful not to molest Jim Free's virile style. It is the book's greatest charm. The first time I revised it Jim Free said, after reading my manuscript, "I can't tell where Free leaves off and David begins. It all looks fine to me."

I thought that was one of the finest professional compliments I ever received. I'd like to believe Mr. Free would be as fully satisfied with this effort.

Part III of this edition is enriched by expert descriptions of the two top stakes in retrieverdom. S. Alan Williams' report of the National Amateur Retriever Championship is especially helpful to an understanding of such competitions, since it is accompanied by both photographs and diagrams of the individual tests—these by Williams' wife, Joan. Perry E. and Zola R. Pound have contributed a graphic, equally informative account of the National [Open] Retriever Championship.

Appendix I is a supplement to the chapter on "Selecting Your Dog," for it includes a full, detailed, and up-to-date description of the official standards for all retrieving breeds recognized by the American Kennel Club. Appendix II, companion to the chapter on "The Truth About Pedigrees—And How to Read Them," is a list of field-trial point winners that makes it possible for any attentive novice to make a useful evaluation of the field qualities of the ancestors of any Chesapeake, Golden, or Labrador. This list is included to help the reader maximize his chances of getting a good one when he selects his retriever—because, as Jim Free warns, *"You've got to have a decent dog to start with."*

The annotated Bibliography can be a most helpful guide to those who have an expanding interest in retrievers. It will guide you to pertinent periodicals and useful books. Because it is based upon my own collection, specific information relates to that edition of any given book which I have been able to examine. The list is as complete as I have been able to make it—probably the most complete on this subject published to date.

Over the years, since its first publication in 1949, *Training Your Retriever* has come to be regarded as the "Bible" of retrieverdom. Jim Free is gone now, but his book—and its truths—will endure.

—Herm David

# Part I

HOW TO FIND AND BUY YOUR DOG

# 1

## The Great Secret Revealed

IF YOU ALREADY own a retriever—or any other kind of dog for that matter—you may as well save your eyes and skip this stuff about how to go about buying a good one. For unless you have more sense than I had when I acquired my first retriever, you're going to take a whirl at making something of the dog you have before you'll even consider turning him in on a new model. And it's entirely possible you are luckier than I was, and that you stumbled onto a dog worth training. I'd say it's about a fifty-fifty chance. I believe about half of the healthy Labradors, Goldens, and Chesapeakes in this country are worth training. There are field strains that haven't yet been ruined by those who breed *exclusively* for the bench shows, and that's more than you can say for many of the sporting breeds and most of the other breeds that have become too popular with the bench show "fancy."

Now please don't start telling me about your dog—how he fetches your newspaper, and wows your guests by retrieving a kippered herring out of the icebox. You can't win if you start that kind of a bull session with me. For I have owned some of the most charming and utterly useless dogs you ever saw. I can and will retaliate by boring you for hours about my first retriever, old Nell, whose memory I dearly love to this day.

Nell was beautiful to look at, a true bench-type Labrador. She would do all sorts of parlor retrieving tricks. She was affectionate, as long as she had her own way. But—she was as hardheaded as a mother-in-law. For instance, I never did persuade her to deliver a duck to hand, and I spent many—too many—weary and frustrated hours trying. Invariably she would spit out the duck as she came ashore. If I wanted it, I could darned well walk over to the edge of the water and get it for myself. She was an incorrigible shot breaker. Also, I never succeeded in curing her of her conviction that it was more important and much more pleasant to run a rabbit than to retrieve a pheasant.

My old hunting partner, Nate Lord, used to laugh until he cried at some of the races he witnessed. A fast field would disappear over the horizon, with the rabbit leading old Nell by half a length, and with me running third but closing fast on the black bitch, screaming unprintable words. It is astonishing what speed a no-longer-young man with a slight paunch can make, even in heavy hunting boots, if sufficiently inspired and pumping plenty of adrenalin.

There were many other essential lessons Nell refused to learn. But I was nearly as stubborn as she was, and struggled with her three years before it dawned on me that she was really not worth fooling with. At that, it broke my heart to let her go. But I finally had enough sense to sell her to a kindly hunter who wanted a bargain dog, and let him cut his retriever teeth on her. I believe he is now a wiser man, also.

So don't tell me about your dog. Just go ahead and start training him, if he's old enough, and you'll find out shortly how good he really is. I hope you're lucky, and that he's eager to please and quick to learn. But if he doesn't respond very fast to those ten-minute daily lessons, then it would pay you to come back here and read the rest of Part I.

I've read a lot of books on dog training in my life, and tried to follow their instructions, with very poor success. Most of them had me licked before I got fairly started, by assuring me I must have *patience*, a quality I do not possess, in order to teach anything to a dog. It took many years of useless struggle with a procession of lovable but hopeless mutts before a great and simple truth slowly penetrated my thick skull. This I am now passing on to you, and you'll save yourself a lot of grief if you'll just take my word for it.

For any ordinary mortal to train a dog, *you've got to have a decent dog to start with.*

That looks asinine in print, it seems so obvious—and yet, believe it or not, that is the theme, the "message," of this book. That is the great secret.

Most Americans, including me, are born with a sentimental and unrealistic attitude toward dogs. During childhood years this attitude is further developed by a procession of pets. A boy takes in a stray cur. He feeds it. The mongrel wags his tail and licks the boy's face. From then on, that dog can do no wrong. It is the smartest, the best dog in the world. The chances are it never actually performs one useful function in its life before being killed chasing a car, shot by an angry farmer for killing chickens, or poisoned by a neighbor weary of replanting his garden. But to the boy that is a wonderful dog. It's *his* dog.

In later years the boy is further misled by the more commercial bench-show racketeers and the backyard breeders. They sell him a "pedigreed" dog, and along with it the false impression that a dog is necessarily worth something because it has a pedigree.

Before you set out to buy an intelligent, easy-to-train pup or young dog, the most important thing for you to do is firmly determine to skip the sentiment, and try to get into a realistic frame of mind. A working cowpuncher takes good care of his horse. He feeds and waters it before he will sit down to his own chow. Sometimes he gets very fond of a top pony. But don't believe what you see in the Western pictures. He doesn't croon "Old Pal" ballads to his mount, walking over a ridge at sunset. And he doesn't waste much feed on a pony that doesn't earn it doing his job.

A dog is a domesticated wild animal. Each breed was originally developed to perform a definite service for man. Many of them have now degenerated under the tender mercies of the kind of bench-show breeder who selects and breeds mainly for looks and conformation, and does not bother much about intelligence, or working qualities. If a dog can win a blue ribbon merely by walking around a ring on a leash, and being posed by his handler, why worry about brains or tractability?

But all dogs, at one time, were bred and selected for one common trait: *eagerness to please a man.*

And that is the first and most important trait you want to look for in the dog you buy—in the dog himself, *and in his immediate ancestors.*

If you want to have a trained retriever quickly and easily, there is just one way to begin. Spend a little time choosing your dog, instead of letting the dog choose you. Get a pup or young dog that is intelligent, eager to please the man, easy to train, a dog that has been bred and selected for these qualities—as well as for the natural instincts of hunting and retrieving game—for many generations. Get yourself one of these, and his training will take no more than ten minutes a day.

He eats no more horsemeat than a brainless, contrary, hammer-headed, although possibly lovable mutt. And here's another great discovery I've made:

*It's just as easy to love a good one.*

# 2

## Bargain Dogs

SO LET'S ASSUME you're sold on my "message." You want to end up with a well-trained, useful retriever, and you don't want to waste a lot of time reaching that goal. You're willing to take my word for it, and start out with the best material you can find. You're ready to buy, and you want to know where and how to go about it.

Well, the first thing to do is to loosen up. Most of us are incredible cheapskates when it comes to buying a dog, and we get just about what we pay for and what we deserve. And when you pause to figure out the economics of owning a dog—which few dog owners seem to do—it is obviously downright silly to be bargain hunting.

So now we come to secret number two, another simple but very important truth.

*A cheap dog is the most expensive in the long run.*

The only thing worse than a bargain dog is a *gift dog.* You have about the same chance of getting a good one this way as you have of making a seven-horse parlay. If you like to play odds like those, go ahead, chum. Go ahead and take a dog as a gift. One of two things happens. You lose a friend, the donor, when you finally harden your heart and get rid of the beast. Or else you lose a *lot* of friends by keeping an unruly mutt for the rest of *his* life, and a good chunk of *yours.* He will alienate your shooting partners, running wild and flushing pheasant out of range. He will ruin every hunt for everybody. And he will eat you out of house and home for at least eighteen years. All gift dogs seem to bear charmed lives, and achieve very ripe old ages.

If you want a dog worth training, you've got to think of the original cost as unimportant. Whatever it is, it constitutes only a small down payment on the overall cost of owning a dog and maintaining it properly over the years of its life. The price of a dog is like the price of a safety razor. They get you on the blades.

Today, using commercially prepared dog food, it costs eighteen to twenty dollars a month to nourish a retriever properly. But if you have three or more dogs, you can purchase their food in bulk at considerably lower prices. In addition, you must also consider the cost of a small kennel and wire-enclosed run(s) to keep the retriever(s) properly confined. Other predictable expenses are distemper and heartworm shots, and occasional veterinary bills. Of course these expenses include no professional training, which can vary from one hundred and fifty dollars a month up to many hundreds, depending on the locality, and the goals you set for your retriever. I'm assuming the dog yourself, right from the start.

If you go about it right, you can buy a *good retriever* pup for as low as two hundred dollars. You can probably find a bargain, from unproven breeding, for seventy-five, and kid yourself that you're saving a hundred and a quarter. You'll keep this little longshot ticket at least a year, trying to make up your mind about him. Feed costs, two hundred and sixteen dollars, or more. A smart deal. Additional losses, one year of your life; possibly a somewhat shortened life, due to hardened arteries acquired in attempting to train a meatheaded pup.

Starting with a good pup at age two months, it takes over a year to have him in shape to take hunting. It wouldn't take this long to train him, but, after all, the pup has to grow up. So if you're sufficiently impatient you might want to try to find an older, trained dog, a proven performer.

But, brother, if you want to buy a finished retriever, you'll really have to get the fishhooks out of your pocket. When people ask me what they would have to pay for such a dog, my favorite answer is the gag about J. P. Morgan.

Some upstart had just made a killing in Wall Street, and approached Mr. Morgan for advice. He was wondering if he could afford to own a yacht.

"Young man," replied Mr. Morgan, "if you even have to ask that question, you can't afford it."

You might as well concentrate on finding a pup or a young untrained dog, unless you're prepared to pay approximately five hundred dollars or more for a trained retriever worth owning. You might get a reasonably good, trained shooting dog for that. If your ambition is to own a field-trial winner, a really superior animal, proven in competition, you'll dig a lot deeper. These—depending on their records of wins in trials—change hands at prices of two thousand to fifteen thousand dollars.

But you don't need a potential field-trial champion to have a perfectly satisfactory shooting dog and companion, and these, when available, can be had at prices ranging from five hundred to a thousand dollars.

There is a man I know in California who thinks he has been trying intelligently for at least six years to get himself a good retriever. He doesn't want to wait for a pup to develop. He wants a finished performer, right now. He's been wanting it for six years, and still wants it.

Now this character makes a lot of money, and he spends it freely. He'll wrestle your arm off in a nightclub, trying to pick up and pay a hundred-dollar check. But he won't pay a decent price to get a decent dog. He has a policy. Someone told him once that no dog is worth more than two hundred dollars. So that's his ceiling price.

He is an ardent hunter, and has the kind of job that allows him plenty of time for shooting everything that flies—quail, pheasant, doves, wild pigeon, sage hen, ducks, and geese. He belongs to a fine duck club, and shoots there every week in season. He takes several hunting trips to other states, and after everything is closed in this country, he goes gunning down in Mexico through the winter. He must spend well over two thousand dollars a year on hunting—on his club and his numerous trips.

He loses an enormous number of killed and crippled birds that he can't find without a good dog. He hates this. He's a sportsman, and a conservationist, at heart. He also enjoys bringing home the meat. If anyone ever needed a real retrieving dog, he's the man. He's always asking me to find him a good one.

The first time I bit. I wrote a lot of letters, and finally located a breeder friend of mine near Chicago, who was willing to part with a good four-year-old bitch, a Labrador. She had proved disappointing as a brood bitch, and my letter hit this breeder at just the right psychological moment. He was willing to let her go for five hundred dollars. I had shot over her, seen her place in a few junior stakes in trials, and knew her well. She would have been perfect for my California friend, and she was more than worth that price.

But do you think he bought her? No.

Instead he bought another two-hundred-dollar bargain from some backyard breeder. So far, to my knowledge, he's had eight of these—none of them worth keeping. But I will say this for him. He doesn't keep these hammerheads long. He writes them off, gets rid of them, sells them for what he can get, or gives them away to anyone who is sap enough to take them. Sixteen hundred dollars he has spent for these bargains. He could have had that one good bitch all these years, enjoying her, for five hundred dollars. A very smart guy. A close man with his dog dollar.

One day last fall he called me in great excitement. He had hit the jackpot at last. One of his long shots had finally come in, this time from somewhere in Missouri. A fine-looking Labrador emerged from the crate. It was bold and keen and eager to retrieve. In the yard it handled perfectly for its new owner, marked well, did a very fast and stylish job of retrieving training dummies.

This dog got me an invitation to a good duck club, anyway. We rushed up there. I was to see the living proof that a superior retriever can be bought by mail for two hundred dollars. I was due for quite a ribbing.

The dog was well behaved, and sat quietly in the blind. Presently a pair of mallards circled our decoys.

"Take them," whispered my friend, and I got lucky and made the double. Both fell far across the pond in heavy tules. Now if you haven't seen California tules you don't know what rugged cover is. A man without a retriever doesn't even bother to look for a bird that falls in them. And it needs a really top-notch dog to cope with them. A powerful dog who can force his way through them. A dog with guts, to take the cutting punishment they give him about the eyes and nose. And a dog with a real nose, to smell and find a bird amid the stench that invariably rises from a stagnant tule marsh.

But this dog marked those difficult falls perfectly. When sent, he tore through those tough tules like a wounded boar making his charge. Very quickly he emerged with the drake in his mouth. He started back toward the blind. The water in the pond was too shallow for swimming, and the clinging adobe mud was two feet deep, but it didn't bother *this* dog. He plowed through it so fast he didn't have time to get mired. He looked like a field-trial champion. I was getting my mouth set to eat a large dish of crow.

Suddenly, halfway back to the blind, he came to a small island in the middle of the pond. He climbed up on it.

Then he sat down, and proceeded to eat that duck. He ate it calmly, and very thoroughly, while his disillusioned owner screamed and cursed and blasted on his whistle. The dog paid no attention. He ate everything but the feathers and the feet.

Then he arose, licked his chops, stretched, and went back into the tules for the hen. He remembered that fall perfectly, and he ate her, too. There was nothing wrong with his appetite.

Now "hard mouth" is still a rare fault to find in a Labrador. The better breeders eliminate for this ruthlessly, and in all the retriever trials I've seen and judged, I can recall only one of the black dogs that was clearly guilty of this blackest of all retriever crimes.

But my bargain-hunting friend managed to find one.

Whether it's a retriever you're after, or a trainable, intelligent dog of any breed for any purpose, it pays to loosen your purse strings before you start, even if it kills you.

If you honestly can't afford to pay the price a reputable breeder asks for an older, trained dog, then content yourself with a pup or a young untrained dog.

If you can't afford to pay the price for the pup, you can't afford to keep him anyway.

If you're just plain tight, to hell with you.

# 3

## The Truth About Pedigrees — and How to Read Them

THIS CHAPTER WILL win me no friends among the more commercial elements in the dog racket. But if you're to buy a decent dog, you must first understand the plain, unvarnished facts about so-called "pedigreed" dogs.

I'm always meeting someone who tells me proudly about the big price he paid for his pedigreed dog. And usually he doesn't know any of the names in the pedigree—not even the names of the sire and dam.

Now the sad truth is that merely because you loosen up and pay a good price for a purebred—or pedigreed—dog of any breed whatever, this is no guarantee that the dog is worth anything. It is no guarantee that the animal has any of the easy-to-train qualities you want—intelligence, tractability, eagerness to please, or even a decent disposition.

In fact, many pedigrees, if you know how to read them, virtaully guarantee qualities that are just the reverse—stupidity, stubbornness, and a generally ornery nature.

Some of the more venal bench breeders, along with some careless and ignorant backyard breeders, have for many years peddled and publicized a whopper to the general dog-buying public. I mean this fiction that just any "pedigreed dog" is somehow a mysteriously superior and desirable critter.

"Pedigree:" says the dictionary, "a table presenting a line of ancestors; a genealogical tree."

And that is *all* it is.

You could provide a pedigree for any mongrel, if you wanted to take the time and trouble to trace down his ancestors for three generations or more, and write down their names on a piece of paper.

It is simply easier to get the names of the ancestors of a pure-bred dog, because they are recorded in the studbook of his particular breed. *But this doesn't mean any of them necessarily had any desirable qualities to transmit to their descendants.*

To say, "This is a pedigreed dog," means little or nothing.

Yet the *right* pedigree means so much.

The immense popularity of bench shows in this country, in my opinion, has ruined many fine breeds of dogs, and has greatly added to the confusion of the ordinary mortal who wants to buy an intelligent, easy-to-train pup. To win ribbons in bench shows, a dog needs to take no real obedience training. (To forestall the angry mail from the bench show "fancy," I hasten to except those dogs that are entered in obedience classes and tracking tests at some of the shows. They have to *do* something, at least. But these are a very small minority of the show dogs.)

Most of the ribbons in these shows are won by dogs that have to do nothing but submit to being led by a leash—sometimes dragged—around the ring by their handlers. I've seen some pretty unruly specimens become bench champions, judged purely on such things as general appearance, physical conformation, coat, and color. Some breed standards recommend "a kindly, intelligent eye," which is all right as far as it goes. But hell's bells! What is a kindly, intelligent eye? In hiring people, I've looked into the kindly, intelligent eyes of plenty of humans who turned out to be horrible nincompoops when it came to doing a job of any kind.

Now I'm not saying physical conformation isn't important. It is. You need a strong, healthy retriever to be able to do his useful work. And surely part of the pleasure of owning any sort of dog is being able to look at him without nausea.

Most good breeders of working dogs try to conform to the breed standards as closely as possible. Many somehow find the time to prove their stock in *both* field trials and bench shows, and for these I have nothing but respect and envy. Some day I hope to have sufficient leisure to show some of my working dogs myself.

But to be a top-notch worker, a dog *has* to be a pretty good physical specimen, automatically. And, unfortunately, the reverse is not true.

My only quarrel with the bench shows is that they have become too popular with people who care nothing about what's inside a dog. The so-called bench "fancy," which blithely ignores the innate qualities, instincts, and tendencies that govern what a dog *does*. The best way to judge a man, or a dog, is not by the way he looks, but how he *acts*. You can't do that in the bench-show ring. And neither can the judges who award the ribbons.

If you lump all breeds of purebred or pedigreed dogs, the vast majority now descend from generation of strictly bench-show stock—from ancestors that had to do nothing useful to earn their keep. Fortunately the retriever breeds have as yet been relatively less spoiled by the bench shows, and by indiscriminate and careless breeding, than any other breeds in America. But even with the retrievers, a pedigree as such is apt to mean nothing, and you should examine *any* dog's pedigree with a bilious eye.

Let me throw in a few fast statistics here for the reader who may be thinking of some other breed, but who wants a pup easily and quickly trained to obedience.

Let's face it. The American Kennel Club is primarily in the dog-show or the show-dog business. It also has a tight hold on the retriever-trial business and it registers and regulates the field-trial Beagles. It also encourages and licenses the obedience trials. Most of the other functional dogs have their own studbooks and trial rules. The bird dogs have the *American Field's Field Dog Stud Book*. The racing Greyhounds have their *National Coursing Association*. The formal-type foxhounds have the *Foxhound Kennel Stud Book*. There are at least two additional studbooks for foot-hunted foxhounds. The Border Collies have two studbooks of their own. The coon hounds have two or more registries apart from the AKC. Even our old farm dog friend "Shep," known formally as an "English Shepherd," has his own studbook. For the most part, breeders of fighting dogs use a registry other than the AKC—although such things are only whispered about.

In 1977 the AKC registered 1,013,650 dogs. There were 991,159 conformation entries in 1,911 licensed and member shows. There were 98,216 entries in the regular classes in 1,136 obedience trials with an additional 941 entries in 101 tracking tests. For 1,106 licensed and member field trials there were 122,318 entries. That figures out to four and one-half AKC entries judged on looks alone to every entry judged on working ability and accomplishment.

The AKC awarded 11,207 obedience degrees and 347 tracking degrees in 1977. That sounds like a lot—but since the degrees are progressive, as many as three plus the tracking degree may have gone to a single dog. Of these, 1,360 obedience and 63 tracking degrees went to breeds eligible for retriever trials.

Effective July 1, 1977, the AKC offered a new title, that of Obedience Trial Champion. The first dog to earn this title did so in just three weeks after the title was offered. She was a Golden Retriever, O.T.Ch. Moreland's Golden Tonka. For the six-month period, a total of 16 dogs earned the new title. Seven of these were among the retrieving breeds—all Goldens.

In 1977 the AKC made 10,963 show champions, of which 380 came from the 37,098 entries of retriever breeds.

But let's keep that figure of 380 retriever show champions from 37,098 entries in mind. That is one new retriever show champion from every 98 entries. Now, from the 29,115 entries in 184 licensed and member retriever field trials during 1977, the AKC awarded 36 Open Field Championships and 34 Amateur Field Championships.

Which championship means the most? An average of 98 retriever show entries for a show title as against an average of 416 entries for each of the retriever field championships: It would seem to be more than four times as easy to win a show title as an open or amateur field title!

I hope this clears up a common source of confusion. Many people think a registered dog is a registered dog—and a champion a champion. But they don't know there are several respected stud-books in the United States beyond the American Kennel Club's—and many kinds of champions.

If you are buying a *working* dog, look for him to be registered with the studbook most respected for working stock in the breed concerned. If you are buying a retriever, I would definitely advise you to insist it be registered in the AKC. This has a substantial effect on the value of any pups it might sire or whelp in the future, and on the value of the dog if you should ever want to sell it. Further, you might decide later that you like retriever trialing, and AKC registration is an absolute requirement for participation in these events.

Now then, what does all this stuff about registration and pedigrees mean to you in achieving your objective—an easy-to-train dog with such other working instincts and qualities as you want?

If you are buying a mature, trained dog, his work can be demonstrated to you, and you can base your judgment to a considerable extent on just what he *does* as an individual. But his breeding is still important also, and I would not buy an individual dog, no matter how impressive his work appeared at the moment, unless he also had some good working ancestors close up in his pedigree. He might be a sport, a throwback. If you ever bred him, the chances of his transmitting his accidental good qualities to his pups would be fairly poor. And, if a young dog, he might have latent bad qualities himself that would crop up later.

And, of course, if you are buying a puppy at any age up to nine months or so, you are almost entirely dependent on his pedigree. But cheer up. The whole secret of reading a pup's pedigree is really quite simple.

You merely want to know, from sources you feel you can trust, just who were his mammy and pappy, and secondarily his grandparents. What did they do? Were they trained dogs? Did they take training easily? Were they used for hunting? If so, *who* shot over them, and what does *he* say about the way they worked? Were any of them field-trial dogs? If so, what were their field-trial records? Were any of them field-trial champions?

Some backyard breeders whose only interest is selling pups will show you a five- or six-generation pedigree, point a grimy finger at a famous name or two on the right side of the page, and give you nothing but double-talk about the unknown individuals on the left, or close-up side of the family tree. Now, it's fun to brag to your friends about Glenairlie Rover or Blind of Arden or some other great field-trial champion being the great-great-grand-father of your Labrador. But if that's *all* you can boast about in the pedigree, it means very little.

To find out why this is true, we don't need to go into a long-winded discussion of Mendel's Law. We just need to realize this:

Sire and dam (two individuals) each contributed an average of 50 percent to the traits, instincts, and makeup of your dog. Grandparents (four individuals) each contributed an average of 25 percent.

Fourth generation (eight individuals) each contributed an average of only 12½ percent.

Fifth generation (sixteen individuals) an average of only 6¼ percent each.

If you will think about this for a moment, you'll readily recognize how silly it is to buy a pup on the strength of one great dog's appearing in his pedigree in the fourth or fifth generation. Yet how many people do it! A fifth-generation ancestor contributes, on an average, only 6¼ percent. Fifteen others in that generation average to the remaining 93¾ percent. If they are unknown quantities, you'd better assume they weren't much good. What chance have the great qualities of that one illustrious dog to filter down to your pup, if his parents and grandparents are also unknown quantities?

And remember, *bad qualities are inherited*, just like the good ones. Sometimes, to a conscientious breeder, they seem to be the dominant ones, as far as transmittal is concerned.

So all you want to see is a three-generation pedigree. But you want to know all you can learn about *every* individual in it. The sire and dam, and the grandparents. That's enough. You want to know not only that these six dogs all were easily trainable and intelligent workers, but also that *none of them had serious faults.*

Now, let's clear up one more small but important item in the reading of pedigrees. When the prefix "Ch." appears before the name of a dog, it means *bench champion*. It means only that the dog has won enough points in bench shows to be awarded that title by the AKC. It doesn't necessarily mean the dog could *do* anything except stand up and walk around the ring.

"Ch." means only that this was a good-looking animal, according to the current standard of that particular breed club. It is no assurance that he had a brain in his head.

There is just one exception that I know of. In 1939 the Labrador Retriever Club incorporated a rule in its constitution and by-laws that no *member of the club* shall use the title "Ch." until a dog, having won a bench-show championship, shall receive a working certificate or better at a field trial. This has been interpreted by the officers of the club to mean that any Labrador, entered in a field trial licensed by the AKC, which has satisfactorily completed both a land and a water series in the same trial, is deemed to have obtained a working certificate.

So *if* you're looking at the pedigree of a Labrador and *if* you're dealing with a member in good standing of the Labrador Club (the rule of course is not binding on other Labrador breeders) and *if* the title was acquired since June 1, 1939, then the prefix "Ch." before a dog's name means a little more. It means that dog had to take a certain amount of training, enough to go successfully through two series of a regular licensed trial. It means he had to be steady to sit quietly on the line and in the blind. And it probably means he had to find and retrieve at least two pheasant and two ducks, and do a satisfactory job of it.

If more sporting-breed clubs would adopt similar rules, it would do much to halt and even reverse the sad downward trend of these dogs on the bench.

Any retriever that has earned any field-trial title has *done* something, and he's done it against top competition. He has clearly demonstrated his great intelligence, his desire to work for his handler, his ability to take training. He's your best bet. He should be at least *one* worthy parent or grandparent for the dog you want, and you need inquire no further about *him*.

Let's just sum this pedigree business up.

The man who says proudly, "My dog is pedigreed," is merely exposing his ignorance.

If he says, "My dog is by So-and-so out of Such-and-such," naming two outstanding *working* individuals of the breed, he's beginning to make sense.

If he then tells you about all four grandparents, he's cooking with gas.

For our present purpose—finding an easy-to-train pup—pay no attention to "Ch." on a pedigree (unless it's a Labrador with a working certificate, or you otherwise know it was also a trained dog).

But pay plenty of attention to any field-trial championship title.

Look no further than second and third generations. But take a good look at all of those six dogs—both parents and four grandparents. In Appendix II you will find the records of those retrievers that have distinguished themselves in meaningful trials recognized by the American and Canadian Kennel Clubs. With this information, any novice can get a useful idea of a pup's field promise from what the public record has to say about the ancestors shown in any American or Canadian retriever's pedigree. There are listed all of the retrievers which have placed in open all-age competition since retriever trials began to be recorded in the United States, through 1967. Amateur field-trial champions, National Derby Champions, and all Canadian Champions are also included, as are all retrievers which have placed in Amateur All-Age stakes since September 14, 1951, when qualifications for amateur field-trial championships began, through 1967. These are the candy kids, the ancestors you want for your dog. And you want at least a couple of them among the parents and grandparents of your puppy.

For your convenience in checking pedigrees, the names are arranged alphabetically, by breed, along with each dog's registration number, year of birth, and totals of open and amateur championship points. As completely and accurately as possible, all recognized field titles have also been given.

Give careful attention to the point totals shown—appreciating that each half point was hard-earned in very rugged competition. Only since July, 1947, have fourth placements earned the half point. Thus there are a number of dogs listed which placed fourth in one or more trials, but are credited with no points. Don't sell them short. Any dog that has gone clear through an open stake to place fourth is quite a dog. Veteran field trialers are very happy to get a fourth.

You will find many achievement titles listed. Most are real nuggets. Look for them. Rated in order of the respect due their holders, they are:

Natl. Field Ch. (National Retriever Field Trial Champion)*

Natl. Am. Field Ch. (National Amateur Retriever Field Trial Champion)

Dual Ch. (dogs holding both open field-trial championships and bench championships)

FC (Retriever Open Field Trial Champion)

AFC (Amateur Retriever Field Trial Champion)

Can. Nat. Ch. (Canadian National Retriever Field Trial Champion)

Can. FTC (Canadian Retriever Field Trial Champion)

Eng. FTC (English Retriever Field Trial Champion)

Natl. Derby Ch. (National Derby Retriever Field Trial Champion)

Sh. Ch. (The AKC, being primarily in the dog-show business, lists show champions as "champions," qualifies all other titles. In this book, to avoid any risk of confusing bench champions with field-trial champions, show championships are also qualified, being shown as "Sh. Ch." or "Show Ch.")

Lesser nuggets, but worthy of respect because they indicate a degree of trainability, are the obedience titles. In order, they are: "U.D." (for Utility Dog), "C.D.X." (for Companion Dog Excellent), and "C.D." (for Companion Dog). There is also an obedience degree "T," awarded for completing a tracking test. Retrievers are questers, specialist hunting dogs which take the scent of their game from the air. I feel it is an indignity to ask them to do a hound's work, and therefore place no value on a tracking degree held by a retriever.

Subject to minor modification by the AKC, to acquire an Open

---

*In January, 1963, the AKC dropped the word Trial from all of the various forms of its Field Championships. Thus, you will find some dogs identified as Field Trial Champions, others as Field Champions. These titles have the same meaning and value—except that the latter titles were earned after the change.

Field Championship a retriever must win a National Championship stake or a total of ten points, which may be acquired as follows: In each Open All-Age, Limited All-Age, or Special All-Age stake, there must be a minimum of 12 starters, each of which is eligible for entry in a Limited All-Age stake, and the winner of first place shall be credited with five points, second place three points, third place one point, and fourth place one half point. However, before acquiring a championship, a dog must win first place and acquire at least five points in at least one Open All-Age, Limited All-Age, or Special All-Age stake open to all breeds of retrievers, and not more than five points of the required ten shall be acquired in trials not open to all breeds of retrievers. You will note that, by this definition, one of the dogs was a Field Trial Champion eighteen times over.

In 1935 the Chesapeake, Skipper Bob, became the first retriever field-trial champion in the United States. On September 11, 1951, the AKC approved a new kind of titlist, the Amateur Field Champion. Originally a retriever had to win a place in an Open, Limited, or Special All-Age, under an amateur handler, to qualify for the Amateur title. Now the requirements are identical to those required of Open Field Trial Champions except that 15 points are needed and all of the points *may* be acquired in amateur stakes and the placements must be under an amateur handler.

A dog may also gain an Amateur Field Trial Championship by winning the National Amateur Retriever Championship stake, sponsored by the National Amateur Retriever Club, an association of member clubs. Its first trial was held in 1957. Contestants must qualify.and be run under amateurs.

Some of the Amateur Field Champions and stake placers have either not competed in or have not placed in open stakes. Therefore you will find some of these do not carry open points. You will also note that some of the dogs have sufficient point totals—but no titles. This means they have not won a qualifying first—or they do not have enough points in breed-open stakes.

Remember, you will want to find the available dog or pup with the *most* of the *best possible* ancestors as close up as possible in the pedigree.

In a general way, the dogs and bitches that have become field-trial champions and then gone on to amass a much larger point total—being the most thoroughly proven performers—have also been the greatest sires and dams, and have produced the most outstanding progeny. There are many exceptions, of course. But you can't go far wrong if you buy a pup whose pedigree is well sprinkled with the names of the big point winners.

These are not too easy to find, but you may as well set your sights high. A man can dream, can't he?

Now one more thing about the list. A few of the dogs have no registration numbers, which means for one reason or another they were not registered in the AKC studbook at the time they last placed. Until recently, a purebred but unregistered dog could be entered by paying an extra "listing" fee.

These were included in our list because it is quite possible some of them have been registered since, or that some of their descendants have been successfully registered, by going through the necessary red tape, tracing down their ancestors, getting affidavits, and supplying evidence to satisfy completely the AKC of their purebred origin.

However, if you run across any of those names on a pedigree, you should make very sure the pup or dog you are considering is eligible for AKC registration. If the breeder can show you the litter *registration* certificate, or the *registration* certificates of *both* sire and dam, that's all you need to see. If not, you'd better buy the dog only subject to his AKC registration. All conditional agreements should be in writing. And avoid disappointment—don't get too attached to the dog until you have his registration papers.

So, if you want an easy-to-train, lazy-man's pup, study Appendix II with care and avoid strictly bench stock of any breed like the plague.

Bench shows seem to bring pleasure to a great many people, and I am glad these folks are enjoying themselves. However, there are those who say—and I can't bring myself to disagree with them—that bench selection is artificial selection. There is considerable evidence that bench-show selection, incomplete as it must be, has robbed many fine breeds of their utility. Now, recent researches seem to indicate we are beginning to pay a heavy price for our methods of bench selection. And that brings us to the subject of hip dysplasia.

There is an element of risk in every enterprise—and this seems the proper place to inform you of a little-publicized risk in dog buying. It is a defect in the way the leg and the hip bones of some dogs fit together, and it is called hip dysplasia. It must be dealt with firmly and realistically. In all breeds of dogs maturing at over 25 pounds, except track Greyhounds, this defect is found in varying degrees of severity. This includes too many otherwise admirable strains of Labradors, Goldens, Chesapeakes, and Irish Water Spaniels.

Dr. Wayne Riser of the University of Pennsylvania's School of Veterinary Medicine is a co-founder of the Orthopedic Foundation for Animals (OFA), which was formed to conduct and finance hip dysplasia research. After intensive investigation, Dr. Riser wrote: "Hip dysplasia is abnormal development of the hip joint. In general in a dysplastic hip the socket is less concave and more shallow than normal. If this ball-and-socket joint is abnormally formed, its working efficiency is lowered, and related ailments such as arthritis develop, thus lowering the usefulness of the dog."

Save yourself heartache, expense, and wasted time by taking what precautions are available when you are buying either a puppy or a grown dog. In most instances of hip dysplasia the defect is not evident in a very young puppy. Radiographs, expertly taken and read, are the only positive means of diagnosis, except in some of the very worst cases. Dr. Riser writes: "Radiologically, the worst cases can be detected at the age of three or four months, but usually it is six months—or even a year—before a definite opinion can be given. Hip dysplasia is difficult to deal with because it seems to be an inherited weakness, due to a lack of sufficient muscle mass to properly hold the ball of the femur in the hip socket through the growth period of the puppy."

Dr. Riser continues: "I believe the incidence of hip dysplasia is quite high in all large breeds, as great as 50 percent in some breeds. The problem evidently centers around a lack of pelvic abductor muscle mass. And, if this is not corrected by breed selection, hip dysplasia will continue to be a serious handicap. Pelvic radiographs [X rays] are our surest guide in selecting breeding stock which will produce the lowest incidence of dysplastic puppies. However, an eye trained to evaluate the mass of pelvic abductor muscle—

or its lack—can be meaningful in reducing both the incidence and the severity of this disease.

"Some people talk about dominant and recessive characteristics when discussing hip dysplasia, and want to put this disease in the same category as directly inherited congenital defects such as cleft palate, monorchidism, and so forth. It does not appear this defect is of that nature. The disease is 'polygenic,' meaning 'many genes.' Most polygenic traits are subject to environmental modification.

"Most large breeds reproduce with a deficiency of mass of pelvic muscle. Any pup will acquire defective hip joints if it does not have enough musculature to hold the head of the femur firmly in the socket. All pups we have examined have had normal joints at birth, and the socket changes form when the musculature fails. Too many of us have bred for size and conformation, but have forgotten about pelvic muscle mass and strength."

At this point you certainly do not wish to become an expert on hip dysplasia. You *do* want to know how to avoid buying a puppy or dog which has, or will evidence, this defect at a later date.

The answer is that there is no certain, guaranteed method at the present time. There are procedures which you can and should take to protect yourself.

Step one would be to deal only with the highest type of dedicated, ethical breeder who understands the problem of hip dysplasia and is extremely alert to avoid it. The OFA certifies dogs as being dysplasia free when expert analysis of their radiographs, voluntarily submitted, are judged to be "clear." A conscientious breeder should have OFA certificates for both sire and dam—or equally qualified certification. Ask to see these written statements. Truly dedicated breeders will respect your discrimination if your request is politely put.

Step two would be to get a written commitment from the breeder to replace the puppy with one of equal quality should it develop hip dysplasia—or any other congenital disease. The best breeders would want to do this anyway.

I prefer to start giving individual attention to a puppy as early in his life as possible, believing that in that way I can develop the maximum of his potentialities. While the possibility of hip dysplasia might make a cautious buyer of me, it wouldn't dissuade me from preferring a puppy to a grown or partly grown dog. I prefer puppies, and the incidence of hip dysplasia from nondysplasic parents is so low I would consider the risk a very minor one.*

An inherited disease which any responsible breeder should also be willing to "make right" if it evidences itself after purchase is progressive retinal atrophy. The inaccurate common name for this disease is "night blindness." It seems to be transmitted as a simple recessive—meaning it could affect neither of the parents but could be transmitted by both of them. Progressive retinal atrophy might take anywhere from months to years to reveal itself. Once it begins, a veterinarian familiar with it can make a diagnosis. Or, should you suspect its incidence in your retriever, a dog-loving ophthalmologist can be consulted. Fortunately, at this time the disease is relatively rare in most retrieving breeds.

There is another "hidden defect" for which you should be alert when buying a male. Be sure the dog has all his masculine equipment. Monorchidism (only one testicle descended) and cryptorchidism (both testicles undescended) are inherited defects which must be avoided. Monorchids are usually fertile, capable of producing more monorchids and cryptorchids, as well as females which carry the genetic factor for the defect. Cryptorchids are sterile, likely unreliable in temperament, sometimes lack normal male vigor and verve, age faster and are somewhat more apt to develop malignancies.

Testicles may be a bit difficult to detect in a very young puppy, but if he has them they can be found.

There is one more defect for which you might be alert. Sometimes the dam, or whoever is helping her, severs the cord too roughly and causes a hernia at the pup's navel. An umbilical hernia is easily detected, since the navel protrudes noticeably. A simple operation can correct this injury when the puppy is young, but this should be the breeder's responsibility.

If you are an impatient man in a hurry and have no interest in being knowledgeable about various canine medical pitfalls, find and

---

*Buyers and breeders wanting a working knowledge of hip dysplasia can consult the book *Canine Hip Dysplasia and How to Control It,* by Dr. Wayne H. Riser and Harry Miller. It is available from the Orthopedic Foundation for Animals, Inc., Box 8251, Philadelphia, Pa. 19101, for $4.50. Proceeds help support the research and services of the OFA.

rely on a veterinarian who does understand these diseases. But make your selection carefully: not all vets are expert in these matters.

Now, one final caution. Most courts, and all of the studbooks, refuse to recognize any conditional terms of sale unless they are in writing. If *any* part of the transaction is incomplete when dog and money change hands, put the entire agreement in writing.

# 4

## What Breed?

PEOPLE ARE ALWAYS asking, "What is the best retriever breed for a shooting dog?" or, "Which is best just for a pet for my kids?"

Now I hate to see a potentially good gun dog wasted as a house pet. It is like putting Cleopatra in a hash house instead of a harem. Her natural talents would be largely unused. Yet she would be easier on your eyes, and no doubt on your digestion, than some haggard slut of a waitress slinging your food at you.

In a moment of slightly alcoholic enthusiasm, a fellow retriever nut, a breeder, once said to me, "These dogs are much too good for the common people."

The retriever-happy fraternity feels this way about these remarkable dogs. It amounts to a special brand of snobbishness, which has nothing to do with money or social position.

In the Midwest Field Trial Club of Chicago, in which I was active for many years before moving to California, one of the most prominent members was a Chicago cop. And as far as the dogs were concerned, he was one of the greatest snobs. He simply hated to see a well-bred working retriever get into the hands of anyone who would not fully appreciate it. And he would never think of selling one of his pups to anyone but a gunning man.

When you stop to think of it, this attitude is understandable. If a man has devoted years of his life, plus a good deal of money, to the improvement of a working breed, carefully selecting for superior dogs with many valuable qualities, he naturally wants to see *all* of those qualities used. If the youngsters from his kennel are not used for hunting or in field trials, he can't be sure his breeding program is right. For the only way to prove a sire or dam is by keeping track of what his or her progeny *do* in the field.

So here's a tip, for anyone trying to buy a retriever pup just for a house pet, from a serious breeder of working dogs. You'd better forget what you learned in Sunday school. You'd better tell a lie, and tell it pretty convincingly. You'd better look him in the eye, and tell him you'll train the pup and use it, at least for hunting. Though that may not be enough, with some breeders. You may even have to act interested in field trials, to get your hands on a pup of particularly good breeding.

The above is treason, and won't increase my popularity with my retriever-breeder friends. But if the truth is told, the best working retrievers *do* make wonderful pets. They can't be beat as easy-to-train, intelligent companions.

But from here on we'll discuss these breeds in terms of their working qualities, for the man who wants a shooting dog or a field-trial prospect. The house-pet seeker can ride along, knowing that the same qualities that make a dog a great worker make him a superior companion for a lazy man.

It is, however, impossible to overemphasize the fact that *individual differences within any breed are far greater than any differences between the average dogs of the different retriever breeds*. It is not so much which breed you get, but which dog. Bearing that in mind, hold your hats and here we go.

*What is the best breed of retriever?*

Well, this is supposed to be a democracy. Let's start by determining which breed is the most popular—which gets the most votes from retriever owners.

Allowing for the fact that in the earliest years of American retriever trials most of the dogs were registered with the Field Dog Stud Book (many are still dual registered), here are the figures for American Kennel Club registrations from 1931 (date of earliest trials recognized by the AKC) through 1966. Included are the six trial-eligible retrieving breeds and the American Water Spaniels.

From the above we might reasonably conclude that among the owners of purebred, registered retrievers in this country, the Labrador is:

In recent years, more than twice as popular as the six remaining breeds combined.

| Year | Labrador Re-triever | Chesa-peake Bay Re-triever | Golden Re-triever | Irish Water Spaniel | Curly-Coated Re-triever | Flat-Coated Re-triever | Amer. Water Spaniel | Annual Total |
|---|---|---|---|---|---|---|---|---|
| 1931 | 40 | 51 | — | — | — | — | | 91 |
| 1932 | 58 | 36 | 20 | 17 | — | 1 | | 132 |
| 1933 | 84 | 70 | 28 | 10 | 1 | 3 | | 196 |
| 1934 | 121 | 103 | 32 | 24 | — | 3 | | 283 |
| 1935 | 126 | 178 | 35 | 18 | 4 | 2 | | 363 |
| 1936 | 174 | 167 | 68 | 31 | 7 | 3 | | 450 |
| 1937 | 277 | 200 | 65 | 58 | 12 | 6 | | 618 |
| 1938 | 283 | 267 | 120 | 57 | 9 | 7 | | 743 |
| 1939 | 392 | 298 | 147 | 43 | 10 | 8 | | 898 |
| 1940 | 473 | 327 | 171 | 43 | 1 | 7 | 70* | 1092 |
| 1941 | 523 | 323 | 183 | 46 | 2 | 2 | 114 | 1193 |
| 1942 | 460 | 350 | 185 | 46 | 5 | 5 | 105 | 1156 |
| 1943 | 362 | 221 | 153 | 31 | 4 | — | 81 | 852 |
| 1944 | 515 | 172 | 248 | 44 | 1 | — | 60 | 1040 |
| 1945 | 956 | 427 | 511 | 59 | 2 | — | 86 | 2041 |
| 1946 | 1736 | 780 | 994 | 95 | 2 | — | 205 | 3812 |
| 1947 | 2035 | 787 | 1187 | 99 | 1 | 1 | 211 | 4321 |
| 1948 | 2190 | 685 | 1218 | 121 | 2 | 7 | 171 | 4394 |
| 1949 | 2154 | 628 | 1321 | 102 | 2 | 1 | 146 | 4354 |
| 1950 | 2442 | 543 | 1411 | 88 | 2 | — | 98 | 4584 |
| 1951 | 2915 | 622 | 1672 | 108 | 1 | — | 115 | 5433 |
| 1952 | 3320 | 652 | 1827 | 103 | 7 | 1 | 149 | 6059 |
| 1953 | 4152 | 751 | 2036 | 116 | 7 | 1 | 116 | 7179 |
| 1954 | 4529 | 791 | 2109 | 155 | 6 | 2 | 155 | 7747 |
| 1955 | 4777 | 746 | 2142 | 161 | 6 | — | 161 | 7993 |
| 1956 | 5510 | 803 | 2604 | 103 | 6 | 4 | 167 | 9197 |
| 1957 | 5744 | 823 | 2527 | 84 | 6 | 19 | 153 | 9356 |
| 1958 | 6111 | 757 | 2761 | 128 | 3 | 1 | 146 | 9907 |
| 1959 | 6520 | 870 | 2754 | 67 | — | 9 | 145 | 10365 |
| 1960 | 6549 | 703 | 2445 | 100 | — | 17 | 128 | 9942 |
| 1961 | 7526 | 626 | 2876 | 76 | — | 10 | 129 | 11243 |
| 1962 | 7865 | 610 | 2800 | 72 | 2 | 9 | 135 | 11313 |
| 1963 | 9125 | 608 | 3467 | 37 | 2 | 24 | 156 | 13419 |
| 1964 | 10340 | 721 | 3993 | 75 | 2 | 27 | 198 | 15356 |
| 1965 | 12370 | 873 | 4703 | 71 | 3 | 32 | 164 | 18216 |
| 1966 | 13686 | 972 | 5644 | 47 | 6 | 47 | 246 | 20648 |
| Totals | 126260 | 18541 | 54457 | 2535 | 124 | 259 | 3810 | 205986 |
| being | 61.3% | 9% | 26.4% | 1.23% | .06% | .12% | 1.85% | of the Grand Total |
| and | 67.3% | 4.8% | 26.1% | 0.38% | 0.21% | 0.17% | 1.14% | of total |

for the most recent five years on the above table.**

*First American Water Spaniel registrations in AKC Stud Book appeared in October, 1940.

**For 1977 and 1978, the AKC's registration totals were, respectively: Labradors 41,275 and 43,500; Chesapeakes 2,906 and 3,059; Goldens 30,263 and 34,249; Irish Water Spaniels 142 and 86; Curly-Coats 45 and 76; Flat-Coats 156 and 122; and American Water Spaniels 323 and 289.

More than two and one half times as popular as the Golden.

More than fourteen times as popular as the Chesapeake.

Still outdistancing the American Water Spaniels by nearly 60 to 1, the Irish Water Spaniels in popularity by 116 to 1, the Flat-Coats by better than 380 to 1 and the Curly-Coats by more than 3,500 to 1.*

There is pleasure to be found in the companionship, training, and hunting of the right dog from *any* of the breeds available.

This is a training book for the impatient man in a hurry—and it is true that it *is* easier to locate a good litter of Labs because there are so many more of them. It is probable that a *good* Lab pup could be located somewhere at any given time. Finding a top quality litter in any of the remaining breeds could mean a more difficult search and a longer wait.

Most, but not quite all, of the Irish Water Spaniels are in the hands of bench-minded breeders. The Curly-Coat is just beginning to be seen again in the United States and Canada. There has been, in recent years, a boomlet in Flat-Coats—but it would take decades under the most favorable circumstances before they could begin to reestablish the dominance they had over Labs in England before the dawn of modern field trials.

It would be difficult, probably impossible, to gauge the percentage of Goldens registered that are hunted. They make such excellent pets, companions, and obedience-trained dogs that they have earned popularity beyond considerations for their much respected prowess as retrievers.

The American Water Spaniel is included here even though it is not eligible for entry in retriever trials. It would probably be too small to compete in these on anything like equal terms with the larger retrieving breeds. But, it does make a dandy little hunting companion. Its AKC registrations have been running about twice those of the Irish Water Spaniel, Flat-Coat, and Curly-Coat combined. And almost every one of these economy-sized retrievers is being actively hunted and is the favorite of an appreciative hunter.

*The public is given to fads in dogs—and the Labrador has proven himself such a fine retriever that it has become something of a fashion to own a Labrador, preferably a black Labrador. Perhaps, the reviser feels, the late Jim Free's writings have been partly responsible for this development. Some readers apparently interpreted his cbjective advice as a suggestion to get any kind of retriever, so long as it was trainable, worth training—and a black Lab. I know this was never Jim Free's intention.—H. D.

A Labrador doesn't know what color he is. And there is nothing in the book of genetics that says a yellow or a chocolate Lab can't be as good as the best of the blacks. In fact, the field trial records book says they can be as good as any. At this writing the yellow, Field Ch. and Amateur Field Ch. Sir Mike of Orchardview stands eleventh in the all-time list of amateur stake winners with 129½ points. Adding his 49 open points, almost all of them under amateur handling, he stands twenty-fourth in combined amateur and open points. Right behind him in combined points is another yellow, Field Ch., Amateur Field Ch., Canadian Field Trial Ch. Brandy Spirit of Netley, that has 84½ amateur and 58½ open points for a total of 143.

The chocolate Field Trial Ch., Amateur Field Trial Ch., Canadian Field Trial Ch. Kimbrow General Ike was a respected campaigner. Currently winning chocolates include Field Ch. Gun Thunder Oly, Canadian Field Trial Ch. Choc of San Juan, and Amateur Field Ch. Oscar's Petite Lightning.

Now then, all of the foregoing considered, which breed has done the most to prove itself *in action?* Which has done best in retriever field-trial competition?

Through the first half of 1967 the top ten scorers of open points, all black Labradors, had totaled 1,431½ points, enough for 143 Field Championships—plus two National Field Championships. Just one of them has enough points for 18 Open Championships.

Here is a summary of placings in those top stakes which produce the Open Championship points, and which were open to all of the full-sized breeds of retrievers, covering the years 1934–1966, based upon the records of *Retriever Field Trial News:*

OPEN PLACINGS BY BREEDS 1934–1966 (1978)

| | % of AKC Regs. | First Places | % of First Places | Total Places | % of Places | Total Points | % of Points |
|---|---|---|---|---|---|---|---|
| Labradors | 62.5 | 1,870 | 88.6 | 7,237 | 86.6 | 17,465.5 | 87.5 |
| | (53.4) | (157) | (92.3) | (632) | (93.8) | (1,480) | (93.2) |
| Goldens | 26.9 | 178 | 8.4 | 772 | 9.2 | 1,792.0 | 8.9 |
| | (42.0) | (10) | (5.9) | (28) | (4.15) | (75) | (4.7) |
| Chesapeakes | 9.2 | 62 | 3.0 | 335 | 4.0 | 694.5 | 3.5 |
| | (3.7) | (3) | (1.8) | (14) | (2.07) | (32.5) | (2.1) |
| Curly-Coats | .06 | 0 | — | 5 | .06 | 8.0 | .04 |
| | (.09) | (0) | (—) | (0) | (—) | (0) | (—) |
| Irish | 1.25 | 0 | — | 3 | 0.35 | 3.0 | .015 |
| | (.1) | (0) | (—) | (0) | (—) | (0) | (—) |
| Flat-Coats | .13 | 0 | — | 1 | .012 | .5 | .005 |
| | (.14) | (0) | (—) | (0) | (—) | (0) | (—) |

Labradors, comprising just over 62 percent of the registered retrievers, won nearly 89 percent of the first places in open championship stakes for which all of the larger retrieving breeds were eligible. They won 86.6 percent of all the placings.

For this period, covering the entire era of American retriever trials, from the beginning until 1968, the Chesapeakes are now second in the wins-to-registrations ratio. Recent trial records have propelled them past the Goldens on this basis—a convincing demonstration of what the right kind of push can do for a breed. The Flat-Coats' win of a fourth in 1959 was the only open placement by any other breed in the previous 25 years. Another Flat-Coat placed in a Midwestern amateur stake during the fall of 1967.

Among the *best* dogs of the three most prominent breeds there is a much smaller degree of variation. And, if you want the best dog obtainable, the following figures should be the most meaningful for you. Here are included only those dogs good enough to have placed in breed-open competition.

These figures should provide useful perspective on the relative merits of the best field-trial dogs of each of the competing breeds, and afford an insight into current trends:

### PERFORMANCES, BY BREEDS, OF SCORING DOGS IN OPEN STAKES 1959–1966

|  | Lab-radors | % of Total | Chesa-peakes | % of Total | Gold-ens | % of Total | Total for All Breeds |
|---|---|---|---|---|---|---|---|
| Starts by Scorers | 16,855 | 91.1 | 482 | 2.6 | 1,165 | 6.3 | 18,518* |
| Placements | 3,260 | 90.7 | 122 | 3.4 | 212 | 5.9 | 3,596* |
| First Places | 822 | 91.1 | 31 | 3.4 | 49 | 5.4 | 902 |
| Points Earned | 7,800 | 90.8 | 294 | 3.4 | 490 | 5.7 | 8,584.5* |
| Points Per Start by Scoring Dogs | .4627 |  | .6099 |  | .4206 |  | .4635 Average for Four Breeds |

*Includes ½ point for one fourth place in 16 starts by a placing Flat-Coat.

These figures reveal, first, that Labradors dominate retriever trials in entries, winners, and virtually every other respect by better than 9 to 1; second, that the Chesapeake has the highest batting average, winning more than its proportional share of first places, of placements, and of points in open competition among the best dogs of all four competing breeds.

PERFORMANCES, BY BREEDS, OF SCORING DOGS
IN OPEN STAKES, 1961–1966

| | Lab-radors | % of Total | Chesa-peakes | % of Total | Gold-ens | % of Total | Total for All Three Scoring Breeds |
|---|---|---|---|---|---|---|---|
| Starts by Scorers | 11,366 | 92.1 | 315 | 2.5 | 670 | 5.4 | 12,351 |
| Placements | 2,159 | 91.4 | 82 | 3.5 | 122 | 5.1 | 2,363 |
| First Places | 543 | 91.4 | 23 | 3.9 | 28 | 4.7 | 594 |
| Points Earned | 5,167.0 | 91.3 | 213.5 | 3.8 | 278.0 | 4.9 | 5658.5 |
| Points Per Start by Scoring Dogs | .4627 | | .6777 | | .4149 | | .4635 |

Average for
Three Breeds

Even though these figures were included in the previous table, thus diluting the more current trends, the Labs show an increase of 1 full percent in starts by scorers—and that's difficult to do when you're as close to 100 percent as they are.

The Chesapeakes showed an even further gain in all except the percentage of starts by scoring dogs. According to these results, it's almost half again as easy to score with a really good Chesapeake as it is with a top quality Lab—and chances with a first-quality Chesie are nearly two-thirds again better than they would be with a trial-worthy Golden.

## FIELD TRIAL CHAMPIONS

From 1931 through 1966 a total of 458 retrievers were awarded open Field Championships.

Of these, 383 (83.6 percent) were Labradors.

Fifty-two (11.4 percent) were Goldens.

Twenty-three (5 percent) were Chesapeakes. None of the three remaining eligible breeds has ever produced any kind of a field-trial championship in the United States.

Through its first 26 runnings, the National (Open) Retriever Championship stake had been won 22 times by Labradors and 4 times by Goldens. The first 11 runnings of the National Amateur Retriever Championship were all won by Labradors.

The Labrador has the momentum and it is far easier to locate excellently bred Lab puppies than it would be to find equal quality in any of the other breeds. However, differences of coat, color, and refinement of form are connoisseurs' delights, and there will always be those who find a challenge in variation.

Obviously, the "minority" retrieving breeds* need the support of organized and determined sportsmen who enjoy challenge to champion and develop them. No one wants to see retriever trials become "Labrador trials." *Any* of these breeds—including the yellow and chocolate Labs—could improve its position significantly if new owners and breeders in sufficient numbers and energies could be added to those already supporting it. Intelligent, enthusiastic, well-financed promotional and breeding programs could, within a very few dog generations, make any of the "minority" breeds the equal of any other.

Having put all these facts and opinions on the record, let me briefly compare the *average* qualities of the three leading breeds, based on my experience with them in the field, in the blind, competing with them in trials, and judging them in trials.

Before I start, I'll confess that for my own purposes I prefer the Labrador. My friends who are Golden and Chesapeake enthusiasts sometimes accuse me of prejudice, and I have trouble convincing them that I love any good dog, regardless of his color or breed. For instance, I was one of the three judges at the first National Championship Trial, in 1941, who gladly and unanimously awarded the coveted title to a wonderful little Golden, King Midas of Woodend. He competed for three solid days with the best Labradors and Chesapeakes in the country, and for those days he was the best dog. And he was a dog I would be proud to own, and to shoot over under any conditions.

Anyway, I'll do my best here to give you my honest observations on the relative advantages and disadvantages of the three breeds, as objectively as possible.

*See Illustrations 126–133.

## THE GOLDEN RETRIEVER

### (See Illustrations 1–4)

To most people, the Golden is by far the prettiest dog to look at, and he is a beautiful animal by any standards. If I were just looking for a pet for myself or the kids, I would go no further. The Golden is very affectionate, being in disposition much like a setter or spaniel. One of the good ones is always tractable. He is the easiest of the three breeds for an impatient amateur to train to obedience and manners.

Usually he can't take much corporal punishment for his misdeeds without the danger of becoming cowed and crawling on his belly. Therefore, if you're apt to lose your temper with a dog, I wouldn't recommend a Golden. On the other hand, he's so eager to please, he doesn't really need any severe treatment to stay in line.

A Golden whose ancestors rank high on the list of field winners is hard to beat as a retriever on land, for any kind of upland game. He has a splendid nose, often winding game from distances up to 40 or 50 yards. He has a very tender mouth, and will never damage your game.

He is usually inferior to the Labradors and Chesapeakes in water. His ancestors were not natural water dogs, as the others were. He is often reluctant to take the water at first, and needs more careful handling to get him to enjoy swimming. Also, his long, wavy coat is a distinct handicap in this element. He is like a man going swimming in a coonskin coat. In spite of this, I've seen some Goldens that became great duck dogs. But they are the exceptions, not the average. And the best Golden is seldom as fast or powerful a swimmer as just a good average Labrador or Chesapeake.

If I did most of my hunting on land, with very little duck or goose shooting, I would seriously consider a Golden, particularly if I did most of my gunning in lighter cover, free from cockleburs. It *can* get to be something of a nuisance, after coming in from a hard day in the field, to spend a couple of hours extricating the tangled wads of burrs from the long, silky hair of a Golden. Some strains, however, have been bred with moderate coats to

make this job easier for owners—and to make swimming easier
for the dogs.

## THE CHESAPEAKE BAY RETRIEVER

(See Illustrations 5–8)

Among retrievers, the typical Chesapeake is at the far extreme
from the Golden in comparing most qualities and traits, with the
Labrador somewhere in between. The Chesapeake is a big, tough,
rugged dog, in body *and* disposition.

If most of your hunting is duck and goose shooting, and particularly if much of it is in saltwater, you'll make no mistake by
getting a good Chesapeake. He was originally developed and used
by the market hunters around Chesapeake Bay, where he had to
battle all day and half the night through the icy surf. For generations he has been bred and selected to take the severest punishment in the water, and he is really a *tough egg*.*

Compared to the Golden and the Labrador, he is not so easy
for an amateur to train. He is apt to be a bit hardheaded. But
a good one is intelligent, and knows when he's licked; if you're
a fairly hard-boiled character yourself, you can train one all right.
You have to keep ahead of him, and insist on obedience at all
times. When he defies you, as he may occasionally, you'll have to
be ready to impose your will by whatever means the situation demands, in order to "clean his ears out so he'll hear you better the
next time you give an order." If this means giving him a trim-
ming, then you'd better be ready to deliver your message in such a
manner that there will be no doubt of its being remembered.

At this point I can hear indignant screams, not only from the
ladies of the SPCA, but also from some of my Chesapeake-owning
friends. Sure, there are exceptions to anything. I've seen some
representatives of the breed that never needed a licking in their
lives. But on the average a Chesapeake is a rugged individualist,
about as tender and sensitive as a locomotive.

*This is still generally true. However, some breeders of Chesapeakes, in-
terpreting this as a criticism of their dogs, have been breeding so diligently
and expertly to produce milder temperaments that, in the opinion of some
old-time breeders, they are now breeding Chesapeakes that are too soft.
—H. D.

This has one important compensation. The Chesapeake requires a firm and sometimes even a heavy hand from his trainer, and I don't enjoy chastising a dog any more than you do. But it is almost impossible to cow him. I've never seen one crawl on his belly after the most severe punishment. Indeed, he's more likely to give you a playful nip if you turn your back on him.

Now here's another thing that must be said that will bring more yelps from the Chesapeake people. Some individuals of the breed show a tendency to hard mouth—the one unforgivable fault in a retriever. If a dog eats your game, or merely crushes it so it's unfit for the table, he's of no use whatever.

In retriever trials I've seen several clear-cut cases of hard mouth among Chesapeakes. I have seen only one Labrador unmistakably guilty of this crime, and no Goldens.

I think many of these cases could have been avoided if these dogs, when young, had been properly and carefully introduced to feathers in the first place. But the fact remains that Chesapeakes seem to have this tendency a little more than the other retrievers; if you get a young one, you must be very careful to avoid letting the fault get started.

Chesapeake enthusiasts will argue that their dogs take a good firm hold on their birds, and seldom drop them. And that many Goldens, and some Labradors, are tender-mouthed to a fault, taking sissy holds on big ducks and pheasant, constantly dropping them and stopping to fiddle around, rolling the birds in the mud, stopping to get a fresh hold on the way in. Well, they have a point there, too.

But I believe it is easier to teach a tender-mouthed dog to take a sufficiently firm hold than it is to dissuade his opposite number from flattening his birds. In fact, most professional trainers say it is virtually impossible to cure a really hard-mouthed dog once this vicious habit is firmly entrenched.

This book is primarily for the impatient man, the busy man, or the just plain lazy man, who wants to know the quickest and easiest way to end up with a well-trained retriever. For him, I'd be inclined to advise against a Chesapeake.

Now please don't misunderstand. This is all comparative, and some of it may even be hair-splitting. The Chesapeake from working stock is still much easier to train than the average dog of *any* breed that has been bred for bench shows rather than useful work. But of these three wonderful retriever breeds, you may as well know he is apt to be the least tractable, the least eager to please, the most inclined to be hardheaded, and even hardmouthed.

More than 35 years of selection for field trials from the most plastic of the Chesapeakes has made the traditional Chesapeake temperament and character something less than unanimous. Here's what his owner, Mrs. Eloise Heller, wrote about her FTC, AFTC, Can. FTC Nelgard's Baron, C.D., all-time high-scoring Chesapeake of a few years back: "I was told, when I bought this seven-year-old dog, he was as tough as they come. He had been violently beaten, shot with shotguns, and generally mistreated. . . . Just a month of living in my house, really becoming *my* dog, made all the difference in the world. Although he had always been happy to work, and was crazy for birds, he 'belonged' now, and was doing his best to please me. It wasn't at all necessary to hit him, for if he disobeyed in a handling test I could just walk out in the field and scold him. If I said 'Shame, shame on you,' I could drop him to the ground with dejection. I praised him when he did well, scolded him when he didn't, and he gave me his all. In one year we won three all-breed, open all-age firsts and, of course, made his Field Trial Championship."

Baron was a son, grandson, and a great-grandson of field champions. When the records he established for his breed in both open and amateur points were broken, it was Baron's son, Dual Ch., Amateur Field Ch. Baron's Tule Tiger that did it. So, it is quite likely that the selective influence of trial competition can be given some of the credit for this amiability and trainability.

## THE LABRADOR RETRIEVER

(See Illustrations 9–12)

We have said that the Golden is the easiest of the three breeds for an amateur to train to obedience. But on that score, the Labrador runs him a fairly close second.

There are a few hardheaded Labradors, but the great majority are very tractable. A good one is easy enough to train. If I can train one—and I've trained a good many—anybody should be able to do it.

I suppose there are some pansies in the breed, too, but personally I've never seen a Labrador crawl on his belly. He's not likely to need it, but if necessary the average Lab can stand up and take a well-deserved licking. On him, you can usually make a sufficient impression without resorting to really severe punishment. Even the toughest of the Labradors is not apt to defy you and need a walloping more than about once a year, for basically he wants to do the right thing. After punishment, he's more likely to jump up and lick your face, as if to say, "Okay, boss, you win," than he is to take a bite at your leg.

If you think you might want to have some fun with your dog in retriever trials, as well as using him for hunting, the records say your chances of picking up some ribbons are best with a Labrador.

And for the man who takes his hunting where he can find it, shooting everything that flies, over land or marsh or water, the Labrador is in my opinion the best all-round choice.

He has an excellent nose, perhaps not quite as spectacular as the Golden's, but plenty of nose to find all the upland game you can shoot for him. He'll trail a crippled, running cock pheasant a mile, and bring it to bag. His short, straight coat sheds burrs, which at times saves you a lot of work and a lot of cussing. In addition to retrieving, he takes naturally to working like a spaniel, quartering close in ahead of the gun to flush upland birds. He is rugged and tough enough to go all day in the heaviest and most punishing cover. I've never seen a Labrador wear out or quit in the hunting field.

He loves the water, his ancestors having been natural water dogs. When sent, he hits the water with a great splash that is a joy to see. He is a fast, strong swimmer. His short, oily coat is no drag in the water. He is not quite as rugged as the Chesapeake for battling icy surf all day, but you'd have a tough time ever drowning a Labrador under the worst conditions, at that. For the ordinary duck hunter's needs, he is all that can be desired.

Personally I like to see a dog *or* a man who seems to love his job. And the average Labrador seems to have this quality even more than the Golden or the Chesapeake. In the trials, the fastest dogs are the Labradors. They go at a sizzling run, not only until they find the bird, but they come in with it almost as fast as they go out. Too often you see the Goldens and Chesapeakes coming in at a slow trot, or even a walk. Perhaps this is a minor point. But part of the pleasure of watching a good dog work is found in the style with which he does his work, whether in trials or in the hunting field.

Now, a word about color. Most of the Labradors are black. Most of the biggest trial winners are black—although not necessarily beyond the approximate 90 percent of the entries they comprise.

The man who breeds, or buys, for color is handicapping himself because it is impossible to concentrate on this one genetic factor without neglecting other, more vital considerations in the makeup of a field dog. I had a friend who was determined to develop a strain of yellows. We often debated far into the night over the desirability of a yellow versus a black coat on a duck dog.

His argument, of course, was that the yellow coat blends with the dead-grass color of a duck blind, or other available cover to hide a dog from waterfowl. (The Chesapeake and Golden enthusiasts use the same argument in favor of their dogs, which have coats ranging from light yellow to golden to dark brown.)

My contention was, and still is, that this is of no practical importance, because ducks pay no attention to a black dog anyway. I've hunted all kinds of ducks under all sorts of conditions, using black Labradors to retrieve them. More often than not, I don't even have the dog in the blind with me, but set him out in the open, right on top of a muskrat house, or on any other dry spot available, where he has a better opportunity to mark falls in any direction. Even the wariest mallards, which flare and shy off if they see so much as a tip of *my* ear, will come straight in to the decoys with a black dog sitting right out in plain sight watching them. I have never had ducks flare, nor lost an opportunity for a shot, because they saw a black dog, whether he was in the blind or out of it.

I have discussed this with dozens of other duck hunters who have had the same experience, and have yet to hear firsthand testimony for a single case where ducks have shied from a black Labrador.

Therefore it seems silly to me to struggle to produce a recessive color trait. The breeder's problems are sufficient without adding the pointless complication of color breeding. One of the reasons the Labrador, the *black* Labrador, has outdistanced his fellow retrievers in a relatively short breed history is that his breeders have been able to concentrate on intelligence, trainability, nose, eagerness to hunt, boldness, endurance, guts, speed, and style—and let the fancy genetic appearance factors be hanged. The black Labrador is an unparalleled combination of dominant *appearance* factors such as black, short hair, broad skull, chunky body, and a rather gaily carried tail. His breeders have not been handicapped by dedication to fancy factors, profitless in a gun dog.

The beauty of a good retriever is not in the color, length, or texture of his coat. Nor is it in the set of his ear or the shape of his muzzle. His beauty is in a sound body, strong legs, and good feet, and in intelligence and alertness. It's in his power, his alertness, his proud bearing, and his efficient motion—his class!

I'm not willing to yield one bit of class for the sake of non-functional attributes. I want a hunting dog, not an ornament.

## WHICH IS THE BEST ALL-ROUND DOG?

People often ask which breed makes the best combined hunting dog, pet, and watchdog.

We've pretty well covered the first two categories. Now how do the three breeds stack up as watchdogs?

Before going further, it is important to stress the fact that I am referring to the average dog of each breed, as I've known them. Extremes in any direction can almost always be found within a given breed.

Now, to answer the question. If I were a postman, I'd have no fear of a Golden or a Labrador as I went about my legitimate business, but I would give a Chesapeake a wide berth.

If I were planning to burgle a house with no people, but with a dog in it, *I* wouldn't tackle one containing either a Chesapeake or a Labrador, but would be fairly confident of my ability to make friends with a Golden, or bluff him into submission. *I* would not attempt to break and enter a house containing a man with a gun *and* a Golden, for the dog would probably give the alarm. He is not apt to bite, but he will bark, and that's really all you ordinarily need in a watchdog. What I might do as a theoretical burglar isn't necessarily what a professional thief might do. They are cowards, sneaking about in the night, taking their livings by what appears to them as the "easiest way." With a streetful of houses to choose from, they'll probably try to find one without a dog, regardless of breed.

All three of these breeds are being used successfully as guide dogs for the blind. The intelligence and the trainability of retrievers is well above the average for the various breeds of dogs. The Goldens, especially, have distinguished themselves in obedience competition.

In summation, these are *my* recommendations.

For a companion or a pet I recommend a Golden.

For a dog that excels on upland game in fairly light cover, where burrs are not apt to be a serious problem, you might very well select a Golden.

For retrieving ducks and geese under rugged conditions and/or if you relish the challenge of training what could be a most challenging dog, try a Chesapeake. If yours is like those I've known, you may have to be ready to go a long way to convince him you are going to be the boss. I cannot recommend the Chesapeake for a pet. This breed was evolved by the Eastern Shore ducking clubs, with emphasis upon qualities needed by an open-water retriever. The dogs were kept in club kennels and were seldom taken home by their originators. They weren't designed to be companions.

For a versatile dog on land and water, for the average hunter, I consider the Labrador to be the best bet.

And for a combined hunting dog, pet, and watchdog—an all-round dog—your chances of finding the individual you want are much better in choosing a Labrador than from the other breeds.

Now let me repeat—the foregoing generalities apply to the

*average* representatives of the *top half* of these three wonderful breeds. They apply to the dogs from *close-up working ancestors,* not from bench-show stock. And even among the top half, there are exceptions in each of the breeds—outstanding and poor individuals. *I* favor the Labradors, but I've seen plenty of these to which I would not now give kennel space. Remember this when you set out to find your retriever:

You are going to buy one individual dog—a *good* dog—not a breed of dogs.

# 5

---

# How to Find Your Dog

ALL YOU NEED to do is to find *the* reputable breeder who has available the pup or dog you want, and this is easy if you go about it right.

The best marketplace for the best retrievers is in *Retriever Field Trial News,* 4213 S. Howell Avenue, Milwaukee, Wisconsin 53207. It is published by the National Retriever Field Trial Club and the National Amateur Retriever Club. The annual subscription price for ten issues is $20.00, and sample copies of the current issue or back issues may be had for $2.10 or $2.20.

A rather complete listing of pertinent periodicals may be found in the Bibliography. You can also obtain information from the secretaries of the national and local clubs which are listed in Appendix III.

At present there are no clubs affiliated with the AKC for American Water Spaniels or Curly-Coats.

Write the secretaries of the clubs in which you have a possible interest. Enclose a stamped, addressed return envelope.

I do urge you, however, not to lose sight of "The Great Secret" which I spelled out for you in Chapter 1: if you are going to train a dog, start with one worth training, and one that wants to be trained.

Now, if you want to indulge yourself in a sportsman's challenge with a "minority" breed, or if you find fascination in perfected form and color, I can appreciate that there is room and there is reason for many tastes. Certainly the world of retrieverdom is more pleasurable and colorful, offers a greater competitive zest for the fact of the presence and/or existence of yellow and chocolate Labradors, Goldens, Chesapeake Bays, Flat-Coated and Curly-Coated Retrievers and American and Irish Water Spaniels.

Choose your own pleasure. As an impatient, nonprofessional trainer, I've found my pleasure in worthwhile, trainable, black Labradors.

If you still haven't been able to make up your mind as to which breed you prefer, write all five clubs, and be an opportunist. Look at whatever is available and buy the pup or dog you like the best, whatever he is. You can't go too far wrong, if you get a really good individual, from trial-proven breeding.

The next thing—or perhaps the first thing to do, since the experience will season your judgment—is to locate and go to a retriever field trial, if this is practical or possible.

At this writing there are nearly 135 AKC-licensed trials spread over the country each year. There are also 300 or 400 informal or "picnic" trials. You shouldn't have much difficulty in getting to one of them. *Retriever Field Trial News* will tell you when and where you can find a licensed trial near you. All licensed trials are also listed in the AKC's monthly, *Pure-Bred Dogs*. This publication is found in many public libraries.

You might also try asking your local gunsmith or outdoor-equipment dealer or outdoors editor if he can tell you who is known in your area as a retriever field-trial enthusiast. Having located such an individual, phone him and see the welcome you'll get.

Trials will offer a triple service. Watching the dogs perform, in competition, will help you decide which breed you want, if you are on the fence, or will confirm or possibly cause you to question the decision you've already made. They will demonstrate to you what the standards of performance are. And they will enable you to meet the leading retriever people of your territory, including possibly the man who has the dog you want.

Owners and handlers at retriever trials are a splendid bunch of people. There you will find a melting pot, from all walks of life—wealthy sportsmen who are captains of industry rubbing elbows with clerks and laboring men. And the ladies are right in there also, training, handling, and sometimes judging—all on even terms with the men. All are held together by their great enthusiasm for these dogs which they consider "much too good for the common people."

Most of them are very friendly to interested newcomers, and many will talk your arm off, giving you a great opportunity to listen and learn. Try to meet the president and the secretary of the club, and any of the other officers you can. These leaders are usually amateur sportsmen who love the dogs for their own sake, and they will steer you right.

You might even stumble onto a good young dog, whose work you see yourself at the trial, that can be bought for one reason or another. This won't necessarily happen at your first trial, but it could. And if your object is to buy a trained dog, sooner or later you'll find one available around the trials.

Most of them are very friendly to interested newcomers, and because they are "retriever happy." But in any group you'll find a few poor losers. Sometimes you can buy a superior dog from one of these, if you're right on the spot to make an offer when the dog has had a poor series and is out of the stake. The greatest dogs in the world have their off days, but some of these characters who care only for winning don't realize this, and will impulsively sell a fine young dog at the moment he loses out in a trial.

Between your letters to the parent breed clubs, the advertisements in *Retriever Field Trial News,* and your contacts made at field trials, you should have no trouble locating reliable breeders within reasonable driving distances of your home. And let me re-emphasize what I mean by a "reliable" breeder. In buying your first retriever, you want to be fussy. Pick a man who not only has a reputation as a square shooter, but who has other visible means of support than just *selling* dogs. And preferably a man who proves his own stock in field trials. You want no truck with breeders for bench shows *only,* backyard breeders, or pet shops.

Now just a word to explain what the term "backyard breeder," uttered in scornful tone, means among the enthusiasts for good working dogs. It means the man or woman who does not hunt, who has no interest in these dogs for their working qualities, who sees an opportunity for profit in selling pups. These people know nothing of bloodlines, field-trial records, or scientific breeding, and care less. They usually start with a pet or the cheapest bitch they can buy. No matter her quality, so long as she is registered.

Then they breed her to the dog with the cheapest stud fee they can find, and sit back and pray for a huge litter. Retrievers often whelp ten or more pups, and breeders of this ilk don't go to the extra pains necessary to raise a large litter. Somehow they find somebody for every pup they manage to raise, and because of improper nourishment of the dam or the pups, or both, none of the pups gets a sufficient start in life. Without extra help, few bitches can give more than eight pups a decent start. With a powdered bitch's milk such as Ebsilac, a feeding tube and hypodermic syringe (or a regular human baby bottle), anyone who wishes to make an effort can help a bitch to nourish any number of puppies properly. But backyard breeders seldom extend themselves. I would want to *know* that any pup I was buying had been properly nourished from the moment of its conception onward.

The type of backyard breeder I'm talking about usually advertises pups for sale at bargain prices in the classified columns of the local newspaper. Many of them are women. They erect cheap and inadequate pens and runs in the yard, and the pups are often raised in filth. It is impossible to rear strong, healthy pups under such conditions.

However, there are some fine pups occasionally raised in backyards, by sincere enthusiasts, hunters, or field-trial people who have a fine bitch, breed her correctly to a great stud, and raise the litter carefully under sanitary conditions. They will tell you all about the sire and dam, the grandparents, their *working* qualities and their field-trial records. I don't call those people backyard breeders, simply because they live in a city, town, or suburb instead of out in the country. In fact, you're quite likely to have one or more of these on your list, as well as some of the larger breeders with country kennels.

After you have located your breeders, it will save your time and theirs if you write or phone them first, inquiring if they have anything available to suit your needs, before going to see them. Usually the best dogs or pups are obtained from the least commercial breeders, men and women who are doing their bit to improve the breed, purely as a hobby. Although they charge good prices for the occasional pups and dogs they sell, very few make anything but a substantial annual loss on their kennels. They have a big investment in sanitary kennels and runs. They feed their dogs the best food obtainable, and plenty of it. They raise healthy litters, assuring the pups a good start. They reluctantly but firmly have the poor specimens put to sleep—instead of selling them for what they can get.

Many of their pups they keep themselves for field-trial prospects. Others are earmarked for friends in the game, people they *know* will appreciate and do right by a worthy pup, and give him an opportunity to show what he can do in trials. So don't be disappointed if breeders of this type don't have a pup you can buy and take home whenever you happen to drop in.

But the law of averages says that from your list, you'll find at least one good breeder with something available. If you impress him as honest and as a man able to appreciate a real dog, he'll probably let you have the pup or dog on approval for a few days, and return your money if you return the dog in good health. Some will even go so far as to guarantee their dogs unconditionally, allowing you to return them at any time if you don't like them. You won't find any backyard breeders or pet shops doing that. This privilege could be horribly abused, of course, but if you're the kind who would do so, such a breeder wouldn't sell you a dog anyway. He's interested in placing his animals with the right people.

By the time you've located your breeder, you've probably decided whether you want a male or female, but perhaps we should have a little discussion of this before you make your selection.

## MALE OR FEMALE?

You sometimes hear it said that a female makes the better hunting dog. I have not found it so. I've had some wonderful bitches I've used as shooting dogs, and some wonderful males, too. If you have no strong preference either way, perhaps you'll do best by being an opportunist on this score also—buying the best available retriever you can find, whether it is male or female.

The drawback to a female, of course, is that she does come in season twice a year, and you have to be careful at those times to have her confined in a stout pen that she cannot get out of—and that dogs cannot get into. Some astonishing feats of climbing can be accomplished at such times, for love. Freehaven Jay once went over three nine-foot fences, believe it or not, in order to fix us up with an unplanned litter from a bitch who was that way.

There are good odor-disguising preparations than can be doused on a bitch. Many times I have taken a bitch in season out shooting with no trouble, fooling farm dogs, and even male shooting dogs in the same party.

Even unplanned litters are no longer the kind of mental threat they once were. If you know the act has been done—and if you act quickly enough—your veterinarian can give your bitch a series of two injections which will possibly abort any conception which may have taken place. These injections have the slight disadvantage of prolonging the bitch's heat.

Although there have been some great field-trial bitches, most of the trial campaigners are males—simply because their sex and reproductive lives do not conflict with their competitive careers. You cannot enter a bitch in season in a trial. It is unfair to the males and it is definitely against the rules. If you are interested in competing in trials, or think you might be, you had probably best take the uncomplicated path and start with a male. (This is good advice, but the late Dr. Bliss A. Finlayson of Seattle, Washington, bought the first edition of this book *after* he had purchased a puppy bitch named Ace's Sheba of Ardyn. With Dr. Finlayson training and handling, she has become 1961 National Amateur Field Trial Champion, Field Trial Champion, Amateur Field Trial Champion, and 1959 Co-National Derby Champion Ace's Sheba of Ardyn.)

If you think you might be interested in becoming a breeder, then of course you want a female.

Sometimes you hear people say a female is better because she doesn't wander away like a male—stays close to home. This is perfect nonsense. Nobody in his right mind will allow a valuable retriever—male or female—to roam at will, to be stolen, killed by a truck, poisoned by an angry neighbor, or just to accumulate bad habits that ruin it for any good use. So if the dog is kept properly confined and under control, this question is beside the point.

# 6

## Selecting Your Dog

NOW LET'S ASSUME you've found your breeder, decided on the breed and sex you prefer, and whether a pup or an older dog.

### HOW TO PICK A PUP
### (See Illustrations 13–14)

Many retriever-happy people, including me, get to kidding themselves that they can pick the best one out of a litter of young pups. We all have different systems, and go through our own sets of motions.

But actually, with pups up to three or four months old, you're almost entirely dependent on the pedigree. Given a litter of good healthy pups, with the right breeding behind them, you're about as well off to shut your eyes and reach in and grab one, as to go through all the nonsense I do.

Many times you'll be given no choice. The breeder will point out one particular male, or a female, and tell you that is the only one available. He is keeping the others, or they are already spoken for by other people. Well, if you're dealing with the kind of breeder you'd better be, go ahead and take the pup that's left. He wouldn't sell it to you if there was anything wrong with it. And you'll have just as good a chance as he has—maybe better—to end up with the prize of the litter. Arnold Rothstein did pretty well, just betting that the wise guys were wrong.

Anyone who raises a litter of pups, and sees them every day, is bound to pick some favorites as he goes along—and even the most experienced dog men will often pick them for foolish reasons, or no reasons. Pups change so fast, even from day to day, it is impossible for anyone to look into a crystal ball and know exactly what a pup will turn out to be when it grows up.

So spend your time studying the pedigree, and asking questions about it, instead of mooning over the individual pups. Exactly who were the father, mother, and the four grandparents? What did each of them *do*? In field trials? As shooting dogs? What were their dominant good qualities? What faults, if any? A good breeder will know these answers, and will tell them to you quite frankly.

After you are satisfied with the breeding behind the litter, go ahead and grab yourself a pup out of it, and take it home.

Of course you want a healthy-looking pup, with good bones, and reasonably straight legs. We'll assume you have taken the recommended precautions to insure, as nearly as possible, that congenital hip dysplasia will not be a future problem for you. (See page 24, Chapter 3.) If your pup is a Labrador, don't let the color bother you so long as it is an allowable black, yellow, or chocolate. The same can be said of any of the other retriever breeds. Pick the dog, let the color fall where it may—just so long as it is within the breed standard. All of the retriever standards, except Irish Water Spaniels and Flat-Coats, permit a few white hairs on the chest. Chesapeakes and American Water Spaniels may even have bits of white on their feet. There's a good practical reason for this stern suppressing of large white spots in retrievers. If they are allowed to degenerate into a lot of white-spotted dogs, they *might* be too conspicuous for duck-shooting companions. Also the lovers of these distinctive animals just don't care to have them lose their identity and be confused with coach dogs or bird dogs.

But if you're in the hands of a good retriever breeder, there will be no weak, sickly, or deformed pups, and none with excess white to choose from. All these will have long since joined their ancestors in canine heaven, wearing small extra halos for having done their bit toward maintaining and improving the standard of the breed.

Complete, official standards for all of the retrieving breeds recognized by the American Kennel Club will be found in Appendix I. Read them if you like, but for a new retriever enthusiast trying to buy his first pup, these detailed standards may prove more confusing than helpful.

Don't spend too much time worrying over breed standards, if you're after a pup. Almost any jerk can recognize a reasonably well-put-together pup when he sees one, without studying a table of points. And that's all you want, from an appearance standpoint. Sure, you want a decent-looking dog. But you are mainly interested in what's inside.

I honestly believe that with young pups it's impossible to tell which member of the litter has the most desirable stuff inside. Yet, knowing it's a waste of time, I usually toss something for each pup to retrieve, presumably to determine which is naturally most interested in retrieving. This is about the same as trying to decide whether a two-year-old baby might grow up to be a pitcher for the Dodgers, by handing him a baseball and seeing if he throws it.

In many young retrievers the powerful desire and instinct for retrieving seems to lie dormant, and often does not bloom until age eight or nine months, or even a year. This was true of Freehaven Jay, that, according to the record, is one of the field-trial greats of all time.

He was three months old when I picked him blindly out of a litter sired by the illustrious Glenairlie Rover. I took him home, and in my ignorance was greatly distressed when I could not get him to retrieve or even to chase a ball or a training dummy. He just wasn't interested. At last, in despair, when he was nine months old, I put him in training with Jim Hogan. Evidently he was just about ready by then to come to life. Also, Jim Hogan was the lad who knew how to wake up his natural instincts and speed his progress. At any rate, just three months later he won his first stake in a field trial, and from then on was sufficiently precocious, winning the title Field Trial Champion before his second birthday.

That started me on my "retriever-happy" career. Since then, I've raised and trained many good dogs that weren't much interested in retrieving as young pups.

Another fairly useless thing I do in picking a pup is to try to find the one that is boldest, most alert, and presumably most intelligent. For instance, I run away from them, calling, whistling, and clapping hands—to see which chases me most aggressively. But the little character who yawns, curls up under a bush, and goes to sleep today might easily be the one that would win the race tomorrow. Puppies are mercurial. They do a lot of napping between their violent fits of play. At any given moment, trying to pick the brightest of the lot is virtually impossible.

So let's just sum up this matter of picking a pup.

Deal with a good breeder, preferably a field-trial man, but at any rate someone with field-trial stock.

Study the parents and the grandparents in the pedigree. If they had the right stuff inside, you can be as sure as it's possible to be that the pups will have it also. The one you grab may never be a field-trial champion, but after all there aren't many of those, and just who do you think you are, anyway? Your pup is likely to grow up to be the finest gun dog you ever dreamed of owning, at the very least.


## BUYING AN OLDER DOG

### (See Illustrations 15–22)

In buying an adult dog—a year old or more—you'd better study the breed description and standard of points a bit more carefully— at least enough to recognize a fairly good physical specimen when you see him. You don't need a potential bench champion, but you do want an animal with no serious defects from the conformation standards set up by the breed club, which presumably had practical reasons for most of them.

Then, whether the dog is trained, partly trained, or untrained, you should be just as fussy about the parents and the grandparents in the pedigree as if you were selecting a young pup. This is important for several reasons. You may not think you'll ever be interested in using the dog for breeding. Neither did I, when I bought Jay, "just for a shooting dog." Since then he has sired several field-trial champions, and I have at times been wading in black pups up to my ears.

Right now you probably are positive you would never think of selling your dog. I was equally sure I would never part with my first retriever. But then Jay gave me the field-trial fever, which led to the incurable disease of breeding. And I have been obliged to sell many dogs I was attached to. You can't keep them all.

Being human, our ideas are subject to change, and it is smart whenever possible to buy anything, whether it's a dog or a house, with an eye to its resale value. No matter how good an individual retriever may be, an impressive pedigree with well-known working ancestors behind him will make him much more valuable if you want to sell him. And of course the pedigree has an even more important effect on the value of his pups, and the stud fee he can command.

First, let's assume you are buying a young, untrained dog of *twelve months or more*. You are satisfied with his pedigree. Even though the dog is untrained, and priced accordingly (possibly from two to three hundred dollars), by that age you can tell something about his natural traits and characteristics. By now he should naturally be keen to retrieve. Ask the owner to toss a training dummy in cover sufficient to hide it. It doesn't need to be a long retrieve. You can tell a lot just from a bundle thrown in a yard. I like to see a youngster that scorches the ground in his eagerness, going out. If he misses the dummy on the first cast, he should show some persistence about hunting until he finds it. You should see him at least showing signs of discovering that he has a nose, sniffing the breeze, and working his way upwind to the fall. The important things to watch are what he does *until he finds the dummy*. That's what reveals the most desirable of his natural, inherited characteristics. Don't worry too much if he doesn't come right in and deliver to hand, or even if he wants to run away and lie down and play with the dummy. That's just puppy stuff, and easily corrected in the course of training—if he has the right stuff in him.

With a reasonably tractable dog, it is easy to take undesirable things out of him. But it is impossible to put things into him that should be there in the first place. Such things as keenness, fire, desire to hunt, persistence, guts, and a good nose to smell with. When a youngster who has these things goes out to retrieve a training dummy, it doesn't take an expert to recognize him. You'll know. Quality will stick out all over him.

If you're a duck hunter, before buying such a young dog you should also see him go in the water. It doesn't need to be big water, for a long swim. A swimming pool or a small pond will do.

When a floating dummy is thrown in, he should hit the water enthusiastically, without hesitation. If he runs up and down shore, trying to make up his mind, and finally tiptoes in as if he hates to get his feet wet, he's not the duck dog for you. By careful training and encouragement, you *might* improve his water work a lot, and you might not. But to do that heartwarming and spectacular job in the water that a good retriever should do, he should be pretty enthusiastic about it to start with. You don't want to spend your life sitting in duck blinds, cussing your dog just to get him to go in the water.

So in buying a young untrained dog you need to see only three things: the pedigree, one land retrieve, and one in the water. You'll know whether he's for you.

But if you're putting out the money for a *trained* retriever, you should see a good deal more. You should see him do all of the retrieving chores that he can *reasonably be expected to do, at his attained age, and at his price.*

Many new retriever enthusiasts, after seeing the open all-age dogs perform in a field trial, make the mistake of expecting a young, trained dog to do the same stuff that the hot competitors make look so easy. You wouldn't expect a high-school ballplayer to measure up to big-league standards. No more should you demand that a young retriever be able to do blind retrieves and take whistle and hand signals like a five-year-old field-trial champion.

In Part III you will find descriptions of the typical tests usually encountered in trials, both on land and in water. In buying a trained dog, it isn't fair to ask the owner to show the dog doing more than he would have to do in a trial.

If the dog is under twelve months, you should be satisfied to see him do the simple marked retrieves, a single shot pigeon on land, a shackled duck in the water, which used to be the tests expected in the Puppy Stake, now discontinued.

If he is a little older—up to about two years old—Derby Stake standards should be applied. These include the ability to make double retrieves on land and water.

Now if the dog is older than two, and the owner is offering him as a good shooting dog but frankly says he doesn't think he'll ever be an Open All-Age dog, he will be priced accordingly, and you should judge him by the typical tests of a Qualifying Stake. That is the stake for the faithful duck and pheasant dogs, the meat dogs, that are wonderful hunting companions but don't quite have that extra something that makes a possible field-trial champion.

Of course if you want a field-trial winner, and are digging down for a price running into four figures, then you want to see that dog do everything he would be asked to do in an Open All-Age Stake. As a matter of fact, before buying such a dog you would be wise to see him compete in one or more trials as well.

Any sincere retriever enthusiast who sells you a trained dog of any age will want to spend sufficient time with you and the dog to be sure you understand how to handle him and get the most out of him.

It is nearly always a mistake for anyone not experienced in training and handling retrievers to buy his first trained dog by mail. In fact, it can be tragic. Many fine dogs have been ruined this way.

Most of the leading retriever trainers use the commands, the hand signals, and the whistle signals given in Part II of this book. But the dog you buy may have been trained quite differently. And the smallest misunderstanding in this respect can be terribly important.

A duck hunter I used to know, an impatient and choleric man, once bought his first and last retriever, a dog I happened to know, a good one. He paid a thousand dollars for it, and it was shipped to him by air. He grabbed the dog out of the crate, and left at once for a duck-hunting trip.

He could not get that dog to retrieve a duck. He would scream, "Fetch," and "Go fetch," and, "Get the hell out there," and everything else he could think of. The dog would just sit quietly in the boat and look at him patiently. The man lost his temper. His companions ribbed him unmercifully about his thousand-dollar dog.

At last, in a rage, he impulsively gave the dog away to his guide. And to this day he is convinced that retrievers are utterly useless.

Now there was nothing wrong with that dog. He had been

trained, as most retrievers are, to go in and retrieve *only when his name was spoken*. To him, the command "fetch" meant something quite different, as you will see in Part II.

It is almost impossible for the seller of a trained dog to give you in a letter everything you should know about that dog, the commands to which he responds, his little idiosyncrasies, and the tricks of handling him. Furthermore, a trained retriever is almost human, and instinctively he can spot a greenhorn, and will take perverse delight in playing you for a sucker sometimes, if he can get away with it.

So, if you want to put out important money for a trained dog, it is much better to buy your first one at least in person rather than by mail. Then the owner can demonstrate the dog thoroughly, *show* you what you can reasonably expect the dog to do, and *show* you how to handle him properly.

Thus, after you get the dog home, you will know what has gone before in his education, and it will be simple for you to carry on from that point with his training—with no waste motions—enough to keep him improving with age and experience, instead of slipping backward. For a dog, like a man, does one or the other. Which it will be, with a good trained dog, depends on his new owner.

But don't let this alarm you. It takes very little time, and it's easy, to keep a trained retriever in the groove.

# 7

# Special Retriever Care

MOST GOOD RETRIEVERS are about as hardy as civilized dogs get—but they are flesh and bone and their work carries them into situations which can produce medical problems and injuries seldom encountered by less active or strictly land-working dogs. A little care before and after a hunt or trial can often help to avoid infection and sickness. The following is a consensus from three veterinarian friends.

Any new dog, puppy or grown, should be taken to your veterinarian at once for a physical examination. If it is a puppy, ask your veterinarian to inaugurate an immunization program for such diseases as distemper, hepatitis, leptospirosis, and rabies.

If you are or become a breeder, have the extra "dewclaws" removed from the puppies while they are still weanlings. It is an extremely simple operation for any veterinarian then—much more difficult later. If allowed to remain, dewclaws are subject to being torn loose afield when such an injury can be painful to the dog and ruin an otherwise good hunt for you. Dewclaws have no function, and, at best, represent potential trouble.

Keep the ears of all flap-eared dogs clean. Use some baby oil on a piece of clean cotton. Do not attempt to reach in farther than you can go with your finger. Check the ears frequently. If, when you massage the soft cartilage at the base of the ear, you hear a watery sound—or if the ear has a sour smell—do not delay a trip to your veterinarian.

Dogs retrieving from the water are almost certain to get some water in their ears. Sprinkle a little BFI powder into the *outer* ear, and then let the dog shake it out. Lay the dog on his side and let the water drain out.

Never go probing into the inner ear. If it gets packed with wax and dirt, have a veterinarian flush it out.

After each workout, give your dog's eyes a brief but careful look. In some seasons weed seeds tend to collect under the eyelids and in the corners of the eye. Wipe these out with a bit of cotton. Use some eyedrops if the dog evidences irritation in his eyes. Watch for eye congestion or corneal injury. These call for professional treatment.

Roll the dog's lip up occasionally and note the color of his gums. If he doesn't show a good, healthy red color consistently, you can suspect some form of anemia, possibly induced by a hookworm infestation. Never worm a dog unless you know what you are worming a dog for. Let a veterinarian do the job after he has determined from a stool examination what kind of worming, if any, is needed.

Run your hands over the dog's body to detect any imbedded thorns. Check his feet, especially if he is a long-coated dog, for thorns or burrs between the toes. Run your fingers under the dog's armpits to make sure there are no burrs there to make his every stride painful.

If possible, condition a dog gradually for hard work. Give him a chance to work his muscles and his pads hard before you ask him to deliver a full day's effort. Especially when age begins to slow a dog does he need this conditioning.

If your dog is wet and the weather cold or the wind high, rub him down before you put him in the car or his crate. Pin an old blanket on the tired and wet brute so his own body heat can dry him. One big safety pin under the neck and another under the belly should do the trick.

A few minutes of concern and care each time you take your dog afield will earn his appreciation—and help keep him out of the veterinarian's office.

# Part II

HOW TO TRAIN YOUR DOG THE EASY WAY

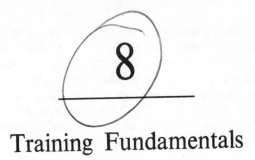

# 8

# Training Fundamentals

OF COURSE the *very easiest* way to get a dog trained is to duck the job entirely and send him to a professional trainer. But good retriever men are scarce and busy. They won't take more dogs than they can comfortably handle. and give each owner his money's worth. Some of the very best ones have at times had to require that reservations be made months in advance for spots in their training strings. At this writing, good professionals charge prices ranging from seventy-five to one hundred dollars per month for board and training (bird bills and trial expenses can skyrocket the bill). Believe me, the pros earn every cent of what they get. To start a twelve-month-old retriever properly, a trainer should have him at least two or three months, depending on the individual dog and on how fast he can safely be pushed. (Here's where a worthwhile, trainable dog becomes an economy. He's cheaper to train, because he learns faster—and better.)

If, as is quite possible, you can't find a well-recommended retriever specialist in your vicinity, able and willing to take on your dog, then you'd better do your own training. Don't make the mistake of compromising on a strictly bird-dog trainer. Some of these are very fine men, but unless they have taken the trouble to learn the retriever specialty—and *have done some actual handling in retriever trials*—they can't do as good a job on your retriever as you can do yourself. They don't know how. For the main job of pointers and setters is finding and pointing live birds—on land. With them, retrieving is strictly secondary. And they are rarely asked to retrieve waterfowl.

So your average bird-dog trainer has no idea what a good retriever can and should be asked to do. He seldom has adequate
water, or even land cover, to train retrievers at his home kennel
at all times of year. And he is likely to be too easily satisfied
with sloppy obedience to commands—since this phase of training
is not so important in pointer and setter work, and usually is not
emphasized with bird dogs as it must be with retrievers.

At the other extreme are the "obedience trainers," to be found
in almost every community, who undertake to teach manners to
any kind of dog. Some of these will assure you they can train a
finished retriever, but unless such a man has had a good deal of
actual experience in AKC-licensed retriever trials, I wouldn't en-
trust a good young prospect to him. A trainer of this type probably
has even less adequate land and water facilities than the bird-dog
man.

He'll teach your dog the obedience commands, all right. That's
his business. But he knows even less than the bird-dog man about
retriever work. And he's all too likely to slow down a promising
youngster, take the steam out of him, and spoil his enthusiasm
for his work—by trying to make him *too steady too soon.* He'll
take on anything from a Scottie to a Great Dane, and most of
the pets he gets aren't really worth training. So to get results, he
often has to use very severe methods.

These aren't necessary for a tractable, intelligent young retriever. It's so easy to train such a dog to the obedience commands, you might as well do it yourself. And after just reading
this book and perhaps attending one field trial, you'll know more
about training a dog to retrieve than some of these obedience
trainers. They aren't much on reading books. They're more inclined
to think they wrote them.

I wouldn't send even a young retriever to a spaniel trainer, no
matter how good his reputation in that field—unless he is one of
those who also handles a lot of retrievers, and has done well with
the latter dogs in trials.

Now even if you are lucky enough to have a *good* retriever
trainer start your dog, you still need to understand how to carry
on his education. And if you have the professional go on and finish the job, you still should know how to keep the dog up to
snuff and how to handle him to get the most pleasure from your

educated shooting companion. If you're going to *own* a retriever, you should understand the principles of training.

But with the good trainers so scarce, the chances are you'll have to train the dog yourself, if you want the job done right.

Can you do it? Let me quote a paragraph from *Field Trial News'* report of the 1960 National Retriever Championship trial: " 'Smoke' has had but one master and one trainer in his nine years and two months. If ever the old adage, 'look out for the one-man dog,' proved true, it was at the 1960 National Retriever Championship Trial. A great dog, a great team—we salute the 1960 National Retriever Champion Dolobran's Smoke Tail and his owner, trainer, and handler, 'Dick' Hecker."

Look at "Smoke's" record in Appendix II (Labrador Retriever Dogs) and see what an amateur owner-trainer-handler and the right dog *can* accomplish. In the earlier days of the National (1942, 1946, and 1949) amateur owner Paul Bakewell III won three National Retriever [Open] Championships as a handler.

There's nothing to it, and it's fun—*if* you don't start backward, as I did. Before you start, just get a few simple fundamentals firmly ensconced in your noggin. Then it will be a breeze—about as taxing to the brain as learning to play gin rummy.

## FUNDAMENTAL NO. 1

*Get a decent dog to start with.*

We have already harped on this enough. If you're still with me, and haven't angrily tossed this book in the ashcan—then I assume you're sold on the principle, in theory, at least. Now then, just how do you determine whether you have a dog worth training?

Here is a very simple and practical yardstick:

If the dog does not respond to his lessons *before you run out of time and patience and feel like chucking the whole thing,* then he's not the dog for you to train. Get smart, and get rid of him. Write him off. Sell him to a bargain hunter. Or give him to your Aunt Minnie for a house pet. Get yourself another dog.

Yes, I know. This is easy to say, and tough to do. You become attached to *any* dog very fast, and love him in spite of everything. The longer you keep him around, the harder it is to banish a useless dog. But until you bring yourself to do it, you're yielding to sentiment instead of using your head. And that, friend, is your problem. I had to battle it out for myself, and so will you.

## FUNDAMENTAL NO. 2

*Everything a dog learns depends on his memory, and only his memory.*

Contrary to sentimental dog fiction, he has no reasoning power. When we speak of an intelligent dog, we really mean a dog blessed with plenty of memory cells in his brain.

In his obedience training, you put him through an action, and speak a command. You repeat this. He associates the action with the command. The better his memory, the less repetition is required. That's all there is to the obedience training.

In the more advanced exercises, in retrieving, the same principle applies. You arrange it so that when a dog goes through a certain action, a pleasant result occurs. He finds the dummy, or the bird. With a little repetition, he quickly associates in his memory the action and the exciting result. He learns to mark falls. To use the wind and use his nose. To take a line. And finally to take whistle and hand signals to blind retrieves.

He learns all this purely through *repetition* and *memory.* Remember those two words. Paste them in your hat. Keep them in mind, and every lesson in this book will not only make sense, but will seem childishly simple. As you go along you'll find yourself improvising new stunts and shortcuts of your own—based on this principle—to get faster results with your own dog. Remember those two words, and you're already a better dog trainer than *some* of the men who call themselves professionals.

## FUNDAMENTAL NO. 3

*This principle I call doubling up, and pyramiding.*

Most of the training books I've read have thrown me for a loss by saying you must teach a dog only one thing at a time. Probably this is sound advice if you're struggling with a stupid mutt. I wouldn't know. I never lasted long enough to train a dog of that type to come in out of the rain.

But for a good, young retriever, or any dog with a good memory, this is utter nonsense. It would take forever.

With a *good* dog, in every lesson you can and should work him on two or more commands. This is like teaching the touch system on the typewriter. Each day you keep adding letters, until suddenly the student knows them all. In the advanced retrieving exercises, you'll be working your dog on five or six different things simultaneously, within a ten-minute session. That's the secret of the good professional trainers. That's how one man can do a good job every day on twenty or thirty dogs. And that's how *you* can train *one* dog in an average of only ten minutes a day.

## FUNDAMENTAL NO. 4

*Don't start the serious training too early.*

This is the most common and the most costly mistake of the enthusiastic amateur with his first retriever pup. I've found it the hardest wrong practice to discourage.

You won't gain a thing by starting a pup on the retrieving work before he is a year old. If he happens to be unusually slow to mature, you can do him much harm by starting earlier.

At every trial of our Southern California Retriever Club, at least one eager newcomer shows up with a four- or five- or six-month-old pup, determined to enter and run him in stakes for older dogs. When, for the good of the pup, we refuse the entry, the owner is vastly indignant.

Quite likely the pup has never retrieved anything but a glove or a tennis ball. He's never seen a pigeon, or a live shackled duck, nor heard a gunshot. We try to explain to the owner that the pup is too likely to toss and play with a pigeon, and needlessly become hard-mouthed, if he hasn't been properly introduced to feathers before being sent to retrieve his first shot bird.

A big, live, mallard drake, with only his feet and wings tied, squawking and pecking indignantly as the youngster approaches the water, can badly frighten a young pup, and even make him permanently cripple shy.

The rude and abrupt introduction to the gun *might* make him gun shy.

But the biggest danger is in requiring the youngster to be steady to shot much too soon.

Now let me emphasize—all this applies to the training in *retriev-*

*ing*. It won't hurt a good young pup to give him some of the simpler obedience training, whenever you like, if you don't get too tough about it. Never give a young pup any severe punishment. Let him grow out of his diapers before you spank him for disobedience.

However, nearly all well-bred retriever pups can be taught quite easily and painlessly to "sit" on command; walk at "heel"; stop jumping on people when you say "down"; and to go into the pen or leap in the car when you say "kennel." And if a pup does respond reasonably well to these commands, he is much less of a nuisance to have around while you're waiting for him to grow up.

But don't, please, try to *combine* the command "sit" with retrieving. Many pups are ruined this way—by your not only rushing their retrieving, but making them sit and wait before being sent. Some greenhorns go much further. I recently narrowly escaped a stroke when I saw the new owner of a *four-month-old* pup working him on whistle and hand signals, and blind retrieves. At four months, mind you! You'll better understand the idiocy of this after you've read the later chapters on training. For now, let me say only that what this clown was trying to do was about like putting a three-year-old child in school—and then starting him right out with calculus, before he's had arithmetic, algebra, geometry, and whatever else you need before attempting calculus.

With some pups, more precocious than the average, it is safe to start them doing a few simple retrieves at eight or nine months, *provided you do not require steadiness*. But even with such a pup you will lose nothing, and save your own time, by waiting until he is a full twelve months old. At successive six-month intervals, he'll be just as far advanced—possibly further—than if you'd started earlier.

The big danger in rushing the retrieving is that of boring the pup —ruining his natural keenness to hunt and to retrieve. And brother, that is important. That quality, you want to keep. *All* of it.

## FUNDAMENTAL NO. 5

*Give short, frequent lessons.*

If you're in a hurry about this thing, it's perfectly all right to give your dog a little work every day—or even twice a day. But don't overdo it at any one time. Don't give him a chance to become bored. A retriever's work should be his fun.

An average of ten minutes a day is plenty, particularly in the obedience training and the earlier stages of the retrieving work. Now obviously there will be times when you'll have your dog out considerably more than ten minutes, for *some* of the more advanced work. But try to keep that average in mind—ten minutes a day. It's much better to underwork than to overwork a young dog. And if at times you get busy and can't take him out for several days, don't worry about it. He won't lose any ground, and it won't do him a bit of harm to sit in his pen for a few days, thinking how nice it's going to be when he gets back to school.

It's a great temptation, when you get a new young dog and you're full of enthusiasm, to take him out and work him silly. Practically all newcomers to the retriever-happy ranks are guilty of this, to some degree. It is responsible for most of the sloppy, indifferent retriever work that you see.

## FUNDAMENTAL NO. 6

*Be alone with your dog when you're training.*

Tell the kids to go fly their kites, and try to find a place where you can have privacy. For all of the obedience training, and even the first simple retrieves, the garage is a good place.

Until the youngster is well along in junior high school and his work has become more important to him than anything else and also until you have become firmly entrenched as the boss, you want no admiring audience distracting and confusing him.

Particularly during the early obedience training, be sure to have him in a closed room or small fenced-in yard, where you can easily catch him if necessary. Which leads to:

## FUNDAMENTAL NO. 7

*Never give a command you're not in a position to enforce.*

This seems so obvious it needs no discussion. Yet everyone, including me, is guilty of this mistake all too often. If you do your best to avoid it, you'll save yourself and the dog a lot of useless arguments.

It's a lot easier to avoid letting the dog become disobedient than to cure it after this fault becomes a habit.

## FUNDAMENTAL NO. 8

*The tone of voice is more important than the words of the command.*

Now I've read that you should always speak quietly to a dog. Bunk! At times I find it very useful to holler. And I mean *holler*.

When a dog is cutting up, it is often more effective than a licking, and much less painful to dog and man, to say loudly and sternly: "Aah—*aah*—AAH——"

If you make this sound on a rising tone, and with rising volume, it has a positively magic effect on a dog. If you really give out with it, it seems to say very clearly to your canine pupil, "You stop that nonsense, now. You be careful. You know better than that. I'm fed up, and you'd better behave, bud—or else."

Another favorite of mine, which for some reason seems to give a lot of belly laughs to my hunting partners, is suddenly to bellow at the top of my lungs: *"WHAT* ARE YOU DOING?"

I use this when a dog is at some distance out in the field, fiddling around, hunting mice, or otherwise not tending to business. Or when he ignores the whistle. You'd be amazed at the instant results usually accomplished by this inquiry, when the inflection is just right, and the voice choking with emotion.

Now all this is no doubt very funny to you at first, and possibly even silly. But it will pay you to think it over.

Why do you suppose the Army spends so much time drilling its officers in the "tone of command"—teaching them to bellow orders in a parade-ground voice?

I'll tell you why. It gets results.

It get results with men, and it gets results with dogs.

Nearly all beginning trainers just sound too damn wishy-washy when they give a command. I don't mean you should yell every time you speak to a dog. Certainly not. But you should always speak with plenty of firmness in your voice, and when necessary, even sternness. You should sound as though you mean it, and as though you expect instant obedience, as a matter of course. You'll get it, if you can put this over in your tone.

Think of it this way. You're not begging a dog to do something. You're not requesting it. You're not even asking. You're *telling* him.

In this one respect, a woman is at a disadvantage in dog training. Her voice is simply weaker, and higher pitched, than a man's. She can't bellow like a top sergeant. But even so, if she really tries she can get that ring of authority into her commands. And when necessary, she can get fine results by throwing away her inhibitions and yelling like a fishwife.

One thing a woman can do as well as any man is to learn to blow the whistle properly, and this is just as important as the voice. When a dog is working at some distance out in the field, you control him entirely with whistle signals and hand motions.

He can hear that whistle at great distances—if he wants to. Many times I've demonstrated this by taking out a wise old retriever, handing my whistle to a greenhorn handler, and telling him to blow it. He trills it sweetly. The dog pays no attention. He doesn't even look around.

Then I take the same whistle. I blast it just once. The dog spins, his ears go up, and his fanny goes down—right now.

He has heard the tone of command in the tone of the whistle. That sound wave just reaches out, spins the dog around, and pushes his rear end down.

There's nothing much to learning to blow a whistle this way. Just forget your bashfulness, and give it everything you've got. What you want is a note as sharp, abrupt, and high as you can get. Also loud.

Block the opening in the mouthpiece with your tongue. Build up air pressure in your mouth—say about 60 pounds—or until you feel your eardrums are about to go out, or you're going to have a stroke. Then move your tongue aside quickly, and let her blast!

As soon as you get your new whistle, practice this a little, before you try it on the dog. It's a fine way to become unpopular around the house. Even better than practicing on your duck call.


## FUNDAMENTAL NO. 9

*No tidbits. No tipping.*

The other day I was working some young dogs in the yard. A nice-looking old gentleman came along, and hung over the fence, watching. Every time one of the dogs retrieved a training dummy, the old man muttered and sadly shook his head. At last he could stand it no longer.

"When they *do* it," he said indignantly, "why don't you *give* them something?"

I tried to explain that this was not a trained-seal act; that there is no need to throw a frozen fish to a Labrador every time he does the job he was born and bred to do; that a retriever needs and expects no more reward for doing his job than a friendly word of praise, or a pat on the head. But the old man was unconvinced. As he stalked off down the road I could hear him grumbling, "He ought to *give* them something."

Give your dog a cooky every time he does what he's supposed to, if you like. But it's a useless precedent you're starting, and will become a nuisance. If he learns to expect these tips, there will come a time, out in the field, when you run out of tidbits. If you never start this practice, he'll be just as happy without it.

## SOME USEFUL PROPS

### (See Illustration 23)

The essential training tools you need don't amount to much, and are easily obtained.

1. *Whistle.* There are two good makes known to me. I've always insisted upon the Acme Thunderer, made in England, because it has a high, sharp note. A dog can hear it at a great distance, and it seems to do something authoritative to his ear. At least equally popular with retriever trialers are the whistles invented by professional handler Roy Gonia. Either of these makes of good whistles are so inexpensive—about a dollar—that you should insist on one of them. Once you've accustomed your dog to a particular whistle, hang onto it so you won't have to accustom him to another.

Put the whistle on a cord, and form the habit of wearing it around your neck, whenever you're training or when you go hunting. No matter how good you think you are at whistling through your fingers or your teeth, I advise you to use a good whistle anyway. Get your dog used to it. You can get a lot more authority into its tone than you possibly can into any unaided mouth signal you can make yourself. And it will still work, even if your mouth is dry —or you suddenly see someone sucking a lemon.

2. *Short Leather Leash.* The handiest kind, I've never seen in a store. Any harness maker will make one up for you at small cost, using a good piece of harness leather about one inch wide. The finished leash should be about eighteen inches long, the leather doubled and sewed together, leaving a loop for your hand at one end, and sewing in an ordinary harness snap at the other. This is just the right length for leading a big dog at heel. You can wad it up and put in in your pocket. And it's about right to use for corporal punishment, if such should be necessary.

3. *Slip-Chain Collar.* The sporting-goods stores have these, but be sure you get a fairly heavy one, and with *welded* rings on each end. Sometimes you're offered one that has only soldered rings. These are too risky, likely to pull apart, and if you leave your dog chained to one, you could lose him. Measure your dog around the biggest part of his head, and get a collar just large enough to slip over his head comfortably, without much space to spare. Some people call these "choke" collars, and think they are cruel, and that trainers use them to administer punishment by choking a dog. This is nonsense. The collar tightens only when the dog pulls against it, and he quickly learns not to make himself uncomfortable. These retrievers have heavy necks. To keep an ordinary collar tight enough so it can't pull over the head is more uncomfortable than the occasional squeeze from a slip collar. It looks better, too, than a big, wide, leather affair, and it doesn't wear off as much hair.

4. *Long Chain Leash and Corkscrew Stake.* Almost any sporting-goods house, pet supply or hardware store, or mail-order service has the right kind of these. Get a fairly heavy chain, five or six feet long, with a good, big harness snap on each end. A heavy swivel in the middle is a good idea. I prefer the welded-link type of chain to the twisted link. The latter scratches, rubs, and tears, and is heavier for the same strength. Also get a corkscrew stake, the kind they use to nail calves to one spot. These twist into the ground quite easily—and are relatively easy for you to untwist when the time comes to leave. Never rely upon a stake driven into soft or rain-soaked earth. Never chain a dog near a fence or other obstruction which he might attempt to jump and thereby hang himself.

The chain and stake will come in handy whenever you take your dog away from home. Use them to tie him securely and safely. Don't ever depend upon a piece of rope, if you're going to leave him for even five minutes. One of these critters will chew through a piece of rope like an ear of sweet corn.

5.   *Land-Training Dummy.* Make this yourself out of an old gunny sack. For starting a young dog, it should be small enough so that he can pick it up easily without stretching his mouth, but not so small that he might inhale it when he makes a fast pickup, and get it halfway down his throat. Take enough of the burlap to fold and roll into a cylinder about twelve inches long, and from two to two and a half inches in diameter. Tie it up securely with a stout cord, so it won't come apart. No need to tie any feathers on it, or to doctor it with artificial scent. Your hand scent on the dummy will be plenty, by the time the dog gets to using his nose. At the outset, it will be mainly sight retrieving anyway, while the dummy is new. Later you'll need two more dummies, larger and heavier, but the one small one is plenty for a while.

6.   *Water-Training Dummy.* The best thing I've ever found is a small boat fender, filled with cork, and covered with heavy canvas. You can get these in many sporting-goods and hardware stores, and in any event in marine-supply stores. Get a small one, not more than two and a half inches in diameter, to start off with. These are light, float, of course, don't get soggy, and have some resilience. Later you'll want two larger and much heavier boat fenders, more like the size and weight of the body of a big mallard duck. You can also buy these, filled with plastic foam, from three to three and a half inches in diameter. *Always* use the training dummies. *Never* throw a stick in the water for your dog to retrieve. That would be a fine way to start hard mouth.

# Spare the Rod

NOW WE COME to a very ticklish subject, one that is tactfully ignored in most of the books, pamphlets, and articles about training man's best friend.

Well, here goes my neck. I'm going to devote *a whole chapter* to it. I'm going to discuss it frankly and realistically. And already I can hear the chorus of shrill, outraged screams from some of the more hysterical unclaimed maidens of the SPCA.

They'll just have to go ahead and scream. For to anyone seriously interested in training any kind of a dog, this question of punishment is important. So let's haul it out on the table. If you're still with me, I assume you're the type who is willing to face the facts of life.

First, let's get this in the record: I'm not a sadist, and I don't enjoy giving a dog a licking. Neither do I enjoy spanking my kids.

But a famous public-opinion poll shows that even today most American parents occasionally spank their children when they persistently misbehave and forget their manners, before they reach the age of reason. These parents feel they are doing their offspring a favor to raise them as decent citizens who are liked, instead of despised as little varmints, by the people around them.

Most modern psychiatrists agree.

Well, remember this: a dog—unlike a child—*never* reaches the age of reason.

When the owner of an unruly dog asks what to do, I like to remind him of that old but good story about the eminent child psychiatrist and the spoiled brat who refused to get off the hobbyhorse. The illustrious doctor finally whispered in the little monster's ear,

"You nasty little so-and-so, you get down off that hobbyhorse right now or I'll knock your goddam teeth out."

The surprised kid climbed down like a little man.

This gag contains a pearl of psychology for any overindulgent mama, *or* dog owner.

If you convince your dog you are ready and willing for a showdown, you probably won't need to have one. At any rate, not more than one. But *if he needs it,* a good old-fashioned thrashing won't hurt him a bit, will clear the air, and will save both you and the dog a lot of time and trouble.

Be sure you administer any such needed corporal punishment in private. Most people just don't understand the occasional necessity for it in dog training. A retriever has a hide ten times as thick as the tender behind of a child. Yet a parent who thinks nothing of walloping his kids, if he sees you administering a well-deserved licking to a 70-pound Labrador, is likely to yell for the humane society, and want to put you in the jailhouse. You'll be scornfully accused of "beating a poor dumb brute." For some reason, this is considered worse than spanking a human child.

I guess the answer is that many people have devoted some serious attention to properly raising their kids, but none to the matter of training decent dogs. These are the people who tolerate perfectly horrible animals for house pets—untrammeled mutts who bark insanely at friends who come to call, nip their ankles, and jump up on them with muddy feet. Such spoiled dogs chase cars, dump the neighbor's garbage can, dig up his garden, kill his chickens, and generally scourge the neighborhood. They are cordially hated by everyone but their softheaded owners, receive many surreptitious kicks, and end up being shot or poisoned by a fed-up neighbor, or flattened by a truck.

Now I don't think their owners are doing these dogs a favor, any more than those parents are doing their children a favor when for lack of needed discipline they allow them to become juvenile delinquents.

*Any* dog should be obedient, and should receive whatever kind and amount of punishment is needed to make and keep him so. And of course, a working retriever *must* be under perfect and quiet control—or he is worse than useless. A hardheaded, defiant dog in the field is a nuisance, and an imposition on your hunting companions. Unless you're willing to do whatever is necessary to keep your dog in line, you are better off without one.

An earnest but misinformed "dog lover" once told me flatly that *all* dog training for *any* purpose is cruel. Also, that all dog trainers are cruel people, who enjoy inflicting punishment on helpless animals.

Obviously this is utter nonsense.

Take the amateur trainers, for instance—the hobbyists. No amateur in his right mind would go to the trouble and expense of keeping and training a kennel full of dogs, unless he really loved dogs. He might keep one meat dog just for practical purposes, but not a dozen.

The same is true of the better professional trainers and handlers. Most of these men could make twice as much money in other jobs or businesses. Why do you suppose they stay in the dog business?

They don't talk baby talk to dogs, and they don't proclaim themselves as "dog lovers." But take my word for it, they love and appreciate a good working dog much more deeply than any spinster lady loves her little, yapping lap dog.

Beyond that, common sense tells you that men who know dogs are not going to ruin promising material with cruelty, or too much punishment. A hunting dog that is not keen for his job, and not supremely happy when doing it, is worthless. You can't beat a dog into doing all that a good retriever must do in the course of a day afield. It is impossible. A dog that has been "trained" this way will quit on you every time, when the going gets tough.

Of course, there are skunks in every group, and there are some self-styled trainers who are stupid enough to be too severe with dogs. They don't get any of my dogs, and I don't like them any better than you do.

Your good trainers—amateur and professional alike—administer corporal punishment only to those dogs that clearly need and deserve it, and even then very sparingly. They try never to lose their tempers. When they have a bad day, and are in a foul mood, they just leave the dogs in the kennel.

When it becomes necessary to give a dog a walloping, they do so only when the dog is caught right in the act of disobedience—

so that the punishment will be clearly associated with the crime in the dog's memory.

A common mistake of beginning amateurs when a dog defies a command at some distance out in the field is to call the dog in and *then* punish him. This is useless, unjust, only confuses the dog, and might even ruin him if done repeatedly. For the *last* thing he did was to come in to his handler when called—a correct, obedient action. And in his memory the licking is associated with that. Next time he is called, he probably will be reluctant to come, and you can't blame him for that.

The only way to punish a dog for a misdeed out in the field is to stir your stumps, *run out to him,* catch him, and thus make him understand that he is getting his medicine for whatever he just did or failed to do. That illustrates an important training principle. In his memory, a dog will always associate punishment with the *last* thing he has been doing.*

If your dog ever demands a showdown, apply only as much pressure as needed to win the argument and command obedience. There are dogs so sensitive that a disgusted look and harsh words are sufficient to do the job. This is not true of most retrievers. When it has become plain that you must deal out punishment, do it. But remember that *every form of canine punishment is effective less by virtue of the pain it causes than by revelation of the power of the administrator.* If it does not instill in the dog an appreciation of the power of the trainer to impose his will, it has missed its mark—and has probably thrown the training program backward.

Here's the best way I know of instilling this respect into a dog without really hurting him. If you are big enough and strong enough, or if the dog is small enough, grab a handful of the loose skin above his rump. Grab another handful of loose skin on his neck, right behind the ears if possible. (If you grab too far back he'll be able to turn enough to bite you.) Now, pick him up and

---

*There is a rather expensive electronic radio-controlled device which is advertised as being able to save you this running. The reviser was the inventor of this tool and built the first one. Forget it. This kind of push-button training can ruin a dog in a flash. This device should be actively avoided by all but the most expert amateurs. In fact, none but the most discriminating of professionals should ever use it. —H. D.

# WHICH BREED?

## The Golden Retriever

### 1.

By any standards, the Golden is a beautiful dog to look at.

### 2.

Tractable, eager-to-please, easy for the amateur to train to obedience.

### 3.

Handles his birds gently—in fact is tender mouthed almost to a fault.

### 4.

Has a spectacular nose, and excels at retrieving upland game.

# WHICH BREED?

## The Chesapeake Bay Retriever

### 5.

A big, tough, rugged dog—both in body and disposition.

### 6.

Bred to battle the icy surf of Chesapeake Bay all day, without tiring.

### 7.

He is sometimes inclined to have a mind of his own, and to need—

### 8.

—a bit more firmness from his trainer than the Golden or the Labrador

# WHICH BREED?

## The Labrador Retriever

**9.**

An aggressive worker, fast, stylish; equally good on land or in the water.

**10.**

The leading winner in the trials, he is also most popular with hunters.

**11.**

It won't hurt your eyes to look at a good specimen of this breed, either.

**12.**

He is tender mouthed, and very easy for **an amateur** to train and handle.

13. Don't waste time mooning over the individual pups in the litter.

## 14.

Instead, study the pedigree. Ask questions about the sire and dam, and the grandparents. Then, if you are satisfied with the ancestors, just shut your eyes and grab a pup.

# BUYING
# AN UNTRAINED DOG

### 15.

A dog of 12 months or more should be naturally keen to retrieve. Ask the owner to toss a dummy in light cover.

### 16.

You want a youngster who fairly sizzles with speed and eagerness as he dashes out after it.

### 17.

Who hunts fast, aggressively, and persistently in vicinity of the fall.

### 18.

And who sniffs the breeze, and shows signs of knowing what his nose is for.

# BUYING
# AN UNTRAINED DOG

**19.**

That thrilling, heart-stopping splash

**20.**

—you see when a dummy is thrown

**21.**

- -and a keen young dog hurls himself

**22.**

—into the water to make the retrieve.

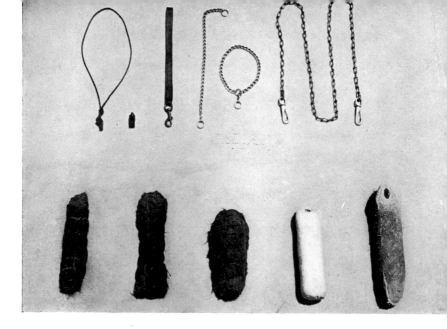

## 23. SOME USEFUL TRAINING PROPS

*Top Row*, from left: (1) Small Acme Thunderer plastic whistle, with cord. (2) Top view of whistle. (3) Short leather leash. (4) Slip chain collar. (5) Collar arranged to slip over dog's head. (6) Long chain tethering leash.

*Bottom Row*, from left: (1) 2½-inch burlap training dummy. (2) 3-inch dummy. (3) 3½-inch dummy. (4) 2½-inch lightweight floating dummy, filled with cork. (5) 3¼-inch heavy floating dummy, filled with sponge rubber.

## HOUSING YOUR DOG

### 24.

Your training job will be much easier if you keep your dog in an outside kennel, and he'll

### 25.

get plenty of exercise racing up and down a small but properly proportioned kennel run.

### 26.

"Chin up, puppy."
*The author's 12-year-old son, Johnnie,*

### 27.

"SIT! Fanny down, puppy."
*teaching command to a 2-month-old*

### 28.

"SIT! Ah-ah-ah!"
*Labrador pup. If a boy can do it with*

### 29.

"SIT. Good puppy!"
*a playful pup, surely a grown man can*

(continued on next page)

# OBEDIENCE TRAINING

## The Command "SIT"
## (continued)

### 30.

"SIT!"
—*do it with a ready-to-learn dog.*

### 31.

"SIT! Stern down."
*The author giving actual first lesson*

### 32.

"SIT. Careful now!"
*to Freehaven Muscles, age 12 months.*

### 33.

"SIT! And stay there."
*Elapsed time, five minutes.*

# OBEDIENCE TRAINING

## The Command "CHARGE" (which means "Lie Down")

**34.**

"SIT"

Grasp front paws—

**35.**

"CHARGE!"

and pull them forward.

**36.**

"CHARGE!"

Steady now, old boy.

**37.**

"CHARGE!"

Nothing to this one.

# OBEDIENCE TRAINING

## The Command "KENNEL"

**38.**

"KENNEL!"
Take dog by scruff of neck—

**39.**

"KENNEL!"
and gently but firmly propel him—

**40.**

"KENNEL!"
into his kennel, doghouse, or pen.

**41.**

KENNEL?
Why certainly, boss.

## The Command "COME"

### 42.

This stuff is unnecessary. There is no need to have a struggle, hauling your dog around on a rope.

### 43.

#### "COME"

Any young dog will chase you, if you will pick them up and lay them down.

### 44.

#### "COME ALONG"

Run away from him briskly, calling "COME" and clapping your hands—

### 45.

—and also blowing *several* quick blasts on your whistle.

# OBEDIENCE TRAINING

## The Command "HEEL"

### 46.

#### "COME ALONG"
Step out briskly with dog on leash. Pull him up firmly if he lags behind.

### 47.

#### "HEEL!"
Walk on, repeating "HEEL" constantly. Hold a stick across his nose if he tries to forge ahead of your knee.

### 48.

#### "HEEL!"
At last, take off the leash. Keep patting your leg to keep him coming.

### 49.

#### "HEEL!"
No leash, no stick, no hands. After only 10 minutes of this, Muscles HEELS! Well, *almost* heels, then.

# SIMPLE CITIZENSHIP

### 50.
"STOP  THAT NOISE!"
Hold dog's mouth firmly closed.

### 51.
"HIE ON"
Useful for hunting *and* housebreaking.

### 52.
"DOWN"
Squeeze *front* paws and push dog down.

### 53.
"NO!—DOWN!"
Stay down. Be a good dog.

# STARTING
# A YOUNG DOG
# RETRIEVING
# A DUMMY

## 54.

**Tease** him with the smaller training dummy until he is frantic to grab it—

## 55.

Then throw it, and call HIS NAME, which is the command to retrieve.

## 56.

When he picks it up, run away clapping your hands and calling "COME."

## 57.

Keep running away until you can grab dummy from him as he catches you.

# TO CURE CHEWING
# OR PLAYING
# WITH DUMMY

### 58.

*If* youngster has tendency to toss, mouth, chew, or play with dummy—tease him with it—

### 59.

say "AH, AH, AH"—let him grab it, but hold your hand around it so he can't clamp down on it—

### 60.

without biting you. Surely, I hope, your own dog won't wish to bite the hand that feeds him. "AH-AH-AH!"

### 61.

"YOU BE CAREFUL NOW!" He'll quickly understand dummy is to be handled as carefully as a dozen eggs.

# BEGINNING TO STEADY A YOUNG DOG

## 62.

Have him SIT. Hold him by the collar while throwing the dummy, but then send him for it quickly.

## 63.

Next step: stand in front of dog while throwing, between him and dummy. Make him SIT a bit longer now.

## 64.

At last, stand beside him. Make him SIT until dummy is down. Then send him by "giving a line" with your hand.

## 65.

Don't bother with this. Sitting to deliver is unnecessary. Take dummy from him at once when he returns.

# INTRODUCING A PUP
# TO WATER

### 66.

Never push or throw him in. Don't even toss a dummy the first time. Put on your waders, or swimming trunks.

### 67.

Wade out in shallow water. Call the pup to you with great enthusiasm. Clap your hands. Blow your whistle.

### 68.

Romp with him in the water. He'll quickly learn he loves it. *Then* lure him to deeper water, and he'll swim.

### 69.

Now you can toss a dummy from shore, and watch him hit the water with that spectacular, all-out splash.

# LEARNING
# ABOUT DECOYS
## The Command
## "LEAVE IT"

### 70.

**"NO!"**

Set out a few decoys, on *land*. There is no need to get your feet wet.

### 71.

**"LEAVE IT!"**

Walk the dog through them, back and forth, on leash. Watch him closely.

### 72.

**"LEAVE IT!"**

If he tries to grab one, restrain him with leash and command LEAVE IT.

### 73.

**THE LIGHT DAWNS**

After 5 minutes: "I get it, boss. You don't want these *wooden* ducks!"

# FORCE TRAINING TO HOLD
## The Command "FETCH"
### (Which means "Don't drop it")

### 74.

"SIT!"

Force open the dog's mouth. Stuff in the smaller training dummy.

### 75.

"FETCH!"

When he tries to spit it out, support lower jaw, very firmly at first.

### 76.

"FETCH!"

Take it from him. Then repeat, supporting jaw more and more lightly.

### 77.

"FETCH!"

Keep repeating this until finally you can take away hand entirely.

# INTRODUCTION TO FEATHERS
## (Ounce of Prevention Division)

### 78.

"AH—AH—Careful, now—"
Use a *dead* pigeon, freshly killed. Tease dog with it to arouse interest, but protect it with your hand.

### 79.

"FETCH—Careful, now—"
Place it gently in his mouth. Have him hold it a moment. There is no excuse for having a hard-mouthed dog—

### 80.

"FETCH—Easy, boy—"
—if you just take this precaution before a bird is ever shot for him. He gets the point quickly.

### 81.

"FETCH it up"
Now back away, call him to you, and receive the pigeon from him. Then toss it out for a short retrieve.

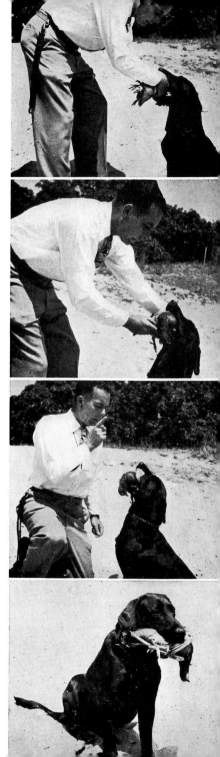

# INTRODUCTION TO
# SHACKLED DUCKS

### 82.

"Good grief! What *now*, boss?" Run through the same routine as with the dead pigeon, but using a *live* duck—

### 83.

—with wings and legs securely tied. This introduction also teaches dog to take proper body hold on a big duck.

### 84.

Now toss duck for *short* retrieve in *shallow* water. Get out there quickly if he offers to play with it. But no!

### 85.

No need for wet feet. Dog takes **firm** but gentle hold, delivers to **hand**. Happy man, happy dog, happy **duck**.

# WORKING FROM
# A BLIND

### 86.

Lead dog into portable blind with
side wings (type used in trials).
Have him SIT, well forward—

### 87.

—facing hole. Then toss dummy
through hole, to land on *ground,* just
in front of blind. Send dog at once.

### 88.

He'll jump through hole to retrieve
it before he has a chance to shy at
this strange contraption. Repeat this.

### 89.

Then throw dummy out in water.
Dog should go out for it through
hole, but may *return* around side.

# TO SPEED UP
# A DOG ON LAND
# AND WATER

### 90.

Have him SIT. Walk away, a little farther each time, finally 100 yards or more. Wait until he is fairly frantic to come to you—

### 91.

—then call him, blowing *several* whistle blasts, and just watch him come! Excellent for a dog which has a tendency to putter coming in.

### 92.

Have him SIT on shore, while you go out in boat. Give him plenty of suspense before you call him. Soon he'll be hitting water with a fine splash.

### 93.

Row around a few minutes, and let him follow the boat. This further develops his liking for the water, as well as his swimming muscles.

# TEACHING
# HAND SIGNALS
## (Baseball Diamond Method)

### 94.

Use a lawn or yard with no cover to hide dummy. Starting from imaginary home plate, walk with dog at HEEL—

### 95.

—out to pitcher's mound. Give command SIT, followed by *one* sharp blast on whistle, meaning STOP and SIT.

### 96.

Then toss the dummy toward second base, being sure the dog sees it, and that it lands in plain sight.

### 97.

Keep commanding SIT, followed by *one* whistle blast, as you leave dog out there, and return to home plate.

(continued on next page)

### 98.

Make overhead arm signal like a *girl* throwing a ball toward second. Call his NAME and shout "GET BACK."

### 99.

Dog will probably hesitate, remember the dummy, then turn his head, see it, and GET BACK to retrieve it.

### 100.

The instant he picks it up, encourage him with *several* quick whistle blasts to come in with it fast—

### 101.

—all the way to home plate. After only 10 minutes of this, he should be ready to proceed the next day to—

(continued on next page)

### 102.

—*Hand signal to right.* Walk dog **out** to pitcher's mound. Blast whistle, **say** "SIT," toss dummy to *first* base.

### 103.

You return to home plate. Call dog's *name* to send him, and throw your arm straight *right* from the shoulder—

### 104.

—at the same time swaying your whole body to *right*. Whistle him in. Work on this for a full 10-minute lesson.

### 105.

The next day, work on *hand signal to left*. Use same routine, in reverse. This time, toss dummy to *third* base.

(continued on next page)

### 106.

You return to home plate. Make **arm signal to LEFT**, call dog's **NAME** *only* if this still necessary to send him.

### 107.

But by now he should be well on his way to associating these arm signals with the direction of the fall, and—

### 108.

—with *permission to go* and retrieve. Work him only to *left* for 10 minutes. Then try *right*, and *get back*.

### 109.

As soon as he is smartly obeying all three signals, without your calling his **NAME**, it is time to move to—

(continued on next page)

### 110.

—a field with sufficient cover to hide the dummy. Toss it to second base. Dog should no longer need aid—

### 111.

—of seeing dummy on bare ground. Call "GET BACK" and give overhead arm signal. If he takes it—

### 112.

—then work him to LEFT and RIGHT, mixing them up. After 10 minutes of this, you should be able—

### 113.

—next day to start real blind retrieves. Plant dummy without dog seeing it. Direct him to it with hand signals.

### 114.

Good judges make a good trial. They plan the tests carefully, trying to give each dog an equal opportunity.

### 115.

Experienced amateur handlers usually are good judges. They are sympathetic but they see every move of every dog.

### 116.

The birds should be thrown *high*. And *both* gunners should always shoot, no matter how good they think they are.

### 117.

In land tests, a retriever must sit quietly on the line until his number is called by one of the judges.

# RETRIEVER
# FIELD TRIALS
## Water Tests

### 118.

In water, the older dogs work from a "blind," and over decoys. *Over* is the word. See that Labrador take off!

### 119.

A shot is fired as a dead or shackled duck is thrown from a boat. Sometimes live ducks are released and shot.

### 120.

Dog must deliver duck to his handler in the blind. But in the informal training stakes for younger dogs—

### 121.

—the judges sometimes dispense with blind and decoys. Here a keen young Golden hits water with enthusiasm.

# RETRIEVER FIELD TRIALS
## Gallery Scenes

### 122.

Scene at 1947 National. At the trials you meet a nice bunch—all sorts of people from various walks of life.

### 123.

Especially at the "picnic" trials in California, informal—you might even say *exotic*—costumes are in order.

### 124.

According to trial etiquette, gallery should applaud only *after* each dog has completed his whole performance.

### 125.

And *please* don't fondle, pet, talk baby-talk to, or feed a ham sandwich to another man's dog. Very bad form.

126.

The Chocolate Labrador.

127.

The Yellow Labrador.

128.

A pair of eager Irish Water Spaniel pups.

129.

The Irish Water Spaniel.

130.

The Curly-Coat.

131.

The American Water Spaniel.

132.

The Flat-Coat.

133.

The Retrieving Spaniel.

# RETRIEVER FIELD TRIAL CHAMPIONSHIPS

## The National Amateur Championship Trial

### 134.

1st Series—A double land mark.

### 135.

2nd Series—A cold land blind, combining land and water work.

### 136.

3rd Series—This triple water mark produced some spectacular work.

### 137.

4th Series—Just over half of the starters were back for this cold water blind.

**138.**

5th Series—This triple land mark with honoring resulted in the elimination of four more contenders.

**139.**

6th Series—A triple land blind with the birds to be retrieved in order proved a demanding test for dogs and handlers alike.

**140.**

7th Series—Sixteen dogs remained in contention to face this triple water mark with honoring.

**141.**

8th Series—This difficult cold water, floating blind involved several obstacles, including a noticeable incoming current, logs, and heavy brush.

**142.**

9th Series—A triple water mark run from atop a steep hill— all birds were shackled ducks.

**143.**

10th Series—The final test was a demanding triple land mark plus a double land blind.

## The National Open Retriever Championship Trial

**144.**

1st Series—A double land mark in which both birds were in alfalfa. Irrigation checks proved perplexing to some of the contenders.

**145.**

3rd Series—A mixed bag triple, water and land.

### 146.

5th Series—Thirty-three **dogs** were back to face this **triple** land mark and honor.

### 147.

5th Series—The line was **on** a dike and perpendicular **to** rows of irrigation **checks** lacing an alfalfa field. **This** challenging series saw the elimination of eight contenders.

### 148.

6th Series—Nearly one-third the field departed after this difficult double water blind.

### 149.

10th Series—The final test **was** a triple land mark and blind.

shake him while you scold. When you are through, set him down ungently, but do not throw him. Continue the lecture.

This is similar to the form of punishment many bitches use on their whelps and that which is used by the leaders of packs of wild dogs. It is also used by many professional trainers. It usually gets full respect quickly.

If you aren't crowding your trainee too fast—and if the dog is worth training—he will soon begin to look forward eagerly to his training sessions. So much so that it is often a severe punishment just to end the session abruptly and put him up for the day.

It is very easy to overdo any form of punishment. It is also a mistake to underdo it. Constant attrition becomes a more painful procedure than the correct method and measure of punishment at the right time. If you can't manage the shaking routine, or if it proves insufficient, try a rolled-up newspaper. Wallop your trainee with it, hard, several times, across the big muscle of the flank. It is impossible really to hurt any dog this way—and a retriever scarcely feels it through his heavy coat. But the rolled-up newspaper makes quite a startling noise, and one good application often gets amazing results, even with a Labrador or Chesapeake—and likely is all that will ever be needed with a Golden.

But if your dog needs it to "get the message," use the strap and use it intelligently, which includes doing the job well enough that it won't have to be repeated in a hurry.

Whatever the punishment, other than cutting off his fun, do not leave the dog. Stay with him at least until he understands that it is what he did that displeased you, and not that you don't like him. This can be the touch that makes the difference.

The correct time to stop the punishment is at the instant when you have convinced the dog that you are capable of enforcing your will. Any punishment beyond that point is unjustified—and it will harm your training program, perhaps irreparably. Look at it this way: whenever two ordinary dogs get in a fight, the victor will quit when the loser yields. Dogs are fair about dealing out punishment. I think they have a right to expect you to be equally fair and considerate.

Hold the dog firmly by the scruff or collar with one hand, so he can't get away from you, and administer the licking with the other, always on that big flank muscle. There is little chance of injuring him there, even in extreme cases where a very heavy strap is needed.

Most retrievers can take, and like, a lot more punishment than they ever need, without any danger of being cowed. But if you should be unlucky enough to get one who *can't take as much as he needs,* and shows signs of being cowed—then you'd better get rid of him at once. He just isn't worth fooling with, unless you like to see a dog crawl up to you on his belly.

At the other extreme is the occasional retriever that just can't seem to remember and profit by a licking—yet seems to have a good memory otherwise, and all the other qualities needed to make a great worker. When I first did this book, in 1948, I wrote: "Such a one is a youngster I'm training now—or perhaps he's training me. His name is Freehaven Muscles, and he is built like a jeep. Also, he can happily absorb as much pounding as a jeep.

"There isn't a mean hair in him, and in most ways he is quick to learn. His fault is too much eagerness, to the point of madness. His instinct to go and retrieve is so powerful that I honestly believe he hovers on the borderline of insanity. A slight understatement would be to say he has an obsession. When a gun goes off, and he sees something fall, he's gone—right now. He knows he's supposed to wait until he's sent. He's had plenty of spectacular wallopings for breaking. They don't mean a thing. When that bird falls, he just can't stand it. Whether I'll be able to steady him before my right arm wears out is the big question."

Well, the question has long since been answered and Muscles has found his reward. I'm sure it must be in a canine heaven where retrievers can break whenever they're ready. He won his first all-age placement at just under three years of age. It was a first—and he had two more of those top awards, plus other placements sufficient to build his point total to 22 points. The dog that became Field Champion Freehaven Muscles took a good bit of solving—but he made it fairly big. And, through such sons as Field Ch., Amateur Field Ch. Paha Sapa Chief II—and grandsons like 1965 National Amateur Ch. Super Chief—he contributed greatly to the quality of many of the finest of today's Labradors.

I wouldn't recommend such a dog for most amateurs to train, including me. As the horse trainers say, he was just too hot. It isn't likely, but if your pup should grow up to be one of these lunatics—unless you're a very determined and rugged character yourself—you'd better do one of two things:

Let a good professional get him under control for you.

Or—you guessed it—get another dog.

But the chances are your dog will be in tractability somewhere between Jay and Molly, and will require little or no corporal punishment. No retriever ever loved his work more than Freehaven Jay. But he was an individualist, and occasionally decided he had a better way of doing it than mine. About once a year he always tried me out, to see if maybe the boss was going a little soft. And he always found out, promptly. He was a tough dog, and I really had to lay on that leash a bit, to win this annual debate. There were never any hard feelings. After it was over, he would jump up and lick my face, and you could almost hear him say, "Okay, chief. You win."

Among the retrievers, there are plenty of such splendid, spirited dogs that (like some children) occasionally need a firm hand. But the kind you pray for is an individual like Molly.

The finest working bitch I ever owned or hope to own was Freehaven Molly, a Labrador, strangely enough. She was keen, fast, had everything. I ran her in only three trials, and she placed in two of them. She would easily have finished her field-trial championship if I had not been obliged to retire from competition during the war—and before the war was over a rattlesnake got her. She was a wonderful shooting dog, too—had just as much guts as any Chesapeake in Maryland. But she had more of that eagerness to please than any animal I ever saw. In the seven years that we were hunting pals, I never so much as whapped her with a newspaper. She didn't need it, and she didn't get it.

I hope you get one like her.

Now I've devoted a lot of space to this subject of punishment because it has been largely neglected and avoided. This very silence has fed wild rumors about the cruel methods of dog trainers. It has been the source of much unnecessary hysteria and confusion.

I definitely don't want to give you the impression that if you set out to train your retriever, you're going to be spending all your time beating up on him. The chances are you'll have to deal out very little or no severe punishment if you get the kind of dog you should in the first place.

The main thing is to sell yourself on being *willing* and *ready*, if necessary, to administer just punishment. If you make this sale, your dog will know it instinctively. He'll get it from your tone of voice, and from the way you blow your whistle. These retrievers are amazing critters. They know if you're bluffing, and sometimes seem to take great delight in calling your bluff.

But a good one, with plenty of that eagerness to please, if he also feels in his bones that you'll stand no nonsense, won't push you too far. And even one of the tougher individuals, if you offer in a firm tone to knock his teeth out, will usually climb right down off the hobbyhorse.

# 10

## Housing Your Dog

SO YOU'VE BOUGHT your dog or pup, and you bring him home. The thing to decide right now is—where is he going to live? In the house? Or outside, in a simple kennel?

It is perfectly possible to raise a retriever as a house dog, and still make a good shooting dog of him. But if you're like I am, you're not man enough to do it this way. It is definitely doing it the hard way.

If you're going to train the youngster quickly and easily, you want to deliberately make a one-man dog of him. He will be one naturally, if given half a chance. You want to be his one and only hero. You don't want him to become a tramp—everybody's pal, nobody's friend. While he's in the early stages of training, at least, you don't want anybody else even to speak a kind word to him— much less fondle and pet him, and make a lap dog out of him.

This rule is almost impossible to enforce, no matter how tough you are willing to get, if the dog lives in the house. Your kids will play with him, and maul him, until he's just too tired to take much interest when you suddenly come home and take him out for his retrieving lesson. Then, too, all guests consider themselves great hands with dogs, and they will toss him tidbits from the table, call him when you've ordered him to sit in the corner, confuse him, and generally undo the obedience teaching you've given him.

As a house dog, he is bound to pick up sloppy habits, and to become confused as to whether his purpose in life is to be a play-boy, or to work for a living at the job for which he was born.

A friend of mine had a half-grown retriever, and while he was away at the office his kids enjoyed, among other things, throwing croquet balls for the pup to retrieve. After a while they would tire of the sport, and leave the pup in the yard to chew up these solid wooden balls. Now that his serious training has begun, it is still a question whether he can be broken of the notion that ducks are like croquet balls—something to be tossed around and played with, and finally dismantled.

If your dog has the run of the house, you simply cannot control what happens to him while you are away. He will be much better off, at least for a year or so, if you keep him in a proper pen out in the yard—*and keep it locked, with the key in your pocket.* But a pup *must* be "socialized." He needs and *must* have attention and handling *every* day.

Contrary to general opinion, you don't need a big place in the country to keep a retriever. There is plenty of room in any suburban or even city backyard for an adequate kennel and run. I live on 34 acres, but my dogs live in individual kennel runs that are only 4 feet wide and 24 feet long. These are much better for a dog than being confined in a large yard. He gets more exercise, running up and down a relatively small and narrow runway. (See Illustrations 24 and 25.) In a large yard, he'll spend most of his time just lying in a corner.

The best arrangement for a single dog—which is also adequate for two dogs—is a narrow run, roughly 4 feet by 24 feet, enclosed with heavy wire fence, and *completely fenced over the top.* You may not believe the wire on top is necessary, but take my word for it. Most retrievers will go over a 6-foot fence sooner or later— and probably sooner. It's best to have the fence 6 feet high, and higher if you're over 6 feet yourself, so you don't have to bend your neck every time you go in to clean the run. Use wire at least as heavy as hog wire, with a mesh no coarser than 2 by 4 inches.

I like a brushed concrete floor in a run. This will cost up to one hundred dollars, unless you prepare the base and forms yourself, and spread the mix after it's delivered. Ready-mix for a run 24 feet by 4 feet by 4 inches will cost about forty dollars, delivered a reasonable distance. A concrete run is well worth the extra expense. It's much easier to keep clean than anything else, and to keep the dog free of worms. If you don't use concrete, then your fence wire must go down into the ground an extra 2 feet, to assure that the dog can't dig under.

I've heard some bench-show breeders say they don't like to keep their dogs on concrete, because it tends to spread their feet. Some say it even does something bad to their legs. But I've kept Labradors on concrete for ten years, and have never seen any evidence that it affected their feet *or* legs. The rough, brushed surface is best.

Even if it did spread their feet a bit, I doubt if I could work up much excitement over it. The important thing, it seems to me, is to keep a dog in clean and sanitary surroundings, where it's easy to keep him healthy and free of worms. An earth or even a sand or gravel run is bound to become foul and infested in time, no matter how you try to keep it clean. But with brushed concrete, it's easy to pick up the stools with a small shovel, and hose down the run once a day. The sun does the rest, keeping it dry and sterile.

The sun is the best medicine for wormy stools, sterilizing them quickly on the hot concrete, and helping to prevent the dog from reinfesting himself. Therefore the run should be carefully located so the sun strikes every part of it sometime during the day.

But it should also have a moving patch of shade somewhere in it at any time of day, for the dog's comfort during the hot weather. If the long way of the run goes east and west, and there is one small tree near the middle of the south side, this double purpose will be nicely accomplished. If no tree is in the right spot, you may have to cover one small section of the run with a canvas tarpaulin to provide the needed bit of shade.

The only other shelter needed by a retriever is a small doghouse in one end of the run. If you're in a cold climate, this should be just barely large enough for the dog to curl up in comfortably. In the winter, it should have a swinging dog door, to close the opening and keep body heat inside. That's all the heat a retriever needs. He is naturally a cold-weather animal. He'll be much healthier, and his coat will be better, if he is not kept in artificial heat.

Now on the matter of chewing up wooden doghouses, I've had very little experience with Goldens and Chesapeakes, but almost any dog, when confined, will chew on any wood he can get his teeth on. And if you have a Labrador, I can sincerely advise you to protect every exposed corner of a wooden house with tin or galvanized metal. The edges of the dog door should definitely be so protected. If you don't the dog will eat it. And one of these big critters can masticate an amazing quantity of carpentry work in one day.

If you sensibly decide to keep your dog properly confined when you're not with him, you'll have a certain amount of trouble at first. If you have young children there will probably be some tears before you make them understand, and you may even have to go to the pound and get them a mongrel of their own to play with and maul, so they'll let your dog alone. Your sentimental friends won't understand, will think you are cruel to keep "that poor beast" penned up in a "cage," and will scoff at your not allowing them to pet him and make a bum out of him.

Well, they don't expect to paw your wife, and talk baby talk to her, do they? Why should they do it to your dog?

If you explain this, some people will understand. But there is always a smart aleck in the crowd who can't see why it's much easier to train a young dog if he worships only you, and is not expecting a lot of babying from every Tom, Dick, or Harry who comes along. You can save yourself the embarrassment of telling people to let the dog alone—by just leaving him in his pen when unbelievers are around.

Many horrified visitors, seeing my retrievers in their "cages," are firmly convinced that these poor animals never get any love and affection. This of course is nonsense. They get plenty. But they get it from me, exclusively.

Whenever you're at home in the evening, with no guests around, by all means bring the dog in the house. Let him lie quietly beside your chair, while you read your book. Talk to him. Pet him. Take him with you when you go for a walk. Make a pal of him. Just don't let anyone else do it. And when you have him out of his run, *always* keep him under control, pleasantly but firmly.

It is best, at least until you are solidly entrenched as the boss, to feed the dog yourself, if you possibly can. If you travel, or for any reason have to delegate this job part of the time, probably your wife is a better bet than a child or a servant. But whoever does it, you must try to indoctrinate thoroughly—persuade him or her just to give the dog his food, and not try to pet or baby him, or divide his allegiance.

This won't make so much difference after you get to giving the dog his real retrieving work. For he soon discovers that this is even more important and much more fun than eating. And after you once take him hunting and shoot birds for him, he's your dog —and you're the number one hero, no matter who feeds him.

This is a thing the SPCA ladies will never believe. They are incapable of understanding it. But it's true just the same.

My retrievers, which spend much of their time in their "cages," are far *happier* dogs than any pampered and spoiled Pekingese with no particular purpose in life. Like a good man, a good dog gets his supreme pleasure from doing the job he was born to do, and doing it well. To believe this, all you have to do is watch the dogs competing in a retriever trial. Just show me one of these that isn't getting a bigger kick out of life than any bored and useless house pet, and I'll eat him.

Your dog will get more plain fun out of the high spot of his day—the ten minutes you take him out for his work—than an ordinary pet finds in twenty-four hours of lying around the yard, wondering what mischief he can get into next.

Now if you're still not convinced that you and your dog will both be better off if you keep him properly confined, here's the topper. If he's any good, you have a substantial investment in him. You don't want to lose him.

There is no such thing as a male dog, of any breed, that sooner or later won't wander off in quest of love, if he has the chance. He may seem quite content for a while, at large in a yard with an ordinary fence around it. But eventually he'll turn up missing. And it is just a question of time before he's killed by a car, or stolen by a dog thief.

Some females will stay at home, except when they come in season. But nobody will remember to examine a bitch every day. She'll come in season unexpectedly, and then she'll be gone over the fence, too. If she comes back at all, and unless you can get her to a veterinarian quickly enough, and unless his shots work, she will present you with a litter of mongrel pups—and this is almost worse than not coming back at all.

So never mind Aunt Minnie. Even though she and her friends think you are peculiar, eccentric, and cruel, build a nice, tight run in your yard. Put a good padlock on it. Keep your dog in it, *except when you have him out for yourself.*

# 11

# Kindergarten—Simple Citizenship

IT IS BEST to have your outside run and doghouse all ready, and pop your dog right in it the night you bring him home. Almost any pup, or any dog of any age, will do some howling and barking his first night alone in strange new surroundings, no matter whether he's in the house, or outside in a yard kennel. So you may as well have his permanent quarters ready, and break him of his noise-making only once, instead of twice.

The first command he must learn, to be a good citizen, is *"Stop that noise."* It is also important to have him understand thoroughly what this means, for another reason. Later, when he gets to retrieving, and birds are actually shot for him, he quite likely will have a tendency to whine, or even to bark, from pure excitement, while waiting to be sent. If this is not curbed at once, it can develop into a serious fault.

A dog that makes a racket in a duck blind just as a bunch of mallards set their wings and come in to your decoys will obviously spoil many shots for you. This is an easy fault to prevent, right from the start, but a hard one to correct after it becomes established and a dog gets to giving mouth like a hound every time he sees a bird in the air or hears a shot.

For this reason, in the retriever trials the judges are quite severe on a dog even for whining softly on the line or in the blind. They penalize for this, and sometimese even disqualify the dog entirely, in open all-age stakes. The easiest way to avoid this trouble is to make sure your dog understands what you mean when you say, "Stop that noise."

## COMMAND: STOP THAT NOISE
### (See Illustration 50)

Whether it's a pup or an older dog, the first procedure is the same. When he starts making a racket, try to sneak up on him, and catch him right in the act of howling or barking.

Hold his mouth shut with one hand, waggle a stern finger at him with the other, and tell him firmly, in the tone of command, *"Stop that noise."* Repeat this admonition several times, then go back in the house.

If he tunes up again, as he probably will, go out and repeat the above procedure, and then lock him in his little doghouse for the night. You should of course have a bolt on the door of the house for this purpose. Let him go ahead and howl himself to sleep. The noise will be sufficiently muffled by the house that it won't quite drive you crazy, or be bad enough that the neighbors will bring down the law on you—for a night or two, anyway.

Many young retrievers will be pretty well cured in one night, some will take two or three. Just be sure, until you win this argument, that the dog associates two unpleasant things in his memory each time he sets up a racket. First, having his mouth held shut and being scolded by the boss. Second, being confined in his house for the night.

This treatment will probably be sufficient for your dog. But if you should draw one that thinks he throws back to a wolf or coyote ancestor, that persists in howling at the moon, and you begin to run out of patience—then it's time to go a bit further. One way or another, *"Stop that noise"* must be learned.

With a young pup, say under nine months, I would hesitate to apply any severe treatment, but would simply continue the scoldings and locking him in his house. This is almost sure to win, fairly soon, with a puppy.

But with an older dog, after you know darned well he knows what is meant by *"Stop that noise,"* I wouldn't fool around more than three nights before beginning to apply more pressure. I enjoy my own sleep too well to spend very many nights arguing with a noisy dog.

First, try really squeezing when you hold his mouth closed, hard enough to pinch his lip against his teeth, while you're repeating the command. This won't actually hurt him much, but every dog hates it, and this likely will be enough punishment to win the debate.

I can remember owning only one Labrador that needed more drastic treatment, and she was my first one—old Nell. We lived in a Chicago suburb then, and the neighbors were beginning to get pretty tired of nightly music, after about a week of it.

She knew perfectly well what I wanted when I staggered out there in my pajamas in the middle of the night, pinched her lip, and told her in no uncertain terms to stop that noise. Each time she would pipe down for about half an hour, but just as I was getting back to sleep, the singing would start again, louder than ever. She was rapidly alienating the whole block, not to mention my long-suffering wife. When I locked Nell in her house it did no good. She just howled twice as loudly.

I was still green enough to be pretty squeamish about licking a dog, but at last was driven to a choice between this, a possible divorce, and a quite probable tar-and-feather party, with me as guest of honor. So at last I went out there with a heavy leather leash, and really gave her a housecleaning—what you would call a good old-fashioned thrashing. She took it in stride, but for the rest of that night she was quiet.

I thought I had won—but I didn't know Nell. Remember—she is the one I struggled with three years before waking up to the obvious truth she wasn't worth fooling with.

Anyway, the very next night after her licking, she was at it again, howling like a zombie. And then, in desperation, I invented my Bomb. I strung together, on a long, strong cord, a nest of assorted tin cans. I suspended this on a small pulley just above the spot at the end of the run where she liked to sit and do her nocturnal singing to the moon. I secured the other end of the cord to the railing of a sleeping porch just outside my bedroom.

That night when she started the music, I leaned out the window and shouted, *"Stop that noise."* As usual, she paid no attention. I waited five minutes, smoked a cigarette, then crept out on the porch, untied the cord, and dropped the Bomb. The tin cans landed right beside old Nell, on the concrete run. In the quiet of the night they made an unearthly racket. It scared hell out of her. She scuttled into her house, and was quiet for the rest of the night.

I was obliged to drop the Bomb only once more, and then Nell was convinced that it paid to heed the command. After that, when she would occasionally try a couple of tentative yips, it was enough to shout *"Stop that noise."* She would scurry for her house, sure that the Bomb would follow.

If your dog is stubborn about this command, another useful stunt is to shout it out the window first, then turn on a light that the dog can see—a yard light, back-porch light, or even some light inside the house. Wait five minutes, and *then* go out to administer the licking, or drop the Bomb, or do whatever unpleasant thing you're going to do. After that, it will usually be sufficient just to turn on the light to quiet the varmint. He'll associate this with the punishment, and figure that's coming next.

But if you have to resort to these severe measures, and it takes more than two or three nights for the dog to respond to this command, the chances are you have a hardheaded individual that will be just as stubborn in all his later training—and your best bet is to get rid of him and get another dog. At this early stage, you probably won't do it. But friend, you'll find out—just as I did.

## HOUSEBREAKING

I'm going to include here what I've learned about housebreaking not only retrievers, but all the miscellaneous house pets we've been guilty of harboring and cherishing.

Even if your retriever lives in an outside kennel, as he should, you'll have him in the house with you at times. Also, you don't want him messing up hotel rooms when you have him on hunting trips. Hotel and motel keepers are inclined to be ugly about this.

I think I've tried most of the recommended methods for housebreaking. A very common one is training the pup to do his business on a newspaper. This is easy to do, but I don't see much sense in it. Every dog I've ever trained this way, sooner or later, when I was taking my ease of a Sunday, with the paper strewn comfortably around the living-room floor, would fix up the sporting section before I had a chance to read it.

Even if your family is neater than mine, and you never have papers on the floor except the one the dog is supposed to use, it is still a damn nuisance to have to bundle up these savory little packages and dispose of them several times a day. In my opinion there is only one sensible place for a dog to relieve himself, and that is outside.

And there is only one way to teach that. During the first few days you have the dog in the house—*never give him a chance to make a mistake.* Until he understands he should never do it in the house, someone must be watching him every minute. The instant he starts sniffing around, acting as if he has to go, take him out immediately. Take him to the same place, every time, right from the start. You don't want dog messes all over your nice lawn, or flower garden. Take him behind the garage, or to a vacant lot next door, or to some place he can use as a toilet area without being a nuisance to *anyone.*

Don't let him start doing it on a neighbor's lawn or garden. This is likely to start a feud that will make the Hatfields' and the McCoys' little squabble seem like a mild disagreement between Boy Scouts. You think it's silly to mention this? You'd be surprised how many thoughtless dog owners are guilty of this imposition on their neighbors.

Always, when you take him out to the proper place, give the command "hie on." (Rhymes with *lie.* See Illustration 51.) Then say, "Be a good dog." Say this in a cheery, encouraging voice. You'll be surprised how quickly he'll get it, and it will speed up his performance, and save you a lot of standing around and waiting.

This command comes in particularly handy when you have him on a hunting trip, and take him out of your hotel room to a strange place to do his business. If he understands then what you mean by "be a good dog," he'll get down to business with much less preliminary sniffing of bushes. You'll be able to get back to your highball that much faster, and to explaining to the gang just how you happened to miss that cock pheasant you needed to fill your limit.

Now it's a nuisance, especially if—tsk—you keep your dog in the house all the time, to have to watch him every minute he's awake during the first two or three days. But this is the only real way to housebreak him, and in the long run it's by far the easiest way. In addition to taking him right out whenever he shows signs of having the urge, you should take him out anyway at regular intervals, whether he wants to or not. With a young pup this should be every two hours. With an older dog, every three hours is often enough. If you simply don't give him the chance to start the habit of doing wrong in the house, you'll be amazed at how quickly he'll form the good habit of doing it in the proper place outside. Dogs are such slaves to habit, and form them so quickly, that he'll soon be reluctant to do his business anywhere but at the regular specified place.

Quite likely you yourself can't be there to watch the pup constantly for the first few days he's in the house, and if so you have to delegate the job part of the time to a servant or another member of the family. Someone has to do it. And whoever has the duty, it is his fault if the dog is permitted to make his first mistake.

If this should happen, there is nothing to do but show him the crime, scold him sternly, say "no" several times, and then take him right out to the proper place, and tell him to "be a good dog." I've never accomplished anything by rubbing a dog's nose in a mess he made in the house. It seems to be much harder on the rug and on me than on the dog. This is ineffective as punishment, and sometimes leads to depraved appetite, getting a pup started eating his own stools.

After a very few times of doing his stuff at the correct place outside, the dog prefers to do it there, and will start telling you when he wants to go out, either by whining or by scratching at the door. When he once starts this, you can begin relaxing your vigilance. But for several weeks, as a precaution, he should be taken out at least two or three times a day, whether he asks or not.

Now nobody in his right mind is going to get up to take a dog out every two or three hours, all through the night. And fortunately this isn't necessary, even with a quite young pup.

A good retriever, or any dog worth keeping, of any breed, is naturally clean, and instinctively will not foul the place where he sleeps. So, until he is thoroughly housebroken, all you have to do at night is to tie the dog on a short chain, not over four or five feet long—wherever he is to sleep. This serves as a double purpose. In addition to housebreaking him to hold everything through the night, it also gets him in the habit of sleeping where you want him to, whether it's in a corner of the kitchen, the basement, or the master's bedroom. But the minute you get up in the morning, take him out instantly to "be a good dog."

If you should be unlucky enough to draw a dirty individual that will persistently foul his own nest, then you will have to do one of three things:

1. Resort to severe punishment, including walloping if necessary.

2. Give up, and keep him outside in a kennel run, where he really belongs anyway. This will save you all this trouble about house-breaking, because even the dirtiest dog will eventually learn he's more comfortable if he doesn't foul the small house where he sleeps, and will finally get to using the run. He will housebreak himself, in effect. Then, when you take him hunting, if you tie him short in a corner of your bedroom, you'll probably have no difficulty. He will have taught himself not to foul his nest.

3. Or—yes—get rid of the dog.

Before we leave the kindergarten stuff, just a few words for the people who are always asking how to train a dog to stop chasing cars, tipping over the neighbor's garbage can, biting people, and being a general neighborhood nuisance.

## CHASING CARS

If your dog is properly confined, this problem will never come up, and that is the best solution. But if you're going to be knuckle-headed about this thing, and insist on trying to give your dog the run of the place; if you claim he never leaves the yard *except* to chase cars—and you want to cure that—there's only one method I can recommend for you to try.

That is to set a trap for him. Get a friend to drive you up and down the street in front of your place, in a strange car. Conceal yourself on the floor, in back. When your dog gives chase, have the driver slam on the brakes and stop quickly. You come roaring out of the car, and chase the dog home. Try to give him the sur-prise of his life. If this doesn't work the first time, then make yourself a tin-can bomb, and hurl this at the dog, from the car. As a last resort, jump out, catch him, and give him a walloping he'll remember the rest of his life. It may require very severe treatment to cure this craze. It's up to you whether you want to dish it out, or keep the dog penned up after all, or let him ultimately die under the wheels of an automobile.

If that doesn't work, and if you are still unwilling to keep your car-chaser confined, and if you don't want to see him get killed or, worse, cause an accident, then take him to a professional for treatment. The good pros have tools and techniques which I wouldn't try myself, and which I wouldn't recommend to any amateur.

## RAIDING GARBAGE CANS

If a dog gets to roaming the neighborhood and becoming a nuisance, he is automatically accumulating many bad habits that will utterly ruin him as a working retriever. But if you don't care about this, and are keeping him just as a pet, and if you are determined to give him his "freedom," then you'd better try to cure him of his more offensive tricks. If you don't, the problem will be solved anyway. You will lose the dog. He will be poisoned, or shot.

Did somebody else's dog ever get to raiding your garbage can? If so, you know how annoying this can become. A dog that forms this habit invariably tips over the can, spreads the contents all over your yard, and paws through it for selected delicacies. If a dog keeps coming back to yours, night after night, I suppose it's a nice compliment to the quality of your garbage. But it gets to be something of a nuisance, cleaning up the mess every morning, and can finally bring a man to a pretty violent frame of mind.

If a neighbor should complain that *your* dog is doing this to him, you'd better take steps to stop it, fast. If you like, you can try setting another trap. If you're silly enough to lose all the time and sleep, go ahead and stake out in the neighbor's yard—try to catch the dog in the act, and punish him severely. This may mean many hours, or even nights of waiting. Personally I don't have that much time to waste on any dog. And even a severe licking may not cure this nasty habit. It probably will relieve that particular neighbor. But everyone has a garbage can. The dog will probably start working a different one the very next night.

A friend of mine had this problem with his dog. At last in desperation he bought an air rifle, loaned it to the currently aggrieved neighbor, and authorized him to use it on the dog—with certain specified precautions.

They moved the garbage can from the back porch to the rear of the yard, and carefully stepped off the distance. It was a good 150 feet—50 yards—from the house. The neighbor, a hunter and a careful man with a gun, agreed to shoot from his bedroom window only when the dog was presenting his stern as a target, to avoid any possibility of hitting an eye.

That same night the dog found the can in its new location with no trouble at all. The neighbor heard the clatter as it went over. He crept to the bedroom window with the air gun.

In the bright moonlight he could clearly see the dog, with his head down among the pork-chop bones, and his south end presented temptingly toward the house. *Target for tonight!* He let the dog have it. The shot was a beauty, a bull's-eye on the big muscle of a rear flank.

It produced instant results. With a starled yip, the dog leaped high in the air. He came down running. He went away from that dangerous garbage can, but fast.

Of course at that distance he couldn't really be hurt by a BB gun. The pellet didn't even break the skin. But it stung enough to startle and frighten him, and to implant in his memory a mighty unpleasant association with the business of raiding garbage cans.

My friend claims this permanently cured the dog of the garbage-can craze. He says it was better for the dog to be carefully shot by a BB gun than eventually to have his head blown off with a real weapon, by some less forbearing neighbor.

Such a solution is a bit risky at best. And it depends on your dog's locating a cooperative garbage-can owner, who is also a good shot.

Personally I would prefer just to keep the dog at home nights, in his pen, where he belongs.


## BITING PEOPLE

Most retrievers have no meanness in them, and you rarely find one that will bite unless greatly provoked. But occasionally even one of these gives his owner a great surprise. Often it is the mildest-mannered dog—of any breed—around home, that is most dangerous to other people when he roams.

The only really painful dog bite I ever received was from an Irish Setter, a mild-mannered breed if there ever was one. This was a beautiful dog, with limpid brown eyes. But in his soul he was no good. He was a wandering mutt, a spoiled and pampered pet.

When I was working in my garden in my own backyard, he would come in there, and bark and snarl at me, insanely. I was naturally a bit annoyed, but would always chase him out by tossing a clod of dirt at him, and think no more about it. One day he changed his tactics. Without making a sound, he sneaked up behind me, and sunk his teeth in my leg. This was too much.

I carried him home by the ears. When his owner saw and heard us coming, he was greatly indignant over my method of returning his pet. He wanted to make something of it.

Speechless with rage, I showed him my bleeding leg. He simply didn't believe his dog did it.

He shouted. "You're crazy. Rex never bites. He wouldn't bite anybody."

For some reason the dog owners who neglect their pets most are always the surest they can do no wrong. Naturally, a sneak like Rex won't bite anybody when his master is around. But the so-and-so bit me, without provocation. And in my own yard. That, I didn't like. I told his owner so. I told him if it ever happened again, I thought Rex's dark red hide would make me a nice rug. Such conversation doesn't help neighborhood relations.

Nobody has the right to keep a dog and allow it to become a nuisance to others. If you don't know where your dog is, you don't know what he's doing. And the chances are, whatever it is. it isn't good. If he starts wandering, there is only one decent thing to do—and one safe thing for the dog himself.

That—once more—is to keep him confined except when you are with him.

# 12

# Grade School—Obedience Training

WITH ONLY EIGHT basic obedience commands you can keep your dog under easy and quiet control, whether he's a working retriever or a house pet of any breed.

Before you start teaching these, it is best to wait a few days after bringing home a new dog or pup. Give him a chance to get over his shyness, and to become accustomed to his new surroundings. If you have much argument over *"Stop that noise,"* wait until he's reasonably happy about that before going on with his further schooling. Try to feed him yourself during this period. Pet him, and talk to him, and build up his confidence in you. This will take very little time, and will make the whole training job easier.

After you have become well acquainted, you can start teaching these obedience commands any time you're ready—to a pup of three months or more, or to a dog of any age. Contrary to popular impression, these commands can even be taught to a very old dog that has been spoiled, if he has a reasonably good memory and an inherent desire to please a man.

Obviously it may take a bit longer for a young and playful pup to grasp them, but a dog of twelve months or so, if he's worth training at all, should be responding within *two weeks* at the most to these eight commands. Furthermore, you can accomplish this magic result in only ten minutes a day, through the simple principle of *doubling up* and *pyramiding*.

Most people just can't believe this. But I've done it myself, many times, and so can you. Ten minutes a day for fourteen days—a total of two hours and twenty minutes of your valuable time—is all you need to spend to have a dog with perfect manners, and to convince your astonished friends and family that you are one hell of an animal tamer.

There is just one catch. Don't expect these fast results if your dog is exhausted by play, or just plain bored, when you take him out for his first lesson, or any lesson. If you insist on making a house pet of him, then you should pen him up or tie him up on a short chain, and allow nobody to go near him, for at least two hours before you try to teach him anything.

Any decent retriever—even a young pup—should then be able to take a ten-minute stretch of intensive training without becoming indifferent or sulky. If he shows signs of wanting to quit on you too soon, he may be sick, and you should have a good vet examine him. But if he's healthy—and isn't keen enough to take ten minutes of serious work a day—then he isn't worth fooling with.

## 1. THE COMMAND: SIT

### (See Illustrations 26–33)

This command is now used by virtually all retriever trainers in this country, and is preferred to the old country command "hup." I've never discovered how the latter word originated, what it meant, or why it was used. But many English trainers still use it.

If you should import a trained dog from England, and he just looks blank when you say "sit," see what happens on "hup." If he responds, I would recommend switching him over, teaching him "sit," anyway.

Why? Because it is almost impossible to say "hup" quietly, and still make the sound convey authority. If the dog is trained to "sit," you can eventually have him sit by just hissing through your teeth—making an "s" sound. This comes in handy in the blind, when ducks are coming in, to be able to remind your dog to be steady without making a big racket. And it is *mighty* useful if you ever handle him in a field trial. The judges can scarcely hear a little soft hissing, and they won't penalize the dog for unsteadiness unless they hear you making a lot of noise, loudly nagging at him for the apparent purpose of keeping him steady.

To teach your dog "sit," just hold him by the scruff or the collar with one hand, and push his fanny down with the other. As you do this, say "Sit!" in a firm tone.

If you have any trouble pushing his hindquarters down, use a rocking motion from fore to aft, exerting rearward and downward pressure simultaneously. This way you can easily tip a big dog over into a sitting position, without having to force him to bend his hind legs.

Keep repeating the command "sit," while you hold him firmly in the sitting position for a few seconds. Then release him. Praise him and pet him for a moment. Then repeat the whole routine two or three times. By now he should begin to associate the command with the simple action. Try it, without touching him.

Speak the command firmly, at the same time holding up one hand with extended index finger. (See illustration.) This admonitory hand signal will come in handy later at times, if right from the start the dog associates it with the command to sit. There will be times when he is far out in the field with a strong wind blowing, when he can't hear the whistle, and then it's useful to be able to stop him with the motionless upstretched arm.

If he doesn't sit at once on the spoken command, push him down again. But a good dog should be doing it, without help, before the first ten-minute lesson is over.

The first few times he does it, make him stay in the sitting position only a few seconds. Then release him by jumping up, moving a few steps away, clapping your hands and calling "Come." He'll be delighted by his release, bound after you, and thus make a start also on learning the command "come," within the very first brief lesson. Each time after he *sits,* then *comes* a few steps to you, pet him and make a fuss over him, and tell him he's a fine dog.

After the ten minutes are up, put him back in his kennel, no matter how much fun you're having. If you're determined to cram the obedience training into him, it's all right to take him out again the same day for one more ten-minute lesson—*but only after an intermission of several hours.* And actually, you'll get fast enough results to satisfy anyone with just one lesson a day.

The next time you take him out, tell him to sit at once. If he's at all slow about it, remind him by pushing him down. Keep at it until he obeys at once, without help.

A dog should know darned well what the command means after that first lesson. But if he's a little slow, give him the benefit of the doubt, and continue during the second and third lessons just to push him down, if necessary.

After that, I wouldn't fool around much. If he is slow at all about putting it down, whack him on the fanny with the flat of your hand. This should be enough, unless—unhappy man—you should be struggling with a hammerhead like Old Nell. I finally had to resort to the strap, even to convince her it was a sound idea to *sit* when I suggested it.

Every time you take the dog out, after that first lesson, start out by having him sit before going on with the main business of the day. Gradually increase the time you require him to stay in that position, without moving, until you have him up to a minute or so.

When he seems quite steady, move back a step or two, holding up that finger and telling him firmly to sit, as you move away. Keep gradually increasing the distance, until you can move 10 or 12 feet away from him. If he chisels or moves at all, put him back on the exact spot where he belongs—scold him, and sternly tell him to "sit." *Never* let him get away with chiseling.

This can develop into a bad fault. Sometimes you see an itchy retriever that can cover an astonishing amount of territory without ever lifting his fanny off the ground. This is a nuisance when hunting, and very bad in field trials.

## 2. THE COMMAND: COME

### (See Illustrations 42–45)

The dog should sit well enough at the beginning of the second lesson so that you need devote only two or three minutes to this, and can bear down for the rest of the session on "come."

Have him sit for a few seconds. Then suddenly turn, run *away* from him, clapping your hands and calling "Come." (This is the conventional command. I use "come along," myself. Either is perfectly all right, and you can take your choice.)

It is the natural thing for any young dog, or young puppy, to chase you when you run away from him. This should be all that's necessary to teach him to "come." I've never yet had to resort to forcing methods on any Labrador I've trained, even including Nell.

However, some trainers tell me they occasionally have to resort to the rope—and we may as well include this method here—just in case you should be unlucky enough to need it. If the dog simply won't chase you when you run away, get yourself 20 or 30 feet of clothesline. Tie a harness snap on one end of it. Lay the line on the floor, across the room. Have the dog sit. Quietly attach the snap to his collar. Move away, and get the rope in your hand.

Then clap your hands, and call "Come," enthusiastically. If he doesn't respond, give a light jerk on the rope. Don't haul him in, hand over hand. Keep giving smart jerks, calling "Come" each time, until you have moved him up to you. He'll soon give up, and come under his own power. Then pet him, praise him, and make a fuss over him.

Now try it a few times, attempting to confuse him as to whether the rope is attached or not. Have it laid out on the floor, but do some sleight of hand with the snap, sometimes attaching it to his collar, sometimes not. You can teach the dumbest dog to come this way, if you want to bother with it. Personally, I don't.

The chances are this won't be necessary, if you are careful to be alone with your dog when you are teaching him to "come," so there's nothing else for him to do but chase after you when you run away. If there is a large, admiring audience, any pup might be distracted, and run around sniffing all the nice people, instead of paying attention to his new boss' antics.

Each time you run away, stoop down quickly just as he catches up to you, take him in your arms, and pet him and praise him. After he has done this three or four times, try calling "Come" and clapping your hands—without running away. But be ready to jump up and start moving away, if he slows up or stops before he gets clear up to you.

He should be coming to you fast, on command, within two or three lessons at the most.

As soon as he is responding well to the spoken command, begin also using the whistle. Say "Come," clap your hands, and quickly blow *two or more* fast blasts on the whistle. Be sure you *never* blow just one blast to have the dog come. Most handlers blow *four* times, in quick succession.

Later, when your dog is ready to learn to take directions from your hand signals, you'll be teaching him to stop and *sit* when you blow just *one* whistle blast. So you can avoid later confusion between the two uses of the whistle by being careful right from the start to use the correct whistle signal for "come."

To a properly trained retriever the sound of the whistle means just one of two things:

1. Several quick blasts mean *come* right now, and fast.

2. One sharp blast means stop and *sit* instantly, and look at the boss for further directions.

### 3. THE COMMAND: KENNEL

#### (See Illustration 38–41)

This command means, "Go in your kennel"; or, "Jump in the car"; or, "Get in the duck boat."

There is no need to devote any separate lessons to this. Every time you put him away, have him *sit* before the door of his house, or the gate to his run. Then point to the opening and say "Kennel." The first two or three times you'll have to take him by the scruff or the collar and heave him in. But he'll learn what this command means very quickly, and after that you should insist on instant obedience to it every time. Sometimes a dog will want to stall on this one, like a child procrastinating about going to bed. A whack or two on the rear end with a rolled newspaper should be enough to convince him that when pappy says "Kennel," he means it.

The first time you want him to get in the back of the car, or into a shipping crate, or a boat, or any strange place or conveyance, have him sit first, then point where you want him to go, and say "Kennel." Toss him in, if necessary. He'll soon learn to get into any place or any thing, when you give this command.

This is easy to teach, yet for some reason it makes a spectacular impression on people when they see a dog smartly obey this simple command.

## 4. THE COMMAND: HEEL

### (See Illustrations 46–49)

If you are right-handed, train your dog to walk at heel on your left side, so there will be no danger of accidentally shooting him when you carry your gun under your right arm. If you shoot from the left side, of course, you'll want him to "heel" on the right side.

Actually on this command he should walk along smartly, his head held high, with his nose beside your knee, neither forging ahead nor lagging behind. Insist on perfect performance to this command, and don't allow him to start getting sloppy, wandering away from your side to sniff bushes. This can be a nuisance to you, and also very dangerous to the dog when you're hunting heavy cover—particularly if there is a trigger-happy member of your party who shoots at rabbits on the ground.

As soon as your pupil is responding reasonably well to "sit" and "come," you can start teaching "heel"—surely by the fourth or fifth lesson.

Let him out of his kennel and have him *sit* for a moment. Then move away, and have him *come*. (In this and all succeeding lessons, give him a quick refresher course in all the commands he *has* learned, before going on with the new one.)

Now attach your short leash to his collar. Get him on your left side, pat your left leg, and step off briskly—saying "Come." Try, through repeating this command, and plenty of encouragement by patting your leg, to get him coming along beside you without even realizing he is under the restraint of leash and collar.

But if he doesn't get it this easily, and pulls back against the leash, don't then start dragging him around the yard, choking him with the collar. Any young dog is likely to be somewhat panicky the first time he feels the restraint of leash and a tightening slip collar, and may plunge around, fighting it, like a calf on the end of a cowpuncher's rope.

Don't let it get this far. If he pulls back, hold him there just long enough for you to get to him. Then release the pressure on the collar, and take him in your arms and talk to him and pet him. If you do this two or three times, he'll quickly find you mean to do him no damage with the collar—and you'll avoid a knockdown drag-out argument.

In one lesson he should get to walking along beside you, on the leash, without pressure on the leash. But if he's a little stubborn about it, apply pressure only in quick tugs, pulling him up beside you, then releasing the pressure on the collar immediately. Keep using the command "come," which he already knows, until he is going along cheerfully beside you on a slack leash.

Then it is time to start saying "Heel" as he walks in correct position. Keep repeating this constantly, in a cheery tone when he's right, sternly when he lags or forges ahead. Pull him into position with a short jerk on the leash.

Sometimes with an eager lunatic like, for instance, Field Champion Muscles in his younger days, when he would insist on forging ahead, you need to jerk back until your arm is tired and your patience begins to wear thin. A simple cure for this is to hold a stick in front of the dog's nose. If he tries to push ahead of it, rap him on the nose with it, lightly. This will soon convince him that when you say "Heel," you don't mean "lead the parade."

As soon as he is responding to the "heel" command on leash, take it off. Step along briskly, patting your leg and repeating the command constantly. Use the stick, if necessary, to keep him from getting ahead.

A dog should learn to heel in one lesson, so you can even dispense with the stick in front of his nose. The four pictures (Illustrations 46–49) are actual photographs of the first ten-minute session I had with Muscles on this command. I'll admit I had to give him a few reminders with the stick later, but he was doing pretty well at the end of the first lesson. Any *normal* dog should do much better.

Thereafter, every time you take him out, give him some walking at heel and insist that he do it perfectly—just as you do with each of the other commands.

## 5. THE COMMAND HIE ON

### (See Illustration 51)

You need devote no particular lesson time to this. Eventually it will come to mean to the dog, "Never mind walking at heel. *At ease.*

Run on ahead. Beat it. Go hunting. Use your nose." Or, "Do your business."

Whenever you have the dog where it is safe for him to run a bit, without getting on a street or highway, send him on with this command. First have him walk at heel, then wave him ahead with a sweeping arm motion, and say, "Hie on!" You should begin this before he gets too good at heeling. If you wait too long before he begins to understand this one, he may be reluctant to leave your side.

Then you might have to run ahead, get him running, and stop suddenly, to convince him it's actually okay for him to get out in front of you.

It is good for a pup or young dog to take him for a walk in open country and give him a chance to run, whenever it is convenient for you. If you live in a crowded city, you can still give him a run occasionally in a big vacant lot, in a park or a golf course, or on a beach.

But when you do this, don't let him get too far away from you. If you prevent him from ranging too far out, right from the start, you won't have to break this bad habit later when you begin using him to hunt ahead of you, and want him to flush birds within easy gun range.

When you tell him to hie on, call him back whenever he gets more than 25 yards away from you. A fast youngster that is eager to run will sometimes discover the only way he can do so, without being called in all the time, is to dash back and forth in front of you, like a windshield wiper. Thus, he'll be teaching himself to quarter ahead of the gun, while he's just out for a romp. Some dogs will do this—some won't. Don't worry about it if yours doesn't. It's simple enough to teach him to quarter correctly, after he's learned in college to take directions from hand signals.

For now, just don't allow him to get more than 25 yards from you, after the command "hie on." The only time a retriever should be permitted to go farther afield is when he is sent to retrieve. And for that, of course, the command "hie on" will never be used.

## 6. THE COMMAND: NO

This is a very useful and important command, but here again no formal lesson time need be wasted on it. Whenever the dog does a wrong thing, and you wish him to stop it, simply restrain him or stop him, using whatever physical force is necessary—at the same time saying "No!" Say it as sternly as you can. Shout it if necessary.

He will understand what it means very quickly. Then you must insist on instant obedience, even if you have to resort to severe punishment to convince him you mean it. For this command—in addition to making him a decent citizen—will quite likely save his life, sooner or later. It will save him from a truck, or a mowing machine, or a rattlesnake, or quicksand, or some other form of sudden death. It is one command on which I will not compromise with any dog.

## 7. THE COMMAND: DOWN

### (See Illustrations 52 and 53)

No dog should be permitted to jump up on people. And for a gun dog, it must be absolutely forbidden. It is exceedingly dangerous to both man and beast for a big retriever suddenly to leap up on you when you have a loaded shotgun in your hands.

Probably the most commonly recommended cure is to step on the dog's hind toes when he jumps up on you. I've never had much luck with this. Maybe I'm not fast enough on my feet. Either I miss those hind toes entirely, or in lunging for them, throw myself off balance. About that time I'm hit on the chest by those big forepaws —with eighty pounds or so of projectile behind them, and I land flat on my back.

I've found it much easier and more effective simply to grab those *forepaws* as they come up, and squeeze them—at the same time saying "No!"—immediately followed by "Down!" Each time the dog jumps up, squeeze the paws a little harder. They are quite sensitive, and you'll be surprised how few times it will be necessary to squeeze them before "down" is thoroughly understood.

Each time, as you squeeze his toes and push him down, scold him a little, and repeat the command a few times. Tell him he's a bad dog. He'll get it.

This same command should also be used for keeping any dog down off the furniture. Whenever he gets up on something, throw him off, at the same time saying "Down!" Bothering to do this is cheap insurance for a continuing happy marriage.

## 8. THE COMMAND: CHARGE

### (See Illustrations 34–37)

This command means "lie down," but don't ask me why. It is used by many of the obedience trainers, and is part of the customary jargon in the obedience classes in bench shows. Use it if you like, or if you feel too silly saying it, it's perfectly all right just to say "lie down" instead.

The professional retriever trainers don't usually bother to teach this command. There is little practical reason for it in retriever work, if the dog is kept confined in a kennel most of the time. I've heard people say it is useful at times to have a retriever lie down beside you in cover, to hide him from ducks.

I claim any cover that will hide me from a duck will hide a dog sitting up. I also claim ducks pay no attention to a sitting dog, even right out in the open. And I like to have my dog sitting up, so he can mark falls. I can't recall a single time in my own hunting experience when it would have been of any value to have a dog respond instantly to the command "charge."

If you have your dog in the house a lot, you may want to teach him this command. Of course if you just have him sit, he'll lie down anyway, when he sees nothing exciting is going to happen, after a few minutes. But if you enjoy showing your friends how he will instantly flatten out like a rug before the fire, there's no harm in it, and it will take only a few minutes to teach this one.

First have him sit. Then pull his front paws out from under him, toward you—and he's lying down. At the same time say "Charge!" Repeat it two or three times, and he has it. That's all there is to it.

## REPETITION OF OBEDIENCE COMMANDS

Your dog now knows what you mean by these commands. To keep improving his response to them, all you need is a little repetition every time you take him out.

This will require no special effort on your part, for you'll automatically give him all the reminding he needs if you simply keep him under control, as you should anyway if you want a decent hunting dog.

When he's out with you he should either be walking at *heel, sitting, lying down,* ranging just ahead of you after the command *hie on,* or *coming* to your command or to your whistle.

Never just let him wander around aimlessly, either inside or outside the house, on his own. Even when you have him out for a walk, and have told him to "hie on," leave him out in front only as long as he runs around and hunts happily and aggressively. The minute he gets listless and appears indifferent, bring him right in and finish the walk with him at heel.

Likely you won't see the importance of this at first—but take my word for it. If you want a really keen performer in the field—a dog you can be proud of—then form this habit right now. Keep him under control every minute he's out of his kennel.

Order him "Down" every time he jumps on you, a guest, or the living-room couch.

Say "No" whenever he does any undesirable thing, and make it stick.

Say "Kennel" whenever you put him away, or want him to get in the car.

All this will seem a bit stuffy right at first, but if you stay with it you'll be surprised how fast you're doing it unconsciously, like shifting gears in a car. Then, with no particular effort on your part, you'll be improving your dog every time you are with him.

# 13

## Junior High—Single
## Marked Retrieves

FOR MANY GENERATIONS retrievers have been bred and selected for the powerful instinct to do one special job–to go out and retrieve anything that falls. It should never be necessary to "force break" one of these dogs to perform this function.

Pointers and setters, whose main purpose is finding and pointing live birds, often lack interest in retrieving, and must be force trained. I have shot quail over many such dogs whose work was a joy to see –until dead birds were down–but that then were indifferent and even downright sulky about bringing them to bag. You could make these dogs do it, but you couldn't make them like it.

There is some excuse for putting up with slovenly retrieving work from a good pointing dog. But I certainly wouldn't give a nickel for a *retriever* that must be forced to go out and do the thing he was born to do. I wouldn't waste time on such a dog, and I wouldn't recommend that you do, either.

Force training such a dog is really a job for a top-notch professional trainer. But if you insist on trying it yourself, there are many good books listed in the bibliography that will tell you how.

So I won't waste space here on detailed methods of force training. They are all fundamentally the same. One way or another, you force the dog to go out to the dummy–either by dragging him out there yourself, or by having a helper haul him out on a rope. Then you put the dummy in his mouth, and make him hold it. Then you haul him back to where you were in the first place.

113

This can be a long-drawn-out process that *really* requires a lot of time and patience. And even when you get through, you'll probably have at best a slow, sloppy, indifferent performer. It's no fun to hunt with a dog like that.

I would hang him in the smokehouse, and get a dog that is downright delighted to be given the opportunity to retrieve.

## STARTING A DOG TO RETRIEVE

### (See Illustrations 54–57)

If your dog is a year old or more, and has had his two-week course in obedience, he's ready to start retrieving. Even at eight or nine months, if he's really keen for it, it won't hurt a pup to give him two or three simple retrieves a day—but no more than that, *please.*

*Never* throw a stick or a ball for him, or anything else but his regular dummy. Never send him to fetch a bottle of beer, or your bedroom slippers. Such parlor tricks are amusing to your friends, but are confusing to the dog. In the field you don't want him bringing you a stick or an empty bottle when you've sent him to trail a crippled pheasant.

Let him know right from the start that the training dummy means business. When you send him after it, he's to hunt until he finds it—and nothing else.

The land dummy, made of an old gunny sack, should be rolled quite tightly into a cylinder about a foot long and two inches in diameter. Bind it together securely with strong cord, so there are no loose edges by which the dog can pick it up. You want him to start right out by taking a proper "body hold" on it.

For the first lesson in retrieving, be sure to be alone with the dog, in an enclosed place. A two-car garage, with doors closed, is big enough. Or a well-fenced yard, containing no cats to chase, or other distractions.

Hold the dummy in your hand, and tease the dog with it. Wave it around, and try to get him jumping and grabbing at it. Don't frighten him by shaking it too close to his nose. You don't want him to get the notion you're going to hit him with it. Some youngsters take a little more time than others to get the idea that this is a new and exciting game.

It often helps to jump around yourself as you wave the dummy, and occasionally feint at throwing it. Keep up a running fire of excited conversation. Such as, "Oh, boy! What's this? Some fun, hey keed?" It doesn't matter what you say. Your tone of voice will help to fire the dog with excitement, and to awaken his fierce instinct to retrieve. Keep up this teasing until he is fairly frantic to get the dummy.

Then maneuver yourself to the middle of the room or yard, so you will have plenty of room to run *away* from the dog the instant he picks up the dummy. Throw it a short distance, only 10 or 12 feet the first time. If you have teased him enough, the dog will leap after it, very aggressively.

Pop your whistle in your mouth, and start blowing one sharp blast after another as soon as he grabs the dummy. Run away from him, keep running until he catches up to you, and lean down suddenly and snatch the dummy out of his mouth as he passes.

The only difficult part of this routine seems to be running away from the dog until he *completely* catches up and is about to pass you. A new trainer invariably stops too soon, turns around and lunges *at* the dog. This causes him to slow up, or even stop, and quite likely to drop the dummy before you can get your hand on it.

So force yourself to keep moving away—until you can scoop the dummy from his mouth as he passes you at full speed. If you do this, you can have your dog doing fast, stylish retrieves, and coming back fast, and *delivering to hand*—within a ten-minute lesson.

You may wonder why this running away business is necessary, when the dog has already been trained to come to your whistle. The main reason is literally to give him no chance even to *think* of dropping the dummy, after he has picked it up. If the first few times he retrieves, he delivers to your hand, this good habit will be established. Also, he will become accustomed to returning with the dummy just as fast as he goes out after it.

These habits can be well started in the first retrieving lesson. And by stirring your stumps a bit, you will have saved yourself a lot of later work, such as force training the dog to deliver to hand—and giving him exercises to speed up his return.

However, if you aren't a very classy fielder, and fumble the dummy, and the dog gets to dropping it somewhere near you, don't worry about it too much at this stage of the game. Don't try to make him pick it up again, or to force him to hold it in his mouth.

It is much more important for the present to develop fully his enthusiasm for retrieving, before you attempt any fussing or arguing about delivering to hand. You want no unpleasant association with that training dummy until he has reached the point where he would rather sail out to fetch it than go to heaven.

That's the easy, happy way to train a retriever. If he sizzles out when you throw the dummy, and brings it even part way back before dropping it—you're doing fine. Just pick it up. Pet and praise him, and assure him he's an elegant dog.

Then tease him with the dummy, and throw it again, and this time try to improve your own footwork, as well as your fielding. You're almost sure to have him retrieving to hand very soon.

The first day, quit after four or five retrieves, no matter how eager the dog is for more. Let him think it over for twenty-four hours. The next day he'll be fairly busting to go.

It is unlikely, but if by the end of the second lesson he is still dropping the dummy before you can grab it, then try using a much smaller one—say about an inch in diameter. After he gets to delivering this, you can then switch him back to the larger dummy. Of all the Labradors I've trained, I had to resort to this with only one—a young bitch with a very small mouth.

## THE COMMAND FOR RETRIEVING

There is only one proper command for sending a retriever to make a retrieve. That is to speak his name. Whether you see any sense in it now or not, you'll be happy later if you train your dog this way.

Bird-dog trainers commonly use "fetch," or "go fetch," or "dead bird!" Obviously the big drawback to any of these is that when the command is spoken, every dog within earshot will go for the bird. Results: a spectacular dog fight, and a torn-up bird. For any kind of hunting, when there is more than one dog in the party, it's best if they're trained to go only on their names. And this is a must if you think you might ever wish to run your dog in a field trial.

No matter what sort of a long-winded and fancy registered name he has, select a short training name for him–a word of one or two syllables that is easy to say and to understand. Avoid a name starting with "s." Reason: you'll want to hiss at him to keep him steady. If his name is Sam, and you use that to send him, he's likely to end up with a nervous breakdown–trying to decide whether you mean *sit* or *Sam*.

After the first lesson in retrieving, begin speaking his name every time you throw the dummy. Say it with excitement and enthusiasm in your voice. Thus he will begin immediately to associate the name command with your permission to go and retrieve.

## PLAYING WITH THE TRAINING DUMMY

### (See Illustrations 58–61)

Sometimes an aggressive pup or young dog will have a tendency to shake the dummy like a rat, play with it, or even run away into a corner and lie down and chew on it. This must be corrected at once.

The easiest cure is simply to redouble your own exertions, which have already been described. Don't give him a chance to play with the dummy. Start blowing that whistle a split second *before* he reaches the dummy. Yell and clap your hands and run away as if the devil himself was after you. Make so much racket that it's more exciting for the rascal to chase you than to play with the dummy.

This will almost always work. When the dog has thus been kidded and coaxed into delivering to hand just a few times, he discovers that if he doesn't waste time playing with the dummy, you'll throw it again for him just that much sooner. And that, after all, is the big treat. It's much more fun chasing the dummy than chewing it.

However, I'll admit this method involves a few minutes of strenuous exercise for you. If you run out of wind, perhaps you'd better have a small argument with the dog, and get it over with.

Tease him with the dummy, but hold your hand around it in such a way that he can't clamp down on it without biting you. When he tries to snap at it, scold him severely. Say "No" each time he tries to handle it too roughly. This is a good time also to start using that warning command "ah, ah, ah." (Like the "a" in cat.)

He will soon understand he must not bite that dummy, any more than he would bite your hand. But don't do more than two or three minutes of this exercise at one time, unless you have a very tough and aggressive dog who is really rough on the dummy. The danger, with an average young retriever, is that too much of this might make him dummy shy, and reluctant even to pick it up.

## THE COMMAND: LEAVE IT

On training dummies, and later on birds, a retriever should take a sufficiently firm hold so that he won't drop even the heaviest cock pheasant. According to the late Martin Hogan's definition, a retriever is not "hard-mouthed" if the birds he brings in are not crushed, and are fit for the table. However, he should give up a bird readily when you take it from him.

This is no problem with most Goldens or with at least half the Labradors, which are apt to be tender-mouthed almost to a fault. But if your dog shows any tendency to hang onto the dummy when you try to take it, you should teach the command "leave it," starting early in the game.

Take hold of the dummy with one hand. Say "Leave it!" very firmly. At the same time grasp the dog's lower jaw with your other hand, and force his mouth open. If he needs more pressure than this to give up the dummy readily, then wrap your hand around his *upper* jaw, and press his upper lips against his teeth. Usually a very little of this will have him gently depositing the dummy in your hand when you say "Leave it!"

Later on, when you introduce him to real birds, you may need to give him a brief refresher course on this, using the same technique exactly.

## TAKING A LINE

For the first three or four retrieving lessons, just keep tossing the dummy, gradually increasing the distance until you are throwing it as far as you can. Keep at this until the dog is retrieving it perfectly, going out *and* coming back with it as fast as he can run. With a really keen dog, you should be able to stop violently running away from him after the first or second lesson, without slowing his return. But please continue to *move backward* a step or two, just as he is approaching you, and snatch the dummy from his mouth *as you are moving away.*

If you begin standing still too soon, or lunging a step or two *toward* the dog to grab the dummy—you're just building up unnecessary trouble. This will cause almost any youngster to slow the last few yards of his return, and may start him dropping the dummy in front of you. If this fault is allowed to start, it can become progressively serious. At last, like old Nell, your dog will be spitting out the duck at the edge of the water, and telling you if you want it you can damn well walk over there and get it.

It can make you mighty mad if, just when you emerge from the blind to finish a retrieve for your dog, you frighten off a new flight of ducks. Also, it's a nuisance if you have to wade in deep mud to get the abandoned bird.

For many practical reasons, a retriever should always deliver right to hand. The easy way to accomplish this is to kid him into always doing so, right from the start.

The next step in his training is to start him taking a line, at the same time giving him longer retrieves. For this you'll need a bit larger area to work in, and a part-time helper to throw the dummy for you.

Most states now license public shooting preserves, and some even grant special licenses for "dog training areas." These facilities are adjacent to most of our large cities. When you need more space, birds, boats, water, a chance to shoot over your dog, or a helper, you might check the "yellow pages" or a local sportswriter or game warden for the location of the preserve nearest you. These facilities can be a great boon in helping you to put a polish on your dog's training.

"Taking a line" means training the dog to follow the exact direction of a gesture you make with your hand, and to stay right on the line all the way to the fall. The simple way to teach this is to begin early giving him this line with your hand, just as you send him for every marked retrieve he makes. Later, when you come to blind retrieves, he will have become so accustomed to finding something right where the boss said it was—and where he knew it was anyway—that he will take your word for it even when he has seen nothing fall.

This is also exceedingly useful for assisting the dog's memory on double and triple retrieves.

If you work your dog from the left side, give the line with your left hand. Reach across and hold him lightly by the collar with your *right* hand. Don't make him sit—yet.

Have your helper walk out about as far as you've been throwing the dummy yourself. If your pitching wing is as old and tired as mine, this will be about 20 or 25 paces.

He should wave the dummy, and shout if necessary to get the dog's attention. But *don't* let him yell the dog's name. He can shout "boo," or make a noise like a gun—anything except any word that you use as a command.

When the dog is looking, the helper should toss the dummy high in the air, so it will land a few feet in front of him. Then he should stand absolutely still, make no motion or sound, while the dog is retrieving.

Let the dog go at once, while the dummy is still in the air. At the same time, speak his name enthusiastically—and give him a line straight toward the spot where the dummy will fall. Do this by letting your left hand hang beside his nose, and jerking your hand sharply forward, in the proper direction, as you send him.

You must time this gesture to keep your hand moving just ahead of his nose as he leaves, so he can see it from the corner of his vision as he takes off on the correct line. Obviously it is useless if you miss the bus, and merely wave good-by at his tail.

Now don't make this a full-armed sweep—a great exaggerated motion—like a desperate bowler trying for a strike. This isn't necessary, and it looks poor in a field trial. Also, you don't want to be pitching yourself out of a duck boat every time you give your dog a line.

Just snap your hand forward, breaking only your elbow and wrist—not the shoulder. Your hand shouldn't move more than two feet. It's better in a trial if it moves less, when you're trying unobtrusively to help your dog remember a fall he's supposed to have marked.

Frank Hogan used to give his dogs a line by moving one finger about three inches. It was spectacular to see his dogs sail out on a perfect line to the most difficult blind retrieves, as a result of that slight gesture of his finger.

But at the start, you'd better give your dog a bit more hand movement than that. As you go along, you can gradually cut it down, if you want to be very fancy in your handling.

Always, from now on, when you send your dog for a retrieve, give him the line with your hand.

The first time a helper throws the dummy, your dog might want to return it to him. After all, he's been accustomed until now to return it to the guy who threw it. So be ready with your whistle, and if necessary take to your heels once more. Run away. Call him to you. He'll quickly understand that, no matter who throws the dummy, he's to bring it only to the boss.

Which brings up another point. Later, when yours is the only dog in a hunting party, never allow even your best friend to take a bird from him. Even if this means you have to lug forty pounds of other people's pheasant in your coat, while you finish walking a mile-long cornfield—insist that *your* dog retrieve only to *you*. Conversely, of course, never accept a bird from another man's dog. A retriever that gets to wandering around, trying to deliver to everybody, won't do a decent job for anybody. He'll end up as a no-good tramp.

You'll need a helper for only a few retrieving lessons, until it's safe to require the dog to be steady. After that you can have him sit while you walk forward and throw the dummy yourself.

For these first few lessons it's best to stick with sight retrieving. Use a big lawn, a golf course, a sand beach—any place where the dummy will always fall in plain sight. Have the helper gradually move out farther, just two or three paces each time, until you have the dog doing retrieves up to 100 yards. Then start mixing them up, long ones and short ones. Don't give him the chance to form the habit of just going out a certain distance, and then stopping and hunting short. Let him learn to keep going out on the line of the fall until he sees or smells the dummy. Most dogs have poor close vision, and even on bare ground they often won't see a dummy or a bird until very close to it.

In each of these lessons, quit after four or five retrieves. Quit while he's still frantic for more. Spend the rest of the ten minutes brushing him up on the obedience commands.

## CURING INDIFFERENCE

If, after you have thoroughly teased your dog with the dummy, he won't go after it when you throw it or if he goes after it half-heartedly—call the whole thing off right then and there. Put him back in his kennel, and let him think things over for at least a week. Don't take him out for *anything*.

You'll probably be surprised at how he wakes up, after a week of solitary. (This is also good medicine for any dog at any age, who goes stale, slow, or sulky.) But if this still doesn't do the trick, try to find someone in your vicinity who will let your pup watch him work his trained retriever. Sometimes this will make a youngster jealous, and arouse his instinct to retrieve.

If this doesn't wake him up, you can resort to force training if you like. I wouldn't. For the dog will never make a happy worker.

## WHEN TO REQUIRE STEADINESS
### (See Illustrations 62–64)

As soon as you feel your dog is a retrieving fiend—when he is sailing out and sailing in with every dummy tossed for him at any distance up to 100 yards—that is the proper time to begin requiring steadiness. When in doubt, wait a little longer. Don't risk spoiling his enthusiasm, or slowing him up.

Have the dog sit, beside you. Hold his collar with your left hand. Toss the dummy with your right. Or if you have a helper handy, he can toss it. But make it a short retrieve.

Make the dog sit after the dummy is on the ground, only until you count five. Then send him, with all the enthusiasm you can. Fairly shout his name as you let go of his collar, and swing that hand out fast, giving him the line.

The first day of this, don't give him any retrieves longer than 30 yards, no matter how well he's doing. Remember, until now he's been charging out while the dummy was in the air, and was half-way to it before it hit the ground.

If he shows any confusion or hesitation about going out, don't make him wait so long. If necessary, send him a few times while the dummy is still in the air. Or make the retrieves still shorter. Or both. During this first period of making him steady, don't allow him to lose any of his steam. Actually, this is the most crucial moment in his training, and about the only one that may need a little special care on your part.

But a keen young dog should sit there quivering, straining to go, his eyes glued on the spot where the dummy fell. He should go like an exploding rocket when you send him, straight to the fall. If he doesn't, it means you're pushing him too fast, and then you should simply put him back a grade in school.

If all goes well the first day, you can then make him stay steady without your hand on his collar. Stand out in front of him when you throw the dummy. Keep saying "Sit!" as you throw it. Be ready to grab him as he goes by, if he tries to break. If necessary, do a flying tackle. But stop him if you possibly can before he gets to the dummy. Scold him, put him back on the exact spot he left and make him *sit* there, but don't be more severe than that for now. You don't want to give him the idea that *retrieving* is a bad thing.

Pick the dummy up and throw it again. Keep at this until he doesn't offer to break. Then gradually move back, until you're standing beside his head. Even from this position you can grab him if he starts to leave, if you're quick about it.

It's much easier never to let him break than to fight it out with him after he's once gotten away with it. And remember this: if he *should* get away from you, and run clear out and retrieve the dummy, *you cannot whip him or even scold him then.* That is the surest way to confuse him, and spoil his enthusiasm for getting the dummy.

From now on, always require him to be steady. Wait at least a couple of seconds before sending him to make every retrieve.

## SITTING TO DELIVER

### (See Illustration 65)

Some trainers require their dogs to *sit* to deliver the bird. I never saw any practical use for this. With some dogs I believe it is even harmful, causing them to slow down the last few yards of their return.

The "AKC Standard Procedure For Retriever Trials" says that a dog sitting to deliver should not outscore a dog that delivers cleanly to hand without sitting. My advice is not to bother with it.

## HUNTING WITH NOSE

After a dog is doing faultless retrieves up to 100 yards on bare ground—is marking the falls perfectly—it is time to start switching him from sight retrieving to using his nose. By now there will be plenty of your hand scent on the training dummy so he can smell it easily from amazing distances.

Start throwing it in fairly light cover at first, just enough to hide the dummy. The first retrieves should be very short, not more than 15 or 20 yards, and *straight into the wind*. If your dog has a nose, he'll discover what it's for very quickly. Keep gradually increasing the length of the retrieves, into the wind, until he is going out 100 yards.

Then you can move around and give him a crosswind, but be sure to start this again with much shorter falls. He may have a little trouble with these, either hunting short, or passing the falls on the upwind side. But he should soon learn from experience to use the wind by swinging a little to the downwind side of the line as he goes out, and keeping on until his nose stops him.

Until he is doing these perfectly, don't give him any work straight downwind. This, of course, is the most difficult retrieve of all. For the dog must not only get clear out beyond the fall, but also must be right on the line of fall in order to smell the dummy.

## HUNTING SHORT

Hunting short, particularly in fairly high cover, is a common puppy tendency. To understand why, squat down beside your dog so your eyes are on the same level as his, and have your helper throw the dummy far out in the field. It will appear to fall much closer than it actually does, because you get no perspective on it, when your eyes are so close to the top of the cover.

To compensate for this, a dog must learn to keep going out on the line until his nose stops him. This can be taught with a simple exercise. For this you will need three training dummies and a helper. Let's use an imaginary baseball diamond to describe it.

The dog sits beside you, at home plate. A crosswind is blowing, from third base toward first. The helper walks out to the pitcher's mound. He stands facing third. Then he throws one of the dummies straight up in the air, to land right at his feet. Send the dog at once, while the dummy is still in the air. At the same time the helper should step backward five paces, toward first base. The dog will have a tendency to swing slightly toward him, which will pull him to the downwind side of the fall. By simply running out to the helper, he will be where he must wind the dummy, spin around, and retrieve it fast.

The helper then moves back to the pitcher's mound, and out five steps toward second base, and throws another dummy. He moves backward, straight downwind, the same as the first time.

Each time the dog goes out and makes a perfect retrieve, without hunting short, move the next one out another 5 yards—on exactly the same line. Thus you can soon have the dog sailing out 100 yards or more—swerving slightly to use the wind—and going at a sizzling run until his nose stops him.

But don't overdo this exercise at any one time. And don't get him swinging too far off the actual line, for this might give him trouble later, when he gets to doing straight downwind retrieves. You can regulate this by the distance the helper moves back from the fall.

This is good corrective medicine for any dog of any age that falls into the habit of hunting short. At the same time it improves his marking ability and gives him good practice at taking a line from your hand signal.

## INTRODUCING TO THE GUN

Retrievers are not likely to be gun shy, no matter how rudely they are first introduced to the gun. But it is so little trouble to do it right, there is no sense in taking chances on ruining a particularly sensitive individual.

Have your helper fire the first few shots at a considerable distance from the dog—at least 100 yards. And have them associated with something pleasant, either retrieving or eating. Use a .22 pistol or rifle. If the dog pays no attention to this, keep increasing the noise, until at last the helper can fire a 12-gauge shotgun just as he is throwing a dummy to be retrieved. The whole job shouldn't take more than five minutes.

## INTRODUCING TO WATER

### (See Illustrations 66–69)

Young Goldens are sometimes hesitant about going in water. Chesapeakes and Labradors are more likely to plunge right in and start swimming the first time they get near a pond.

But with any of them, it is well worthwhile to start them correctly, so they will love the water and go in enthusiastically, instead of grudgingly. It is best, if possible, to use a freshwater pond for the introduction of a young dog to this element. Try to avoid saltwater, as he is likely to drink some of it, become sick, and form an aversion to all water. And by all means, avoid putting him through surf until he is a seasoned swimmer. At the outset, don't use a pond with deep mud at the edges, as this might slow up and even frighten a potentially fine water dog.

Pick a spot where the dog can wade out some distance on a fairly hard bottom, and play around in shallow water, before he must start swimming.

Don't start by throwing something for him to retrieve. There's no reason to risk his refusing. And don't *ever* throw the *dog* in the water.

Just put on your waders or swimming trunks and wade out in the water *yourself,* while the dog sits on shore. Have him wait until he is busting to follow you. Then call him, with great enthusiasm. Blow hell out of your whistle. He'll come in. Even a very shy pup will soon be over any fear of the water, plunging around, romping and playing in it. Before he knows it, he'll venture out over his head, and be swimming.

## SINGLE RETRIEVES FROM WATER

### (See Illustration 69)

Only after the dog is thoroughly at home in the water, and follows you in with no hestiation, should you give him his first water retrieve. For this, use the smaller water dummy.

Toss it from the shore, only a short distance, to land in shallow water where the dog will not have to swim. Send him at once. Don't give him time to hesitate. Call his name while the dummy is still in the air.

Thus he will form the habit of hitting that water with a spectacular splash every time he goes in to retrieve. Throw the dummy a bit farther each time, until it is landing well out in swimming water. While he is retrieving it as far as you can throw it, have your helper throw it from a boat. Keep moving it out just a little farther each time, always on the same line, until at last he is doing 100-yard retrieves from water.

Probably your dog will have a tendency to drop the dummy just as he comes out of the water, stop there, and shake. You can kid him out of this by standing right on shore yourself while he is retrieving. As he returns, when he reaches the shallow water, start blowing your whistle vigorously. Then move away, calling him, and try to get him to run after you, so you can grab the dummy out of his mouth before he drops it.

This is all that is needed to get most dogs delivering to hand, even from the water. But if your dog persists in dropping the dummy at the shore, don't worry about it at this stage. You can easily force him to hold it, a little later. The important thing now is to develop his enthusiasm for water retrieves.

Gradually increase the time you make him sit before sending him, until you are counting five *after* the dummy is down on the water. But do this only as long as he is hitting the water enthusiastically and marking the falls perfectly. If he begins slowing up, or marking short, start sending him again while the dummy is in the air. And don't give him more than five retrieves in one session.

Never allow your dog at any age to become lackadaisical, to hesitate, or to tiptoe slowly into the water. If he starts this, give him the solitary treatment. Lock him up for a week. Then start over. Have him sit on shore. You wade out, or go out in a boat. Make him wait until he is dying of suspense. Then call him. If this doesn't get him hitting the water with a splendid splash, he just wasn't meant to be a water dog.

## USING A YOUNG DOG AT STUD

Along about now, some local yokel will want to use your dog at stud. The candidate is almost sure to be an unworthy bitch, for an experienced breeder wouldn't use an unproven stud, no matter how good his pedigree.

But you're nutty about your dog, and the temptation will be strong to carry on his line. Don't do it, friend. Not yet. Don't breed him until he's at least two years old. If you have field-trial ambitions for him, don't do it until after he's made his field-trial championship.

Love is a mighty potent thing. It will distract a youngster from his schoolwork, if he gets interested in the girls too soon. Wait until he's thoroughly trained, and doing his main job well, before you risk dividing his interest..

While he's still in junior high, you don't want him walking with a swagger, smoking big black cigars, and whistling at every girl who goes by the drugstore.

# 14

---

# High School—Double Marked Retrieves

AFTER YOUR DOG has learned to do a perfect job of marking and remembering single falls, that is the proper time to start him on doubles. If you rush this, there is danger of causing indecision, having him run out between the falls, and not really mark either of them. This can develop into a nasty fault. The cure is to put him back on singles for a while.

## DOUBLE MARKED RETRIEVES

No matter how well he's been doing with the singles in cover, start the doubles on bare ground, where both dummies will land in plain sight.

Again using the imaginary baseball diamond, stand beside the dog at home plate. Toss one dummy toward third base, not more than 15 feet. Then turn and toss the other toward first, the same distance. Be sure the dog sees you toss the second one. Then send him for it at once, giving him the line with your hand.

When he returns, take the dummy from him, and hold it out of sight, behind your back. Turn the dog around and have him sit so he directly faces the first dummy. Let him sit until he sees it lying there. Then send him, with great enthusiasm. Repeat this a few times, until he begins to get the idea of going back for a second dummy.

From now on it is simply a matter of gradually lengthening the falls, just as you did with the singles, until at last he is doing doubles, widely separated, each at least 100 yards out. Normally, the *last* fall, being freshest in the dog's memory, will be the *first* retrieve. So the first fall is the difficult one. If at any stage the dog has difficulty remembering it, shorten up on the first fall for a while.

Until he is doing a perfect job on long doubles, keep the falls widely separated, so there will be no temptation to him to switch dummies, or to attempt to bring in both at once. To avoid this further, arrange the falls so he can't possibly wind the first while bringing in the second dummy.

For example, the crosswind is blowing from left to right. Throw the first dummy toward first base—the other toward third (which he will retrieve first). Thus, as he is coming in with that one, he can't possibly smell the other, being upwind of it.

## DOUBLES IN LINE

After he is doing nicely on wide-angle doubles, try a long and a short, exactly on the same line. Have your helper throw one out about 30 yards, run out and throw the other 30 yards farther, and then stand perfectly still. The dog will sail out toward the far fall, but likely spin on the short one when he runs over it and retrieve that one first. Whistle him in with it.

Then send him back for the far one. He should remember it, particularly with the helper standing out there, to remind him how far out it is. But if he should start hunting short, have the helper pick up the far dummy at once and throw it up in the air again. Continue this, until you have him doing a faultless job on both dummies.

Then reverse the routine. Throw the far one first, then the short one. You may again have trouble getting him out far enough for the far fall. If so, have the helper walk out, pick it up, and toss it in the air again at the same spot. Keep at this until the dog is sailing out for that far one, even after the diversion of the short one. He should learn to keep going out on that line until his nose stops him.

This is excellent exercise for the dog's memory—and also constitutes fine high-school work on taking a line. But don't overdo it at any one time. Occasionally mix it up, throwing in a widespread double, to keep reminding him of those, so he doesn't expect *always* to find the second bird on the same line as the one he has just retrieved.

After he is sharp at both types of double retrieves, the next step is to start doing them in cover. Again starting with short falls, keep at this practice until he can do them up to 100 yards. Always give him the line with your hand, to each fall. If, as young dogs often do, he has a tendency to forget the second fall, and swing back toward the one he has already retrieved—take him right back to bare ground for a while. Shorten the retrieves. Lengthen them again only as fast as he will go directly to the second fall, without swinging off the line.

If he has a reasonably good memory, he will learn to use it very fast. At the same time, he'll be learning to rely on the line you give him. That will be very important a bit later, when you get ready for blind retrieves. So never fool him. Be sure he *always* finds a dummy when he takes the line you give him.

## DOUBLES ON WATER

Don't give him doubles in water until he is doing them perfectly on land. Then start all over, with very short retrieves, with plenty of spread between the falls. If necessary, it is worth one trip to a large enough body of water so that you can get up to 50 yards between falls. If he starts switching dummies in the water, it's hard to stop him. Personally, I'm poor at walking on water.

Stand at the edge of the water, and toss a dummy toward third base, another toward first. Then the routine is pretty much the same as when you started the doubles on land. Allow the dog to shake the water from his coat after the first retrieve. Then have him sit, facing the other fall. This should be close enough so he can easily see it. Wait until he does. Then send him with violent enthusiasm. This way you will give him no chance to start hesitating about entering the water for a second fall. Lengthen the retrieves *very* gradually. After you are throwing them as far as you can from shore, call in that patient helper again.

Have him throw the dummies from a boat, or from the far shore of the pond, if that can be done without making the retrieves too long. A long, narrow pond from 75 to 100 yards wide is ideal.

You can work across it, and there is no temptation for the dog to return by land. In a small, round pond, when widespread falls are near the side shores, any sensible dog is likely to go ashore after each retrieve, and run back by land. A dog that is started in such a pond, and has most of his practice there, is likely to form this habit.

Then, when you get him suddenly into big water—whether duck hunting or in a field trial—he is likely to make enormous detours, trying to find a way back to you by land. This can become a bad fault, and it's best to avoid letting it get started.

One word of caution. Don't start your double retrieves in a river with a swift current. Obviously, if the dummies drift far from where the dog sees them fall, he'll be badly confused. No retriever should be sent for doubles in a swift current until he's finished college. Then you can correct him with hand signals, and help him to learn about current drift.

Do not give him doubles in line, in the water, until later—after he has been thoroughly broken of any notion of switching dummies. For the present keep the falls well separated, at a wide angle.

## RETRIEVING TO HAND: "FETCH"

### (See Illustrations 74–77)

Until now you've done nothing to *force* the dog to hold the dummy firmly in his mouth until you take it from him. If your footwork has been good, you probably have kidded him into chasing after you and doing a pretty fair job of delivering to hand, on land at least.

By moving away from him briskly as he comes out of the water, and calling him, you may even have him waiting to shake himself until after delivering. But it's a big temptation to any dog, when coming out of cold water, to drop the dummy as soon as he gets out into the air, in order to shake.

Even though he isn't doing it now, he may slide into this nasty habit later, if he is not taught the command "fetch." In retriever language, this means, "Don't drop it. Hold it. Put it right in my hand."

It sounds much better in a field trial, or to your admiring hunting companions, if when your dog emerges from the water you quietly say, *"Fetch* it here, old boy," than if you bellow, "Don't drop that duck, you such-and-such of a so-and-so!"

You should teach the command "fetch" only after the dog is a confirmed retriever, hurling himself out enthusiastically after double falls, on land and water. By then there's no danger of slowing him, or spoiling his enthusiasm for his main job.

Strangely, I personally have never had a serious argument over "fetch" with a male dog, but have had to fight it out with several bitches. For some reason, they often hate it. Like women, they resent being forced to do anything.

Have the dog sit. Force open his mouth and quickly pop the smaller training dummy in it. When he tries to spit it out, support his lower jaw, firmly at first. Hold both jaws together if necessary, so he can't spit out the dummy. Meanwhile keep saying "Fetch!"

The first time, make him hold the dummy only while you count five. Then say, "Leave it," very cheerily, and take it from him. Pet him a moment. Tell him he's a fine dog.

Then repeat the process. Each time should require less physical force on your part. The third time, you can probably get him to hold the dummy by very light pressure with a finger under his chin. Keep repeating the command, and then try taking your finger away entirely.

An eager-to-please dog will learn this command in eight minutes. To prove this, at the risk of slowing up a promising pup, I used Freehaven Rook, age ten months, for the demonstration shown in Illustrations 74–77. With an older dog, already accustomed to delivering naturally to hand, it can be done even faster.

Don't overdo this exercise at any one session. But give him a minute or two of practice at it every time you take him out from now on, until he is perfect. At last, you should be able to put the dummy in his mouth, say "Fetch!" and walk away. He should hold it for several minutes, until you return and take it from him.

Then it is time to start using the larger and heavier dummies, to prepare him for handling big ducks and pheasant without dropping them.

## SWITCHING BIRDS

Every retriever should be taught at this point that he must never switch birds. He should go for the bird he's sent for, and return with it, even if he stumbles over another on the way in.

Some old hunters will debate this. "I want my dog to leave a dead bird and go after a cripple," they say. "That shows good sense."

Well, in the first place, a dog has no sense. He does what he's in the habit of doing. True, there is a rare situation when it might be best for him to drop a dead bird and get a fast start after a runner. But there are many more times when he'll be dropping *your* bird to go after another man's cripple. And if the other man has sent his own dog for it, yours may return minus his ears. Most retrievers won't go out of their way to pick a fight, but they won't back away from one, either.

A dog should never be permitted to try to bring in two birds at once. This is a sure way to start hard mouth. No dog has a big enough mouth to hold two mallards or cock pheasant without damaging them.

Another thing. A dog that once starts switching usually develops indecision. On a double retrieve, he will start out between the falls, and swim around all day trying to make up his mind which to get first.

If these arguments aren't enough to convince the wise characters, here's the topper. Virutally all judges in retriever trials penalize severely for switching birds. Sometimes they even disqualify for it. They must have reasons. They are the men who have the most experience at actually hunting over good retrievers.

To teach your dog about this, throw two dummies just 15 feet rom you, to fall about 10 feet apart. Send your dog for the *last* one thrown. If at any time, going out or coming in, he moves even one step toward the other dummy—run out there at him, roaring, "No!"

Drag him back to the exact spot where he picked up the correct dummy. Put it in his mouth. Tell him to "fetch." Have him sit right there, holding it. Walk back to your original position. Then whistle him in with it. Then take it, and send him for the other.

Keep at this exercise until he will do it perfectly, coming

straight in with the one dummy without even looking at the other.

Then it is time to increase the temptation. Throw one dummy as far as you can. Send the dog for it. As he is returning toss the other to fall just 5 feet in front of him. Be ready to roar "No!" if he tries to switch. If he persists, and actually switches, rush out there, take the second dummy away from him, and put it back on the exact spot where it fell. Drag him back out to where he picked up the first one, put it in his mouth, and make him sit there. Go back to your original position, and whistle him in. Keep at this until you have him coming in, running right over the other dummy, without offering to switch.

You can accomplish this lesson in less time than it has taken me to tell you how, and it is well worth doing.

## RETRIEVING DECOYS: "LEAVE IT"

### (See Illustrations 70–73)

Unless you like to get your feet wet, the simple way to teach a dog about decoys is to set out a few on *land*.

Put your dog on leash, and walk him through the decoys. When he offers to grab one, jerk him back sharply, and say, "No! Leave it!" Keep doing this, back and forth, until he will walk through without even offering to look at one of the blocks. The light will dawn for him suddenly.

Then he'll look up at you as if to say, "I get it boss. You don't want these *wooden* ducks!"

After that, toss a dummy across the decoys, and send him for it, straight through them. Keep at it until he will go and return without paying the slightest attention to the decoys. Then place them in shallow water, and repeat the routine. You may occasionally have to remind him by shouting, "Leave it!" but you should be able to keep your feet dry.

## WORKING FROM A BLIND

### (See Illustrations 86–89)

In the retriever trials, dogs are required to work from a portable "blind," which bears little resemblance to any real duck blind you ever saw. This is made of plywood, standing as high as a man's chest. It has wings on either side. There is a hole in the front section, large enough for a dog to jump through. If your dog will work from one of these—he'll have no shyness about going into any blind you can imagine under hunting conditions.

It is hardly worthwhile to make one of these just to train one dog, for you can teach him to work from the blind in one brief lesson. The first time you go to an informal field trial, you can borrow the blind they have there, while it is not in use.

Set it well back from the edge of the water. Lead your dog in on leash. He may be a little shy about going in this strange contraption. Say "Kennel!" and pull him clear up front, and have him sit squarely in front of the hole. Pet him for a moment and let him relax.

Then toss a dummy *through the hole,* to land on the ground just 3 or 4 feet in front of the blind. Send the dog immediately. He'll jump through the hole to retrieve it.

Don't try to make him return through the hole. Let him come around the side. But you stay in the blind to receive the dummy from him.

Repeat this two or three times. Then throw the dummy clear out in the water. The dog will leap through the hole like a veteran, and from then on, you'll find he'll march right into the blind at heel, and take his position before the hole, with no trouble.

## WORKING FROM A BOAT

Retrievers are not asked to work from a boat at the trials, but this is often necessary when you're duck hunting. It's a good idea to get your dog used to it before the opening day. If you don't own a boat, you can borrow one of these when you go to a trial.

Put it well up on shore. Say "Kennel!" and make the dog jump in it. Get in and stand beside him, and have him sit. Toss a floating dummy in the shallow water. Send him for it. He will readily leap out after it, with the boat stationary on shore. When he returns, don't let him jump in the boat with it. Reach out and take the dummy, saying "Leave it!" just as he reaches the side of the boat. Then call him on in, and have him sit. Repeat this two or three times.

Now move the boat out into about 6 inches of water. Go through the same routine there. It won't bother him to jump directly into the shallow water. Gradually move out farther, until finally you have him taking off into deep water, with no hesitation. When he swims back to the side of the boat with the dummy, reach out to take it from him. Then grab him by the scruff and help him in. Just pull him up until he can hook his front legs over the side of the boat. Then push down on the top of his head, to give him leverage. He'll do the rest. This is much easier than trying to lift 80 pounds of dog plus many pounds of water clear into the boat.

Never try to get him clear in the boat with a duck in his mouth. He can't help clamping down on it as he struggles into the boat, and this might make him hard-mouthed.

## INTRODUCTION TO FEATHERS

### (See Illustrations 78–81)

Before you send your dog to pick up his first shot bird, spend a couple of minutes properly introducing him to feathers. This is the cheapest possible insurance against hard mouth.

Use a freshly killed pigeon. If you live in the city, and a pigeon is a hard prop to come by—go to an informal field trial, once more. The field-trial chairman will gladly loan you a slightly used pigeon.

Go out behind a hill where you won't bother anyone. Wrap a piece of string around the dead pigeon, so the wings won't flop around when you throw it. Bind it up tight, so it's pretty much like a training dummy—only with feathers on it.

Tease the dog with it. Get him interested. He probably will grab at it. Hold your hand around it so he can't bite it without biting you—just as you did to keep him from roughing the training dummy. Say "No!" whenever he tries to bite it. Tell him to be careful.

After he has calmed down, have him sit. Place the pigeon in his mouth. Say "Fetch." Watch him carefully, and if he starts to bite it, be ready to pinch his lip against his teeth, and say "No!" very sternly. He'll quickly get the idea that the pigeon is for fetch—not for food.

As soon as he sits quietly, hold it gently in his mouth, back away from him a few steps. Then call him to you, and take the pigeon from him. If he is at all reluctant to let go, pinch his lip against his teeth and say "Leave it!"

Now throw it for him, just a few feet away. Have him retrieve it. If he offers to treat it roughly when he picks it up, scold him severely, and take the bird away from him. Have him sit, put the bird in his mouth, and make him hold it gently for several minutes. As soon as you make him understand the pigeon is to be considered just as a training dummy, he'll handle it gently. With a good dog, this should take only a few minutes.

Gradually increase the length of the retrieves, until you're throwing it as far as you can. At last, take the string off the pigeon. Throw it, flopping wings and all. By now the dog is accustomed to this new taste and smell, and the feel of the feathers in his mouth. He'll retrieve it like a veteran. And now, you have a bird retriever. He should never offer to damage your game.

Live pigeons can be shot for him to retrieve any time you have the opportunity, from now on.

## INTRODUCTION TO SHACKLED DUCKS

### (See Illustrations 82–85)

After your dog is handling dead pigeons, it is time to introduce him to live shackled ducks. If it is too much trouble for you to keep a couple of these on hand, you can also borrow a live duck for the purpose at an informal trial.

At most of the Eastern trials, full-flying ducks are shot for the dogs to retrieve on water. But in many of the trials throughout the country, shackled ducks are used. These of course are birds legally raised on game farms, and purchased for this purpose.

But whether or not you have field-trial ambitions, your dog should be taught to handle a shackled duck before you take him shooting. Again, this is cheap insurance against hard mouth. If you neglect it, and you have a fairly tough, aggressive dog, he's likely to flatten the first crippled duck you send him for. Once he starts killing cripples, he may be too rough on dead birds as well.

On the other hand, a sensitive youngster may become cripple shy, if his first experience with live birds is rudely thrust upon him when you take him hunting. A big, old greenhead with nothing wrong but a broken wing can put up quite a bluff.

Before you introduce your dog to a big duck, you should have him easily handling the big and heavy training dummies, without dropping them.

Then the routine is exactly the same as with the pigeon, except that the duck is very much alive. The wings are tied securely, at the base. The legs are tied together, near the feet.

Tease the dog with the duck. Get him interested. But don't let him grab it. Protect it with your hand. Make him understand this strange live critter is in exactly the same category as the training dummy and the dead pigeon.

Then force his mouth open, very wide, and stuff in the duck. Be sure he has a good, full body hold on it. Tell him to "fetch." Don't make him hold it more than a couple of seconds at first. Repeat two or three times, each time having him hold it a bit longer. He'll get used to it quickly, and get the knack of getting a firm but gentle hold on this big bird. Then you can toss it in the water for a short retrieve, and from then on, he's a cripple retriever. If he picks up the duck by the neck, the feet, or by a wing tip, always correct his hold. Put the body of the bird squarely in his mouth. Tell him to "fetch." Make him hold it correctly for a moment, before you take it from him again.

## TAKE HIM HUNTING

Now you can take your dog hunting any time. He is ready for everything but blind retrieves, and he should be a real help to you in the field or in the blind. Don't hesitate to send him for anything on land or water, *provided you're sure he saw it fall.*

But don't, please, expect him at this stage to do blind retrieves. If you're shooting over decoys, take a little trouble to get the dog placed so he can see where the ducks are likely to fall. If you're in a shore blind, or even a boat blind, make a hole in it big enough for the dog to see through, and to jump through when he goes out to retrieve.

If you're in a sunken barrel, try to find a dry spot nearby where the dog can sit and mark the falls. Even if he's right out in the open, the ducks won't pay any attention to him. If you are out in a marsh, the top of a muskrat house is a good place for the dog. However, if you set him out at some distance from you, he has to be mighty steady.

Don't let him start breaking shot. Many hunters make this mistake. Some even encourage their dogs to do it. If you do, you'll regret it. Once started, it's a tough fault to cure.

The first time you take a green dog hunting, pay more attention to him than you do to your shooting, even if you thereby miss some shots. This is hard to do, I know, but it's the best investment you can make in the future of your dog. You won't have to do this many times. He'll quickly understand hunting is just like the practice at home, and that the boss will stand no nonsense.

Once you get that across, you can forget you have him with you except when you need him. You can go ahead and tend to your shooting, confident that the dog is walking smartly at heel, or sitting right where you put him, and that he isn't going any place until you send him.

# 15

## College Stuff—Blind Retrieves

THE OLD DUCK HUNTER, in his beat-up shooting coat, had the air of a man who was slumming. He was about to witness his first and last retriever field trial, and he didn't care who knew it.

Before the first stake got under way, I heard this old character talking loudly to a crony in the gallery. He sneered, "If this is like the bird-dog trials, it's nothing but a lot of fluff and guff. These fancy trial dogs are no good for bringing home the meat."

Late the following afternoon, when the trial was nearly over, I saw him again. He was watching the final series of the open all-age stake, a difficult handling test. On the far side of the lake, a good 300 yards away, a dead duck was being planted for each dog to retrieve. It was placed well up on the land, in heavy cover, some 50 yards beyond the far shore.

The competing dogs were held behind the gallery, and called up one at a time as their turns came. They heard no shots, saw nothing fall. This was a blind retrieve to end all blind retrieves.

The old duck hunter watched intently as a black dog sat beside his handler, waiting. One of the judges spoke his number. Then his handler quietly said the dog's name, and gave him the line with a very slight hand gesture. The dog sprang forward, hit the water with a mighty splash, and started straight across the lake. He swam powerfully, and never deviated from that line.

The old duck hunter moaned softly. There was a dazed look about his eye.

"Well," I said, "how do you like these 'fancy trial dogs' by now?"

He didn't even turn his head. He was watching a dog. A duck dog.

"Lord," he muttered, "what I'd give for a dog like that."

Soon the dog climbed up the bank on that far shore. He was just a black speck in the distance. He began hunting up the shore, to the left. The handler blasted sharply, once, on his whistle. The black speck stopped instantly, and stayed motionless. The man made a hand signal to the right. The black speck scuttled fast to the right, down the shore. Then the whistle blasted once more. The black speck stopped, exactly on the line of the fall.

Now this retrieve was straight downwind, the toughest kind there is. The handler waved his arm in the "get back" signal. The dog turned and went straight back on the land, hell bent. But the heavy cover threw him slightly off the line, and he swerved a bit to the left. When he was just beyond the hidden duck the handler hit him with one more whistle blast, and gave him a hand signal to the right. The dog spun into the wind, nailed the bird not 5 yards away, scooped it up, and started back with it at a dead run.

The old duck hunter was breathing hard, through his mouth.

"How do you like that?" he croaked. "Why, it's like retrieving your ducks with a guided missile!"

One of his cronies was still unconvinced. He said, "Yeah, but what for? *My* ducks fall right in the decoys."

The old duck hunter turned on him scornfully. "Don't give me that," he snorted. "I've seen some of your cripples fall a lot farther than that there duck."

It is a thrilling and spectacular sight to see a finished retriever respond perfectly, at great distances, to hand and whistle signals. But more than this, it is very useful to own a dog that can do it.

Whether you want a field-trial prospect or just a meat dog, you should teach him to handle on blind retrieves. Then you can place him just downwind of any fall that he hasn't seen, as much as a quarter of a mile away. This looks like black magic when you first see a retriever obeying quiet hand signals from a fabulous distance.

Actually, it's a cinch for the greenest amateur to teach a good dog to "handle" perfectly on blind retrieves—and to do it furthermore with no arguments, no sulks, no lost tempers, no hauling the dog around by a rope, no army of assistant trainers—and with everybody happy.

The main danger is in teaching this too soon. Try to resist this temptation. Wait until the dog is two years old, or until he has had a full season of hunting experience, before you give him hand signals. First let him fully develop his powerful instinct to hunt on his own, and to mark and remember falls. Then there will be little danger of his becoming too dependent on your help, getting sloppy about his marking, and asking you for directions to falls he should damn well remember for himself. The ideal retriever is a dog that finds every bird he has seen fall, without help from his handler, yet will handle perfectly the falls he had no opportunity to see.

My method of teaching hand signals is like a jigsaw puzzle—simple when you see it all assembled. But it took me several years to put it together, out of pieces "borrowed" from Frank Hogan, Jim Hogan, and other good trainers—plus a few I whittled out for myself. The routine is easy to demonstrate, but I always had difficulty *describing* it to people, until finally I hit upon this baseball gag.

Now I call it The Baseball Diamond Method of Teaching Hand Signals. If you've ever seen a ball field, you'll understand it. (See Illustrations 94–113.)

For your purpose, of course, the baseball diamond is purely imaginary. There is no need to put out any bases, or markers such as I have used in the photographic illustrations.

To begin, use a yard with no cover, so the dummy will always land in plain sight. Start at home plate. Walk out toward second base, with the dog at heel. As you cross the pitcher's mound, suddenly say "Sit," and immediately blow *one* sharp blast on your whistle. The dog should sit instantly and stay on the pitcher's mound, while you walk on a few steps toward second before you stop. Thus he will begin learning to stop and stay put on one whistle blast, no matter where you are or what you are doing. From now on, one whistle blast means stop and *sit*. (Two or more mean *come*.)

Now toss the dummy toward second base, to fall not more than 15 or 20 feet from the dog, where he can see it plainly. Leaving the dog on the pitcher's mound, you return to home plate. As you do, keep looking back and commanding "Sit," followed by one whistle blast, if the dog shows any inclination to move.

Stand at the plate a moment while the dog watches you, wondering what in the world the boss is up to *now*. Then suddenly make an overhead arm signal, like a *girl* throwing a ball toward second base. At the same time shout the dog's name, followed immediately by the command "Get back!" The dog may hesitate a moment, slightly confused by these strange doings. But then he will remember the dummy, then look around and see it, and *get back* to retrieve it. The instant he picks it up, encourage him with *several* quick whistle blasts to come in with it fast, all the way to you at home plate.

For the first lesson, concentrate on this one direction. Each time the dog performs perfectly, make the next retrieve a bit longer, until at last he is *getting back* smartly, clear out into center field. Before this session is over, you should be able to stop calling his name to send him. The overhead arm signal, plus the command "get back," will be all the permission he needs, very quickly.

The next day you can teach him the arm signal to the right. Start at home plate. Walk out and again have him *sit* on one whistle blast, at the pitcher's mound. Toss the dummy toward *first base*. Return to home plate, again leaving the dog out there on the mound, of course.

Then call his name, and throw your arm straight to the right, from the shoulder. At the same time, sway your whole body to the right. Keep at this until the dog will go straight right to the dummy, just on the arm signal, and you can stop calling his name. And, of course, gradually increase the length of the falls, until they are far out in right field.

To teach the arm signal to the left, simply reverse this process, tossing the dummy toward *third* base instead of first. After you have devoted one lesson to each of the three directions, spend a session at mixing them up. First give him a "get back," then a signal to the right, then one to the left. If this confuses him at all, shorten the retrieves, so he can look around and easily spot the dummy. But by now he should be well on his way to associating these arm signals with the exact direction of each fall.

Next, move to a field with sufficient cover to hide the dummy. Thus you are removing the sight aid, and the dog will have only his memory and marking ability to help him respond to the hand signals. Start all over, with very short retrieves. Give him rights, lefts, and "Get backs." Mix them up as long as the dog is doing them perfectly. But if he gets confused, concentrate on one at a time for a while. Continue this practice until he is hitting them all right on the button, in cover, at distances up to 100 yards.

Now, in these exercises, keep your imaginary baseball diamond in exactly the same spot. If the dog beats paths in the cover from the pitcher's mound to first, second and third—so much the better. Let the routes to the falls become thoroughly familiar to him. Then comes the big moment when you remove the *marking* aid.

Take the dog behind a bush, or stand in front of him so he can't see what's going on. Have your helper sneak out and drop the dummy on the line between pitcher's mound and second base.

Then walk the dog out and have him sit as usual (with the customary single whistle blast, of course) at the pitcher's mound. Return to home plate. Then give him the overhead arm signal, and yell "Get back!" with great enthusiasm.

The dog will probably make a take, and wonder whether you have suddenly gone nuts. But if your preliminary work has been well done, he should suddenly remember about that arm signal and that command. He should spin and tear out along the familiar route to second base, and hit the dummy right on the nose. If he doesn't, it simply means you are rushing things too fast, and you should give him another session or two with the marking aid.

But the minute he obeys a hand signal without seeing anything fall, the job is 90 percent done. From then on, you simply give him occasional practice at blind retrieves. Mix them up, on both length and direction. As soon as he is doing them faultlessly on the old familiar baseball diamond, move to fresh ground, and eventually to heavier cover. And then, finally, to water.

As you go along, you can gradually cut down on the exaggerated motions of your arm to the right and left. Finally, you can keep your elbow tight against your side, and just flip your hand slightly to the right, and the dog will respond perfectly. Always use the right hand to send him right, of course, and the left to send him left. Sometimes you see handlers using the right hand for both directions. This looks awkward, and is confusing to the dog.

As you practice the blind retrieves, keep increasing the distance between you and the dog, until you have as much as 100 yards between home plate and the pitcher's mound. The ultimate objective is to have him stop instantly on the whistle, as far away as he can hear it—and to take a hand signal from you from just as far as he can see you.

Then it's time for the final step—to teach him to take a line to a fall he hasn't seen, *starting from your side*. This should now be very easy. In his preliminary training, you've been giving him a line to every market retrieve. He is already well on his way to understanding what this gesture means.

Have your helper plant the dummy between the pitcher's mound and second base. Walk the dog out to the mound and have him sit. This time you stay there beside him, on the mound. Speak his name, and give him the line with your hand. If he hesitates, say "Get back!" and give him the overhand signal. He knows by now what these mean.

He should romp straight out on the now familiar path, straight to the dummy. Keep at this until you can send him just by speaking his name, and giving him the line with a slight underhand gesture. Send him out from the mound in all directions. Keep increasing the length of the falls. If he gets off the line, stop him with the whistle, and direct him with hand signals to a spot just downwind of the fall.

Later, to develop a lining confidence, you can, in an irregular sequence, start to interrupt retrieves to second base at the pitcher's mound. Send the dog, again in an irregular pattern, to first or third base. Use varying distances. This is very advanced work. *It should be attempted only after the basics have been thoroughly mastered.*

In all of your practice, make sure the dog finds the dummy exactly where you told him it was. Then he'll quickly learn to trust you and rely on your directions. Never let him quit before he finds it. If necessary, walk all the way out and show it to him. Have him sit. Put the dummy in his mouth and let him sit there holding it while you walk back to the spot from which you sent him. Then call him in with it. He'll learn to believe what pappy tells him, very fast.

You'll find it's a lot of fun to stand in one spot and direct a guided missile. But don't get so fascinated with this game that you play it all the time. Mix up the blind retrieves with plenty of practice on marked falls. Don't give your dog a chance to get lazy, and start asking for help he doesn't need. If he ever should stop and turn, and ask for a hand signal, on a fall he has seen, just turn your back on him. Wait him out. Make the rascal go on out and find it for himself.

# 16

Finishing Touches and
Minimum Maintenance

NEARLY ANY GOOD retriever will take naturally to working like a spaniel, quartering ahead of the gun, and flushing upland birds. In fact, many retriever-happy people claim these dogs are far superior to the spaniels at their own specialty.

I won't go quite that far. But for heavy work, the big rugged retrievers are hard to beat. They have the stamina to keep going all day, routing pheasant out of the heaviest marsh cover—in the kind of going that wears out a spaniel in two or three hours.

However, before using your dog for this work, it is best to give him one full season of hunting strictly as a retriever, keeping him at heel except when you send him for a shot bird. It is a great temptation to get him out in front too soon. But you'll do the youngster a favor if you resist this. He must be absolutely steady to flush and shot before you start him quartering, and any keen young dog is likely to forget this if, when a bird goes up and guns go off, you are not right beside him to remind him to sit.

And of course if you have field-trial ambitions, you'd better postpone using your dog for flushing birds until after you have retired him from serious competition. There is no question but that this takes the sharp edge off a dog's retrieving performance. Often in a trial you see a dog quartering all the way out to a long fall, instead of sizzling straight out on the line. This invariably proves to be a youngster that was used *too soon* for flushing pheasant.

If you give your dog time to develop fully the *habit* of taking a line direct to a shot bird, then he is not likely to become confused

149

if you begin also using him for quartering and seeking *live* game. Let him learn his main job thoroughly before you teach him what is essentially an entirely different trade.

Give him at least one full season of working only as a retriever. Get him absolutely steady to flush and shot. Then teach him the hand signals. After that, it will be easy to develop his natural instinct to hunt ahead of you, and flush live birds—and without hurting him very much in the retrieving department.

You can introduce him to this new job before the season opens, if you can procure two or three live pigeons, and get a good man with a scatter-gun to shoot them for you. For this exercise you will need to find a fairly good-sized field, with sufficient cover to hide a pigeon.

Tie the dog where he can't see you while you go out to plant the pigeon, at least 150 yards out in the field. Hold the pigeon in both hands, and as you walk out dizzy it by swinging it continuously in a tight circle. Its head will weave drunkenly, and flop over on its chest when it is ready to plant. Drop it quickly in a good patch of cover and keep right on walking away, fast. If you do this, the pigeon won't fly, and will stay put until the dog flushes it.

Now go back to your dog, and smoke a cigarette while the pigeon regains its equilibrium. Then start working slowly across the field, directly toward the pigeon. Have your friend walk beside you, with his gun ready.

Tell the dog to *hie on*. If he runs straight ahead, stop him with the whistle when he gets out about 20 yards. Give him a hand signal to the right. Stop him again with the whistle while he is still well within easy gun range. Give him the hand signal to the left. Continue this, working him back and forth in front of you, just like a windshield wiper, as you walk forward slowly, on the line of the hidden bird.

As the dog gets close to it, have your whistle ready. The instant the pigeon flies, yell "Sit!" and blast once on your whistle. If the dog starts to break, keep yelling "Sit!" and get to him as fast as you can. Put him back on the exact spot he occupied when he flushed the bird. The gunner should hold his fire until he sees the dog is steady. If the dog sits immediately when you yell, the pigeon should be shot, and you should go to your dog, keep him steady for just two or three seconds, and then send him to make the retrieve.

But don't worry if you have to let the first pigeon fly away. The main thing is *not to shoot it* if the dog breaks and gives chase. Thus he will learn he can't catch a flying bird. If this happens, you should go after him, catch him, and reprimand him severely. Drag him back to the exact spot from which he broke, and make him sit there for a good long time, thinking it over. If he breaks a second time, you may as well give him a good walloping, and get it over. For he will be utterly useless as a gun dog if he runs wild, flushing other birds in cover far ahead of you, and chasing them over the horizon.

To cure a chronic breaker, have the dog drag a 50-foot line. When he gets close to the pigeon, sneak up and get the line in your hand. Give the dog enough slack so he can start running when the birds get up. Then give him the surprise of his life, by jerking him end over end.

But this will be unnecessary if your dog is steady and under control, as he should be, before you start him quartering. If you are on your toes you can, with whistle and voice, make him sit and stay the instant he flushes his first bird. The bird can then be shot. And after the first few times, you can stay right where you were, and send the dog to make the retrieve from there, by quietly speaking his name and waving him toward the fall.

You'll be amazed how quickly he will catch on to this exciting new game. After he has quartered correctly across a field only two or three times—each time thereby finding and flushing a live bird, which is then shot for him to retrieve—he will suddenly look up at you as if to say, "Hot damn! How long has *this* been going on?"

If it's too inconvenient to give your dog this preliminary practice, you can do it just as well on wild birds, during the first hour of the opening day of hunting season. But you'll want to pick your hunting partner pretty carefully. Get someone who won't think he's killed if he has to pass up a few shots for the sake of a good dog. It's no job for a game hog. Don't try to shoot these first two or three birds yourself. You may be plenty busy with the dog, without being encumbered with a gun. And don't attempt to start the dog on his quartering career with a large party of hunters. Someone is sure to make you feel uncomfortable about holding up the hunt, and you will hurry and fail to start the dog properly.

If you just take your time that first day, it is so easy to have the dog steady as a rock, to flush and shot. Once he gets this idea, you can begin forgetting him, and tending to your own shooting. And, brother, that is worthwhile. From then on, he'll kick up birds for you that would sit tight while an army of dogless hunters marched right over them.

From then on, you and the dog will both learn from experience, hunting together. If he responds to hand and whistle signals at *any* distance, and if you keep him absolutely steady—never allow him to break under any circumstances—you'll find yourself improvising all sorts of tricky teamwork for bringing game to bag.

Old Freehaven Jay had become fantastically wise about driving pheasant *to me*. One day years ago, in North Dakota, birds were running ahead of us, down the bottom of a big ditch, just beyond gun range. Jay, quartering close ahead of me, was becoming fully as annoyed and frustrated as I was. I decided to try an experiment. Stopping Jay with a quick beep of the whistle, I hand-signaled him to the right, up out of the ditch, at the same time climbing out myself. He looked at me in amazement, but then reluctantly obeyed. Then I waved him back, down the deserted section-line road that paralleled the ditch. He went, but of course kept trying to swing back into the ditch, where he knew the pheasant were. Each time I stopped him with the whistle, and signaled him back onto the road.

When he was 150 yards away, I stopped him, and hand-signaled him back down into the ditch. I went back into it myself, crouched down low in the cover, and softly whistled the dog toward me. He intercepted those running pheasant, busted right into them, and put three beautiful cocks right over me. I shut my eyes, shot, and got two of them. You never saw a more delighted dog. And from then on, we had a new way to work ditches.

After that, with running birds ahead, we needed no whistle signals. Jay would look back, and I swear he'd lift an eyebrow, as if to say, "We've got a trackman here, boss. Shall I head him off?" All I had to do was give him a hand signal to right or left, and he did the rest—circling well ahead of the runner, and flushing him back in my direction.

The stunt was very useful on pheasant, but I later found it came in even handier on California quail, which *really* love to run. If Jay and I could get a covey going up and down the bottom of a canyon, we'd really confuse them. That's all we needed to fill our limit—one big running covey—provided I could hit them.

As you hunt with your dog, you and he will develop a means of communication all your own. When he first starts quartering ahead, you should watch him closely all the time. Be sure you aren't asleep when he flushes a bird for you. Nothing is more discouraging to him than to put up a fine cock, big as a bucket, and have you finally fire two parting salutes as it disappears over the skyline.

But before long, you'll be able to tell, just by looking at the dog, at his tail action and his whole attitude, just what is going on. He'll tell you as clearly as if he could talk whether he's just hunting hopefully, or on a hot trail, and at last whether the bird is sitting tight or running ahead. I can't describe exactly how he'll tell you these things, for different individual dogs do it differently. I can positively assure you that if you watch him closely, you'll soon understand what he's saying. And then you'll know when it's safe to be lighting a cigarette, and when it isn't, and when it's time to throw it away and get your thumb on the safety of your gun. After that you can relax, and let your dog take you hunting.


## MINIMUM MAINTENANCE

Whether you have bought a trained dog, or trained him entirely yourself, you now own a valuable property. He can stand a lot of neglect without depreciating in value, but not total neglect.

In between hunting seasons, spend a few minutes at least once a week giving the dog a little practice. Don't allow him to forget anything he has learned. Don't let him get sloppy about the obedience commands.

Keep him up to snuff on his marking by giving him a few double marked retrieves. Vary the lengths of the falls, so he doesn't get used to finding them at any certain distance. Then give him a good, tough blind retrieve, so he doesn't get rusty on the hand and whistle signals. You can use training dummies for all this. Once the dog has had a season or two of hunting, he'll never forget about the real birds.

But don't fall into the lazy habit of giving him all his practice in the same small yard, where there is no opportunity for variety. A dog can quickly form the habit of going off the porch, around the rosebush, down the garden path, and finding the dummy at the same old corner of the tool house. In any vicinity you can find some strange vacant land not too far away, where you can take the dog occasionally.

Whenever you have the opportunity, put him in the water, to keep him keen, and to keep his swimming muscles in good shape.

If he should, through your neglect, develop some little fault, take a few minutes to pop him back in the proper grade at school, and correct it before it gets serious.

## SLOW RETURN
### (See Illustrations 90–91)

If he starts slowing up as he returns with a bird, give him a refresher course on coming fast to the whistle. It's easy to do this whenever you take him out for a walk. Have him sit. Walk on ahead, 50 yards or so. Stand and look at him, building up the suspense, until he is crazy to catch up to you. Then suddenly blow several blasts on your whistle, and just watch him come! Keep repeating this all through your walk, until you are leaving him behind as much as 100 yards before you call him. This will not only speed his response to your whistle, but is splendid exercise for him.

Also, when you give him practice retrieves, take to your heels once more. As he returns, the moment he slows up at all, run away from him. Keep running until he catches you, and you can take the dummy from him.

## HITTING THE WATER
### (See Illustrations 92–93)

Sometimes an unfortunate experience when duck hunting will make a young dog hesitant about hitting the water with that all-out splash—either an encounter with deep mud, or landing on a submerged stump, or just hitting really cold water for the first time. You can restore his confidence, and get him taking the water with proper enthusiasm again, with very little trouble. Get out in a boat, in a pond with a good hard bottom near shore, but with swimming water out in the middle. Have the dog sit on shore. Make him stay until he is dying of suspense. Then call him suddenly, with your whistle. He should, with a very little of this, get to hitting the water again. Let him swim around a bit, following you in the boat. This is fine for developing his swimming, and making him feel completely at home in the water.

If no boat is easily available, you can do much to get him hitting the water properly simply by standing on shore, tossing a dummy only 10 or 12 feet, and sending the dog immediately, while the dummy is still in the air. Doing this a few times will often get amazing results. All you need do is to change his *habit* of entering the water, to get him hitting it again, with no unpleasant result.

## SLOPPY HOLD

If your dog starts taking a sloppy hold on big ducks, correct this at once, for if neglected it can grow progressively worse, until at last he is *dragging* them in to you through the mud. Whenever he has the bird by the head, neck, wing tip, or feet, take it away from him. Open his mouth wide and jam the duck in, so that he has a full body hold on it. Tell him in a severe tone to "fetch." Make him hold it correctly for a minute or two. Then back away, call him to you, and receive the duck. Usually very little of this is needed to convince a dog to take the right hold in the first place.

## PIDDLING

A retriever is supposed to be so keen for his job that he will stop for *nothing* until he finds and retrieves the bird he's sent for. But sometimes a feisty young male will fall into the unnecessary habit of stopping to piddle on bushes as he goes out. This is a minor fault, which counts only slightly against a dog in a trial, and somewhat reduces your pleasure and pride in him as a hunting companion. But it's easy to correct, and you might as well do so, particularly if you think you might ever run him in a trial.

Always, before you work with him, give him plently of opportunity to run around and "be a good dog." Then, simply don't allow him to get away even once with stopping to do his business while on a retrieve—whether he's going out or even *returning* with the bird or the dummy.

The instant he stops to lift his leg, go roaring out at him, shouting "No!" Jerk him to a sitting position, and immediately send him on to the fall. If he tries to do it coming in, rush out the same way, drag him in with you to your original position, take the dummy from him there. *Then* tell him to "hie on," and "be a good dog." Thus make him understand he is to finish the job at hand before retiring to the gentlemen's restroom.

If some ignoramus sees you correcting this fault, he will probably think you are crazy or cruel, or both. He will sneer, "The poor dog. He's not even allowed to relieve himself."

Actually it takes a dog less than a minute to complete almost any retrieve if he's tending to business. If he can hold everything all through the night, to avoid fouling his bed, he can damn well hold it for one minute while he's doing his job. By now he knows what you mean by "No." If he persists in his leg lifting, it means he is defying you on that matter, and soon he'll be doing it on more important things. So I wouldn't waste too much time on this, before giving him a good licking and winning the argument once and for all.

## WHINING AND YIPPING

We have already touched on the matter of whining, yipping, or giving tongue when on line or in the blind. Sometimes a three- or four-year-old dog will suddenly start this, for no apparent reason. Whenever it starts, crack down on it at once, as severely as necessary to put a stop to it. The dog already understands *"Stop that noise."* All you must do is insist on obedience to this command. Scold him, pinch his lip, or give him a walloping as a last resort. For this can develop into a very serious fault.

## HARD MOUTH

All through the book we've talked of little ways to avoid letting hard mouth get started. But even with these precautions, you will occasionally find a dog that has been tender-mouthed for years, suddenly begins flattening his birds for no apparent reason. This is most unlikely, but if it should happen to you—you must crack down severely and at once. Show the crushed bird to the dog. Scold him severely. Put it in his mouth and make him hold it gently for a long, long time—meanwhile talking to him like a Dutch uncle. If it ever happens a second time—then it's time to get out the persuader. If you don't win this agument right now, you've lost a retriever. When the habit becomes confirmed, hard mouth is almost impossible to cure.

## DEFYING THE WHISTLE

Sometimes a dog that stops instantly on the whistle when he is relatively close to you will develop a convenient deafness when he is out in the field or in the water 100 yards or more. Of course the hearing of individual dogs varies. But if you really give out on an Acme Thunderer, any young dog with clean ears can easily hear it at least a quarter of a mile—unless you are blowing directly into a very strong wind. So don't let your dog kid you. Be reasonably sure before you punish him that he can hear the whistle. If in doubt, send a helper out to see if *he* can hear it.

Then when you're sure, crack down hard, and win this argument. When he defies the whistle, go roaring out there as fast as you can. Catch him. Drag him back to the exact spot where he should have stopped. Blow a single blast. Say, "Do you hear that? *Sit!*" Repeat this several times. Meantime, give him a good licking, between these admonitions. I have found it easier on me and the dog, in the long run, to deal out a really good old-fashioned thrashing when this whistle deafness first appears. That usually ends it, and saves much nagging, yelling, and many lickings in the future.

## BUT CHEER UP

We seem to be ending this chapter on a gloomy note, full of faults to correct, and dogs to be walloped. But these matters had to be included somewhere, just in case you might sometime run into one of them.

I could go on and on, describing many more specific stunts for meeting relatively minor problems that you might conceivably encounter with your dog. But this book is going to be thick enough without them, and by now you can easily figure them out for yourself, if the need arises. They are all based on *repetition and memory*.

When your dog does anything wrong, see that an unpleasant result occurs; repeat it enough so it becomes associated in his memory with the improper action. He will quickly decide that petty crime doesn't pay.

Conversely, be sure that there is always a pleasant result when he does what he should. To him there is nothing finer than triumphantly to find the dummy or the bird, and then to receive a word of praise and a pat on the head from you.

Actually, if you started with a good dog in the first place, and then trained him the easy, happy way—and didn't overtrain him when he was too young—the chances are good that he'll never develop any serious faults for you to correct.

And the most painless way to keep him up to snuff for hunting is to run him in every retriever trial you can conveniently get to. Do it for practice, fun, and experience for your dog. It is well worth the small entry fee, just to work your dog on ducks and shot birds occasionally, as a change from the training dummies.

But remember that out of all the dogs entered, most of them with more experience than yours, only four can win places in each stake. So don't expect to win. Be happily astonished if the lightning strikes, and you get a ribbon.

Even if you never win a place, you'll get plenty out of the trials. You'll be a better handler for this experience. Your dog will be a better meat retriever. And you'll both have more fun when you go hunting together.

# 17

## If the Ladies Can Do It–

THERE'S ENOUGH OF the cavalier in me that I feel I can train and handle any hunting dog as well as any woman who ever lived. This may not be true, as I've seen some very talented ladies operating on the line at trials across the breadth of this nation. When they've placed ahead of me, I've been able to accept my defeat gracefully because the ladies, almost without exception, compete without asking for any considerations not due all competitors.

I can take these defeats gracefully, but I've never been convinced I am any less than better than any woman trainer-handler anywhere.

If you've any reservations about whether you can train and handle a fine hunting dog, consider what the ladies have accomplished. The National Retriever Championship is the toughest competition of them all. No lady handler has ever won it—but you can believe they've been in there swinging, and that they've been close many times. Twenty-five ladies started 49 retrievers in the first 27 National [Open] Championships. For the first twenty years they had averaged just over one start a year. But, during the next seven years they came on strong with 27 starters. Mrs. Walter S. Heller, stalwart supporter of the Chesapeakes, competed in eight of those first 27 Nationals—taking her dogs to the brink of victory in several of them. Valarie Fisher, not yet twenty-one, came very close to winning it in 1969 with her Golden.

In the National Amateur Championships the ladies have been even more active. In the first ten years of that stake 30 ladies

handled 101 of a total of 488 starters. During that period 12
different ladies had 16 finalists. Only once in that decade were the
ladies shut out of the finals. Mrs. Heller was a finalist in '58 and
'59, '66 and '67. Mrs. Theodore E. Fajen, Jr., and Mrs. Warner
L. Atkins have both pressed their way to the finals twice. Miss
Ann A. Fowler competed in all of the first ten National Amateurs and, in 1959, went to the finals with her Golden, Happy
Thanksgiving.

Many of the ladies do much, or all, of their own training. One,
Miss Francis Griscom, has trained professionally.

Women who've tried retriever trialing feel it is one of the very
few sports where a lady can step in and compete on equal terms,
not only with men, but with the best of the professionals. And,
they can do it without losing one bit of their femininity. Some
ladies feel they may yield a small edge in the strength and carrying power of the voice. However, Mrs. George H. Flinn, Jr., the
most active campaigner of Goldens, feels ladies have an advantage
in that they are usually able to get closer to their dogs and understand them better. "Torchy" Flinn was president of the National
Amateur Retriever Club in 1964, a vice-president from 1960
through 1963.

Some of the ladies have compiled distinguished records. Mrs.
Heller carried her Chesapeake, Dual Ch., AFC Baron's Tule Tiger
to the all-time highest total of Amateur All-Age (112) and Open
(96) for his breed—208! Mrs. August Belmont stands second among
the ladies for successful campaigning with an individual dog in
Amateur All-Age stakes. She handled her AFTC Shauna Buck, a
black Lab male, to 90½ Amateur All-Age and 7½ Open points.

Many others have also done extremely well. Consult Appendix
II for the Amateur All-Age records achieved by the following
ladies with these dogs:

| Amateur Handler | Retriever, Color, Breed and Sex |
|---|---|
| Mrs. Theodore E. Fajen, Jr.* | FC, AFC, CFTC Brandy Spirit of Netley (Y.L.M.) |
| Mrs. Clifford V. Brokaw, Jr.* | FTC, AFTC Cindy's Pride of Garfield (B.L.M.) |

| *Amateur Handler* | *Retriever, Color, Breed and Sex* |
|---|---|
| Mrs. Richard Reeve* | FTC, AFTC Bay City Zany Jane (B.L.F.) |
| Mrs. George H. Flinn, Jr. | FC, AFTC, CFTC Stilrovin Tuppee Tee (G.F.) |
| Miss Ann A. Fowler | AFTC Happy Thanksgiving, C.D. (G.M.) |
| Mrs. Milton D. Orowitz* | FTC, AFTC Black Brook's Lady Bimba (B.L.F.) |
| Mrs. Claus P. Johnson | FC, AFC Jetstone Muscles of Claymar (B.L.M.) |
| Mrs. Warner L. Atkins | FC, AFC Sam Frizel of Glenspey, C.D.X. (B.L.M.) |
| Mrs. George H. Flinn, Jr.* shared with John W. McAssey | FC, AFTC Mainliner Mike II (B.L.M.) |
| Mrs. Edward C. Fleishman | FTC, AFTC Mount Joy's Louistoo (C.M.) |
| Mrs. Edward Wylie | AFC Black Jake of Devon (B.L.M.) |
| Mrs. Donald S. Thatcher* | FTC, AFTC Tam O'Shanter of Craignook (B.L.F.) |
| Mrs. Warner L. Atkins* | Dual Ch., AFC Petite Rouge (B.L.M.) |
| Mrs. George H. Flinn | FTC, AFTC, Can. Dual Ch. Rockhaven Raynard of Fo-Go-Ta (G.M.) |
| Mrs. Charles C. B. Stevens | FC, AFTC Bigstone Shady Lile (B.L.F.) |
| Mrs. Albert P. Loening* | FTC, AFTC Medlin's Texas Right (B.L.M.) |
| Miss Ann A. Fowler | FC, AFC Stilrovin Savannah Gay |
| Mrs. Clifford W. Mortensen* | FC, AFTC Bingo's Ringo (B.L.M.) |

(An asterisk indicates that another handler is recorded for one or more of the dog's Amateur All-Age placements. In most, but not all, instances these ladies also handled their dogs to their Open victories.)

These dogs have accumulated point totals sufficient for from 4 to 14 amateur championships each—and several of them were still on the campaign trail when these records were compiled.

In *June, 1970,* Audrey Brokaw won the National Amateur with her black Lab male FC-AFC Andy's Partner Pete.

In *November, 1976,* Judy Weikel was the first woman ever to win the National Open. She won with her black Lab male FC-AFC San Joaquin Honcho (which was the youngest dog ever to win a National).

The following are ladies whose dogs finished the *National Opens:*

In *1971* Louise Belmont w. black Lab male FC-AFC Carr-Lab Penrod;

Dana Brown w. black Lab male FC-AFC Paha Sapa Warpaint,

In *1973* Dana Brown w. black Lab bitch DUAL-AFC Royal Oaks Jill of Burgundy,

In *1977* Delma Hazzard w. black Lab male FC-AFC Dude's Double or Nothin',

In *1978* Judy Weikel w. black Lab male NFC-AFC San Joaquin Honcho.

Ladies whose dogs finished the *National Amateurs*:

In *1973* Valerie Walker w. Golden Retr. male FC-AFC Misty's Sungold Lad;

Joannie Schellinger w. black Lab FC-AFC Spring Farm's Smokey;

Josephine Reeves w. black Lab male FC-AFC Shadow of Provincetown,

In *1974* Dana Brown w. black Lab male FC-AFC Paha Sapa Warpaint,

In *1975* Annette Paterno w. black Lab male AFC Gahonk's Saygo and black Lab bitch AFC Trumarc Shindana;

Debbie Morgan w. black Lab male FC-AFC Watchim Sneak;

Kristin Lende (just a teen-ager) w. black Lab bitch AFC Tidewater Mallard,

In *1976* Audrey Brokaw w. black Lab male FC Invails GunHo;

Joannie Schellinger w. black Lab male FC-AFC Spring Farm's Smokey,

In *1977* Marion Weiss w. black Lab bitch FC-AFC Macariolyn's Feather Tiger;

Judy Weikel w. NFC-AFC Honcho;
Delma Hazzard w. black Lab male FC-AFC Dude's Double or
Nothin',
In *1978* Judy Weikel w. Honcho;
Lesley-Rae Karnes w. black Lab bitch FC-AFC Donnybrooks St.
Jude,
In *1979* Louise Belmont w. black Lab male AFC Carr-Lab Raiders
Gain;
Lesley-Rae Karnes w. black Lab bitch FC-AFC Donnybrooks St.
Jude

Ladies whose dogs have won the *National Derby Championship*:
1971   Debbie Morgan w. Watchim Sneak—black Lab male.
1973   Dottie Ramsey w. Tigathoes Funky Farquar—Golden Retr.
male.
1974   Delma Hazzard w. Dude's Double or Nothin'—black Lab
male.
1975   Lesley-Rae Karnes w. Donnybrooks St. Jude—black Lab
bitch
1976   Louise Belmont w. Carr-Lab Raiders Gain—black Lab
male.

The highest honor that may be paid any retriever trialer is an
invitation to judge the National [Open] Championship. Of the
first 63 individuals so honored, 5 were ladies. Mrs. J. Gould Remick
judged it in 1943, 1945, and 1949. Mrs. Carl Erickson officiated
in 1942 and Mrs. Gaylord Donnelley in 1944. Next honored was
Mrs. Frances Garlock in 1950, followed by Mrs. B. Brannan Reath
II in 1965. Mrs. Reath had judged the National Amateur Championship in 1963. About 4 percent of the experienced judges are
ladies.

The ladies not serving actively as judges are at every trial, everywhere, helping to make them run smoothly—but their participation
considerably exceeds working on the hospitality and food committees. They have played prominent roles as club officers. Mrs. Audrey James Field was, in 1931, the first president of the Labrador
Retriever Club when it ran the first AKC-licensed field trial.

Since that time the ladies have been very instrumental in building retriever clubs. In 1940 they formed their own Women's Field
Trial Club and have staged and managed excellent retriever trials

ever since. Although it is a national organization, the Women's Club holds its trials on Long Island. In the spring of 1956, the Western ladies formed their own group, the Sagehen's Retriever Club.

The men compete in these trials—and usually judge them, but the ladies run them—and often win them.

Whether as breeders, trainers, hunters, or owners—or all of these—the ladies have found in retriever training a healthy, enjoyable, and challenging sport where they compete on equal terms with the very best there is.

# Part III

## RETRIEVER FIELD TRIALS

*What to expect and how to act when you attend your first one.*

# 18

---

## What It's All About

A BALL GAME is pretty dull if you don't understand the rules. It's a lot more fun if you know a little something about the inside stuff—and what to watch. Similarly you'll get more enjoyment from your first retriever trial if you understand what's going on. It really isn't very complicated.

In the United States, the most respected of the retriever trials are run under the rules of the American Kennel Club. These rules insure that competitive conditions are, as nearly as it is possible to make them so, the same throughout the country. These rules are augmented by the recommendations of the Retriever Advisory Committee. From time to time, new rules are introduced and some of the older ones are amended. They are adjusted to meet the gradually changing requirements of trials, trialers—and of the AKC. Between this printing and your reading of this book, it is almost certain some changes, however small, will have been made in these rules. Therefore, rather than risk misleading you by printing possibly obsolete rules here, I strongly urge you to direct a postcard to the AKC, asking for one copy, each, of *Registration and Field Trial Rules for Retrievers,* and *Standing Recommendations of the Retriever Advisory Committee.* These are revised with every change and single copies are free. The AKC's address is 51 Madison Avenue, New York, New York 10010.

Rules changes, proposed or accomplished, are first published in the AKC's official magazine, the monthly *Pure-Bred Dogs.*

The Retriever Advisory Committee is composed of delegates from member clubs. It meets annually and offers an expert consensus on rule interpretation and trial procedures. Like the AKC rules, the "recommendations" are subject to gradual change. Although they do not have the status of "rules," they are respected and followed everywhere in the United States where field trials are run. When the committee feels it is necessary to do so, it recommends a change of rules to the AKC. Thus the AKC is able to adjust rather quickly to the needs of retriever trialers and trials. You will find it extremely worthwhile to study your copy of the Committee's *Recommendations,* which covers such subjects as: Trial Procedure, Evaluation of Dog Work, Natural Abilities, Abilities Acquired Through Training, and Classification of Faults. You'll be glad you sent for your copy.

You will get your basic concepts of trial mechanics and procedures from the AKC rule book and from the Advisory Committee's *Recommendations.* If, in addition to an understanding of these, you absorb a few tips on field-trial etiquette, you will be prepared for the role of sophisticated spectator, right from the start. Here are some suggestions I wrote for distribution to new members and guests of the Southern California Retriever Club.

## ETIQUETTE FOR THE SPECTATOR

1. *Spectator dogs.* At most trials, human spectators are more than welcome—but not spectator dogs. All field-trial committees have been plagued so many times by unruly pets that are not kept under control by their thoughtless owners, that no dogs whatever except those competing are wanted on the trial grounds. Obviously it is unfair to a competing dog if, just as a bird is shot for him, somebody's Pomeranian sets up a loud yapping and causes the retriever to turn his head and fail to mark his fall. I've even seen a Boxer, too trustfully allowed off his leash, suddenly run out and start a fight with a retriever that was in the field and under judgment.

2. *Loud talk in the gallery.* When a dog is sitting on the line or in the blind, it is just as bad form to risk distracting him with loud talk as it is to make a racket when a man is putting in a golf tournament.

3. *The proper time for applause.* (See Illustration 124.) By all means, don't hesitate to applaud a good performance heartily. But

wait until the dog has completed his job. If it is a double or a triple retrieve, wait until he has delivered the final bird to his handler.

4. *Gallery crowding behind handlers*. The gallery should stay at least 20 yards behind the judges, to avoid distracting the dogs on a marking test. On a blind retrieve—or handling test—the gallery is usually requested to split and leave a wide, empty space behind the handler. If a solid mass of people is standing directly behind a handler, it is very difficult for the dog to pick him out of the crowd from far out in the field. And it is well-nigh impossible for the dog to see his hand signals.

So their dogs can pick them out easily, handlers have established the practice of wearing white jackets, but only while they are *handling*. If you plan to attend a retriever trial you would be well advised to wear something other than light, plain-colored clothing—particularly on the upper half of your body. If you find yourself at a trial and garbed in such a manner that a dog could, from a distance, confuse you with his handler, protect your personal popularity by staying out of sight of competing dogs. A trial is a contest between finely fashioned skills and the contest would be irreparably marred if you permitted a dog to confuse you with his handler.

5. *Petting or touching dogs*. (See Illustration 125.) If you've already trained your own retriever, you know about this. You know why the handlers are more jealous about undue attentions to their dogs than to their wives. But most people quite naturally don't understand this. They are accustomed to petting and fondling any dog they see. Nobody wants to offend interested newcomers at the trials, and it is embarrassing to a handler to have to ask a well-meaning person to let his dog alone. So make yourself useful. If you see someone attempting to pet a competing dog, do the handler a favor. Step up and tactfully explain why it's best to let these dogs alone, when they are in competition. Tell the petter he has such a way with animals that the dog might fall in love with him, and try to watch him instead of his handler when his turn comes to be out in the field under judgment.

6. *Feeding tidbits to dogs*. Often there is a well-meaning female going around actually trying to *feed* the dogs. If you see one just

tell her how heartbreaking it is to a man who has spent months getting a young dog ready for a trial—if the pup does a nice retrieve, and then refuses to bring the bird to his owner, but runs all through the gallery looking for that nice lady who slipped him the ham sandwich.

7. *Hysterical old maids, male and female.* At nearly every trial some Sunday driver drops in, attracted by the crowd, just to see what's going on. Such people know nothing of hunting, or dogs, or game conservation. Sometimes one of them becomes hysterical and makes a scene over "cruelty" to pigeons, pheasant, or shackled ducks. Strangely enough, a man who gets this obsession is likely to make more noise and be less reasonable than a woman.

The most annoying of these I ever encountered was a strictly minor-league celebrity with major-league hallucinations. He showed up at a trial, and wasn't getting much attention. The people there were more interested in first-rate dogs than second-rate hams. Suddenly this character became greatly excited over how "cruel" and "unsporting" it was to have *two* men shooting those poor defenseless pigeons with *shotguns*. He gathered a crowd, all right, but he never did make it quite clear just what he wanted—whether we should arm the pigeons to defend themselves, or have our gunners use deer rifles. At last, to everybody's relief, he stormed off, loudly threatening to call the cops.

But most of the people who become concerned about the killing of the feathered livestock are perfectly sincere, nice folks. They usually calm down at once if someone bothers to explain that the relatively few pigeons and pheasant shot at the trials are martyrs to the cause of conservation. That they are killed much more quickly and cleanly by expert gunners, for instance, than squawking and terrorized barnyard chickens that are beheaded by an ax. That for every barnyard pigeon or game-farm pheasant we kill, at least ten wild birds are saved, by retrievers, through finding and bringing to bag thousands of dead and crippled birds that otherwise would rot or die lingering deaths in field or marsh. For the trials are the only means of demonstrating the great value of retrievers to hunters, and encouraging them to use them. Also, the trials are the proving ground for breeding stock, and enable better hunting dogs to be bred.

Some of these people get more excited about the dogs "biting" the live shackled ducks than about shooting the pigeons. Explain to them that these retrievers are very tender-mouthed. They don't hurt the ducks. They carry them gently, and some of the old ducks that are used over and over actually get to enjoying the ride. One maiden lady refused to believe me when I told her this. I finally convinced her by getting one of my dogs out of the car, borrowing a fresh egg from the lunch wagon, and having the dog retrieve it to hand, without breaking it. After that the old gal relaxed, stuck around, and ended up enjoying the trial.

In every state, of course, the use of game-farm pheasant and ducks must be completely legal and approved by the state division of fish and game. But beyond this, most of these state departments thoroughly appreciate the retriever's great contribution to conservation, and heartily encourage and support the retriever trials in every way.

If you encounter a "cruelty" screamer at a trial, you can make yourself useful by explaining all this to him. But if that doesn't satisfy him, and he still wants to make a noise, then he's just a nut. The chances are, he is also a hypocrite. Ask him if he's a vegetarian. Ask him if it's worse to shoot a pheasant than to club a bawling steer to death in the slaughterhouse. Or to stick a pig in the throat with a knife while it's fully conscious, and let it slowly bleed to death. Tell him that's how he gets his bacon and pork chops. Tell him to please go home.

8. *The one-, two- or three-year "expert."* It seems there is always one of these self-proclaimed authorities either coming or going at any amateur sporting event. Sometimes there are exaggerated examples like the "one-week expert." When they've worn out their welcome, these individuals move on to some other activity. Don't buy their misinformation. Politely, ignore them. And, resist all temptations to assume that *you* are able to quickly assimilate all there is that is important to know about retrievers and retriever trials.

9. *The rule book artist.* There are many well-considered rules and procedures governing retriever trials. The responsibility for observing and enforcing them belongs to the judges, the field trial committee, and any AKC representative who might be present.

These people have their own, quiet ways of handling sticky situations. Watch and enjoy, but don't participate unless you are properly doing so in some official capacity.

## SOME INSIDE STUFF TO WATCH

1. *Bird throwers.* (See Illustration 116.) The boys who throw the birds for the official guns to shoot can make a trial an even competition—or a crap game. There is a considerable art in throwing a bird so it will fly in the exact direction wanted. Pigeons are especially ornery and unpredictable, particularly in a strong wind, and are apt to turn most any way except the way they're supposed to go. But a good thrower can hurl each bird out by main force, far enough so the guns can kill it without messing it up, before the bird *can* turn. This takes a strong pitching arm, plus plenty of experience. Watch the falls. If all the dogs get falls of approximately equal length, you're not only watching some good guns— but some expert bird throwers. Sometimes an old hunter is inclined to sneer when he sees the birds thrown—presumably instead of *flushed*—to be shot. But obviously it would be impossible to get anything like equal falls for each dog by flushing the birds to fly wild in all directions.

2. *Official guns.* (See Illustration 116.) The old hunter who thinks it is as unsporting to shoot thrown birds as "shooting fish in a bucket" would get the surprise of his life if he tried just once to shoot for a retriever trial. A pheasant kicked out of heavy cover gets away slowly. If he takes off into the wind, he hangs up there on a string. All the hunter has to do is knock him down, any way and anywhere he can. It doesn't matter where the bird falls.

In the trials the birds are given an instant start at top speed. Usually they are hurled straight downwind. They are really going away from there. They must be shot at just the right distance—not at the most convenient distance for the gunners. The judges are ugly about this. They want equal falls for all dogs, so they can fairly judge and compare their performances. Furthermore they want no birds shot too close, smashed to pieces by a tightly bunched wad of shot, and turned into a mass of bloody, raw hamburger.

Just one of these to pick up can make a valuable young dog hard-mouthed.

On the other hand, the birds must be cleanly killed. If the guns wait a split second too long, and let a cock pheasant ride slightly out of range, a strong running cripple is the likely result. If the dog fails on it, he's had a rough break. But if he works it out, and gets it, the judges can fairly put him above a dog that did a faultless job on a dead bird. Not being crystal gazers, they have no way of knowing what the second dog might have done with a cripple. Perhaps if he'd had the opportunity, he would have done even better.

For most retriever trials the finest wing shots in the territory are drafted to do the shooting. Most judges prefer to have just one gun shoot, with the other backing, in case the first one misses. A man who doesn't appreciate the fact that a trial is a serious contest for the dogs—and not a clambake for the benefit of the guns—has no business being out there.

Even the finest shots, shooting as a team, occasionally miss. This can be a tough break for a keen young dog that watches a missed bird fly away and light in a distant field. He is all too likely to remember and go on a fruitless chase of that one, instead of marking and getting the bird subsequently killed for him. The very pressure not to miss, and the judges yapping about just where the birds should be dropped—and having to worry about not shooting the other gunners or the gallery—can cause even a gunner with iron nerves to tighten up and get off his timing for a moment.

So watch the work of the guns. If they go on all day, killing birds cleanly, dropping them not too close and not too far—you're watching a superlative performance. And if you think it looks easy, just get out there and try it sometime. In some present-day trials the handler will shoot at least one of the birds himself—with the official guns backing him up.

3. *Importance of uniform cover.* One of the biggest headaches of every field-trial committee is trying to get the adequate ground for the land tests, with uniform cover. If a bird falls on bare ground for one dog, while the next gets a fall in a patch of dense weeds, it is hardly an equal contest. But sometimes it is simply

impossible to get even cover, particularly for the spring trials. Then it is interesting to watch how the judges make the best of it, skipping around from one place to another, trying to give all the dogs similar tests.

4. *Equal marking opportunities*. In a marking test, where dogs are scored on their ability to mark and remember one or more falls, it is obviously no contest unless all dogs have equal opportunities to *see* those falls. When hilly or rolling land must be used, good judges are careful to see that one dog is not expected to mark a bird that falls *over* a hill, while others have a clear view straight up a slope—or down—or on the level. Notice also whether the judges move on past a big tree or another obstruction that *might* interfere with a dog's view of the fall. Extra long falls should be avoided.

5. At most trials, live shackled, rather than free-flying, ducks are used for the marked retrieves on water.

Some trialers argue that the shackled ducks are artificial, have no blood scent, and do not simulate actual hunting conditions. Also, a live duck will occasionally squawk, or flap a wing and thus help a lucky dog find it quickly. All of this is true.

However, I still feel that under some conditions the shackled ducks are the lesser of two evils, and on the whole more uniform marking tests can be had with them. Mallards raised on a game farm are not nearly such dependable flyers as pheasant. There are always many of the ducks that, when thrown, drop like a rock. These are very hard to hit, and the best of guns frequently cripple them, particularly when it is necessary to try to shoot them from a boat. A cripple on water is much more serious than on land. A dog can run down a crippled pheasant. But if a wing-tipped duck is out in a big body of deep, open water, he can give the greatest retriever a bad time. He can swim just as fast as any dog, and he can dive deeper than any dog.

At this point I can hear the old duck hunters snorting, "What good is a retriever if he can't handle crippled ducks?"

It's a good question. The answer is that a good retriever can and does get at least nine out of ten cripples, under average duck-hunting conditions, even including those with nothing but a broken wing. In a fairly shallow marsh it's a cinch. The dog will quickly corner and catch the most vigorous cripple, and it can't dive deep enough to elude him. Even in a big lake, if you give the dog enough time, he can often drive the duck ashore and then run it down.

Many Labradors will dive quite deep themselves after a duck. I once knocked down a blackjack that instantly dove in about eight feet of water. I sent Freehaven Jay after it, to the great distress of my guide. He was sure no dog could ever get that duck. But luckily the duck came up within 10 feet of the dog, and immediately dove again. Suddenly one black Labrador completely submerged. Not even the tip of his tail was visible. He stayed under a long time. The guide was convinced I had lost a dog. I was beginning to wonder, myself. At last Jay surfaced, snorting like a whale. He had a very active blackjack in his mouth! To this day the guides at my old duck club in Illinois talk about that "submarine dog."

But that was hunting. A field trial is supposed to be an equal contest for all dogs. I'd have no objection to giving *all* dogs cripples, if someone could guarantee that each cripple would put on the same performance, no matter how tough it might be.

One time Freehaven Jay had done faultless work right up to the final series of a big Eastern trial. No other dog was close to him, and he appeared a cinch to win if he could just pick up two more ducks. Then two of the finest guns in the country fixed him up with a strong cripple. It was strong and it was the meanest duck I ever saw. It fell far out in a huge, deep lake, and the water was ice cold. Jay chased that ornery duck all over the lake. Whenever he got close, it dove in 40 feet of water. He couldn't drive it ashore, and there was no other place to corner it in shallow water. He swam at top speed for *fifty minutes,* while I stood helplessly in the blind, and quietly had a stroke. At last, when I saw he was nearly exhausted, I called him in. No trial is worth drowning a dog.

So perhaps I'm prejudiced. But I've seen this happen to too many fine dogs, and I prefer shackled ducks, even if they occasionally give a dog a slight advantage by giving tongue or flapping a wing.

Another trouble with shooting thrown ducks is that they frequently turn and fly straight back at the gunners, no matter how skillfully they are thrown. This happened in several series at the 1948 National Championship Trial. Many of the ducks were consequently shot much too close—virtually shot to pieces.

In blind retrieves, of course, freshly killed ducks should always be used. The shackled birds are only practical for marking tests, and even then they must be handled correctly. A shackled duck falls so quickly that it will be down on the water before a dog has a chance to see it, if the gun is not fired until the bird is in the air. The shot must be fired *first,* and only then should the duck be thrown, giving the dog time to turn his head and see the fall.

This matter of shot vs. shackled ducks probably will be a lively topic of debate as long as trials are held. So pick your side, and when the trial is over and the post mortem begins, climb right up on that bar stool and start swinging.

# 19

---

# Typical Retriever Trial Tests

TESTS VARY SOMEWHAT because of local conditions, but in general the experienced judges stick to the conventional, tried and true tests. If there is time to give enough of these, they offer plenty of opportunity for the best dog to reveal all of his desirable qualities and abilities. Too often, when a green judge* attempts something tricky, it boomerangs, and he runs into complications that nobody could foresee.

In the early days of the sport in the Middle West we would sometimes see as many as six or seven different stakes in a two-day trial. But now that entries have grown so large (an average of 35 starters in licensed Open All-Age and 25.5 in Amateur All-Age stakes during 1967), the American Kennel Club has a rule that no trial can offer more than one stake yielding open championship points and that no two-day trial offering one of these stakes can offer more than two stakes unless separate judges and grounds are used to run them simultaneously. The favorite "minor" stakes seem to be the Derby (which now has the same age qualifications that used to describe the "Junior," a stake no longer recognized), the Qualifying, and the Amateur All-Age. The Puppy Stake, and—in effect—the *old* Derby, have wisely been dropped by the AKC.

Since this chapter is also to serve as your yardstick when you are buying a dog—to tell you what a retriever can fairly be expected to know and do at a given age—we will include a brief

*AKC rules now require that any combination of two judges for any stake offering championship points must have a total of eight or more previous assignments within the past five years. Thus, if one is a novice, the other must be well-seasoned. Only amateurs may judge.

discussion of *all* the official stakes described by the American Kennel Club.

It is customary to shoot pheasant for land work in Open All-Age Stakes, although any game bird may be used. Because pheasant are so very expensive, most clubs are obliged to use pigeons for the minor stakes. But occasionally a club shoots the works, and provides pheasant for all stakes. Before entering a trial, be sure to find out what birds your dog will have to retrieve. If he has been trained only on pigeons, you should give him a little practice on pheasant before asking him to pick up these much larger birds in a trial. The entry blank and premium list of a licensed trial always specify what birds will be used on land and whether shackled or shot ducks on water. At an informal trial, you can be reasonably sure that only pigeons and shackled ducks will be used.

The names and marginal limitations of the various stakes offered are subject to change with time, but not severely so. If you've sent to the AKC for your own free copy of the latest edition of the booklet *Registration and Rules for Retriever Field Trials,* you will have the very latest information on the subject.

The AKC is quite stiff—some say stuffy—about which dogs may enter trials at which AKC championship points are awarded. All entrants must be AKC registered, or part of an AKC registered litter, or an imported dog registered with a kennel club acceptable to the AKC. Without special permission from the AKC, dogs in the latter two categories may be entered only three times before being registered. Only dogs of the six breeds listed as "retrievers" are eligible for AKC trials.

## DERBY STAKE

*A Derby Stake at a retriever trial shall be for dogs which are over six months of age and not yet two years of age on the first day of the trial at which they are being run.*

This is a stake where the mistakes of youth tend to be forgiven and where the potentialities for future greatness are cherished. The judges want to see the makings of a future champion. They want to see evidence of trainability, but they do not expect polished performance. Speed, desire, style, nose, a willingness to handle, those components of what is called "class," are the "gold" Derby judges seek. There's an average of only four series and each is relatively simple. Usually a Derby Stake starts with a single on land, then one in the water. The third series might be a double on land and/or water. The difficulty of the fourth series, if any, often depends upon how much test the judges need at that point to separate the dogs so they can be placed.

## QUALIFYING STAKE

*A Qualifying Stake at a retriever trial shall be for dogs over six months of age which have never won first, second, third, or fourth place, or a Judges' Award of Merit in an Open All-Age or Limited All-Age, or won first, second, third, or fourth place in an Amateur All-Age Stake, or won two first places in Qualifying Stakes at licensed or member club trials.*

The qualifying stake is an evolvement from the old "nonwinners" stake which used to be jammed with hunters and their meat dogs. Time, however, has become such a treasured commodity at retriever trials, that some of the fat that was fun had to be trimmed off. Now, because this *is* a qualifying stake, judges are reluctant to view it as the relatively informal event it once was. It is the only intermediate stake between the Derby and the Amateur or Open-Point stakes. The tests and the light in which they are evaluated vary with the judges. Even those who choose to look upon it as an intermediate or a "Meat-Dog" Stake are very careful to have rather polished performers for their first- and second-place dogs. These places qualify a dog for Limited All-Age Stakes.

Usually the Qualifying Stake has four tests, including double marks on land and water—with the possibility of a triple mark in the water.

Usually judges have only a half day to run the Qualifying Stake. Therefore they frequently have no choice but to drop many dogs that complete the first series—but in mediocre fashion—in order to have time to give enough additional series so that the best dogs will be thoroughly tested. Probably the most difficult thing in judging is trying to guess how tough to make the first series in a Qualifying Stake.

The object is to plan a chore that will prove something, will separate the top dogs from the also-rans, but will not cause more than half the starters to fail. The judges' most haunting nightmare is that of losing all the dogs in the first series.

This fear is justified because the quality of work in a Qualifying is so unpredictable, and varies so greatly from trial to trial. Sometimes youngsters or experienced old meat dogs get hot and put on a show that looks like an Open All-Age. And sometimes they just plain stink.

So if you enter a Qualifying and have hopes of staying in to the end, you should have your dog prepared for *anything* but a blind retrieve. I have yet to see one of these pulled in a Qualifying, but have seen just about everything else.

You may get a very severe steadiness test, with birds shot right in front of the dog. And with a large entry, the judges may even be obliged to drop dogs in the first series for partial breaks.

Be ready for double marked retrieves of almost any kind. In light cover, the falls might be as far as 150 yards. Another favorite is a *very* long single bird, for a marking test. Sometimes this bird is dropped *beyond* the edge of a field with cover on it, so the fall is out on bare ground, or freshly plowed ground. This nearly always loses many Qualifying dogs, who simply will not leave the cover and hunt the bare ground. If in all his recent practice your dog has been accustomed to finding birds only in cover, you'd better give him a little practice on this test.

Be prepared for long singles up to 300 yards, and try to have your dog sailing out on that line until his nose stops him, so he won't hunt short. Brush him up a bit on the matter of switching birds. You might get a test in which the dog is sent for a long marked bird. Then as he comes in with it, another bird is thrown and shot right in front of him, to tempt him to switch. This test is not used as much as it formerly was, but you'd better be ready for it.

You rarely encounter a "walk-up" test in a Qualifying, so this will be described under Open All-Age, where it properly belongs. But it's easy to be ready even for this, and you might as well do so. The dog will of course work from a blind and through decoys.

You can be reasonably sure you will get no handling test on a blind retrieve, and the dog will get a much higher score in the marking tests if he finds the birds without help from you. Just the same, it may come in very handy if he will obey hand and whistle signals. If he has failed to mark a bird, it is much better to handle him quickly and quietly to the fall—and at least have a fighting chance of staying in the trial—than to let him hunt all day, far from the vicinity of the fall, disturbing too much ground, and finally pick him up at the request of the judges. Then you *know* he's all through.

## AMATEUR ALL-AGE STAKE

*An Amateur All-Age Stake at a retriever trial shall be for any dogs (over six months of age), if handled in that stake by persons who are amateurs (as determined by the Field Trial Committee of the trial-giving club.)*

The most significant and happiest trend in retriever trials during recent years has been the exploding popularity of Amateur All-Age Stakes. The turning point was the AKC's establishment of Amateur Field Trial Championships in September of 1951. This presentment of an achievable goal lent zest to amateur competition which was further heightened by the establishment of the National Amateur Retriever Championship in 1957—and the need to gain qualifying wins for eligibility.

In 1951, 16 clubs offered 16 amateur trials with 355 total entries. The following year there were 26 clubs offering 39 trials—and the total entry had more than doubled to 856.

In 1967 there were 121 Amateur All-Age stakes with 3,089 starters, an average of 25.5 per stake. There were 198 different retrievers sharing the possible 484 placements.

In 1955, the last full year before Amateur All-Age stakes began offering the incentive of qualification for a national amateur championship stake, there were 39 amateur stakes with 967 entries. Qualifications began at midyear in 1956. In 1957 the National Amateur Retriever Club was organized. As illustration of the influence these developments have had, in the 12 years following

1955, amateur trials had an amazing growth of 316 percent. For a control figure, we can compare with the very healthy 142 percent growth shown by Open and Limited All-Age stakes during the same period. In 1978, there were 168 Amateur All-Age stakes with 7,191 starters.

The Amateur All-Age is for the fellow who gets his thrills from handling his own dogs. The tests are approximately the same as those in the Open, Limited, and Special stakes, but the handlers are equal in that each of them is a chap (or a lady) whose livelihood does not depend upon how well he trains and handles. That doesn't mean that the competition isn't keen—and that you won't see handlers who could make their livings as pros if they chose to do so. If you are selecting a stake to enter, I'd suggest you first get your feet wet in informal trials, or in Derby or Qualifying stakes.

## OPEN ALL-AGE AND LIMITED ALL-AGE STAKES

(The Open All-Age and the Limited All-Age stakes are identical except for qualification. The tests are the same and the computation of AKC points is the same. The Limited has entry restrictions and is sometimes used by clubs which anticipate that the major entries at their trials might be more than they can handle in the time available.)

*An Open All-Age Stake at a retriever trial shall be for all dogs (over six months of age).*

*A Limited All-Age Stake at a retriever trial shall be for dogs (over six months of age) that have previously been placed or awarded a Judges' Award of Merit in an Open All-Age Stake, or that have been placed first or second in a Qualifying, or placed, or awarded a Judges' Award of Merit in an Amateur All-Age Stake carrying championship points.*

These, with the Amateur All-Age, are the big-time stakes where the first four placements count points toward the titles of Field Champion or Amateur Field Champion—and sometimes, if the handler is an amateur, toward both titles at the same time. Most of the competitors are also working for placements to qualify for one, or both, of the two national championships. All clubs allow at least one full day for such a stake, frequently longer, so the dogs may be thoroughly tested.

It seems that each year the tests in these stakes have become more difficult until what was once considered a fantastic performance has become commonplace. And why not? Selection of breeding stock through trials has produced superior animals and will continue to do so. Furthermore, each year we have more and better handlers and trainers.

The marking tests are not likely to be much more difficult than those described that you *might* encounter in a Qualifying. You will probably get more of them, since more time is available for the Open Stake.

To have a chance to go clear through the big stake, your dog must mark well, and do doubles, triples, or even four birds, up to 100 yards in the heaviest cover. He must be absolutely steady. Judges have almost no choice but to throw him out if he makes a deliberate move to go before he is sent.

You should be prepared for a test tempting him to switch birds, and a "walk-up." The latter test simulates an ordinary hunting party driving a field for pheasant. Two or more dogs are on line at a time. At a word from a judge, the line moves forward, with guns and bird throwers walking also, out on the wings. Your dog must walk quietly at heel. Suddenly a bird is thrown and shot. The dog must *sit* at once—on your quiet command—and stay until ordered by the judges to retrieve. Actually I don't think this is any more difficult for a jittery dog than sitting on a fixed line while his birds are shot out in front. If your dog is dependable about walking at heel, you'll have no trouble with a walk-up, but it wouldn't do any harm to practice it a little in advance.

In an Open Stake, good judges will do their best to have at least four series, and sometimes five or six if time permits. The best dogs have a way of coming to the top, and automatically placing themselves, if given enough fair opportunities to do their stuff.

Expect at least one series to be a blind handling test on land, and another a blind on water. So unless your dog is quite responsive to the hand and whistle signals, you are wasting your entry fee in an Open All-Age Stake.

You can be sure, too, that almost any stake will, in at least one test, require the dogs to swim past anchored artificial decoys.

In setting up a handling test, the judges try to devise something that will really show them whether or not each dog can be handled —and how well he handles. When a dead bird is planted 100 yards or so straight out in front, it doesn't necessarily show the judges what they want to see. Many of the dogs will take a line, and romp straight out and stumble over the bird, without any handling being necessary. A dog cannot be penalized for this, even though he is suspected of being just lucky. But the judges still don't know whether he will handle.

Therefore they try to devise a handling test that is fair, yet will require the dog to respond to hand and whistle signals. Sometimes this is done by planting two dead birds, one of them out in front 50 yards or so. A crosswind is blowing from right to left. The second bird is planted much farther—100 yards or more—and slightly *to the left of the line of the first bird.*

Each handler is requested by the judges to get the far bird first. To do this, the dog must be sent on a line safely to the right, or upwind side, of the short bird. After he is well beyond it, the handler then stops him with the whistle, and directs him with hand signals back to the left, to the long bird.

I believe this type of test is fairer and usually proves more than having a long blind bird, with a marked bird in another direction that the dog gets first. It is true the marked bird pulls many dogs back to the vicinity of that fall, when they are sent out on the blind retrieve. And this makes it necessary for the dog to be handled. But a wise old campaigner with a good memory knows perfectly well he already has picked up the marked bird. He is likely to take a line, and go straight out and stumble over the blind bird —and still the judges don't know whether he can be stopped on the whistle and directed by hand signals.

Sometimes a disappointed handler, whose dog fails, sets up a beef that a certain test did not represent "hunting conditions." To my mind this is the silliest of all complaints. Anything can happen when hunting. I can't conceive of a place I might not someday want to send a retriever for a fallen bird.

On the other hand, "hunting conditions" should not be used as an excuse for setting up a test that cannot be made approximately the same for every dog. Within that limitation, I feel that any retriever taking up the time of the judges in any All-Age Stake should be expected to do practically anything but answer the telephone and take a message.

The qualifications for championship status are always subject to change—but they almost never do in any truly significant respect. Here they are, as published by the AKC at this writing:

At present, to acquire an Amateur Field Championship, a retriever must be registered with the *American Kennel Club Stud Book* and must win:

(1) a National Championship Stake, handled by an Amateur, or a National Amateur Championship Stake or (2) a total of 10 points in Open All-Age or Limited All-Age Stakes or a total of 15 points in Open All-Age, Limited All-Age or Amateur All-Age Stakes, which may be acquired as follows: In each Open All-Age, or Limited All-Age or Amateur All-Age Stake, there must be at least 12 starters, each of which is eligible for an entry in a Limited All-Age Stake, and the handler must be an Amateur (as determined by the Field Trial Committee of the trial-giving club), and the winner of first place shall be credited with 5 points, second place 3 points, third place 1 point, and fourth place ½ point, but before acquiring a championship, a dog must win a first place and acquire 5 points in at least one Open All-Age, Limited All-Age or Amateur All-Age Stake open to all breeds of Retriever, and not more than 5 points shall be acquired in trials not open to all breeds of Retriever.

At present, to acquire a Field Championship, a retriever must be registered with the *American Kennel Club Stud Book* and must win:

(1) a National Championship Stake or (2) a total of 10 points, which may be acquired as follows:—In each Open All-Age or Limited All-Age Stake there must be at least 12 starters, each of which is eligible for entry in a Limited All-Age Stake, and the winner of first place shall be credited with 5 points, second place 3 points, and third place 1 point, and

fourth place ½ point, but before acquiring a championship, a dog must win first place and acquire 5 points in at least one Open All-Age or Limited All-Age Stake open to all breeds of Retriever, and not more than 5 points of the required 10 shall be acquired in trials not open to all breeds of Retriever.

## NATIONAL AMATEUR CHAMPIONSHIP STAKE

So that there might be a fitting annual culmination of activity for amateur handlers, the National Amateur Retriever Club was formed in 1957. An association of member clubs, it has staged a National Amateur Retriever Field Trial Championship Stake each year, starting in 1957. Contestants are limited to dogs which, when handled by an amateur, win a first place carrying five championship points, plus two additional championship points in Open, Limited, Special or Amateur All-Age stakes recognized by the American Kennel Club during the fiscal year preceding the trial.

The trial was first held in the Central time zone, then the Pacific (or Rocky Mountain) time zone, back to the Central time zone—and then to the Eastern time zone, with the rotation to be continued, in the same manner as the National Championship Stake. The rotation is usually planned so that the two stakes will never be in the same time zone during a single calendar year. Here's the AKC's rule on the subject:

A National Amateur Championship Stake at a Retriever Trial shall be for dogs which by reason of wins previously made, qualify under special rules subject to approval by the Board of Directors of The American Kennel Club. This stake shall be run not more than once in any calendar year by a club or association formed for this purpose, or by the club formed to conduct the National Championship Stake, and the stake shall be duly licensed by The American Kennel Club. The winner of such stake shall become an Amateur Field Champion of Record, if registered in the *American Kennel Club Stud Book,* and shall be entitled to be designated National Amateur Retriever Field Trial Champion of 19—.

At this writing a dog may be qualified for entry in the National Amateur Championship in one of three ways. It can qualify as the defending champion, by winning the previous National [Open] Championship under an amateur handler, or by winning one five-point first place and two additional points during the preceding fiscal year, all under amateur handling. Dogs are qualified for the National [Open] Championship according to the same formula, except that the winner of the previous National Amateur Championship is automatically qualified—and, of course, the winner of the previous Open Championship, regardless of the professional status of its handler.

The AKC's description of the National [Open] Championship Stake is nearly identical to that given above for the National Amateur, except that the word "amateur" does not appear.

# 20

The National Amateur
Championship Trial—*By S. Alan
and Joan Williams*

WHAT IS A National Amateur Championship like? What are the
dogs asked to do? How good must a dog be to win it? Short of
attending yourself, you can rely, as most retriever-folk do, upon
a firsthand report in *Retriever Field Trial News*. Here is Alan
Williams' account of the 1967 National Amateur Retriever Championship, illustrated with Joan Williams' photographs and diagrams
of the tests.

The eleventh annual running of the National Amateur Retriever
Championship was held near McCall, Idaho, on the shores of Big
Payette Lake, on June 21–24, 1967. It is picturesque country with
lush Alpine meadows and unbelievably blue, deep lakes nestled
among tall timber, surrounded on all sides by snow-capped moun-
tains.

Four days were allowed for the trial, and Sunday June 25, could
have been utilized if needed to reach a logical conclusion. The
judges were Bud Orowitz of Roslyn, New York; Hugh Klaren of
Lake Forest, Illinois; and Edward H. Brown of Milwaukie, Oregon, representing, as required by the National Amateur Retriever
Club, the East, Midwest, and Far West. John McAssey of Denver,
Colorado, was trial chairman.

Sixty-one of 73 qualified dogs were entered and one, 1964 National Ch., FC, AFC Ripco's V. C. Morgan, was scratched.

The judges had spent three days on the grounds, first survey-ing the land, then conceiving, planning, and testing the stake's tests. All challenges devised for the contenders were fair and de-manding; if anything, a bit more demanding than the judges had anticipated. But, there was the need to reduce the field of 60 to one champion within the time available. Just in case they were re-quired, four additional tests had been planned.

Of the entries, 38 were black Lab males, 10 black Lab females, 5 yellow Lab males, 3 Golden males, 2 Golden females and 3 Chesapeake males. Seven of the 9 finalists, including the new cham-pion, were black Lab males. The others were AFC Col-Tam of Craignook, a yellow Lab male, and Dual Ch., AFC Baron's Tule Tiger, Chesapeake male.

Two of the entrants had just turned nine. They were FC, AFC Francis Fishtail, and FC, AFC Sam Frizel of Glenspey that lasted through the ninth series. The youngest contender was AFC Guy's Bitterroot Lucky, not yet three—and he went right through the final test. Two others had just turned three. They were Polaris Luke, and Waccamaw's Tinker, a yellow Lab male that also fin-ished all series.

These were the dogs entered:

### Starters In Order of the Draw

| Order of Draw    Name, Color[1], Breed, Sex, Owner | Whelping Date | 1967 Series Complt'd | 1967 Amateur Points[2] | 1967 Amateur Starts | 1967 Amateur First |
|---|---|---|---|---|---|
| 1.  AFC Jilly Girl, L.F.<br>Owner: Frank W. Miller,<br>So. St. Paul, Minn. | 12-25-60 | 3 | 1 | 3 | 0 |
| 2.  Polaris Luke, L.M.<br>Owner: Francis W. Partridge,<br>Boise, Idaho | 4-14-64 | 5 | 13 | 6 | 2 |
| 3.  FC-AFC Frances Fishtail, L.F.<br>Owner: Richard H. Hecker,<br>Tucson, Ariz. | 6-5-56 | 3 | 2 | 9 | 0 |
| 4.  AFC-CFC Irwin's Toby, L.M.<br>Owner: Wm. J. Hutchinson,<br>Hamilton, Ontario, Canada | 1-15-58 | 1 | 11 | 5 | 1 |
| 5.  AFC Jingo Jo's Duckmaster,<br>L.M.<br>Owner: Hugh Adams,<br>Fair Oaks, Calif. | 4-20-62 | 2 | 16 | 16 | 3 |

| Order of Draw | Name, Color[1], Breed, Sex, Owner | Whelping Date | 1967 Series Complt'd | 1967 Amateur Points[2] | 1967 Amateur Starts | 1967 Amateur Firsts |
|---|---|---|---|---|---|---|
| 6. | FC-AFC Sir Mike of Orchardview, Y.L.M. Owner: Roger Vasselais, Remsenburg, L.I., N.Y. | 1-12-59 | 6 | 20 | 11 | 3 |
| 7. | AFC Col-Tam of Craignook, L.M. Owner: Mr. and Mrs. R.O. Bateman, Milwaukee, Wis. | 1-18-61 | 10 | 13½ | 6 | 2 |
| 8. | Waccamaw's Tinker, Y.L.M. Owner: William A. Chandler, Dickinson, Tex. | 1-24-64 | 10 | 11 | 10 | 2 |
| 9. | FC-AFC Ripp'n Ready, Gold. M. Owner: W. D. Connor, Andover, Mass. | 1-23-60 | 8 | 6 | 14 | 1 |
| 10. | Rowdy's Sean of the Corkies, L.M. Owner: S. C. Shea, Grosse Pointe Woods, Mich. | 6-29-63 | 3 | 2 | 12 | 0 |
| 11. | AFC Hoss of Palm Grove, L.M. Owner: George J. Gray, So. Daytona, Florida | 12-20-63 | 9 | 10½ | 14 | 2 |
| 12. | AFC Copper City Buck, L.M. Owner: Bob Sparks, Butte, Mont. | 8-5-60 | 5 | 0 | 0 | 0 |
| 13. | FC-AFC Mount Joy's Louistoo, Ches. M. Owner: E. C. Fleischmann, Sebastopol, Calif. | 11-24-57 | 2 | 9 | 8 | 1 |
| 14. | Gerry's Kaiwa of Rosamond, Gold. F. Owner: Geraldine Miller, Project City, Calif. | 1-20-62 | 3 | 5 | 12 | 0 |
| 15. | AFC Guy's Bitterroot Lucky, L.M. Owner: Guy P. Burnett, Missoula, Mont. | 8-12-64 | 10 | 16½ | 12 | 2 |
| 16. | Black Rocky, L.M. Owner: Roy M. Hutchinson, M.D., Fort Dodge, Iowa | 8-13-62 | 4 | 2 | 10 | 0 |
| 17. | NAFC-FC-CAFC-CNFC Captain of Lomac, L.M. Owner: Rudy R. Deering, West Vancouver, B.C., Canada | 5-24-59 | 7 | 8 | 5 | 1 |
| 18. | FC Jet's Target of Claymore, L.M. Owner: Mr. and Mrs. Bing Grunwald, Omaha, Nebr. | 1-14-62 | 2 | 5½ | 23 | 1 |

| Order of Draw | Name, Color[1], Breed, Sex, Owner | Whelping Date | 1967 Series Complt'd | 1967 Amateur Points[2] | 1967 Amateur Starts | 1967 Amateur Firsts |
|---|---|---|---|---|---|---|
| 19. | AFC Shamrock Acres Simmer Down, L.F. Owner: Jean and Jim Marth, Waukegan, Ill. | 5-10-61 | 7 | 11 | 13 | 1 |
| 20. | AFC Caesar of Swinomish, L.M. Owner: Gene H. Hill, Albany, Ore. | 12-5-58 | 9 | 6 | 6 | 1 |
| 21. | AFC Smoke Tail's Cricket, L.M. Owner: George D. Alt, Los Olivos, Calf. | 4-18-60 | 6 | 0 | 0 | 0 |
| 22. | FC-AFC Dairy Hill's Mike, L.M. Owner: Harold Mack, Jr., Hillsborough, Calif. | 9-21-57 | 10 | 17 | 16 | 2 |
| 23. | DUAL-AFC Baron's Tule Tiger, Ches. M. Owner: Mrs. Walter S. Heller, Sonoma, Calif. | 4-14-59 | 10 | 21 | 19 | 3 |
| 24. | FC-AFC Jetstone Muscles of Claymar, L.M. Owner: Claus and Margie D. Johnson, Lincoln, Nebr. | 1-14-62 | 6 | 9 | 10 | 1 |
| 25. | FC-AFC Tarblood of Absaraka, L.M. Owner: John A. Love, Jr. and Bruce W. Bridgford, Sheridan, Wyo. | 7-15-57 | 2 | 6½ | 14 | 1 |
| 26. | FC-AFC Butte Blue Moon, L.M. Owner: Mr. and Mrs. Bing Grunwald, Omaha, Nebr. | 6-2-63 | 8 | 22½ | 23 | 3 |
| 27. | AFC Golden Rocket's Missle, Gold.M. Owner: Bud Shearer, Tigard, Oregon | 9-29-61 | 2 | 12½ | 10 | 1 |
| 28. | FC-AFC Sir Knight Falcon, L.M. Owner: Perry E. and Zola R. Pound, Englewood, Colo. | 2-5-59 | 6 | 10 | 7 | 2 |
| 29. | Marelvan Mike of Twin Oaks, L.M. Owner: John F. Nash, Gates Mills, Ohio | 4-2-63 | 2 | 16 | 10 | 2 |
| 30. | FC-AFC Glengarven's Mik, L.M. Owner: Roger Vasselais, Remsenburg, L.I., N.Y. | 8-23-59 | 10 | 33½ | 28 | 5 |

| Order of Draw | Name, Color[1], Breed, Sex, Owner | Whelping Date | 1967 Series Complt'd | 1967 Amateur Points[2] | 1967 Amateur Starts | 1967 Amateur Firsts |
|---|---|---|---|---|---|---|
| 31. | FC-AFC Torque of Daingerfield, Y.L.M. Owner: Joan H. Watkins, Seattle, Wash. | 10-1-62 | 3 | 12½ | 15 | 1 |
| 32. | FC-AFC Lord Bomar, L.M. Owner: John A. Love, Jr., Sheridan, Wyo. | 1-6-61 | 10 | 15 | 14 | 1 |
| 33. | FC-AFC Stilrovin Savannah Gay, Gold.F. Owner: Mrs. Ann F. Walters, Council Bluffs, Iowa | 3-28-60 | 1 | 0 | 0 | 0 |
| 34. | FC-AFC Sand Gold Kim, L.F. Owner: Jerome D. Bernstein, Chicago, Ill. | 4-16-60 | 6 | 6½ | 8 | 0 |
| 35. | AFC Black "R" of Birch, L.M. Owner: Richard G. Gardner, M.D., Boise, Idaho | 8-1-59 | 6 | 6½ | 7 | 1 |
| 36. | Moll-Leo Cayenne, Gold.M. Owner: James D. Browning, Eugene, Oregon | 11-7-62 | 3 | ½ | 8 | 0 |
| 37. | AFC Rosehill's Little Dutch Boots, L.F. Owner: Michael R. Flannery, Solon, Ohio | 3-19-61 | 2 | 7½ | 15 | 1 |
| 38. | FC-AFC Super Chief, L.M. Owner: August Belmont, Syosset, New York | 6-27-62 | 10 | 53 | 21 | 8 |
| 39. | FC-AFC Sam Frizel of Glenspey, L.M. Owner: Mrs. Warner Atkins, Pinehurst, No. Carolina | 6-19-56 | 9 | 8½ | 6 | 0 |
| 40. | FC-AFC Carbon Marker, L.M. Owner: Mr. and Mrs. Ted Fajen, Jr., Milwaukee, Wis. | 8-27-60 | 5 | 3½ | 9 | 0 |
| 41. | Alamo Black Jack, L.M. Owner: Noxie M. Romano, Jr., Houston, Tex. | 3-12-62 | 6 | 1 | 9 | 0 |
| 42. | AFC Floodbay's Baron O'Glengarven, L.M. Owner: Austin B. Mason, Needham Heights, Mass. | 3-15-62 | 2 | 14½ | 12 | 2 |
| 43. | AFC Black Michael O'Shea, L.M. Owner: Frank L. Fletcher, M.D., Boise, Idaho | 7-7-61 | 2 | 3½ | 8 | 0 |
| 44. | FC-AFC Fisherman Bill of Delaware, L.M. Mr. and Mrs. Mahlon B. Wallace, Jr., St. Louis, Mo. | 6-13-60 | 3 | 11½ | 11 | 1 |

| Order of Draw | Name, Color[1], Breed, Sex, Owner | Whelping Date | 1967 Series Complt'd | 1967 Amateur Points[2] | 1967 Amateur Starts | 1967 Amateur Firsts |
|---|---|---|---|---|---|---|
| 45. | FC-AFC Samson's George of Glenspey, L.M. Owner: Mrs. Warner Atkins, Pinehurst, No. Carolina | 4-12-63 | 4 | 5 | 11 | 1 |
| 46. | AFC Duke of Teddy Bear, L.M. Owner: Charles J. Bierschied, Denver, Colo. | 5-31-61 | 4 | 0 | 0 | 0 |
| 47. | FC-AFC Dairy Hill's Night Watch, L.M. Owner: Andrieus A. Jones, Hillsborough, Calif. | 2-20-58 | 2 | 2 | 12 | 0 |
| 48. | FC-AFC Rill Shannon's Dark Del, L.F. Owner: Michael R. Flannery, Solon, Ohio | 10-24-60 | 3 | 31½ | 19 | 4 |
| 49. | Rim Rock Roscoe, L.M. Owner: Dr. and Mrs. Gene B. Starkloff, St. Louis, Mo. | 12-29-62 | 10 | 10 | 6 | 0 |
| 50. | FC-AFC Chesanoma's Kodiak, Ches.M. Owner: W. E. Peltzer, M.D., Salt Lake City, Utah | 10-4-59 | 1 | 6½ | 9 | 1 |
| 51. | FC-NAFC Rebel Chief of Heber, L.M. Owner: Gus and Virginia Rathert, Modesto, Calif. | 12-25-60 | 1 | 25 | 13 | 4 |
| 52. | FC-AFC Black Jet XVI, L.M. Owner: Richard S. Humphrey, Water Mill, N.Y. | 3-29-58 | 2 | 5 | 8 | 1 |
| 53. | AFC Bean Ball, L.F. Owner: Richard H. Hecker, Tucson, Ariz. | 4-18-60 | 2 | 12½ | 18 | 1 |
| 54. | NFC-AFC Ripco's V. C. Morgan, L.F. (Scratched) Owner: J. D. Ott, Seattle, Wash. | 10-29-59 | — | 5½ | 9 | 1 |
| 55. | AFC Columbine Loran, Y.L.M. Owner: Jack Hogue, Brighton, Colo. | 7-30-61 | 2 | 6½ | 9 | 1 |
| 56. | AFC Smoke Tail's Chico, L.M. Owner: Howard A. Jacobs, Rapid City, So. Dak. | 4-18-60 | 1 | 6 | 4 | 1 |
| 57. | FC-AFC Stonegate's Arrow, L.M. Owner: Mr. and Mrs. Bing Grunwald, Omaha, Nebr. | 6-22-59 | 3 | 14½ | 23 | 2 |
| 58. | FC-AFC Lucifer's Lady, L.F. Owner: Dr. R. L. Ellis, Redding, Calif. | 3-6-58 | 5 | 1 | 4 | 0 |

| Order of Draw | Name, Color[1], Breed, Sex, Owner | Whelping Date | 1967 Series Complt'd | 1967 Amateur Points[2] | 1967 Amateur Starts | 1967 Amateur Firsts |
|---|---|---|---|---|---|---|
| 59. | FC-AFC Grady's Shadee Ladee, L.F. Owner: W. K. Chilcott, Jr., Sequim, Wash. | 3-24-63 | 3 | 8½ | 14 | 1 |
| 60. | FC-AFC Flood Bay's Boomerang, L.M. Owner: Lewis S. Greenleaf, Jr., Greenwich, Conn. | 3-15-62 | 4 | 22 | 13 | 2 |
| 61. | AFC Gimp of Lakin, Y.L.M. Owner: Robert Sandahl, Des Moines, Iowa | 6-14-61 | 3 | 8 | 9 | 1 |

[1]Where a color is not indicated for a Labrador it can be presumed to be black. Golden Retrievers are, of course, presumed to be golden in color.
[2]Qualifications for the National Amateur Championship are computed on the "fiscal" year following the last previous trial. These are the figures for the calendar year of 1967.

### First Series—8:10 A.M. Wednesday, June 21
### 60 Starters—Dog No. 1 Ran First

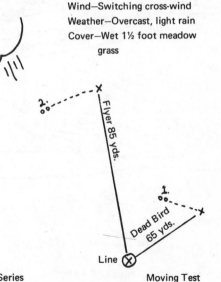

Wind—Switching cross-wind
Weather—Overcast, light rain
Cover—Wet 1½ foot meadow grass

Flyer 85 yds.

Dead Bird 65 yds.

Line

1st Series                    Moving Test

(For photograph, see Illustration 134.)

Dog Number 1 was put on the line at approximately 8:10 A.M. on Wednesday. This was a double land mark, the first of which was a dead bird thrown 65 yards to the right of the dog. The second was a flyer 85 yards straight out.

Scenting was average and many dogs had trouble. When this series ended at 1:00 P.M., five dogs—Numbers 4, 33, 50, 51 and 56—had been eliminated. One of them had won this championship two years earlier.

### Second Series—2:30 P.M. Wednesday, June 21
### 55 Starters—Dog No. 7 Ran First

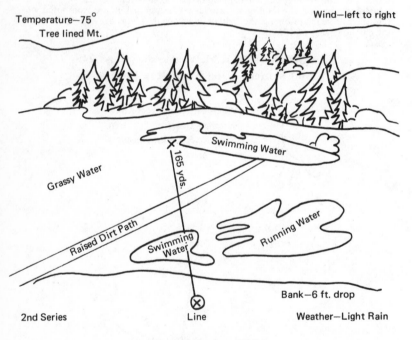

(See Illustration 135.)

Field down to 55 dogs. Number 7 started at 2:30 P.M. This was a cold land blind, a combination of land and water, 165 yards. The line to the blind was down a 6-foot bank, across a pot hole (swimming water), across a raised dirt path, and through grassy water. There was quite a bit of trailing and scent and very little wind. Handlers had to be on their toes in this series which ended at 6:10 P.M. Thirteen dogs were dropped after this test: Numbers 5, 13, 18, 25, 27, 29, 37, 42, 43, 47, 52, 53 and 55.

### Third Series—8 A.M. Thursday, June 22
### 42 Starters—Dog No. 12 Ran First

Temperature: A.M.–50° Overcast
Noon–75° Bright sunshine

(See Illustration 136.)

Forty-two dogs were back for this triple water mark which started at 8:00 A.M. It produced some spectacular work with the first mark a dead duck thrown 60 yards to the left of the dog, across a channel into sparse cover after two shots. The next mark was a shackled duck, 65 yards in front of the dog, but slightly to the left and toward the first bird. The last mark was a shot bird to the right of the dog and from the bank. It was 40 yards away. Guns retired on the first bird. Thirty dogs required handling. One dog switched. Eleven dogs, Numbers 1, 3, 10, 14, 31, 36, 44, 48, 57, 59 and 61, were dropped.

### Fourth Series—Thursday P.M., June 22
### 31 Starters—Dog No. 20 Ran First

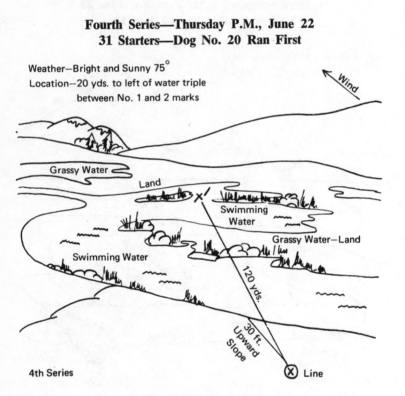

Weather—Bright and Sunny 75°
Location—20 yds. to left of water triple
          between No. 1 and 2 marks

Wind

Grassy Water

Land

X'

Swimming Water

Grassy Water—Land

Swimming Water

120 yds.

30 ft. Upward Slope

4th Series

(X) Line

(See Illustration 137.)

This was a cold water blind. Just over half of the starters were back. The line was down a sloping hill, 30 feet from swimming water, through the first and second marks of the third series, across another strip of swimming water to the floating, dead duck. The total distance was 120 yards. This test eliminated four more dogs, Numbers 16, 45, 46 and 60. Three-quarters of the dogs did well in this series—5 of them were brilliant.

### Fifth Series—8 A.M. Friday, June 23
### 27 Starters—Dog No. 26 Ran First

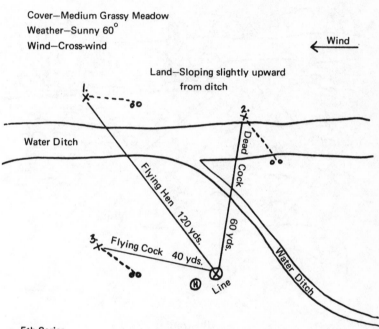

Cover—Medium Grassy Meadow
Weather—Sunny 60°
Wind—Cross-wind

Wind ←

Land—Sloping slightly upward
from ditch

Water Ditch

Flying Hen 120 yds.

Dead Cock

60 yds.

Flying Cock    40 yds.

Water Ditch

Line

**5th Series**

(See Illustration 138.)

This was a triple land mark with honoring. The first mark was a shot hen 120 yards ahead, just slightly to the left. The second was a dead bird, 60 yards from the line to the right. Each of these marks was over a water ditch. A shot rooster, 40 yards from the dog to the left, was the last mark. Four dogs, one of which broke while honoring, were dropped. They were Numbers 2, 12, 40 and 58.

## Sixth Series—12:30 P.M. Friday, June 23
## 23 Starters—Dog No. 35 Ran First

Weather—Warm, sunny 80°

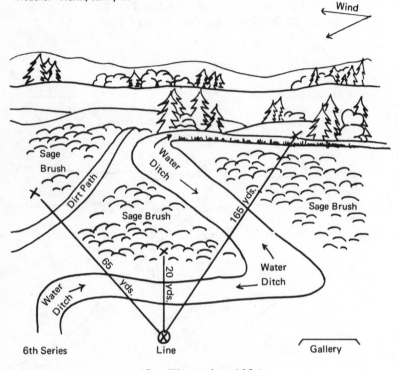

(See Illustration 139.)

For the 23 dogs back, the price of poker was starting to go up. For 7 of these the ante, as expressed in a demand for near faultless performances, was a bit too high. This was a triple land blind with the birds to be retrieved in order. There were many obstacles —a demanding test for dogs and handlers alike. The first blind was 20 yards straight out from the dog, down through a water ditch and into a pocket of sagebrush. The second blind was 65 yards out, to the left, across the water ditch and a dirt path and into some more sage. The third blind was 165 yards out, to the right. First a strip of water had to be crossed, then sage, then a widened water ditch, more sage and a narrow strip of water. With the wind mostly from the right, dogs taking the longer land route around the first two water obstacles were in danger of finding themselves upwind of the third bird. The 7 dogs dropped after this test were Numbers 6, 21, 24, 28, 34, 35, and 41.

### Seventh Series—3:30 P.M. Friday, June 23
### 16 Starters—Dog No. 9 Ran First

Weather—Sunny 75°

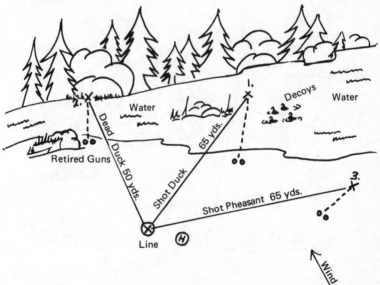

7th Series

(See Illustration 140.)

The weather was sunny, temperature about 75 degrees at 3:30 Friday afternoon for the 16 dogs carried over into this series. Number 9 was first to start this triple water mark with honoring. The line was 40 yards from the water's edge. The first mark was a shot duck, 65 yards out and in the water past decoys, just slightly to the right of the line. The second mark was a dead duck, 50 yards to the left of the dog, across a strip of water and on the far bank. The guns retired on this bird. The third mark was a shot pheasant on land, 65 yards to the right of the dog.

Work in this series was fairly consistent with three dogs handling. Two dogs, Numbers 17 and 19, were dropped at its conclusion. One was a former National Amateur Champion.

### Eighth Series—Saturday Morning, June 24
### 14 Starters—Dog No. 23 Ran First

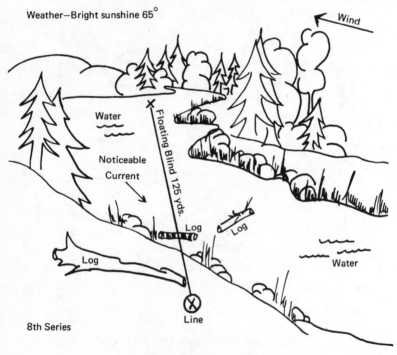

(See Illustration 141.)

This was Saturday morning, the beginning of the fourth day of the stake. The sun was bright and the temperature a comfortable 65 degrees, when the judges, starting with Number 23, began calling the dogs to the line. They now had the field down to a very workable 14 dogs. This was a 125-yard cold water, floating blind. The line was near the bottom of a very steep hill, 20 yards from the water's edge. The dogs had a very critical angle into the water. Among the many obstacles were a noticeable incoming current, logs, brush, inlets—and brush on the far shore that drew most of the dogs. A few tried the near shore. Two more starters were dropped, Numbers 9 and 26, leaving only a dozen contenders.

### Ninth Series—11:15 A.M. Saturday, June 24
### 12 Starters—Dog No. 49 Ran First

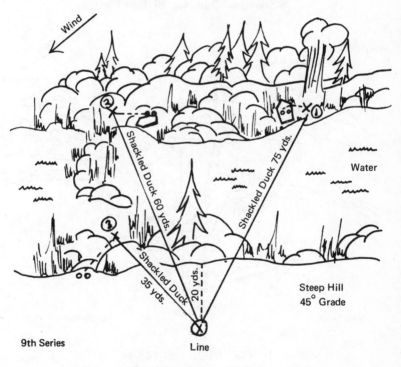

9th Series

(See Illustration 142.)

This was a triple water mark run from the top of a very steep hill, at 11:15 A.M. on Saturday. Number 49 was the first contender to meet its test. All birds were shackled ducks. The line was some 20 yards back from the water's edge. First bird was 75 yards from the line, about 30 degrees to the right across water and into heavy cover. The second was very much the same thing, but to the left and about 15 yards shorter. It was thrown from a boat. The third duck was about 35 yards out on the near shore—and about another 20 degrees to the left. This area was peppered with decoys.

Three dogs handled and three had long hunts on one or another of their birds. Three dogs missed the distinction of being finalists. They were numbers 11, 20 and 39.

### Tenth Series—3:30 P.M. Saturday, June 24
### 9 Starters—Dog No. 30 Ran First

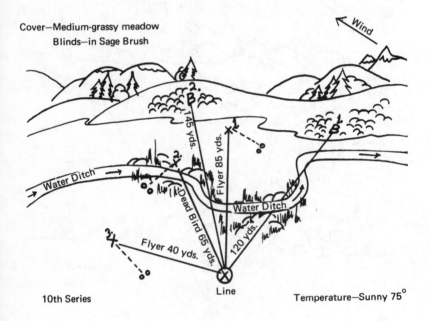

Cover—Medium-grassy meadow
Blinds—in Sage Brush

Wind

145 yds.

Flyer 85 yds.

Water Ditch

Dead Bird 65 yds.

Water Ditch

120 yds.

Flyer 40 yds.

Line

10th Series

Temperature—Sunny 75°

(See Illustration 143.)

The sun was still shining and the temperature had climbed to only 75 degrees when Number 30 was the first of the 9 finalists to be called to the line at 3:30 P.M. on Saturday. This was a triple land mark and a double land blind. For the trial that made a total of 17 marked retrieves and 8 blind retrieves.

A shot hen was the first mark, 85 yards straight out from the line and across a water ditch. The second mark was a dead hen, slightly to the dog's left and across the water ditch. A shot rooster, 40 yards immediately to the left of the dog, was the third mark. The first blind was 120 yards from the line, behind and beyond the first mark—and uphill in sagebrush. A straight line called for a double crossing of the water ditch. The second blind was 145 yards out between the lines of the first and second marks, again the water ditch to cross and then uphill into sagebrush. Five of the dogs handled on marks, but all of them completed the series—and all were warmly applauded on leaving the line.

It was no surprise to close followers of the trial when the judges named Field Champion and Amateur Field Champion Super Chief the 1967 National Amateur Retriever Champion. This five-year-old is owned and was handled by August Belmont, field trial veteran and Wall Street financier—and the newly elected president of the sponsoring National Amateur Retriever Club.

"Soupy" outclassed the field. He was brilliant throughout and won applause from the gallery for spectacular work on the fifth, sixth and ninth series. He faltered in the eighth and was handled sharply in the tenth (as were four others).

Soupy was given to the Belmonts by Wilbur Goode as a replace-ment for a well-bred pup he had sold them earlier. This pup, like Soupy sired by Paha Sapa Chief II, had not lived up to the promise of his breeding, and anxious to make the transaction a happy one for the Belmonts, Goode sent them as a gift an eight-week-old puppy he had taken from the breeder, Thomas H. Stein, as a stud fee puppy. (Soupy is out of Ironwood Cherokee Chica.)

California professional Rex Carr is credited by Belmont as be-ing the trainer of both himself and Soupy.* However, Carr doesn't handle Soupy. The Belmonts have done that since midway through

*The successful teamwork between Belmont and Soupy is eloquent il-lustration of the value of handler and dog having the same trainer. No one should ever send a dog to a trainer unless he plans to spend some time with that trainer himself—to learn the signals, the approach to and the peculiar-ities, with answers, of his own dog. Soupy and the Belmonts went on to top the 1967 scoring in *both* open and amateur stakes. Soupy set new records of 53 points *and* eight first places in Amateur All-Age stakes during that year. (He had 13 placements out of 21 starts.) The same year he also topped the point-winners in Open All-Age stakes with 32½ as a result of four more firsts plus five additional placements out of 20 starts, all under amateur handling. His total accomplishment was 242 amateur points and 212½ open.—H. D.

his derby year. But, each year during winter's off-season, Soupy goes back to Carr for additional polish.

Here are brief comments on the other finalists:

FC, AFC Sir Mike of Orchardview was finishing the Amateur Championship for the second year in a row. He was handled sharply on one mark in each of the first and tenth series and he had a below par blind in the second. The balance of his work was very consistent, with an unusually good line in the tough eighth series.

AFC Col-Tam of Craignook was handled on marks in the third, fifth and sixth series. He also stumbled a little in the eighth. The rest of his work was near-perfect, with brilliant performances in the fourth and ninth series.

AFC Guy's Bitterroot Lucky was the "baby" of the trial. He had a difficult time coming up with a missed mark in the third. His second, eighth and ninth series earned gallery applause. His sixth was simply spectacular. His work was unbelievable for a dog his age.

FC, AFC Dairy Hill's Mike was another that finished for the second year in a row. He had a rough blind in the second and a poor mark in the third series—and was handled on a mark in the tenth. The rest of his work was very consistent, with flashes of brilliance in the fourth and sixth series.

Dual Ch., AFC Baron's Tule Tiger was handled capably by his owner, Mrs. Walter S. Heller, but the Chesie had a shaky start in the first and second series. He had his best job in the fourth, and was one of the few dogs that did not handle on the marks in the tenth. This was his second straight finish.

FC, AFC Glengarven's Mik ran an exceptionally fine National Amateur. He was handled on marks in the third and fifth series. The rest of his work was near-perfect and always stylish and pleasing to watch.

FC, AFC Lord Bomar hurt himself some in the second series, but was in strong contention going into the eighth, where he slipped a bit more—and had to be handled on a mark in the ninth. His excellent recovery in the tenth was not enough.

Rim Rock Roscoe was hurt in the fourth and sixth series because of his lines to the blinds. He dropped further back in the eighth, where he had considerable trouble.

# 21

## The National Open
## Retriever Championship Trial—
## *By Perry E. and Zola R. Pound*

As reported in *Retriever Field Trial News*

THE ORIGINAL CONCEPT of the National [Open] Retriever Championship Trial was to take the top twenty dogs or so of the year, run them through at least ten series in three days, and then average *all* the work and pick the winner. An ordinary Open Stake is frequently decided after only four series. Some have had as few as three.

It is possible for an erratic and unreliable dog to have luck, and get through three or four tests without making a mistake. But a dog that can put together ten faultless performances on difficult tests over a three-day period has to have a good deal more than luck. However, those of us who initiated the National did not feel the winning dog would necessarily make no mistakes in ten series.

Theoretically, it would be possible for a dog to have one or even two poor series, yet do such spectacular work in all the rest that his *average* for the whole trial *might* surpass all his competition.

I've always hated to see good dogs thrown out of a trial after a poor first series. How many times, on the opening day of pheasant season, I've seen a dog do a perfectly miserable job on his first bird —just through overexcitement—then settle down and do beautiful work all the rest of the long day.

Now I prefer that dog to an uninspiring plodder who stumbles around at slow motion and manages to find all his birds, if that's *all* you can say for him.

That was the idea of the National trial. With a small entry of top dogs, and three full days to run them—dogs would be definitely eliminated only for the crimes of breaking or hard mouth. Judges at their discretion could even carry along a dog after a complete failure to find a bird. *This* trial was going to be different. Instead of an elimination contest, it was to be just the opposite. The judges were to keep *all* the dogs in, all through the trial, unless a dog broke, was clearly guilty of hard mouth, or had done such perfectly stinking work that he obviously was unworthy of the title of National Champion, no matter what he might do for the balance of the trial.

A careful reading of this chapter's account of the National by Perry E. and Zola R. Pound will show how the judges, insofar as possible with such a large entry, hewed closely to these founding concepts.

It is a two-headed problem, resulting from a wealth of extremely talented retrievers. Raise the eligibility requirements even further and you risk freezing out potential National Champions. Run all the eligibles through to the most logical possible conclusion and you will require more days than can be spared by judges, owners, handlers, trial officials, and galleryites. It is a rather delicious problem—the result of expanding retriever popularity and improvement.

Over the years, the qualifications for eligibility have been tightened time after time. At present they are: (a) the winner of the preceding National Championship stake, (b) the winner of the preceding National Amateur Championship stake, (c) those dogs winning a first place and a total of seven championship points in Open All-Age stakes during the preceding fiscal year.

Almost every qualifying dog is entered. Since 1961 the sponsoring National Retriever Club has allowed an extra, fifth, day to be used if necessary to bring its trial to a logical, rather than a hurried conclusion. In 1967 there were 59 qualified dogs from 4,370 starters in 126 stakes. Two entries were scratched and three qualified dogs were not entered. That left 54 starters. The trial was held on the McKellips Ranch in the Mohave Valley, just across the Colorado

River from Needles, California. The Southwestern site of the trial allowed longer hours of daylight in mid-November than would have been encountered at a more northerly locale. The judges were able to complete the minimum of ten tests during the scheduled four days for this reason, and also because of fine organization and the selection of good test sites in a relatively compact area.

relatively compact area.

Even under such near-perfect conditions for trial progress, it is obviously impossible for judges to carry most of the dogs through all of the tests. It is a pity, because, with the qualification so difficult, you can bet it is impossible for a sour dog to get into the trial. Every dog dropped is a good one.

It is still a wonderful trial, a spectacle of sparkling dog work to warm the heart of any hunting man.

Before we go on with the play-by-play report, here is the list of starters, in the order of the draw, showing the number of points won by each during 1967 only, and the number of series for which each dog was called back by the judges in the National trial. Open starts and Open firsts are also shown. Handlers, if other than the owner, are shown in parentheses.

Starters in Order of Draw, 1967 National Retriever Championship

| Order of Draw | Name, Color*, Breed, Sex, Owner and Handler | Whelping Date | 1967 Series Compl'td | 1967 Open Points | 1967 Open Starts | 1967 Open Firsts |
|---|---|---|---|---|---|---|
| 1. | FC-AFC Rill Shannon's Dark Del, L.F. Owner: Mr. Michael R. Flannery, Solon, Ohio | 10-24-60 | 8 | 14½ | 11 | 2 |
| 2. | '65 NFC Martens Little Smoky, L.M. Owner: Mr. John M. Olin, Alton, Ill. (T. W. Pershall) | 3-3-59 | 7+ | 15½ | 16 | 1 |
| 3. | FC Martens Scrubby Giant, L.M. Owner: Lawrence R. Martens, Sauk Rapids, Minn. | 5-19-60 | 6 | 10 | 12 | 2 |
| 4. | FC-AFC Shawnee Ace of Spades, L.M. Owner: Perle and Gladys Lewis, Pekin, Ill. (Perle Lewis) | 6-21-61 | 5 | 7½ | 14 | 1 |

*Where color of Labradors is not indicated it can be presumed to be black.

Starters in Order of Draw, 1967 National Retriever Championship

| Order of Draw | Name, Color*, Breed, Sex, Owner and Handler | Whelping Date | 1967 Series Compl'td | 1967 Open Points | 1967 Open Starts | 1967 Open Firsts |
|---|---|---|---|---|---|---|
| 5. | FC Misty of Otter Creek, L.F. Owner: Mr. Robert H. Rovelstad, Elgin, Ill. (Del Huffstutter) | 3-6-64 | 3 | 10½ | 16 | 1 |
| 6. | FC V-Jay's Black Paddle, L.M. Owner: Joseph and Verna Simpson, Danville, Calif. (Joe Simpson) | 6-25-60 | 10 | 11½ | 19 | 2 |
| 7. | FC-AFC Jet's Target of Clamar, L.M. Owner: Mr. and Mrs. Bing Grunwald, Omaha, Nebr. (D.L. Walters) | 1-14-62 | 5 | 9 | 26 | 1 |
| 8. | FC Anzac of Zenith, L.M. Owner: Carnation Farm Kennels, Carnation, Wash. (Doug Orr) | 3-24-63 | 2 | 9 | 23 | 1 |
| 9. | FC-AFC Jetstone Muscles of Claymar, L.M. Owner: Claus P. and Margie D. Johnson, Lincoln, Nebr. (Margie Johnson) | 1-14-62 | 7+ | 13½ | 11 | 2 |
| 10. | FC Michelle, L.F. Owner: Mr. Cyril R. Tobin, San Francisco, Calif. (Ed Minoggie) | 1-29-63 | 2+ | 27 | 22 | 3 |
| 11. | FC-'67 NAFC Super Chief, L.M. Owner: Mr. August Belmont, Syosset, L.I., N.Y. | 6-27-62 | 6 | 32½ | 20 | 4 |
| 12. | FC Ace of Garfield, L.M. Owner: Mr. John M. Olin, Alton, Ill. (T. W. Pershall) | 7-22-59 | 6 | 10½ | 15 | 1 |
| 13. | FC-AFC Torque of Daingerfield, Y.L.M. Owner: Joan H. Watkins, Seattle, Wash. | 12-27-61 | 5 | 17½ | 18 | 2 |
| 14. | FC Royal's Moose's Moe, L.M. Owner: Dr. Earl J. Clayton, Spencer, Iowa (C. J. Schomer) | 3-22-63 | 6 | 16 | 21 | 2 |
| 16. | FC Cimaroc Tang, L.M. Owner: Mr. Wm. K. Laughlin, Southampton, L.I., N.Y. (R. Staudinger) | 6-13-63 | 10 | 22½ | 25 | 3 |
| 17. | FC-AFC Butte Blue Moon, L.M. Owner: Mr. and Mrs. Bing Grunwald, Omaha, Nebr. (D. L. Walters) | 6-2-63 | 10 | 25 | 26 | 4 |

Starters in Order of Draw, 1967 National Retriever Championship

| Order of Draw | Name, Color*, Breed, Sex, Owner and Handler | Whelping Date | 1967 Series Compl'td | 1967 Open Points | 1967 Open Starts | 1967 Open Firsts |
|---|---|---|---|---|---|---|
| 18. | '66 NFC Whygin Cork's Coot, L.M. Owner: Mrs. George Murnane, Syosset, L.I., N.Y. (Joseph Riser) | 6-12-62 | 2+ | 25 | 22 | 3 |
| 19. | Tar Dessa Venture, L.M. Owner: Mr. John M. Preston, Hillsborough, Calif. (Ed Minoggie) | 10-28-63 | 10 | 9 | 27 | 1 |
| 20. | FC-AFC Sand Gold Kim, L.F. Owner: Mr. Jerome D. Bernstein, Chicago, Ill. (Owner: or T. Sorenson) | 4-16-60 | 5 | 9½ | 15 | 1 |
| 21. | AFC Flood Bay's Baron O'Glengarven, L.M. Owner: Mr. Austin B. Mason, Jr., Needham Heights, Mass. (J. Sweezey) | 3-15-62 | 10 | 15½ | 22 | 2 |
| 22. | FC Caliph Obsidian Hobii, L.M. Owner: Messrs. Jay G. Odell and Arthur Ebeling, Woodstock, Ill. (Ed Carey) | 2-1-63 | 2 | 10 | 24 | 2 |
| 23. | FC-AFC Guy's Bitterroot Lucky, L.M. Owner: Mr. Guy P. Burnett, Missoula, Mont. | 8-12-64 | 10 | 16 | 10 | 2 |
| 24. | FC Cinderfella of Stonesthrow, L.M. Owner: Mr. John M. Olin, Alton, Ill. (T. W. Pershall) | 2-28-62 | 4 | 12½ | 17 | 2 |
| 26. | Dual Ch. Happy Playboy, L.M. Owner: Mrs. Grace L. Lambert, Princeton, N.J. (Wm. Wunderlich) | 2-26-64 | 5 | 13½ | 18 | 1 |
| 27. | FC Brazil's Black Jaguar, L.M. Owner: Mrs. Richard S. Humphrey, Water Hill, L.I., N.Y. (R. Staudinger) | 9-19-61 | 7+ | 11 | 24 | 2 |
| 28. | FC Gun Thunder Oly, C.L.M. Owner Mrs. William P. Roth, San Mateo, Calif. (Ed Minoggie) | 12-17-61 | 5 | 15 | 8 | 3 |
| 29. | FC-AFC Lord Bomar, L.M. Owner: Mr. John A. Love, Jr., Sheridan, Wyo. (D. L. Walters) | 1-6-61 | 10 | 22 | 29 | 2 |
| 30. | FC Canuck Crest Cutty Sark, L.F. Owner: Mrs. Albert P. Loening, Southampton, L.I., N.Y. (Jay Sweezey) | 11-11-61 | 10 | 19 | 17 | 2 |

Starters in Order of Draw, 1967 National Retriever Championship

| Order of Draw | Name, Color*, Breed, Sex, Owner and Handler | Whelping Date | 1967 Series Compl'td | 1967 Open Points | 1967 Open Starts | 1967 Open Firsts |
|---|---|---|---|---|---|---|
| 31. | FC Del-Tone Buck, L.M. Owner: Mr. Albert M. Stoll, New Orleans, La. (Tom Sorenson) | 7-30-61 | 2+ | 12 | 18 | 2 |
| 32. | FC Mr. Mac's Billy Boy, L.M. Owner: Mr. George Murnane, Syosset, L.I., N.Y. (Joe Riser) | 3-11-63 | 10 | 11 | 22 | 1 |
| 33. | FC Choc of San Juan, C.L.M. Owner: Mr. Richard C. Cook, Renton, Wash. (Bert Carlson) | 1-3-63 | 5 | 16½ | 16 | 2 |
| 34. | FC Martens Stormy, L.M. Owner: Mr. John M. Olin, Alton, Ill. (T. W. Pershall) | 8-1-59 | 6 | 11 | 14 | 2 |
| 35. | FC-AFC Dessa Rae, L.F. Owner: Mr. A. Scharwat, Cheney, Wash. | 2-6-60 | 4 | 7 | 8 | 1 |
| 36. | FC Duxbak Scooter, L.M. Owner: Mrs. Grace M. Lambert, Princeton, N.J. (Wm. Wunderlich) | 4-11-58 | 5 | 8 | 17 | 1 |
| 37. | FC Cedar Haven Matador, L.M. Owner: Mrs. William P. Roth, San Mateo, Calif. (Ed Minoggie) | 10-20-63 | 7+ | 11½ | 31 | 2 |
| 38. | FC-AFC Fisherman Bill of Delaware, L.M. Owner: Mr. & Mrs. Mahlon B. Wallace, Jr., St. Louis, Mo. (T. Sorenson) | 6-13-60 | 6 | 23 | 17 | 2 |
| 39. | FC-AFC Flood Bay's Boomerang, L.M. Owner: Mr. Lewis S. Greenleaf, Jr., Greenwich, Conn. (Ray Staudinger) | 3-15-62 | 10 | 22 | 26 | 2 |
| 40. | FC-AFC Balsom's Mandy, L.F. Owner: Ben B. Baker, D.V.M., Eureka, Calif. | 10-21-58 | 4 | 10½ | 11 | 2 |
| 41. | FC-AFC Sazerac Mac, L.M. Owner: Julian J. Fertitta, M.D., Beaumont, Tex. (W. W. Higgs, Sr.) | 12-9-58 | 3 | 11 | 10 | 1 |
| 42. | FC-AFC Paha Sapa Warpath, L.M. Owner: Mr. and Mrs. Bing Grunwald, Omaha, Nebr. (D. L. Walters) | 12-2-60 | 2 | 12 | 24 | 1 |

Starters in Order of Draw, 1967 National Retriever Championship

| Order of Draw | Name, Color*, Breed, Sex, Owner and Handler | Whelping Date | 1967 Series Compl'td | 1967 Open Points | 1967 Open Starts | 1967 Open Firsts |
|---|---|---|---|---|---|---|
| 43. | FC-AFC Glengarven's Mik, L.M. Owner: Mr. Roger Vasselais, Remsenburg, L.I., N.Y. | 8-23-59 | 3 | 15½ | 28 | 1 |
| 44. | FC-'65 NAFC Rebel Chief of Heber, L.M. Owner: Gus and Virginia Rathert, Modesto, Calif. (Gus Rathert) | 12-25-60 | 10 | 21½ | 14 | 2 |
| 45. | I Love Lucy of Audlon, L.F. Owner: Mr. Tim Treadwell III, Memphis, Tenn. (Tom Sorenson) | 5-22-63 | 3 | 8 | 23 | 1 |
| 46. | FC Nethercroft Nemo of Nascopie, L.M. Owner: Mrs. Grace L. Lambert, Princeton, N.J. (Wm. Wunderlich) | 3-10-62 | 0+ | 19½ | 15 | 3 |
| 47. | DUAL-AFC Baron's Tule Tiger, Ches.M. Owner: Mrs. Walter S. Heller, Sonoma, Calif. | 4-14-59 | 4 | 19½ | 20 | 2 |
| 48. | FC Medlin's Otto of Toothache, L.M. Owner: C. Truman Clem, D.D.S., Lewisville, Tex. (Floyd Hayes) | 10-7-62 | 3 | 7½ | 22 | 1 |
| 49. | FC-AFC Cougar's Rocket, L.M. Owner: Mr. James L. Csaey, Palo Alto, Calif. | 2-7-61 | 1 | 10½ | 9 | 2 |
| 50. | FC Sheba's Westmoor Contessa, L.F. Owner: Mrs. S. G. B. Tennant, Houston, Tex. (W. W. Higgs, Sr.) | 2-16-63 | 8 | 8½ | 12 | 1 |
| 51. | FC-AFC Stonegate's Arrow, L.M. Owner: Mr. and Mrs. Bing Grunwald, Omaha, Nebr. (D. L. Walters) | 6-22-59 | 6 | 17½ | 26 | 1 |
| 52. | FC-'66 NAFC-'66 CNFC-CAFC Captain of Lomac, L.M. Owner: Mr. Rudy R. Deering, West Vancouver, B.C., Canada | 5-25-59 | 3 | 10 | 7 | 2 |
| 53. | FC Double Play of Audlon, L.M. Owner: Mrs. Henry G. Keeler, Jr., Clayton, Mo. (Tom Sorenson) | 6-23-61 | 3 | 10 | 23 | 1 |

Starters in Order of Draw, 1967 National Retriever Championship

| Order of Draw | Name, Color*, Breed, Sex, Owner and Handler | Whelping Date | 1967 Series Compl'td | 1967 Open Points | 1967 Open Starts | 1967 Open Firsts |
|---|---|---|---|---|---|---|
| 54. | FC-AFC Tarblood of Absaraka, L.M. Owner: Mr. John A. Love, Jr., Sheridan, Wyo. (Ray Olson) | 7-15-57 | 2+ | 17½ | 28 | 1 |
| 55. | FC-AFC Grady's Shadee Ladee, L.F. Owner: Mr. William K. Chilcott, Jr., Sequim, Wash. | 3-24-63 | 3 | 12 | 14 | 1 |
| 56. | FC-AFC Hoss of Palm Grove, L.M. Owner: Mr. George J. Gray, South Daytona, Fla. | 12-20-63 | 6 | 12 | 24 | 1 |

Of the 56 entries, 44 were males and 12 females. Both scratches were females—the result of normal risks in campaigning that sex. There were two chocolate Lab males, one yellow Lab male, and one Chesapeake Bay male. Owners, including three ladies, handled 18 of the starters. It was the first trial in many years—if ever— without a Golden Retriever competing.

The winner was FC, AFC Butte Blue Moon, a four-year-old black Labrador by Beavercrest Storm Cloud out of Mascushla of Rockmont. He is owned by field-trial stalwarts Bing and Brownie Grunwald of Omaha, Nebraska. Trained and handled by D. L. Walters, he was the youngest dog running in this championship in 1966 and has come on very fast since then. At this trial, he demonstrated exceptional ability on difficult marking and handling tests.

1967 was a good year for Moon. The first week in March he completed his Amateur Field Championship at the Lone Star trial when he was handled to first in the Open and second in the Amateur by Mrs. Grunwald. His Open title was not completed until seven weeks before this victory in the National.

The Grunwald-Walters combination had a first National Retriever Champion in 1962, when their Big Stone Hope won it. In 1958 the Grunwalds' Boley's Tar Baby was National Amateur Champion and their Nodak Cindy was 1957's National Derby Champion.

The trial site in the Mohave Valley offers numerous water sites and a wide variety of cover, plus easy accessibility for handlers, workers, and gallery. The grounds offered a considerable variety of test sites in a rather compact area.

Weather during the trial was clear with morning temperatures of 50 degrees rising to 80 during the afternoon. There was virtually no wind which, while it made for equal conditions for all dogs, had the disadvantage of denying to the judges any real opportunity of testing the dogs' noses—and their aptitude in using them.

Since one-fourth of the Ranch was divided in 1961, nearly a score of retriever owners have bought property because of the excellent dog-training facilities the area affords.

The judges, Harold Mack, Jr., of Hillsborough, California; A. Nelson Sills of Newark, Delaware; and Gene B. Starkloff of St. Louis, Missouri, represented, as required, the three zones of the first 48 States. They spent long hours for several days before the trial in going over the grounds, requesting certain physical changes of land and water cover, and planning a variety of tests which would insure a fair, impartial trial. All who know these three men respect them for their knowledge of dogs and their ability to set tests which will tell them what they need to know. They were congenial and cooperative throughout and never once required anything which was extremely difficult mechanically.

Here's a description of the tests and a log of the trial's progress:

### First Series—8 A.M. Wednesday, November 15
### 54 Starters—Dog No. 1 Started

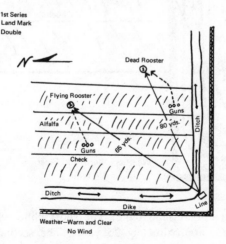

(See Illustration 144.)

There were 56 entries, 2 scratches, 54 starters at 8:00 A.M. on Wednesday, November 15, 1967. This was a double land mark. The first bird was a dead rooster on the right, angled back from the guns, approximately 80 yards from the line. The second bird was a flying rooster on the left, shot to fall approximately 65 yards from the line. Both birds were in alfalfa. From the line they were across a ditch and across several irrigation checks. These checks proved quite perplexing to some dogs. There was practically no wind. Number 46 broke. Number 49 was dropped.

### Second Series—Wednesday Afternoon, November 15
### 52 Starters—Dog No. 6 Started

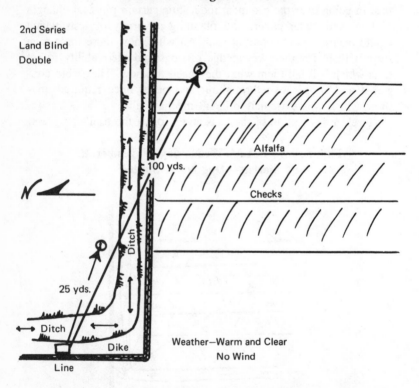

This was a double land blind. The short blind was across an irrigation ditch, approximately 25 yards. The second blind. 100 yards, was at a sharp angle to the first blind. Dogs had to cross an irrigation ditch twice, then through alfalfa and several irrigation checks. Again, there was practically no wind. Numbers 8, 22 and 42 were dropped.

### Third Series—7 A.M. Thursday, November 16
### 49 Starters—Dog No. 12 Started

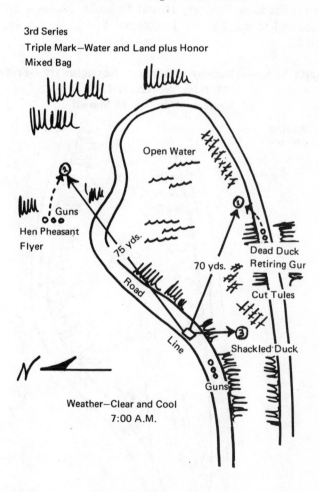

3rd Series
Triple Mark—Water and Land plus Honor
Mixed Bag

Open Water

Guns
Hen Pheasant
Flyer

75 yds.

Road

Line

70 yds.

Dead Duck
Retiring Gun

Cut Tules

Shackled Duck

Guns

N

Weather—Clear and Cool
7:00 A.M.

(See Illustration 145.)

A mixed bag triple, water and land, for this test. There was one shot pheasant, a dead duck, and a shackled duck, plus honoring. First the dead duck was thrown 70 yards, across a small lake to fall in cut tules. The second bird was a flying hen pheasant on the left, shot to fall approximately 75 yards into a sandy area with no cover—and no wind. The third bird was the shackled duck, thrown from the proximity of the line to fall in open water between the cut tules. Numbers 18 and 54 broke. Numbers 10 and 31 were picked up. The judges dropped 5, 41, 43, 45, 48, 52, 53 and 55.

### Fourth Series—Thursday Afternoon, November 16—Friday Morning, November 17.
### 37 Starters—Dog No. 19 Started

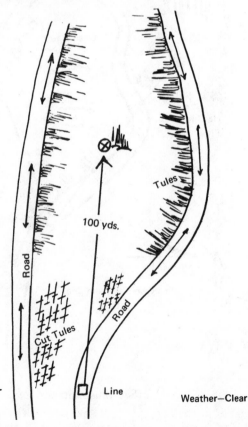

4th Series
Water Blind
"Cold"

Tules

100 yds.

Road

Road

Cut Tules

N

Line

Weather—Clear

This was a cold water blind. The line was approximately 30 yards from the water. There was a very sharp angle of entry. The blind was a floating, anchored duck about 100 yards down a narrow slot between the tules. The judges were unable to complete this series on Thursday afternoon, and six dogs were carried over to Friday morning with a starting time of 6:45. Numbers 24, 35, 40 and 47 were dropped.

### Fifth Series—8 A.M. Friday, November 17
### 33 Starters—Dog No. 27 Started

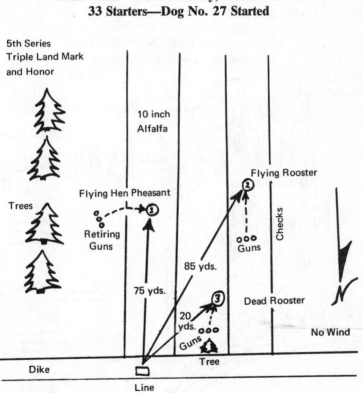

5th Series
Triple Land Mark
and Honor

10 inch Alfalfa

Flying Rooster

Flying Hen Pheasant

Trees

Retiring Guns

Checks

Guns

85 yds.

75 yds.

Dead Rooster

20 yds. Guns

No Wind

N

Guns

Tree

Dike

Line

Weather—Clear
8:00 A.M.

(See Illustrations 146–147.)

Thirty-three dogs back to face this triple land mark and honor. Number 27 was first off at 8:00 A.M. Friday. The line was on a dike and perpendicular to rows of irrigation checks which laced an alfalfa field. The left-hand bird was a flying hen at 75 yards, flighted 45 degrees back from the guns. These guns retired. The second bird, a flying rooster, on the right at 80 to 90 yards, flighted straight down the checks to fall two checks from the line. The third bird, on the right, was a dead rooster at 20 to 25 yards—two popper shots fired. Again, there was practically no wind. This series brought elimination to eight contenders, Numbers 4, 7, 13, 20, 26, 28, 33 and 36.

### Sixth Series—Friday, November 17
### 25 Starters—Dog No. 37 Started

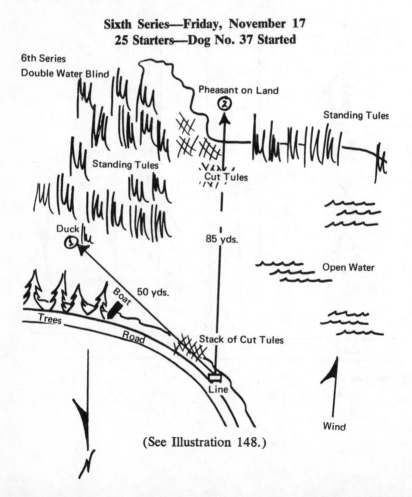

(See Illustration 148.)

Twenty-five dogs were still in contention as this double water blind began. Number 37 led off. The short blind was a dead duck on the left at the edge of the tules, approximately 40 to 50 yards. The long blind was a dead pheasant planted across the lake through a slot of tules up on the land—a total distance of approximately 85 yards. Prior to the beginning of each dog's test, the gunner fired two shots, just before the handler's number was called. It was required that the short blind be picked up first—and the handler was on his own for the second blind. Nearly one-third of the field departed after this one. Dropped were Numbers 3, 11, 12, 14, 34, 38, 51 and 56.

### Seventh Series—Friday Afternoon, November 17
### 17 Starters—Dog No. 2 Started

7th Series
Land Blind
   and
Diversion Bird

Salt Cedar Trees

Light Cover

Dead Hen Pheasant

Pile of
Dead Brush

150 yds.

Guns

50 yds.

Gravel
Draw

Ridge

Line

Road

N

Weather—Clear

No Wind

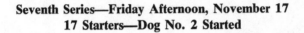

This was to be the last test of a very busy Friday. The judges had reduced the field to a workable 17 dogs—and they started this test with Number 2. This was a land blind with a diversion through a gravel draw. The diversion was a dead pheasant thrown to the left at about a 45-degree angle approximately 50 yards out. The blind was 150 yards through the gravel draw, past a pile of dead brush on a hillside on the opposite side of the draw. Still there was no wind and the situation continued to favor those dogs that took their directions very kindly and accurately. All dogs were called back.

### Eighth Series—8 A.M. Saturday, November 18
### 17 Starters—Dog No. 21 Started

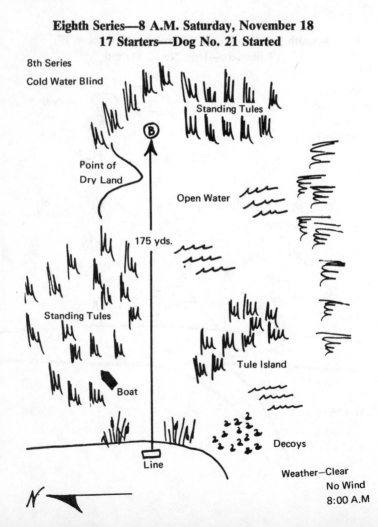

8th Series

Cold Water Blind

Standing Tules

Point of
Dry Land

Open Water

175 yds.

Standing Tules

Tule Island

Boat

Line

Decoys

Weather—Clear
No Wind
8:00 A.M

N

It appeared to all that this was to be the final day of reckoning. This was a cold water blind, 175 yards up a slot through the tules, past a diversion boat 20 yards on the left, two tule points on the left, a bare land point on the left—on the right a tule island. Still there was no wind—and a good nose didn't help much. Numbers 2, 9, 27 and 37 failed to complete and were picked up. In their final cut the judges dropped Numbers 1 and 50.

### Ninth Series—Saturday, November 18
### 11 Starters—Dog No. 39 Started

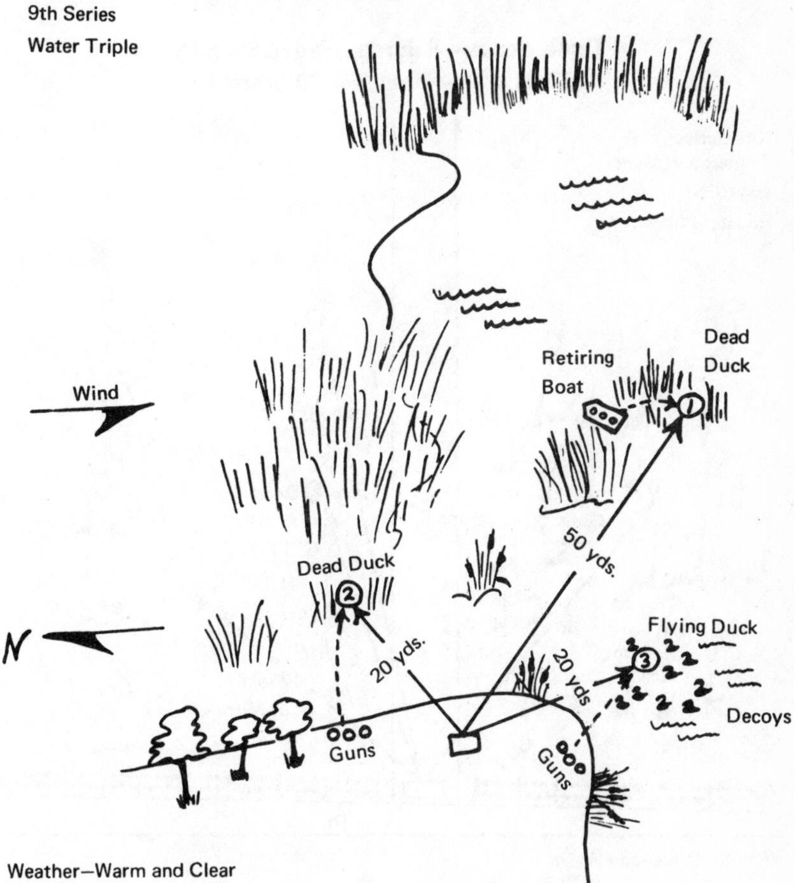

9th Series
Water Triple

Wind

N

Retiring Boat

Dead Duck

Dead Duck

50 yds.

Flying Duck

20 yds.

20 yds.

Guns

Guns

Decoys

Weather—Warm and Clear
Very Light Wind

Eleven dogs back for this water triple in the same area as the previous test. First called to the line was Number 39. A dead duck was thrown from the boat at the tule island. Another dead duck was thrown from the left on the shore and to land in standing and cut tules. A live duck was shot from the right to land in the decoys. The boat retired in behind the tules on the first bird. There was a very slight wind from left to right. The heavy cut tules made this a very "gutty" test as it was difficult to dig the birds out. Several dogs handled—but all were called back for the final scheduled test.

### Tenth Series—Saturday, November 18
### 11 Starters—Dog No. 23 Started

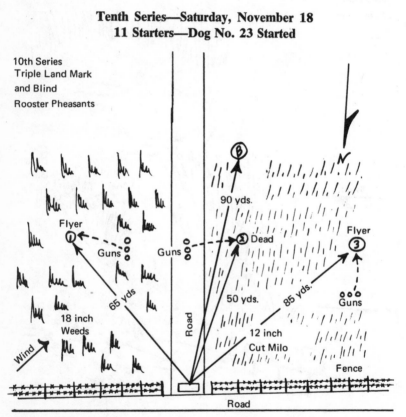

10th Series
Triple Land Mark
and Blind
Rooster Pheasants

Flyer ①

Guns

Guns

Flyer ③

② Dead

90 yds.

65 yds.

50 yds.

85 yds.

Guns

18 inch
Weeds

Wind

Road

12 inch
Cut Milo

Fence

Road

Weather—Clear and Warm

(See Illustration 149.)

Number 23 was first called for this triple land mark and blind. All three sets of guns in a row. The bird on the left was shot flighted to the left, to fall in weed cover approximately 18 inches high. The second bird was a dead pheasant thrown from a set of guns on a road straight away from the line. It was thrown to the right to fall about 50 yards from the line in 12-inch cut milo. The third bird was a flyer on the right about 45 degrees, flighted straight away from the guns and approximately 85 yards from the line. It was also dropped into 12-inch cut milo. The blind was at 90 yards, almost on a line with the second fall, in the cut milo. There was very little wind, quartering from left to right.

Here, as reflected in their notes, is the way the judges evaluated the 11 finalists:

FC, AFC Butte Blue Moon's first four series proved water and land marking and handling ability. He was hurt in the fifth by a poor mark, although he was not handled. The sixth, seventh, and eighth series were demanding and he showed control in difficult water and land blinds. His ninth series was perfect, and he entered the tenth one of the top dogs in strong contention and finished with a perfect job of marking and handling.

FC V-Jay's Black Paddle was hurt in the first series, came back strong. He had some trouble with the long portion of the double blind in the sixth, also hurt in the demanding blind in the eighth, but finished strong.

Tar Dessa Venture had consistently nice work except for a poor bird in the first series, and trouble with the long blind in the sixth. Also some trouble in the seventh series, but finished strong. He had sensational fourth and eighth series. Lined the cold water blind in the fourth series, and hand only two handles in the eighth series water blind.

AFC Flood Bay's Baron O'Glengarven's first five series were consistently good, but he had to be handled into the water on the left-hand blind in the sixth. He was hurt in the demanding long water blind in the eighth, and ended with two near-perfect series.

FC, AFC Guy's Bitterroot Lucky* was the youngest dog in the National Open—just as he was in the National Amateur. And, he made the finals in both 1967 championships. Handles in the fifth and again in the ninth were his major problems. He had a breath-taking land blind in the seventh series.

*1969 Nat. Amateur Champion.

FC Cimaroc Tang had a weak fourth series, was somewhat hurt in the fifth and sixth. From then on he had excellent work, including a fine water blind in the eighth series.

FC, AFC Lord Bomar was consistent with near-perfect work except for trouble on the key bird in the fifth series—and again on the last marked bird in the tenth series.

FC Canuck Crest Cutty Sark is a fast, stylish female with a beautiful water entry. She was hurt in the fifth when she failed to mark the last bird down at approximately 30 yards, overshot, and drifted into the long flyer, then was handled. She was a strong contender at the finish.

Mr. Mac's Billy Boy had three good series, then was hurt on the cold water blind in the fourth. He went out of control on the final blind in the tenth series. Otherwise he had consistently good work.

FC, AFC Flood Bay's Boomerang had consistently fine work. He was somewhat hurt in the long water blind of the sixth, but entered the tenth as one of the top dogs. Unfortunately for him, he did not exhibit good control in the final blind of the tenth.

1965 Nat'l. Amateur Field Ch., FC Rebel Chief of Heber finished with much good work, but he was hurt in the second and again in the seventh. He was one of two dogs with sensational eighth series water blinds.

# 22

## The Wheels in a Judge's Head

NEWCOMERS TO THE trials often wonder just what the judges are writing in those mysterious notebooks—and how they compare and evaluate and score the work of the different dogs. There are different methods of scoring, but all depend on the men who use them, and all seem to arrive at about the same result.

### METHODS OF SCORING AND KEEPING NOTES

Some judges have elaborate score sheets in their notebooks, and on each performance they manage to check off a detailed list of items such as: manners, marking, memory, attention, sagacity, control, steadiness, nose, delivery, courage, perseverance, speed, style, etc. I tried something like this once, but found I was not nimble enough to keep up with it. I was so wrapped up in my bookkeeping work I had no time to watch the dogs.

I think the majority of experienced judges now use a much easier and simpler system. As each dog works, a running diagram is drawn, showing just where he went in relation to the falls. This can be done by simply moving your pencil while watching the dog. This is then supplemented by a few very brief notes—just enough to recall the entire performance later. A single grade, or score, is then jotted down for the overall performance for that series. Some use A-plus for perfect, and grade down with A, B-plus, B, C-plus, etc. Others prefer 10, 9-plus, 9, 8-plus, etc.

A few men with whom I've judged give a separate grade or score for each bird, but in my opinion this is a needless complication. In a double-retrieve marking test, for instance, the important

227

thing is whether a dog remembers the *second* bird for which he is sent, and his performance on that one should count much more heavily than on the first one.

I use the 10-for-perfect method, giving a single score for each entire test. At any stage of the trial you can quickly total the scores of each dog, and get a *rough* idea of how they stand. This is often most useful when the judges are pressed for time, and must quickly decide whether another series is needed, or whether it is possible to place the dogs fairly without seeing further work and without resorting to a lot of hair-splitting on minor faults. If there are at least four top dogs whose total scores are well separated, you're reasonably safe to stop the trial. If several are very close, it's best to get in another series if this can possibly be done before dark.

But let me say right here that after the stake is over, careful judges *never* award the placings just on the basis of the total scores. The performances in each series of every dog which finished the trial are reviewed, discussed, and compared. Scores of one or more judges are sometimes then revised, to make them fair on a *comparative* basis.

In a long-drawn-out series you sometimes discover your scoring has become more lenient, or perhaps more severe, as time dragged on. I try to keep checking this during a series, leafing back through my book to compare what I gave previous performances with that of the current dog. But when all the notebook pages are spread out before you, you sometimes find you have slipped and given a bit higher grade to a dog whose actual work was slightly inferior to that of another. This always comes out in the final discussion, if sufficient time is given to it. On the whole, however, it is surprising how closely the offhand scores given in each series by two or three different judges usually agree with each other.

I am reproducing here a fairly typical page from my notebook. (See page 230.) There is one such looseleaf page for each dog, with room for three series on each side. Dogs are identified and judged only by number.

Offhand this looks like the doodlings of a diseased mind, I grant you. But it makes sense to me. It clearly recalls to my mind, even now, every detail of that dog's performances, in the first three series of the Open at a trial I judged some years ago.

The first series was on land, a marking test (M). In the diagram, X marks position from which dog was sent. The arrow shows wind direction. The circle labeled (1) is the first fall, a shot pheasant, approximately 100 yards. The circle labeled (2), on the right, is a short diversion bird, a fall of about 40 yards.

The diagram, plus the brief notes on the right side of the page, tell me something like this:

On the short bird (2) the dog had a perfect mark, hit it right on the nose. Did a fast, stylish job. There was nothing wrong with his pickup, delivery, or anything else, or mention would have been made of it in the notes. But of course this was the last fall, and merely a short diversion bird. An Open All-Age dog *should* do perfect work on it. The real test here is what he does on the other.

Not so good. He overran it quite badly on the upwind side. Then showed poor memory, because instead of correcting and hunting back to the downwind side of (1), he hunted much too much ground too far out and too far to the right. Then he hunted back almost to the second fall (the one he had already retrieved).

At this point the handler whistled, and handled him twice; he then got the bird quickly, but the main damage had been done. He had badly flunked his marking and memory test. However, he was a "goin' dog," an aggressive, hunting fool. Otherwise he might have drawn an even lower score than 4 on the series.

The second series was in water, a marking and memory test (M). From a point of land, the first duck was thrown and shot to fall out in a saltwater cover, 150 yards from the dog. Then two dead ducks were thrown to land among the decoys, as short diversion birds. After retrieving them, many of the dogs had trouble remembering the long first bird, and needed much help from their handlers.

But not this dog! He had barely stayed in after that poor first series, but now he pulled himself right back into the trial. He hit the water with a great splash, and did a perfect job on the two short birds. Then, with no hesitation, he hit the water once more, and with great enthusiasm. He never even looked back at his handler for encouragement, but swam strongly, straight out to the far bird, showing a perfect memory this time. He made the test look easy and was the first dog so far in this series to do a perfect job and receive the rare mark of 10.

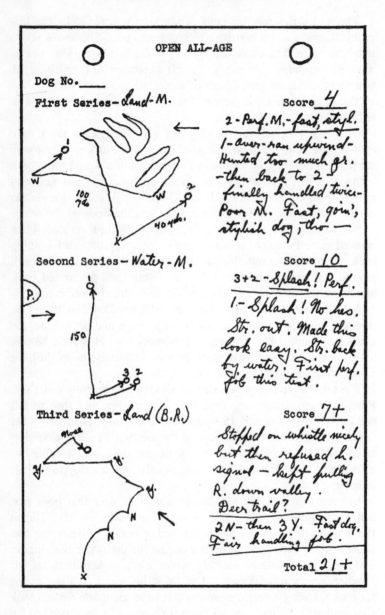

OPEN ALL-AGE

Dog No.____

First Series—Land- M.                    Score _4_

2 - Perf. M.- fast, styl.

1- over-ran upwind-
Hunted too much gr.
-then back to 2 !
finally handled twice-
Poor M. Fast, goin',
stylish dog, tho —

W

100
7%

W

2

40 yds.

X

Second Series — Water - M.              Score _10_

3+2 - Splash! Perf.

1.- Splash! No hes.
Str. out. Made this
look easy. Str. back
by water! First perf.
job this test.

P.

1

150

3  2

X

Third Series—Land (B.R.)                Score _7+_

Stopped on whistle nicely
but then refused h.
signal — kept pulling
R. down valley.
Deer trail?

2 N- then 3 Y. Fast dog.
Fair handling job.

Nose

Y.

Y.

Y.

N

N

X                                       Total _21+_

The third series, on land, was a blind retrieve (B.R.). The dogs worked from a hillside, across a valley, to a dead pheasant that had been dropped from a jeep about halfway up the hill on the other side. Distance, about 200 yards. The cover was very low, stunted scrub oak. Dogs could be seen at all times, and could not see their handlers. But they could not sail out on a line to the bird, being thrown off by necessary detours around dense patches of the scrub oak. The whole area was also full of fresh deer track and sign, the tempting scent of which apparently pulled many dogs off down the valley to the right. Every dog was obliged to show the judges how well he responded to his handler's directions.

The diagram and notes on our hero show that he quickly swung off the line, to the right, but stopped nicely on the whistle. He started to take the hand signal to the left, but stubbornly swung back to the right. Stopped again, he did the same thing. Then on the third try, he took the left signal, stayed with it for a while. Took two more hand signals perfectly, winded the bird, and completed. He obeyed the whistle each time it was blown. But on the hand signals he replied with two "noes" (N) and then three "yeses" (Y). He was fast, and did a fairly quick job of getting his bird. I called it a fair handling performance, and gave him a score of 7-plus.

Well, that's enough, I think, to give a rough idea of how many judges score and keep notes. Some might score a point or so higher than I did on the first and third series described above, and some a bit lower. *But the relation of the scores to all the other dogs in the series would be about the same.*

Watching and scoring the work is easy, if the tests pan out as they are supposed to. By far the hardest part of the judging job is planning the tests, and trying to avoid unpleasant surprises. For when a series is once started, you must go through with it, no matter how it pains you. You can't call it off and do something else after the first dog has run.

## PLANNING THE TESTS

A man judging a retriever trial is—or at least should be—looking for exactly the same sort of work he would like to see his own dog do, from the duck blind, or in the field. However, there is one important limitation in the trials that he must constantly remember.

Retrievers perform some spectacular and astonishing feats in the hunting field, but many of these don't make practical tests in a trial. Unless a test can be controlled so that each dog is given approximately the same job to do, it is useless for a trial competition.

For instance, one of the greatest values of a retriever is in tracking down, catching, and bringing to bag a strong running crippled pheasant. Nobody in his right mind would argue that. Yet I, at least, have never figured out a way to test competing dogs on cripples, and do it fairly for all dogs. A man who has judged trials and should know better actually made the serious proposal that every open all-age stake should include at least one series on running pheasant. He suggested the birds be brailed so they can't fly, a bit of fresh blood smeared on their legs to give them blood scent, then tossed in cover as a shot is fired.

I would be all for this test if there were any way to get these unpredictable cock pheasant to cooperate. But the first one might land running like a jack rabbit and be halfway out of the county in a very few seconds, and give a dog a really rough job of trailing. The next might crawl into a clump of dense cover, sit tight, and be picked up practically where he fell. Now if you were judging, how would you compare the work of two dogs doing such different jobs? It isn't fair to dog Number 2 to penalize him because he had only a simple, marked retrieve to do, if he did it well. You have no way of knowing what he would have done if given the same opportunity as dog Number 1.

A few people in the sport sometimes sneer at my "phobia" for having equal tests for all dogs. But these are usually not the people who have done much training and handling themselves.

If you have ever had a dog of your own knocked out of a trial by an unfair and avoidable "break of the game," you're inclined to develop a rabid sympathy for the dogs and their handlers—and to think it's important to give each dog the same opportunity. That's why experienced amateur handlers make the best and fairest judges.

Of course the top professional handlers would be splendid judges —but it would be unfair to ask them to judge. AKC rules now require that only experienced amateurs judge—and that if one is rather new his partner must be well experienced. No *active* professional is ever asked to judge a licensed trial.

No matter how much experience he's had, a man often yearns for a crystal ball when he's trying to guess right in setting up a test.

On a given day, nobody knows how scenting conditions will be until after they've seen a few dogs work. When dogs can easily wind a bird from a distance of 25 or 30 yards, they often will make two long falls in the heaviest cover look almost too simple to bother with. But if scenting conditions should be nil, and a dog must stumble on a bird to find it, the same falls may cause many top dogs to fail miserably.

Sometimes scenting is fine in one field, and you are amazed to find it very poor in another, later in the day. This may be due to catnip or some other weed hidden in the cover, which gives off a strong odor. But sometimes when this happens, nobody has the slightest notion as to the cause.

Another judge's headache is the matter of wind. If in the middle of a series the wind dies entirely, or if its direction changes, the entire test is different for the later dogs. Good judges do their best to compensate for this, by shortening falls or changing direction of working the dogs, when the terrain and other factors will permit.

Sometimes on an overcast morning a series is started, and before it is over the clouds clear away. Then the remaining dogs may have to mark their falls directly against a blinding sun.

Tests occasionally backfire on the most careful and experienced judges, for no apparent reason. They may plan something which should be perfectly simple for Open All-Age dogs, yet have dog after dog go haywire and fail completely.

The judge's worst nightmare is having a test boomerang so badly that he loses *all* the dogs in the first series, or any series for that matter, of any stake. Even with a huge entry and being pressed for time, I believe any conscientious judge would hate to lose as many as half the dogs through failure in a first series.

Sometimes you hear people in a gallery feeling sorry for the judges because so few dogs fail. This is nonsense. Oh, I suppose there have been a few lazy, incompetent, or inexperienced judges who were happy to see dogs eliminate themselves, to make their own job easier.

But men who train and handle their own dogs are not likely to be planning tests with such an objective. They want to keep the good dogs in as long as possible, for they know that's the only way to be sure of finding the best one at the end of the trial.

He can't win if he isn't still in there.

Such judges, in planning tests, are trying to make them just hard enough to give the dogs a chance to show *how well they can do them,* yet not to make too many of them fail. This is a bit like walking a tightrope. To accomplish it, a man needs experience, ingenuity, sympathy for dogs and handlers—and then he also needs a lot of luck in his guessing.

## CONDUCT OF A TRIAL

Good judges won't stand for very much sloppy gunning. They will usually insist that a pair of gunners who miss more than one bird be relieved instantly. They feel a trial is for the dogs, and not for the amusement of the local skeet shooters. If two men who are good shots take it seriously, and both shoot and both try on every bird, there is little excuse for a pheasant ever flying away.

When a bird is missed, it may sail a half-mile before it goes down. The dogs on line have their eyes glued on it. If another bird is then shot, and one of these dogs sent, he is all too likely to take out cross country after the missed bird. After all, it was shot at by a pair of skeet champions, and it *could* be a cripple.

Therefore, careful judges do the best they can to cancel the effect of a missed bird by excusing the dogs from the line. Or they may give the handlers their choice of being called back later in the series, or just walking their dogs around for a moment, to get their minds off the long fall of the missed bird.

The fussiest judges usually won't allow a dog to be sent for a bird they think might be a runner. When in doubt, they excuse the dogs from the line, and have the bird picked up. They won't even permit a dog to take an unusually long fall. It *might* cause him to fail, unfairly. But even if he does a perfect job on it, he can't be scored higher than dogs which performed perfectly on the shorter falls they were given.

I think this procedure is the lesser of two evils. But picking up hair-trigger dogs after birds have flown and shots have been fired is at best a precarious business. It sometimes causes a dog to break later, even if he doesn't leave right now, as the handler gingerly reaches for his collar.

The best solution is to avoid the whole problem by insisting on good gunning.

In a marking test, the dogs should have equal opportunities to see their falls. Obviously it is unfair if one dog sits up high with a full view, and another is down in a depression, or behind a clump of brush, or attempting to mark a fall over a hill. When you see the line move on beyond such obstructions, or when you see a judge squat down beside a dog to determine just what the dog can see from *his* eye level, you're looking at a man who is trying to run an equal contest for all.

Good judges keep a trial moving. If necessary they keep going straight through the daylight hours, with no time out for lunch or anything else. They expect the field-trial committee to have things organized, and are apt to be ugly about any unnecessary delay.

Their objective is to run enough series so every worthy dog in every stake is given sufficient opportunity to win or place if he is capable of it. Ordinarily, they want at least three series in Derby and Qualifying Stakes, and at least four in the All-Age events. But the number needed will vary greatly in different trials. At a Woman's Club Trial which I was privileged to judge with my good friend the late Howes Burton, the Open dogs were hot, and there were forty-two of them. I never saw such beautiful dog work, and so much of it, in my life.

By Saturday night, after running four series in a day and a half, we felt it would be too ridiculous to try to place the dogs. Too many were too close to perfection. We could have done it, but it would have meant resorting to some very fine distinctions on minor faults. Both of us felt we hated to award championship points on such hair-splitting.

The field-trial committee cooperated splendidly, secured other judges for the Amateur Stake on Sunday, and allowed us to go on with the Open. We kept running and running those marvelous dogs until, after seven series, they finally placed themselves.

If you see enough work, it's easy to place them. But nowadays, with entries growing so large at some of the trials, this matter of having enough tests in the available time is often the biggest problem the judges face.

## GALLERY JUDGES

Many people in the galleries at trials keep brief notes of their own, and score each performance. Sometimes they disagree violently with the decisions of the judges when the awards are announced. Usually these are soreheads, selfishly interested in a dog that failed to win.

I have heard of "raw decisions" that were supposedly obvious to every handler and gallery spectator, but I have never seen one. When I am a spectator or handler at a trial, and people ask me what dog is on top, I usually most honestly answer that I have no idea.

Very rarely does anyone at a trial actually see *all* the work of *every* dog—except the judges themselves. Certainly a handler can't. He must spend much of his time running back and forth to his truck, bringing up his dogs, while other dogs are performing.

Spectators who think they're seeing everything don't realize how much time they spend gossiping with friends, wandering back to the lunch wagon or for a bottle of beer, and how much of the work they thus actually miss.

Then, too, nobody but the judges is close enough to the dogs to see and hear everything that goes on. A dog may whine quite loudly on the line without the gallery knowing it. He may be very unsteady, when the gallery is not in position to see it. He may rough his birds severely, yet not quite badly enough to be disqualified entirely for hard mouth. He may give up his birds so reluctantly that the handler has to pry them out of his mouth. The gallery misses many of these things, and they may have quite a bearing on the final placings in a close trial.

I have done my share of criticizing *tests,* or *trial procedure*. But I have yet to feel competent as a spectator to quarrel with the *final placings* of any judges, in any trial I've ever seen.

So my advice is to go ahead and score the dogs yourself. Be a gallery judge. It's fun, and makes the trial more interesting to watch. But for heaven's sake, be quiet about it. Most of the retriever people are good sports, and lose as gracefully as they win. But if you try you can always find one or two of the other kind, ready to enter into a malicious whispering campaign about who "really should have won." This is almost as bad as beefing directly to the judges about their decisions. The chances are at least 1,000 to 1 that you are wrong and the judges are right. Nobody but a sucker bucks odds like those.

# 23

---

# Tips for the Amateur Handler

MANY AMATEURS, when handling in a trial, are as nervous as if they were appearing for the first time before a huge audience in Hollywood Bowl. But even some of the older pros confess they've always had this same trouble, and probably always will. So if, when you take your dog on line, your hands shake and the bottom of your stomach falls into your shoes, don't worry about it. You have plenty of company.

Don't be afraid of the judges. They're only people. And don't hesitate to ask them questions, if you're not sure what you're supposed to do. They want to see your dog do the best job of which he is capable.

Your purpose as a handler is to help your dog to give his best performance. It is smart to start showing him at his best, right from the time your number is called to summon you up to the line.

## WHEN YOUR DOG IS UNDER JUDGMENT

At just what instant does a dog start being under judgment? The AKC regulation says: "In stakes carrying championship points . . . dogs should be considered under judgment from the time they are called to the line until they have left the line and are back of all of the judges, at which point the dogs may be put on leash."

In the All-Age Stakes it is required to bring the dogs up to the line without either lead or collar, walking at heel. And if a dog does not heel reasonably well, but wanders around sniffing bushes, or if he precedes the handler by 15 or 20 feet to the line or into the blind, many judges will notice and penalize the dog for bad manners.

In minor stakes you are safe to bring the dog to the line on leash, unless you have been specifically instructed to have him at heel. But he should walk along quietly. It looks lousy if he drags you up there like a moldboard plow, and some judges might penalize for this, even in a lesser stake. After all, a retriever is supposed to be under quiet control at all times.

You will want your dog to be able to spot you easily in the gallery when you are giving him signals. Go prepared to make it as easy as possible for him to do so. Get a *white,* lightweight windbreaker. Buy it large enough so that you can put it on over heavy outer clothes. At a trial wear it only while you are handling or awaiting your call to the line. Wear it at every training session so your dog will become accustomed to seeing you in it when he is taking directions.

When you reach the line, have your dog *sit* on the exact spot designated by the judges. If they have neglected to pick a position from which he has a fair chance to see his falls, they'll be glad to have you call it to their attention. Don't hesitate to ask if you may move your dog slightly to avoid an obstruction. But usually the judges will pick a better place for your dog than you know how to do yourself.

Remove leash and collar at once and stuff them in your pocket, so no part of them is showing. Do this without being told. In the old days a few of the trickier handlers tried to use exposed leashes to intimidate unsteady dogs.

Take plenty of time, within reason, to get your dog sitting so he is aimed correctly. He should be facing what will be the most difficult fall, usually the first bird shot. That's the one you want to be sure he sees and remembers. He'll turn his head to see the other one. But in maneuvering him into position, don't grab him and haul him around. Coax him around to where you want him by patting your leg and commanding "Heel." Once you've taken off the leash, don't touch your dog. Judges must penalize for this, because some handlers have attempted all sorts of stunts and subterfuges to hold dogs steady, even to standing on their tails. Of course any handler seen actually holding his dog to keep him steady must be disqualified entirely.

## KEEPING YOUR DOG STEADY

However, you should use every *legitimate* means to help your dog resist the temptation to break. At a trial, excited by the other dogs, the crowd, and general hubbub, he's much more likely to leave you than he is in training workouts at home.

Stand beside him—but *beside his head, not his tail.* Stand far enough forward so that when your arm hangs naturally by your side, your hand is beside the dog's nose. He can see it, and smell it, and it reminds him that pappy is there, too, when those squawking cock pheasant go up and the guns start going off. This is very important. Yet how often you see a careless handler standing back beside a dog's stern, and then being greatly astonished when the dog suddenly leaves.

Watch your dog every minute. Be ready to hiss softly, or even sharply to command "Sit" if necessary, the instant you see those muscles bunching for a takeoff. A young dog that has been reasonably well trained to obedience can be kept steady in a trial if his handler is on the ball, and doesn't go to sleep.

Most judges won't penalize much if you hiss once or twice, or even say "sit" fairly quietly. But if you overdo it, are constantly nagging, and making a good deal of noise about it, they must assume the dog is very unsteady, and penalize quite severely.

If your dog *should* get away from you, try to stop him and get him back, even if you have to bellow "No!" and "Sit" repeatedly. Don't make the common mistake of shouting his name. He'll just go faster, thinking you're sending him. Stop him and get him back as quickly as you can. If he broke only 8 or 10 feet, you might even stay in a minor stake, for the judges don't *have* to throw a dog out for a controlled break except in an All-Age Stake.

But if only for the good of the dog, try to stop him before he goes clear out and retrieves the bird. If he gets away with that once or twice, and learns that at a trial there's nothing the boss can do by way of just retribution, he's well on his way to becoming a chronic breaker. And that can really be tough to cure. It's much easier never to let him get away with a complete break, even once.

Don't get excited and send your dog before a judge calls your number. Does this admonition seem silly? Well, you'll probably forget it, at least once. Nearly everybody does, and nothing makes a handler feel sillier. This, of course, is a technical break.

If a bird is missed and you are told to pick up your dog, be sure to reach for his collar very cautiously and slowly, at the same time commanding "Sit." This is a ticklish moment. A sudden movement of your hand might cause the dog to break, thinking you are giving him a line to the fall. And the rule book says very definitely that you are still under judgment until you have left the line with your dog on leash.

## MARKING YOUR FALLS

Mark your falls. You can't help your dog find them if you don't know where they are yourself. This sounds elementary, too, but it isn't easy. Most humans are very poor markers to start with.

Then, remember, to complicate things further, you must not take your eye off your dog. You have to watch him with one corner of your vision, and with the other mark your falls. This is quite a trick, and has a tendency to make a man walleyed.

Before you go up in line, study the background of the field, at the approximate place from which you'll work. Distant farm buildings, odd-shaped trees, and fence posts are very helpful for remembering the exact *line* of a fall. Have all these possibly useful objects in your mind before you go on line. Then, when your birds are shot, and you see them down out of the *corner* of one eye, you say something like this to yourself, "The left one is on a line with the fourth fence post to the left of that big dead elm. It is out just beyond the second patch of darker green in the cover."

Then you memorize other landmarks for the second fall. But the important one to be sure of is the *first* fall—the one your dog is most likely to have trouble remembering. However, the smart handler marks them all, whether it's two, three, or more birds.

## GIVING YOUR DOG A LINE

Before you go up in line, be sure you know exactly which direction the wind is blowing. Then, when you send your dog for his first retrieve, give him a line with a very slight gesture of your hand, on the downwind side of the fall. This is just a bit of insurance. If the dog marked the fall, he should hit it on the nose anyway. But if he cuts it too thin, he might just miss it on the upwind side, and run on out of the county.

For his second retrieve, always take time to have him *sit* for a second or two, aimed the way you want him to go, and then give him a line for the fall. Don't ever get cocky about the dog's memory and grab the first bird from him, and just vaguely wave him back for the other. I did it once, and it cost me a win in an Open Stake.

Now what sort of line you give on this second retrieve depends on the setup of the test. If the first bird retrieved was on the right, and the wind blowing across from *left* to *right,* then with the average dog you would give him a line straight at the left fall. His tendency will be to swing back to the right a little, because of the right fall he's just retrieved. This will keep him safely on the downwind side of the left fall. But a test set up this way is quite simple, and not likely to be encountered except in very minor stakes.

More likely the wind will be blowing from right to left. And then, when you send him for that second retrieve, you'd best play safe and give him a *false* line—far to the left of the actual fall. Then if he curves in toward the old fall, he still has a margin of safety to keep him on the downwind side of the bird he's after.

More handlers fumble on this matter of giving a smart line than anything else. Study this with your own dog, in practice. Some dogs curve toward the old fall much more than others. See how much he usually curves, and then when you're in a trial don't get rattled and forget to allow for it when you give him his line.

## HANDLING IN MARKING TESTS

Most beginning handlers are whistle happy. If they've trained their dogs to handle, they can't wait to prove it. Usually, they're just penalizing their dogs. In a marking test, any dog that apparently needs a lot of whistle and hand signals to help him find birds he saw fall must be marked down severely.

So, when your dog is hunting the vicinity of a marked fall, let him alone. Keep your whistle in your pocket. Let him hunt it out on his own. Even if it takes slightly longer, he'll get a better score than if you help him.

But this doesn't mean, if he badly overruns the bird and starts aimlessly hunting the whole country far from any fall, that you should let him go on indefinitely. After a reasonable amount of such wild romping, the judges have no choice but to tell you to pick him up. If that happens, you *know* you're all through.

When he overruns, if he does not correct himself quickly and come back to the area of the fall, then you'd better whistle him in, stop him, and with hand signals put him on the bird as quickly as you can. If you get your birds fairly fast, you at least have a chance to stay in the trial for a while. You can't possibly win if you are dropped in an early series.

But if you're not fairly sure he will respond to the whistle, then you'd better not blow it, no matter what he's doing. All you can do is stand there and suffer, silently praying that he will tire of romping the horizon and stumble over the bird on his way back in, before the patience of the judges is exhausted. For the only thing worse than handling on a marked fall is to attempt to do so, and have the dog refuse.

Always watch your dog. Don't ever turn your back on him, to address a pleasantry to the judges. He will invariably choose that moment to start running a rabbit over the hill, and that fleeting instant when you *might* have stopped him with the whistle will be gone forever.

In marking tests it helps sometimes to move forward two or three steps ahead of the line. Most judges won't object to this, within reason. Frank Hogan, the old maestro, used to keep inching forward until the judges told him he'd gone far enough. If you didn't watch him, he would suddenly be halfway out to the dog.

Another useful stunt, when your dog has difficulty seeing you against a gallery, is to move your whole body when you give a hand signal to left or right. Often this motion will help him find you.

In each series, watch carefully what happens to the dogs ahead of you. You can avoid many pitfalls this way. If most of the dogs seem to be having the same kind of trouble, assume that yours will, too, and try to compensate for it in your handling.

If your dog overruns a fall, and you think you'll have to handle, stop him before he gets beyond "range of control." Nearly every dog has one. He'll stop beautifully on the whistle and obey hand signals like a German soldier until he gets out a certain distance. After that, he suddenly goes "deaf." The distance at which this phenomenon occurs varies greatly with different dogs. You'll quickly discover what your dog's is, after he has defied you once or twice.

In a walk-up test, as you move forward, repeat the command "heel" quietly, and only as often as necessary to keep your dog at heel. Watch him with one eye, and keep the other on the boy who will throw the first bird. The instant the pheasant is thrown, stop and command your dog to sit. Be sure you stop beside his head, not his tail. From then on the procedure is usually the same as in a marking test from a stationary line. The other bird is then thrown and shot, you mark your falls, watch your dog and send him only when his number is called.

## HANDLING IN WATER TESTS

In a double retrieve on water, the judges sometimes permit the handler to step outside the blind to send the dog for the second bird. If they so instruct you, take advantage of it. You'll get no extra credit if you show off by sending the dog from inside the blind. And it is, of course, much easier to give him the line from outside than through the hole in the front of the blind.

If the judges don't tell you, play safe and ask them whether they wish you to stay in the blind for both birds.

On a blind retrieve across water, don't attempt to send your dog into the water at very much of an angle to the shoreline. Send him straight in, get him well out past the decoys, and then while he is still within easy "handling range," turn him and handle him to the hidden bird—by water as much as possible.

When a dog has seen no fall—and sometimes even when he has —if you try to send him in at an angle to the shore he very likely will start hunting down the shore instead of entering the water. If he once gets this notion in his head, he may give you a bad time.

Well, that's enough about handling. At least it is enough to get you started, so you won't look or feel silly as I did during my early handling attempts.

Bless you, sucker, and good luck. Perhaps you, too, got into this thing quite innocently, just wanting to have yourself a meat dog to use for hunting. But after you've handled your retriever in his first trial, you'll be hooked. You'll have field-trial fever. And so far as medical science now knows, this disease is incurable.

# Appendix I

The first club formed for each breed is recognized by the American Kennel Club as the "parent" club for that breed. One of the functions of a parent club is the setting of a standard of perfection for its breed. This is meant to serve as guide to breeders and bench judges. Where no parent club exists for a breed, the AKC sets the standard.

Since the AKC does not permit illustrations or drawings as a part of a breed standard, the framers of these descriptions must attempt to do the job with words alone. Imperfect as they are, these standards are essential guides.

From time to time these standards may be modified.

The standard for each of the retrieving breeds is presented here for the benefit of those who may have some occasion to consult it. Standards apply mainly to grown dogs, however, not to immature puppies. Puppies are like babies—they are apt to grow in sections, and at a given moment nobody can tell for sure what their conformation will ultimately be.

## THE LABRADOR RETRIEVER
Description and Standard of Points
*(Adopted by the Labrador Retriever Club, Inc., and Approved by the American Kennel Club, April 9, 1957)*

*General Appearance.* The general appearance of the Labrador should be that of a strongly built, short-coupled, very active dog. He should be fairly wide over the loins, and strong and muscular in the hindquarters. The coat should be close, short, dense, and free from feather.

*Head.* The skull should be wide, giving brain room; there should be a slight stop, i.e., the brow should be slightly pronounced, so that the skull is not absolutely in a straight line with the nose. The head should be clean-cut and free from fleshy cheeks. The jaws should be long and powerful and free from snipiness; the nose should be wide and the nostrils well developed. Teeth should be strong and regular, with a level mouth.

The ears should hang moderately close to the head, rather far back, should be set somewhat low, and not be large and heavy. The eyes should be of a medium size, expressing great intelligence and good temper, and can be brown, yellow, or black, but brown or black is preferred.

*Neck and Chest.* The neck should be medium length, powerful and not throaty. The shoulders should be long and sloping.

The chest must be of good width and depth, the ribs well sprung, and the loins wide and strong, stifles well turned, and the hind-quarters well developed and of great power.

*Legs and Feet.* The legs must be straight from the shoulder to ground, and the feet compact with toes well arched, and pads well developed; the hocks should be well bent, and the dog must be neither cowhocked nor too wide behind; in fact, he must stand and move true all around on legs and feet. Legs should be of medium length, showing good bone and muscle, but not so short as to be out of balance with rest of body. In fact, a dog well balanced in all points is preferable to one with outstanding good qualities and defects.

*Tail.* The tail is a distinctive feature of the breed; it should be very thick toward the base, gradually tapering toward the tip, of medium length, should be free from any feathering, and should be clothed thickly all around with the Labrador's short, thick, dense coat, thus giving that peculiar "rounded" appearance which has been described as the "otter" tail. The tail may be carried gaily but should not curl over the back.

*Coat.* The coat is another very distinctive feature; it should be short, very dense, and without wave, and should give a fairly hard feeling to the hand.

*Color.* The colors are black, yellow, or chocolate, and are evaluated as follows:

(a) Blacks: All black, with a small white spot on chest permissible. Eyes to be of medium size, expressing intelligence and good temper, preferably brown or hazel, although black or yellow is permissible.

(b) Yellows: Yellows may vary in color from fox red to light cream with variations in the shading of the coat on ears, the underparts of the dog, or beneath his tail. A small white spot on chest is permissible. Eye coloring and expression should be the same as that of the blacks, with black or dark-brown eye rims. The nose should also be black or dark brown, although "fading" to pink in winter weather is not serious. A "Dudley" nose (pink without pigmentation) should be penalized.

(c) Chocolates: Shades ranging from light sedge to chocolate. A small white spot on chest is permissible. Eyes to be light brown to clear yellow. Nose and eye-rim pigmentation dark brown or liver colored. "Fading" to pink in winter weather not serious. "Dudley" nose should be penalized.

*Movement.* Movement should be free and effortless. The forelegs should be strong, straight and true, and correctly placed. Watching a dog move toward one, there should be no signs of elbows being out in front, but neatly held to the body with legs not too close together, but moving straight forward without pacing or weaving. Upon viewing the dog from the rear, one should get the impression that the hind legs, which should be well muscled and not cowhocked, move as nearly parallel as possible, with hocks doing their full share of work and flexing well, thus giving the appearance of power and strength.

*Approximate weights of dogs and bitches in working condition.* Dogs—60–75 pounds; Bitches—55–70 pounds.

*Height at Shoulders.* Dogs—22½–24½ inches; Bitches—21½–23½ inches.

## THE GOLDEN RETRIEVER
### Description and Standard of Points
*(By courtesy of the Golden Retriever Club of America, Approved by the American Kennel Club, September 10, 1963)*

A symmetrical, powerful, active dog, sound and well put together, not clumsy or long in the leg, displaying a kindly expression and possessing a personality that is eager, alert and self-confident. Primarily a hunting dog, he should be shown in hard working condition. Over-all appearance, balance, gait and purpose to be given more emphasis than any of his component parts.

*Size.* Males 23–24 inches in height at withers; females 21½–22½. Length from breastbone to buttocks slightly greater than height at withers in ratio of 12–11. Weight for dogs 65–75 pounds; bitches 60–70 pounds.

*Head.* Broad in skull, slightly arched laterally and longitudinally without prominence of frontal or occipital bones. Good stop. Foreface deep and wide, nearly as long as skull. Muzzle, when viewed in profile, slightly deeper at stop than at tip; when viewed from above, slightly wider at stop than at tip. No heaviness in flews. Removal of whiskers for show purposes optional.

*Eyes.* Friendly and intelligent, medium large with dark rims, set well apart and reasonably deep in sockets. Color preferably dark brown, never lighter than color of coat. No white or haw visible when looking straight ahead.

*Teeth.* Scissors bite with lower incisors touching side of upper incisors.

*Nose.* Black or dark brown, though lighter shade in cold weather not serious. Dudley nose (pink without pigmentation) to be faulted.

*Ears.* Rather short, hanging flat against head with rounded tips slightly below jaw. Forward edge attached well behind and just above eye with rear edge slightly below eye. Low, houndlike earset to be faulted.

*Neck.* Medium long, sloping well back into shoulders, giving sturdy muscular appearance with untrimmed natural ruff. No throatiness.

*Body.* Well balanced, short-coupled, deep through the heart. Chest at least as wide as a man's hand, including thumb. Brisket extends to elbows. Ribs long and well sprung but not barrel shaped, extending well to rear of body. Loin short, muscular, wide and deep, with very little tuck-up. Top line level from withers to croup, whether standing or moving. Croup slopes gently. Slabsidedness, narrow chest, lack of depth in brisket, excessive tuck-up, roach or sway back to be faulted.

*Forequarters.* Forequarters well coordinated with hindquarters and capable of free movement. Shoulder blades wide, long and muscular, showing angulation with upper arm of approximately 90 degrees. Legs straight with good bone. Pastern short and strong, sloping slightly forward with no suggestion of weakness.

*Hindquarters.* Well-bent stifles (angulation between femur and pelvis approximately 90 degrees) with hocks well let down. Legs straight when viewed from rear. Cowhocks and sickle hocks to be faulted.

*Feet.* Medium size, round and compact with thick pads. Excess hair may be trimmed to show natural size and contour. Open or splayed feet to be faulted.

*Tail.* Well set on, neither too high nor too low, following natural line of croup. Length extends to hock. Carried with merry action with some upward curve but never curled over back nor between legs.

*Coat and Color.* Dense and water repellent with good undercoat. Texture not as hard as that of a shorthaired dog or silky as that of a setter. Lies flat against body and may be straight or wavy. Moderate feathering on back of forelegs and heavier feathering on front of neck, back of thighs and underside of tail. Feathering may be lighter than rest of coat. Color lustrous golden of various shades. A few white hairs on chest permissible but not desirable. Further white markings to be faulted.

*Gait.* When trotting, gait is free, smooth, powerful, and well coordinated. Viewed from front or rear, legs turn neither in nor out, nor do feet cross or interfere with each other. Increased speed causes tendency of feet to converge toward center line of gravity.

#### DISQUALIFICATIONS

*Deviation in height of more than one inch from standard either way. Undershot or overshot bite. This condition not to be confused with misalignment of teeth. Trichiasis (abnormal position or direction of the eyelashes).*

### THE CHESAPEAKE BAY RETRIEVER
Description and Standard of Points
*(By courtesy of the American Chesapeake Club, Approved by the American Kennel Club, July 9, 1963)*

*Head.* Skull broad and round with medium stop, nose medium short-muzzle, pointed but not sharp. Lips thin, not pendulous. Ears small, set well up on head, hanging loosely and of medium leather. Eyes medium large, very clear, of yellowish color and wide apart.

*Neck.* Of medium length with a strong muscular appearance, tapering to shoulders.

*Shoulders, Chest and Body.* Shoulders, sloping and should have full liberty of action with plenty of power without any restrictions of movement. Chest strong, deep and wide. Barrel round and deep. Body of medium length, neither cobby nor roached, but rather approaching hollowness, flanks well tucked up.

*Back Quarters and Stifles.* Back quarters should be as high or a trifle higher than the shoulders. They should show fully as much power as the forequarters. There should be no tendency to weakness in either fore or hindquarters. Hindquarters should be especially powerful to supply the driving power for swimming. Back should be short, well-coupled and powerful. Good hindquarters are essential.

*Legs, Elbows, Hocks and Feet.* Legs should be medium length and straight, showing good bone and muscle, with well-webbed hare feet of good size. The toes well rounded and close, pasterns slightly bent and both pasterns and hocks medium length—the straighter the legs the better. Dewclaws, if any, must be removed from the hind legs. Dewclaws on the forelegs may be removed. A dog with dewclaws on the hind legs must be disqualified.

*Stern.* Tail should be of medium length—varying from: males, 12 inches to 15 inches, and females from 11 inches to 14 inches; medium heavy at base, moderate feathering on stern and tail permissible.

*Coat and Texture.* Coat should be thick and short, nowhere over 1½ inches long, with a dense fine woolly under coat. Hair on face and legs should be very short and straight with tendency to wave on the shoulders, neck, back and loins only. The curly coat or coat with a tendency to curl not permissible.

*Color.* Any color varying from a dark brown to a faded tan or deadgrass. Deadgrass takes in any shade of deadgrass, varying from a tan to a dull straw color. White spot on breast and toes permissible, but the smaller the spot the better, solid color being preferred.

*Weight.* Males, 65 to 75 pounds; females, 55 to 65 pounds.

*Height.* Males, 23 inches to 26 inches; females, 21 inches to 24 inches.

*Symmetry and Quality.* The Chesapeake dog should show a bright and happy disposition and an intelligent expression, with general outlines impressive and denoting a good worker. The dog should be well proportioned, a dog with a good coat and, well balanced in other points being preferable to the dog excelling in some but weak in others.

The texture of the dog's coat is very important, as the dog is used for hunting under all sorts of adverse weather conditions, often working in ice and snow. The oil in the harsh outer coat and woolly undercoat is of extreme value in preventing the cold water from reaching the dog's skin and aids in quick drying. A Chesapeake's coat should resist the water in the same way that a duck's feathers do. When he leaves the water and shakes himself, his coat should not hold the water at all, being merely moist. Color and coat are extremely important, as the dog is used for duck hunting. The color must be as nearly that of his surroundings as possible and with the fact that dogs are exposed to all kinds of adverse weather conditions, often working in ice and snow, the color of coat and its texture must be given every consideration when judging on the bench or in the ring.

Courage, willingness to work, alertness, nose, intelligence, love of water, general quality, and most of all, disposition should be given primary consideration in the selection and breeding of the Chesapeake Bay dog.

### POSITIVE SCALE OF POINTS

| | | | |
|---|---|---|---|
| Head, inc. lips, ears & eyes | 16 | Color | 4 |
| Neck | 4 | Stern and tail | 10 |
| Shoulders and body | 12 | Coat and texture | 18 |
| Back quarters and stifles | 12 | General conformation | 12 |
| Elbows, legs and feet | 12 | Total | 100 |

*Note:—*The question of coat and general type of balance takes precedence over any scoring table which could be drawn up.

|                                              | Inches |     |      |
| -------------------------------------------- | ------ | --- | ---- |
| Length head, nose to occiput.......... | 9½     | to  | 10   |
| Girth at ears...................... | 20     | to  | 21   |
| Muzzle below eyes.................. | 10     | to  | 10½  |
| Length of ears..................... | 4½     | to  | 5    |
| Width between eyes................. | 2½     | to  | 2¾   |
| Girth neck close to shoulder........... | 20     | to  | 22   |
| Girth of chest to elbows.............. | 35     | to  | 36   |
| Girth at flank...................... | 24     | to  | 25   |
| Length from occiput to tail base....... | 34     | to  | 35   |
| Girth forearms at shoulders........... | 10     | to  | 10½  |
| Girth upper thigh................... | 19     | to  | 20   |
| From root to root of ear, over skull..... | 5      | to  | 6    |
| Occiput to top shoulder blades........ | 9      | to  | 9½   |
| From elbow to elbow over the shoulders. | 25     | to  | 26   |

### DISQUALIFICATIONS

*Black or liver colored. Dewclaws on hind legs, white on any part of body, except breast, belly or spots on feet. Feathering on tail or legs over 1¾ inches long. Undershot, overshot or any deformity. Coat curly or tendency to curl all over body. Specimens unworthy or lacking in breed characteristics.*

### THE AMERICAN WATER SPANIEL
Description and Standard of Points
*(By courtesy of the American Kennel Club)*

*General Appearance.* Medium in size, of sturdy typical spaniel character, curly coat, an active muscular dog, with emphasis placed on proper size and conformation, correct head properties, texture of coat and color. Of amicable disposition; demeanor indicates intelligence, strength and endurance.

*Head.* Moderate in length, skull rather broad and full, stop moderately defined, but not too pronounced. Forehead covered with short smooth hair and without tuft or topknot. Muzzle of medium length, square and with no inclination to snipiness, jaws strong and of good length, and neither undershot nor overshot, teeth straight and well shaped. Nose sufficiently wide and with well developed nostrils to insure good scenting power.

*Faults.* Very flat skull, narrow across the top, long, slender or snipy muzzle.

*Eyes.* Hazel, brown or of dark tone to harmonize with coat; set well apart. Expression alert, attractive, intelligent.

*Fault.* Yellow eyes to disqualify.

*Ears.* Lobular, long and wide, not set too high on head, but slightly above the eyeline. Leather extending to end of nose and well covered with close curls.

*Neck.* Round and of medium length, strong and muscular, free of throatiness, set to carry head with dignity, but arch not accentuated.

*Body Structure.* Well developed, sturdily constructed but not too compactly coupled. General outline is a symmetrical relationship of parts. Shoulders sloping, clean and muscular. Strong loins, lightly arched, and well furnished, deep brisket but not excessively broad. Well-sprung ribs. Legs of medium length and well boned, but not so short as to handicap for field work.

*Legs and Feet.* Forelegs powerful and reasonably straight. Hind legs firm with suitably bent stifles and strong hocks well let down. Feet to harmonize with size of dog. Toes closely grouped and well padded.

*Fault.* Cowhocks.

*Tail.* Moderate in length, curved in a slightly rocker shape, carried slightly below level of back; tapered and covered with hair to tip, action lively.

*Faults.* Rat or shaved tail.

*Coat.* The coat should be closely curled or have marcel effect and should be of sufficient density to be of protection against weather, water or punishing cover, yet not coarse. Legs should have medium short, curly feather.

*Faults.* Coat too straight, soft, fine or tightly kinked.

*Color.* Solid liver or dark chocolate, a little white on toes or chest permissible.

*Height.* 15 to 18 inches at the shoulder.

*Weight.* Males, 28 to 45 pounds; females, 25 to 40 pounds.

DISQUALIFICATION

*Yellow eyes.*

## THE IRISH WATER SPANIEL
Description and Standard of Points
*(By courtesy of the Irish Water Spaniel Club of America,
Approved by the American Kennel Club, June 11, 1940.)*

*Head.* Skull rather large and high in dome with prominent occiput; muzzle square and rather long with deep mouth opening and lips fine in texture. Teeth strong and level. The nose should be large with open nostrils and liver in color. The head should be cleanly chiseled, not cheeky, and should not present a short wedge-shaped appearance. Hair on face should be short and smooth.

*Topknot.* Topknot, a characteristic of the true breed, should consist of long loose curls growing down into a well-defined peak between the eyes and should not be in the form of a wig; *i.e.* growing straight across.

*Eyes.* Medium in size and set almost flush, without eyebrows. Color of eyes hazel, preferably of dark shade. Expression of the eyes should be keenly alert, intelligent, direct and quizzical.

*Ears.* Long, lobular, set low with leathers reaching to about the end of the nose when extended forward. The ears should be abundantly covered with curls becoming longer toward the tips and extending two or more inches below the ends of the leathers.

*Neck.* The neck should be long, arching, strong and muscular, smoothly set into sloping shoulders.

*Shoulders and Chest.* Shoulders should be sloping and clean; chest deep but not too wide between the legs. The entire front should give the impression of strength without heaviness.

*Body, Ribs and Loins.* Body should be of medium length, with ribs well sprung, pear-shaped at the brisket, and rounder toward the hind quarters. Ribs should be carried well back. Loins should be short, wide and muscular. The body should not present a tucked-up appearance.

*Hindquarters.* The hindquarters should be as high as or a trifle higher than the shoulders and should be very powerful and muscular with well-developed upper and second thighs. Hips should be wide; stifles should not be too straight; and hocks low-set and moderately bent. Tail should be set on low enough to give a rather rounded appearance to the hindquarters and should be carried nearly level with the back. Sound hindquarters are of great importance to provide swimming power and drive.

*Forelegs and Feet.* Forelegs medium in length, well boned, straight and muscular with elbows close set. Both fore and hind feet should be large, thick and somewhat spreading, well clothed with hair both over and between the toes, but free from superfluous feather.

*Tail.* The so-called "rat tail" is a striking characteristic of the breed. At the root it is thick and covered for 2 or 3 inches with short curls. It tapers to a fine point at the end, and from the root-curls is covered with short, smooth hair so as to look as if the tail had been clipped. The tail should not be long enough to reach the hock joint.

*Coat.* Proper coat is of vital importance. The neck, back and sides should be densely covered with tight crisp ringlets entirely free from wooliness. Underneath the ribs the hair should be longer. The hair on lower throat should be short. The forelegs should be covered all around with abundant hair falling in curls or waves, but shorter in front than behind. The hind legs should also be abundantly covered by hair falling in curls or waves, but the hair should be short on the front of the legs below the hocks.

*Color.* Solid liver; white on chest objectionable.

*Height and Weight.* Dogs, 22 to 24 inches; bitches, 21 to 23 inches. Dogs, 55 to 65 pounds; bitches, 45 to 58 pounds.

*General Appearance.* That of a smart, upstanding, strongly built but not leggy dog, combining great intelligence and the rugged endurance with a bold, dashing eagerness of temperament.

*Gait.* Should be square, true, precise and not slurring.

### SCALE OF POINTS

| *Head* | | | *Coat* | | |
|---|---|---|---|---|---|
| Skull and topknot. | 6 | | Tightness, denseness of curl | | |
| Ears | 4 | | and general tex- | | |
| Eyes | 4 | | ture | 16 | |
| Muzzle and nose.. | 6 | 20 | Color | 4 | 20 |

SCALE OF POINTS—CONTINUED

*Body*

Neck .......... 5

Chest, shoulders, back, loin
and ribs ...... 12   17

*Driving Gear*

Feet, hips, thighs, stifles and
continuity of hindquarter
muscles ...... 14

Feet, legs, elbows and muscles
of forequarters .   9   23

*Tail*

General appearance and
"set on," length and car-
riage ........ 5   5

*General Conformation and
Action*

Symmetry, style, gait, weight
and size ...... 15   15

———
100

## THE FLAT-COATED RETRIEVER
### Description and Standard of Points
*(By courtesy of the American Kennel Club)*

*General Appearance.* A bright, active dog of medium size
(weighing from 60 pounds to 70 pounds) with an intelligent expression, showing power without lumber and raciness without weed-
iness.

*Head.* This should be long and nicely molded. The skull flat and
moderately broad. There should be a depression or stop between
the eyes, slight and no way accentuated, so as to avoid giving
either a down or a dish-faced appearance. The nose of good size
with open nostrils. The eyes, of medium size, should be dark brown
or hazel, with a very intelligent expression (a round prominent eye
is a disfigurement), and they should not be obliquely placed. The
jaws should be long and strong, with a capacity of carrying a hare
or pheasant. The ears small and well set on close to the side of
the head.

*Neck, Shoulders and Chest.* The head should be well set in the
neck, which latter should be long and free from throatiness, sym-
metrically set and obliquely placed in shoulders running well into
the back to allow of easily seeking for the trail. The chest should
be deep and fairly broad, with a well-defined brisket on which the
elbows should work cleanly and evenly. The fore ribs should be
fairly flat showing a gradual spring and well arched in the center

of the body but rather lighter towards the quarters. Open couplings are to be ruthlessly condemned.

*Back and Quarters.* The back should be short, square and well ribbed up, with muscular quarters. The stern short, and well set on, carried gaily but never much above the level of the back.

*Legs and Feet.* These are of the greatest importance. The fore-legs should be perfectly straight, with bone of good quality carried right down to the feet which should be round and strong. The stifle should not be too straight or too bent and the dog must neither be cowhocked nor move too wide behind, in fact he must stand and move true all round on legs and feet, with toes close and well arched, the soles being thick and strong, and when the dog is in full coat the limbs should be well feathered.

*Coat.* Should be dense, of fine quality and texture, flat as possible. Color: black or liver.

### THE CURLY-COATED RETRIEVER
### Description and Standard of Points
### (By courtesy of the American Kennel Club.)

*Head.* Long and well proportioned, skull not too flat, jaws long and strong but not inclined to snipiness, nose black, in the black coated variety, with wide nostrils. Teeth strong and level.

*Eyes.* Black or brown, but not yellow, rather large but not too prominent.

*Ears.* Rather small, set on low, lying close to the head, and covered with short curls.

*Coat.* Should be one mass of crisp curls all over. A slightly more open coat not to be severely penalized, but a saddle back or patch of uncurled hair behind the shoulder should be penalized, and a prominent white patch on breast is undesirable, but a few white hairs allowed in an otherwise good dog. Color, black or liver.

*Shoulders, Chest, Body and Loins.* Shoulders should be very deep, muscular and obliquely placed. Chest, not too wide, but decidedly deep. Body, rather short, muscular and well ribbed up. Loin, powerful, deep and firm to the grasp.

*Legs and Feet.* Legs should be of moderate length, forelegs straight and set well under the body. Quarters strong and muscular, hocks low to the ground with moderate bend to stifle and hock. Feet round and compact with well-arched toes.

*Tail.* Should be moderately short, carried fairly straight and covered with curls, slightly tapering towards the point.

*General Appearance.* A strong smart upstanding dog, showing activity, endurance and intelligence.

# Appendix II

## RETRIEVER TRIAL WINNERS: SOME NAMES TO SEEK IN PEDIGREES

The idea is to get a retriever that *wants* to be trained—and is *worth* training. There is no need to listen to unsupportable claims. With the aid of the following list *anyone* can make a useful evaluation of the field qualities—as they appear on the public record—of the ancestors in the pedigree of any American- or Canadian-bred retriever.[1] See the chapter "The Truth About Pedigrees—And How to Read Them" for a guide to evaluation.

This is an alphabetical list, by breed and sex, of retrievers that have placed in Open, Limited, and Special[2] All-Age stakes licensed by the AKC from 1931 through 1975, and those that have placed in Amateur All-Age stakes from September 14, 1951, through 1975.[3] Also included, for all of the years for which they have been awarded through 1975, are the National [Open] and National Amateur Retriever Champions, the Canadian National Retriever Champions, Field & Stream Trophy winners (once emblematic of the national championship), AKC Retriever

---

[1] If it is a Chesapeake, Curly-Coat, Flat-Coat, Golden, Irish Water Spaniel, or Labrador—the trial-eligible breeds.

[2] Now discontinued.

[3] Amateur placers and Amateur Field Champions are listed since amateur title qualifications began in 1951, National Derby Champions since 1937, Canadian Field Trial Champions since the first was awarded in 1942, Canadian National Retriever Champions since the first in 1950.

Field Champions and Amateur Field Champions,[4] Canadian Field Trial Champions and Amateur Field Trial Champions—and U.S. National Derby Champions. The last named is not recognized by the AKC, but is a highly sought title. Many of these field trial winners have also been show and/or obedience titlists. These titles, where known, are also shown.

Where so many thousands of facts are incorporated in a single listing it is probable that, despite all efforts, some errors will remain. The reviser is anxious to correct any errors and/or omissions in future printings and editions. He will greatly appreciate reader cooperation in calling them to his attention. He may be addressed in care of the publisher at 200 Madison Avenue, New York, New York 10016.

| Name | Date Birth | AKC Reg. Number | AKC Amateur Points | AKC Open Points |
|---|---|---|---|---|
| *Chesapeake Bay Retriever Dogs* | | | | |
| FC Alamo's Lucias | 1970 | | | 9½ |
| Aleutian Drake's Quest | 1953 | S627743 | ½ | |
| AFTC Aleutian Mike | 1954 | S657646 | 10½ | 8½ |
| Aleutian Ranger | 1956 | S930585 | 5 | |
| FC, AFC Aleutian Surf Breaker | 1972 | | 17 | 10 |
| Alpine Big Butch | 1953 | S655710 | 14½ | |
| Andy's Bullheaded Bulldozer | 1963 | SA244125 | | 2 |
| FTC, AFTC Atom Bob | 1953 | S629714 | 47 | 47½ |
| Aubraes Sand Turk | 1963 | SA227353 | ½ | |
| Auror's Indian Bear | 1975 | | 1 | ½ |
| Babylon Captain Brownie | 1935ᵃ | | | |
| 1956 Can. Nat'l Ch. Dual Ch. Baker's King | 1953 | 333047CKC | | |
| Can. Dual Ch. Baron's Skipper Bob | 1953 | 339514CKC | | |
| Dual Ch. AFC, CFTC Baron's Tule Tiger (All-time highest open and amateur scores for a Chesapeake) | 1959 | SA13353 | 112 | 96 |
| Baronland's Alaska Bob | 1965 | SA370397 | 1½ | 3 |
| FC, AFC Bay City Jake | 1970 | | 34½ | 24½ |
| Sh. Ch. Bayberry Pete | 1947 | S210600 | 6 | 19½ |
| FTC Bayle | 1944 | A789367 | | 17½ |
| Beewacker's Chester | 1952 | S637550 | ½ | 1 |
| Beewacker's Jeff | 1956 | S856789 | ½ | 1 |
| Big Chief | 1937 | A293230 | | |
| Blemton Just Ted | 1936 | A72985 | | 3 |
| Blond Dick | 1948 | S241505 | 1 | |

[4]The AKC titles Field Champion and Field Trial Champion mean exactly the same thing. So do Amateur Field Champion and Amateur Field Trial Champion. The word "Trial" was dropped by the AKC in 1962. In this listing the longer title has been retained for those retrievers that were granted their titles in that form.

| Name | Date Birth | AKC Reg. Number | AKC Amateur Points | AKC Open Points |
|---|---|---|---|---|
| Bob of Montauk | 1936 | A78768 | | 5 |
| Bob's Aleutian Trojan | 1958 | SA107122 | 4 | 1½ |
| Sh. Ch., AFC Bomarc of South Bay, C.D. | 1958 | S930205 | 24 | 2½ |
| Brewster's Laddie | 1934 | A1597 | | 1 |
| Brookhaven Gep | 1930 | | | 1 |
| Bud Parker Bang | 1931 | 881831 | | 3 |
| Buddy Brown | 1940 | A753055 | | 6 |
| Captain Ringo Kid | 1953 | unreg. | 10 | 3 |
| CFTC Ce-Pine Sandy Duke | 1953 | S694010 | 3 | |
| FTC Chesacroft Baron | 1936 | A177853 | | 20 |
| Chesacroft Bob | 1934 | A68453 | | 1 |
| Sh. Ch. Chesacroft Newt | 1933 | 934526 | | 1 |
| Chesapeake Skipper | 1954 | S701363 | 1 | |
| Chesareid Donache Topper | 1961 | SA114854 | 2½ | |
| Chesdel Chippewa Chief | 1971 | | 28 | 12 |
| Chesdel Happy Joe | 1938 | A350334 | | 1 |
| AFTC Chesonoma's Louis | 1953 | S708366 | 28 | 7½ |
| FC, AFC Chesonoma's Kodiak | 1959 | SA90353 | 33½ | 30½ |
| Choptank Coca-Cola | 1953 | S698848 | 3 | 1 |
| AFTC, Sh. Ch. Chuck's Rip Joy | 1950 | S455148 | 17½ | 9½ |
| Coke of Cooa King | 1945 | S8035 | | ½ |
| CFTC Conroy's Golden Arrow | 1949 | 274866CKC | | |
| FC, AFC Copper Topper der Wunderbar | 1968 | SA717131 | 14½ | 9½ |
| FC Cub's Kobi King | 1967 | SA551686 | | 30½ |
| Dale's Cinnamon Chip | 1973 | | ½ | |
| Deerwood Tiger | 1946 | S72127 | 11½ | 12½ |
| Delshore Duke | 1944 | A897745 | | 3 |
| 1937 Nat'l Derby Ch. Dilwyne Chesabob | 1936 | A78769 | | 8 |
| FTC Dilwyne Montauk Point (Field & Stream Trophy, 1936) | 1931 | A63115 | | 26 |
| Fireweed's Aleutian Widgeon | 1975 | | 3 | ½ |
| Fleet of Flat Hummock | 1953 | S654444 | 1 | |
| Flood Tide Pete | 1933 | 960003 | | |
| Gross Schlecht Bark Von Berg | 1971 | | | 3 |
| FTC Guess of Shagwong | 1939 | A410126 | | 19 |
| 1939 Nat'l Derby Ch. Gunnar II | 1938 | A323445 | | 7 |
| CFTC, CAFTC Gypsy's Mallard of Vigloma | 1954 | 451708CKC | | |
| Heller's Hobo | 1952 | S867647 | 1 | 1 |
| Howe's Bonnie Laddie | 1930 | 894667 | | 5 |
| Howe's Pal | 1930 | A68389 | | |
| Ingham Hill Laddie | 1929 | | | |
| Iron's Terry | 1949 | S399164 | | 1 |
| J. J.'s Hy-Wyne Willows | 1963 | SA218887 | 1½ | ½ |
| Jack Pine of Deerwood | 1946 | S105422 | | 3 |
| Sh. Ch. Jordi's Catamaran, U.D. | 1952 | S564711 | 1 | 3 |
| Kimkay Target | 1969 | SA702466 | ½ | |
| King Hanibal of Boomtown, name changed to Heller's Hobo | | | | |
| King of Montauk | 1923 | | | 8 |

| Name | Date Birth | AKC Reg. Number | AKC Amateur Points | AKC Open Points |
|---|---|---|---|---|
| Ko-Ko's Sergeant Rusty | 1957 | S951159 | 8½ | 6 |
| Dual Ch., AFC Koolwater's Colt of Tricrown | 1964 | SA279418 | 15 | 12 |
| Sh. Ch. Laddie's Rowdy | 1944 | A783993 | | 8 |
| Lakewood Ben | 1941 | A600708 | | 5 |
| Lassie's Ace | 1945 | S6260 | 9 | 3 |
| FC, AFC, Can. Sh. Ch. Meg's O'Timothy, Can. C.D. | 1958 | S958562 | 21 | 12½ |
| Michael of Deerwood | 1942 | A678562 | | 1 |
| CFTC Midnapore's Mtn Chum | 1952 | 310549CKC | | |
| Mount Joy's E.C. Bay | 1973 | | 4 | 4 |
| FTC, AFTC Mount Joy's Louistoo | 1957 | S992478 | 60 | 51 |
| Dual Ch., AFTC Mount Joy's Mallard | 1951 | S499258 | 36 | 20½ |
| Mount Joy's Mickey Finn | 1966 | SA399458 | ½ | 5 |
| Mount Joy's Mighty Ike | 1969 | | | 5½ |
| Mount Joy's Tiger | 1951 | S499254 | ½ | ½ |
| Native Shore Mike's Image | 1959 | SA6060 | 5 | |
| FTC, AFTC Nelgard's Baron, C.D. | 1951 | S444283 | 27½ | 48 |
| Nelgard's Brown Bomber | 1945 | A983621 | | 2 |
| FTC, AFTC Nelgard's King Tut | 1947 | S84384 | 19 | 21 |
| CFC, CAFC, AFC Nanuk of Cheslang | 1970 | | 16½ | 9½ |
| Neshoba Trooper Ned | 1961 | SA124497 | ½ | |
| AFTC Odessa Creek Spunky | 1950 | S486686 | 15 | ½ |
| CFTC Oil City Ted | 1950 | 286493CKC | | |
| Pine Ridge of Deerwood | 1946 | S105421 | 2 | 8½ |
| Pride of Montauk | 1926 | | | 1 |
| CC Prince Cocoa of Kent | 1960 | 519712CKC | | |
| AFTC Rip | 1953 | S807131 | 18½ | 3½ |
| CFC Rocky of Cal-Peake | 1966 | SA648330 | | 1 |
| CFTC Rocky View's Radar Duke | 1959 | SA6223 | | |
| Roscoe, CDX | 1955 | S799829 | | ½ |
| St. Jones Chief | 1945 | S23403 | | |
| Sea Bee Brant | 1944 | A794897 | | 1 |
| Sergeant Rex | 1951 | S483431 | 1 | 3½ |
| Shagwong Chief | 1932 | 203853 | | |
| FTC Skipper Bob | 1931 | 984475 | | 26 |
| FC Slow Gin | 1958 | S937058 | 3 | 11½ |
| Dual Ch. Sodak's Gypsy Prince | 1931 | 831195 | | 14 |
| FTC Sodak's Rip | 1938 | A277831 | | 14 |
| Squaw Island Brownie | 1974 | | | 3½ |
| FTC, AFTC Star King of Mount Joy | 1952 | S568417 | 31½ | 10 |
| Storm Cloud | 1932 | 900447 | | |
| Stratte's Norske | 1960 | SA83356 | ½ | 4 |
| Tealwood's Rocky | 1954 | S717649 | 3½ | ½ |
| The Big Fellow | 1964 | SA308517 | ½ | 3 |
| Thor of Ohio | 1954 | S670853 | ½ | |
| Ch. AFC Tiger's Cub C.D. | 1965 | SA360939 | 68 | 24 |
| Tiger's Texas Tiger | 1967 | SA536928 | 1 | 4½ |
| CFTC Timbertown Mick | 1941 | 191029CKC | | |
| CFTC 'Toba Tiger of 'Peake | 1958 | 437415CKC | 4 | |

| Name | Date Birth | AKC Reg. Number | AKC Amateur Points | AKC Open Points |
|---|---|---|---|---|

### Chesapeake Bay Retriever Bitches

| Name | Date Birth | AKC Reg. Number | AKC Amateur Points | AKC Open Points |
|---|---|---|---|---|
| Aleutian Water Spray | 1946 | S141569 | 3 | 2½ |
| Alpine Billie's Chips | 1956 | S886619 | 2 | ½ |
| Alpine Matty | 1962 | SA210376 | 5 | |
| Bea of Blue Hen | 1948 | S319545 | 1½ | 3 |
| Blemton Binnacle | 1940 | A445723 | | |
| Delmonte Giner | 1940 | A548269 | | 1 |
| Dilwyne Donga | 1937 | A217541 | | 1 |
| Dodel Fusty | 1938 | A333257 | | 1 |
| Frosty Milady | 1951 | S482527 | 5 | |
| AFTC Gypsy | 1945 | A963576 | 21 | 10½ |
| Gypsy's Tinker of Viglóma | 1950 | S435887 | 3 | |
| Judy of Apple Valley | 1948 | A285241 | 5 | |
| King Tut's Rose of Random Lake | 1954 | S661640 | 3 | |
| Meg O' My Heart | 1952 | S582627 | 1 | |
| FTC, AFTC Meg's Pattie O'Rourke (1958 Natl. Derby Ch.) | 1956 | S856791 | 51½ | 55½ |
| Meg's Tami O'Hara | 1959 | SA25094 | 8 | 6 |
| FTC Montgomery's Sal | 1946 | S44270 | | 25½ |
| FC, AFC Mount Joy's Bit O'Ginger | 1962 | SA163900 | 49½ | 27 |
| Mount Joy's Dilwyne Jez O'Meg | 1966 | SA488380 | 13½ | 7½ |
| Native Shore Pink Lady | 1945 | S6276 | 5 | 6 |
| Princess Anne | 1933 | 902089 | | 4 |
| FTC, AFTC Raindrop of Deerwood | 1949 | S374290 | 33½ | 20½ |
| Sh. Ch. Shinnecock Belle | 1935 | A42949 | | 6 |
| FTC Tiger of Clipper City | 1943 | A734222 | | 32 |
| Tiger's Samantha | 1968 | | | 1 |
| Tops | 1933 | | | 6 |
| Trofast of Green Valley | 1957 | S898796 | ½ | |

Note: Since 1973, no points have been won by Flat-Coats in Open or Amateur. Those that have placed in Derby or Qualifying Stakes are: Raboff Morinda, Terricroft Dan'l Doll, Copper Caliph of Mantayo, Stolford Black Queen, Mantayo Ramblin Wreck, and Wyndham's Wingover Brunhild.

### Curly-Coated Retriever Dogs

| Name | Date Birth | AKC Reg. Number | AKC Amateur Points | AKC Open Points |
|---|---|---|---|---|
| Sarona Jacob of Marvadel | 1934 | 970212 | | 3 |
| Sarona Sam of Marvadel | 1933 | 988379 | | 4 |

### Flat-Coated Retriever Dogs

| Name | Date Birth | AKC Reg. Number | AKC Amateur Points | AKC Open Points |
|---|---|---|---|---|
| Copper Caliph of Mantayo | 1963 | SA233214 | | 3 |
| Mantayo Rambling Wreck | 1964 | SA285728 | ½ | |
| Rab of Marinda | 1955 | S770543 | | ½ |

### Flat-Coated Retriever Bitches

| Name | Date Birth | AKC Reg. Number | AKC Amateur Points | AKC Open Points |
|---|---|---|---|---|
| Stolford Black Queen | 1963 | SA254626 | ½ | |
| Wyndham's Wingover Brunhild | 1968 | SA596322 | 3 | |

| Name | Date Birth | AKC Reg. Number | AKC Amateur Points | AKC Open Points |
|------|------------|-----------------|--------------------|-----------------|

## *Golden Retriever Dogs*

| Name | Date Birth | AKC Reg. Number | AKC Amateur Points | AKC Open Points |
|------|------------|-----------------|--------------------|-----------------|
| Amber's Diablo Rock | 1972 | SB69141 | 1½ | |
| CFC Angus of Stilrovin | 1964 | SA275874 | ½ | |
| Apache Trigger | 1943 | A732880 | | 2 |
| Bainin of Caernac, C.D. | 1972 | SA915780 | 8 | 3½ |
| Bang Away's Hay Bailer | 1957 | S966698 | | 4 |
| Bangaway's Haymaker | 1959 | SA44304 | ½ | |
| Barry of Laurentide | 1952 | S650368 | ½ | |
| 1950 Nat'l Ch. FTC Beautywood's Tamarack (*Field & Stream* Trophy, 1950) | 1947 | S153955 | | 18½ |
| FC, AFC Benjamin Rajah Frisbie | 1971 | SA933226 | 49½ | 13½ |
| Bingo of Yelme II | 1944 | A833289 | 5 | 1 |
| Bonnie Brooks Barney | 1968 | SA711557 | ½ | |
| Bonnie Brooks Copper | 1965 | SA379862 | ½ | 6 |
| Bonnie Brooks Danny, C.D. | 1967 | SA486567 | 2 | 2 |
| FC, AFC, CFC Bonnie Brooks Elmer | 1965 | SA297157 | 16½ | 11½ |
| AFC Bonnie Brooks Mike | 1965 | SA306961 | 13 | 17½ |
| FC, AFC Bonnie Brooks Red | 1969 | SA766255 | 34 | 13½ |
| FC Bonnie Brooks Tuff & A Half | 1965 | SA297155 | 7 | 45 |
| Bozo of Irgold | 1952 | S598711 | | ½ |
| Brackenhollow's Sungold Rock, C.D. | 1967 | SA460409 | 1½ | |
| FTC, AFTC Brandy Snifter | 1954 | S683575 | 44½ | 47 |
| Brazen Beau | 1947 | S204830 | 8 | |
| Brick of Garfield | 1950 | S375163 | | 3 |
| Brick's Golden Riptide | 1953 | S654267 | | 3 |
| Brigg's Lake Golden Boy | 1962 | SA159959 | 7 | |
| FTC, AFTC Brigg's Lake Mac | 1954 | S792678 | 16 | 11½ |
| Brushaway's Golden Rocket | 1942 | A648755 | | 1 |
| Buck's Golden Nip | 1956 | S807409 | 4 | |
| Buddy Always | 1952 | S620631 | 5 | |
| Can. Dual Ch. Bycober Sir Alexander, Can. C.D. | 1950 | 296939CKC | | |
| Caernac's Mor Sealgair | 1972 | SB77131 | 7 | 4 |
| FC, AFC Chief Sands | 1966 | SA438222 | 53 | 34 |
| Chips of Sands | 1970 | SA876319 | 6 | 8½ |
| Chuck's Victoria Special | 1958 | S977084 | 3 | |
| Dual Ch., AFC Clickety Click | 1963 | SA263912 | 11½ | 20½ |
| FTC Commanche Cayenne | 1951 | S477091 | 12 | 41½ |
| Copper Beau | 1954 | S710440 | 9 | 1 |
| Corrie of Sycan | 1956 | S824962 | ½ | |
| Dual Ch., AFTC Craigmar Dustrack | 1951 | S459592 | 9 | 21 |
| Craigmar's Tagalong | 1955 | S779286 | 2 | |
| Ch. Craigmar's Tule Topper | 1956 | S839490 | | 1 |
| FTC Cresta Chip | 1945 | A994048 | | 12½ |
| Dual Ch., AFTC Cresta Gold Rip | 1950 | S409316 | 3½ | 12 |
| AFC Dorado's Rowdy Hastings | 1971 | SA923957 | 19½ | |
| Duke of Handjem | 1966 | SA403209 | 4 | |
| Duke of Spring Hills | 1953 | S626495 | 3 | |
| Dustrack's Golden Riddle | 1955 | S737876 | 1 | |
| Dutch's Red | 1964 | SA330352 | 3½ | ½ |

| Name | Date Birth | AKC Reg. Number | AKC Amateur Points | AKC Open Points |
|---|---|---|---|---|
| Echo of Maple Lake | 1958 | S928500 | ½ | |
| FTC, AFTC Fairhaven Donner | 1956 | S781503 | 17½ | 15 |
| Flambeau Chip of Handjem | 1969 | SA706142 | 3 | |
| FTC Georgia Boy | 1949 | A708145 | 1 | 20 |
| Gigi's Golden Prince | 1967 | SA560153 | ½ | |
| Gold | 1942 | A708145 | | 1 |
| Gold Mont Sir Nibbs | 1948 | S279892 | ½ | |
| CFTC Golden Achievement | 1960 | SA113007 | | |
| Golden Boy XI | 1950 | S434790 | ½ | |
| CFTC Golden Kingsley Rex | 1959 | 438068CKC | | |
| Goldway Piper | 1967 | SA482069 | | ½ |
| Ch. Golden Knoll's Town Talk, C.D. | 1954 | S693266 | 2 | |
| Golden Opportunity | 1958 | S981264 | 6½ | 1 |
| AFC Golden Rocket VI | 1957 | S976261 | 15½ | 1 |
| FC, AFC Golden Rocket's Missile | 1961 | SA175930 | 37 | 28 |
| Golden Rocket's Raincheck | 1964 | SA356564 | | 3 |
| Golden Rocket's Ruff Boy | 1964 | SA308729 | ½ | |
| AFTC Golden Star of Oak Ridge | 1954 | S758274 | 9 | 8 |
| AFTC Goldenrod's Thanksgiving | 1956 | S862443 | 32½ | 4½ |
| Goldwood Bingo | 1960 | SA57839 | 3 | |
| Goldwood Frisco | 1949 | A872638 | | 13 |
| FTC Goldwood Tuck | 1937 | A205346 | | 31 |
| AFC Gunnerman's Coin of Copper | 1956 | S822112 | 22 | 3½ |
| H.R.H. Timothy | 1941 | A584049 | | ½ |
| AFTC Happy Thanksgiving, C.D. | 1952 | S576101 | 70½ | 1 |
| FTC Harbor City Rebel | 1950 | S405972 | | 26½ |
| Harbor City Shadrack | 1951 | S565674 | | 4 |
| Hathaway Treve | 1951 | S519682 | 3 | |
| Henry J. Livingston | 1959 | SA11955 | 6 | 5 |
| Heydown Rip Tide | 1946 | S132131 | | ½ |
| AFC Holway Barty | 1971 | SB147050 | 11 | 6 |
| Holway Leo | 1955 | S892175 | 3 | |
| AFC, Ch. Honor's Dorado of Spindrift | 1969 | SA707435 | 17 | 9½ |
| FC Igor of Geekowat | 1960 | SA69015 | | 20 |
| Indian Knoll's Gunfire | 1956 | S786818 | 5½ | ½ |
| Ch. J's Golden Gunner, C.D. | 1959 | SA12753 | 1 | |
| FTC, AFTC Joaquin's Nugget | 1952 | S608926 | 29 | 20½ |
| Jolly Again of Ouilmette, C.D. | 1961 | SA159661 | 1½ | 5½ |
| Jolly Too | 1952 | S575901 | ½ | |
| Jupiter's Golden Comet | 1953 | S595617 | 10½ | |
| CFTC Karl of Felsberg | 1956 | 398836CKC | | |
| Kate's Own Rip | 1952 | S706006 | ½ | 6½ |
| Kimberwood's Rock River | 1972 | SB189888 | | ½ |
| Kin Ken | 1946 | S86112 | | 1 |
| King Croesus | 1954 | S661222 | 12½ | |
| King Kinike of Handjem | 1966 | SA403210 | 6 | ½ |
| 1941 Nat'l Ch., FTC King Midas of Woodend | 1937 | A207518 | | 17 |
| FTC Kingdale's Buck | 1943 | A843397 | | 13½ |
| CFTC King's Ransome II | 1952 | 300883CKC | 6 | |
| AFTC King's Red Flame | 1955 | S763789 | 17 | |

| Name | Date Birth | AKC Reg. Number | AKC Amateur Points | AKC Open Points |
|---|---|---|---|---|
| FC, AFC Kinike Chancellor | 1969 | SA708517 | 39½ | 82 |
| Kinike Loki | 1973 | SB443776 | 3½ | ½ |
| FC Kinike Oro 'de Rojo | 1972 | SB253962 | 1½ | 10 |
| Kip of Stonegate | 1948 | S233768 | ½ | |
| Knight of Amber | 1950 | S461544 | 7 | |
| Krystolida's Royal Skyrocket | 1947 | S174298 | 1 | |
| Lakwoia Gold Dandee | 1970 | SA775722 | | ½ |
| Lord Buff of Spring Hills | 1957 | S898444 | ½ | |
| AFTC, Ch. Lorelei's Golden Rockbottom, U.D. | 1948 | S270654 | 14 | 1 |
| Lucky Star Duke | 1959 | SA136046 | 3 | ½ |
| FTC, AFTC Macopin Expectation | 1954 | S702541 | 40½ | 56 |
| Macopin Golden Ducat II | 1960 | SA45221 | | 8 |
| FTC Macopin Maximum | 1956 | S836811 | | 86 |
| Maple Lake's Prairie Fire | 1961 | SA185087 | ½ | |
| Marchall's Texas Duke | 1965 | SA354588 | | 1 |
| Maycock's Duke | 1961 | SA18800 | | 3 |
| Michael of Woodend | 1939 | A327770 | ½ | |
| Mr. Nugget of Redmond | 1968 | SA583809 | ½ | |
| FC, AFC Misty's Sungold Lad, C.D.X. | 1965 | SA327277 | 124 | 88½ |
| FC, AFC Moll-Leo Cayenne | 1962 | SA182290 | 21 | 16 |
| Molly's Cayson Bear | 1964 | SA321388 | 3 | |
| Moody's Rock Point Chevron | 1959 | SA16047 | 3 | |
| Nero of Roedare | 1936 | A112862 | | 13 |
| Nickle, C.D. | 1948 | S338500 | 7 | |
| FTC, AFTC Nickolas of Logan's End | 1958 | S918564 | 123½ | 52 |
| Nimrodorum Duke | 1945 | S191575 | | 5½ |
| FC, AFC Northbreak Kinike Sir Jim | 1972 | SB297944 | 19 | 14 |
| Northbreak's Panacea | 1968 | SA586952 | | ½ |
| FTC, AFTC Oakcreek's Fremont | 1951 | S466782 | 28 | 73½ |
| FTC, AFTC Oakcreek's Sir Dorchester | 1948 | S217227 | 26 | 43½ |
| Oakcreek's Stormy Weather | 1952 | S566713 | 3 | 14½ |
| 1952 Can. Nat'l FTC, FTC, AFTC, CFTC Oakcreek's Van Cleve | 1946 | S49753 | 46½ | 78½ |
| Ojibway Gunner | 1956 | S819330 | ½ | |
| Oleander's Golden Lad | 1946 | S74830 | 1 | |
| Ch. Orchid Hill Chips Bifrenaria | 1959 | SA4983 | | 3 |
| Pajim's Klondyke | 1975 | SB749927 | 1 | 5, |
| Peter Gunn | 1958 | S962225 | ½ | |
| Peter of Woodend | 1939 | A569148 | | 8½ |
| Peter Pan's Herman | 1957 | S931714 | 6½ | ½ |
| Piccolo Pete | 1974 | SB624190 | ½ | |
| FTC Pirate of Golden Valley | 1941 | A507433 | | 33 |
| Pirate of Stonegate | 1946 | S77938 | | ½ |
| Prairie's Golden Bear | 1971 | SA963719 | ½ | |
| AFTC Pride of Roaring Canyon | 1955 | S79938 | 19 | 12½ |
| Rainvalley's One Spot | 1952 | S552542 | 9½ | 5 |
| 1951 Nat'l Ch., FTC, AFTC, CFTC Ready Always of Marianhill (*Field & Stream* Trophy, 1951) | 1946 | S90917 | 26½ | 53½ |
| AFC Ready of Sacramento | 1963 | SA224741 | 14 | 3½ |

| Name | Date Birth | AKC Reg. Number | AKC Amateur Points | AKC Open Points |
|---|---|---|---|---|
| FTC, AFTC Red Ruff | 1951 | S466780 | 45½ | 47 |
| Reddy All Righty | 1956 | S825102 | 7 | |
| Redwing's Tom Tom | 1956 | S849030 | 3 | 1½ |
| Red Rufus of Twin Pines | 1969 | SA766702 | 5½ | |
| Reid's Goldrange Drake | 1960 | SA223499 | | 3 |
| Ribbon of Novato Cain | 1971 | SB45701 | ½ | |
| Right on Dynamite John | 1974 | SB465134 | 17½ | 2 |
| FTC Rip (*Field & Stream* Trophy, 1939 and 1940) | 1935 | A86933 | | 63 |
| FC, AFC Ripp 'n Ready | 1960 | SA81585 | 29½ | 37½ |
| Riverview's Golden Sands | 1974 | SB751298 | ½ | |
| Riverview Hawk's Kiowa, C.D.X. | 1974 | SB453262 | ½ | |
| Robin Hood of North Haven | 1946 | S139043 | 4 | ½ |
| Rock of Courtney | 1951 | S515156 | ½ | 8½ |
| AFTC Rock of Roaring Canyon | 1951 | S517199 | 17½ | 7 |
| Rock of Sun-N-Aire | 1952 | S615672 | | ½ |
| FTC, AFTC, Can. Dual Ch. Rockhaven Raynard of Fo-Go-Ta | 1948 | S469424 | 51½ | 24½ |
| Rocky King of Post Oak, C.D.X. | 1959 | S982375 | 5½ | |
| FTC, AFTC Rocky Mack | 1953 | S655578 | 35½ | 10 |
| Ronaker's Grand Duke | 1972 | SB61152 | 1 | |
| Dual Ch., AFC Ronaker's Novato Cain, C.D. | 1966 | SA380533 | 51 | 35 |
| Royal Flush II | 1952 | S530801 | ½ | 5 |
| FTC Royal Peter Golden Boy | 1941 | A616198 | | 36½ |
| FTC Royal's Royal of Stonegate | 1945 | A814479 | 5 | 15 |
| CFTC Royal's Tuck of Stonegate | 1948 | S228503 | | 1 |
| Rumrunner's Handyman | 1975 | SB784619 | | ½ |
| Ch. Rusina's Mr. Chips | 1952 | S655648 | 3 | |
| Sabe Lo Todo of Stilrovin | 1964 | SA273256 | ½ | |
| FC Sandstorm II | 1972 | SB93797 | 2½ | 21½ |
| CFTC Sandy Knoll Gold Pilot | 1958 | 425163CKC | | |
| CFTC Sandywell Hi Speed | 1953 | 324196CKC | | |
| FTC Sir Arthur | 1953 | S650118 | | 14½ |
| Sir Michael Robert | 1967 | SA541703 | | ½ |
| Sommer's Golden Boy | 1955 | S808398 | | ½ |
| Ch. Spinwick Jim | 1953 | S724618 | 3 | |
| Dual Ch., AFTC Squawkie Hill Dapper Dexter | 1948 | S187838 | 13 | 27½ |
| Stilrovin Chum Fun | 1954 | S704823 | ½ | |
| Stilrovin Clipper Delane II | 1966 | SA429014 | 6 | 6½ |
| FTC, AFTC Stilrovin Luke Adew | 1957 | S951922 | 18 | 34 |
| Dual Ch. Stilrovin Nitro Express (1941 Nat'l Derby Ch.) | 1940 | A396107 | | 54½ |
| Dual Ch. Stilrovin Rip's Pride | 1941 | A396107 | | 54½ |
| FTC Stilrovin Super Speed | 1940 | A396108 | | 34 |
| CFTC, CAFTC Stonegate's Golden Tamarack, C.D., Can. C.D. | 1956 | 392775CKC | | |
| FC, AFC Sungold Lad's Talisman | 1971 | SB49314 | 20 | 14½ |
| AFTC Sunshine Cake | 1954 | S699147 | 33 | 13½ |
| Synsto's Provencal Pal | 1955 | S755953 | ½ | |
| Thanksgiving's Everready | 1959 | SA18543 | 11½ | |

| Name | Date Birth | AKC Reg. Number | AKC Amateur Points | AKC Open Points |
|---|---|---|---|---|
| FTC The Golden Kidd | 1945 | S20621 | 1 | 63½ |
| The Reddy Fox | 1950 | S523072 | 2½ | 8 |
| Thornwood's Ray De Oro | 1959 | SA27830 | 2 | |
| Tigathoe's Choptank Child | 1973 | SB364031 | | 3 |
| Dual Ch., AFC Tigathoe's Funky Farquar | 1971 | SB170187 | 37 | 15 |
| Tigathoe's Jicarilla | 1971 | SB41008 | | 5½ |
| FC, AFC Tigathoe's Kiowa II | 1971 | SB45105 | 33 | 10½ |
| Tigathoe's Planters Punch | 1968 | SA650286 | 1 | |
| Tigathoe's Teetotaler | 1962 | SA131935 | 1 | |
| FC, AFC Tigathoe's Tonga | 1971 | SA928990 | 46½ | 21 |
| Tink's Ben of Pennywise | 1965 | SA427637 | | 5 |
| Tioga's Gold Mica | 1973 | SB326101 | 1 | |
| FC, AFC Tioga Joe | 1965 | SA352221 | 37½ | 25½ |
| Ch. Topaz Highlight, C.D.X. | 1947 | S17848 | | 4 |
| Ch. Tri-Strada Autumn Hugh | 1961 | SA112928 | 9 | |
| FTC Tri-Strada Upset | 1948 | S215251 | | 23½ |
| Ty's Skipper of Stonegate | 1952 | S604294 | 1 | |
| FTC, AFTC Tyson Rowdy | 1956 | S869708 | 24 | 18 |
| CFTC Walker's Kim | 1950 | 310076CKC | | |
| CFTC Walker's Rhett | 1950 | 309590CKC | | |
| Webkap's Buster Brown | 1956 | S845764 | 3 | |
| FTC Whitebridge Walley | 1937 | A226373 | 28 | |
| Wilhaggin's Ready Poacher | 1968 | SA561611 | 1 | |
| Winsome Rajah | 1946 | S317536 | | ½ |
| Wraith's Gelt, C.D.X. | 1971 | SA975570 | ½ | |
| Yankee Rebel | 1971 | SA970703 | 8½ | 4½ |
| FTC Zip | 1948 | S257272 | 1 | 28½ |
| Zipper of Lakeview | 1945 | A979798 | | 2 |

## Golden Retriever Bitches

| Name | Date Birth | AKC Reg. Number | AKC Amateur Points | AKC Open Points |
|---|---|---|---|---|
| FTC April Showers | 1941 | A532502 | | 12 |
| FTC Banty of Woodend | 1938 | A299293 | | 12 |
| FTC Beauty of Sunburg | 1948 | S277182 | 7 | 10 |
| AFC Bonnie Belle of Hunt Trails | 1973 | SB256566 | 22½ | |
| Bonnie of Golden Valley | 1941 | A507427 | | 3 |
| Butch's Bonnie Bell | 1948 | S285275 | | ½ |
| AFC Cazador's Hermanita | 1967 | SA521851 | 10½ | 5 |
| Cherryhill Hawtdaugh | 1975 | SB803218 | | ½ |
| Colonel's Chip of Kristan | 1959 | S983164 | 1 | 3 |
| Destiny's Ready Ripple | 1963 | SA228213 | 6 | 2½ |
| Ch. Fieldale's Nike of Honeyhill, C.D.X. | 1973 | SB269110 | ½ | |
| FC, AFC Gerry's Kiawa of Rosamond | 1962 | SA172780 | 16 | 11 |
| FTC Golden Beauty of Roedare | 1937 | A246295 | | 15 |
| Golden Token of Goldrun | 1971 | SB91606 | | ½ |
| Ch. Hornet of Tigathoe | 1949 | S306991 | ½ | |
| Howe's Peggy | 1948 | S378988 | 3 | |
| Ch. J's Teeko of Tigathoe | 1959 | SA12754 | 3½ | |
| Jacqueline of Robin Way, C.D. | 1965 | SA365753 | ½ | 3 |
| FC, AFC Kate of Rocky-Vue | 1970 | SA866355 | 33 | 17½ |

| Name | Date Birth | AKC Reg. Number | AKC Amateur Points | AKC Open Points |
|---|---|---|---|---|
| Kingdale's Goldie | 1943 | A843396 | | 3 |
| FC, AFC Kinike Coquette, C.D. | 1966 | SA378622 | 30 | 20 |
| Kinike Mystique | 1969 | SA706021 | 6½ | ½ |
| CFTC Lady Bess | 1953 | 335495CKC | | |
| Ch. Lady Butterscotch, U.D.T. | 1966 | SA437695 | | 1 |
| CFTC Lady Ricki of Hillhaven | 1951 | S713795 | ½ | |
| Lorelei's Lucky Nan | 1949 | S339175 | | ½ |
| Maggie Happydaugh, U.D. | 1973 | SB328397 | 5 | |
| Mickey of Tiger Dale | 1957 | S966356 | | 1 |
| Mioak's Ginger | 1975 | SB852208 | 1 | |
| Mol-Leo Ginger Snap | 1962 | SA197628 | 3 | |
| Molly of Crooked River | 1959 | SA19766 | 1 | |
| Moneya of Geekowat | 1957 | S894596 | ½ | |
| My Flicka | 1950 | S434719 | 5 | 1 |
| Northbreak's Jazzy Classic | 1974 | SB726282 | | 1 |
| Oakcreek's Golden Spirit | 1949 | S300495 | 8½ | 2 |
| FTC Patricia of Roedare | 1937 | A300261 | | 14 |
| Princess Tammy II | 1958 | S940114 | 1 | |
| Ready About of Northbreak | 1968 | SA587584 | ½ | |
| Red's Lakwoia Ty | 1974 | SB475054 | 1 | 1 |
| Ch., AFC Riverview's Chickasaw Thistle, U.D.T. | 1961 | SA96205 | 16 | 6 |
| Ch. Rockcrest Golden Nugget | 1956 | S787384 | ½ | |
| Royal Golden Teal | 1949 | S329944 | | 3 |
| Royalridge Games Up, C.D. | 1967 | SA511729 | 4 | 2½ |
| Sam's Northbreak Lemon Cookie | 1972 | SB116669 | 5 | 3 |
| Sandy II | 1946 | S76139 | | 8½ |
| Ch. Saratoga of Tigathoe II | 1949 | S306988 | 3 | |
| 1944 Nat'l Field Ch., FTC Sheltercove Beauty (1942 Nat'l Derby Ch., *Field & Stream* Trophy, 1944) | 1941 | A487805 | 29 | |
| Shirayuki | 1945 | A975510 | | ½ |
| Sorehon Sabra, C.D. | 1973 | SB423636 | 1 | 3 |
| Ch., CFTC Stalingrad Express | 1942 | A642163 | | 5½ |
| FTC, CFTC Stilrovin Katherine | 1940 | A396109 | | 12 |
| FC, AFC Stilrovin Savannah Gay | 1960 | SA44248 | 48 | 46 |
| FC, AFTC, CFTC Stilrovin Tuppee Tee | 1957 | S798112 | 72 | 11 |
| Stilrovin Vee | 1942 | A598386 | | 3 |
| Sudden Sandy | 1946 | S75176 | | 4 |
| Ch. Sunburst Miss Polaris | 1963 | SA196995 | ½ | |
| AFC Sun Dance's Babe | 1969 | SA701869 | 10 | 5½ |
| FC, AFC Sungold Sprite, C.D. | 1966 | SA382654 | 29 | 21½ |
| Susie Q of Deer Creek | 1939 | A316352 | | 1 |
| Tigathoe's Chickasaw | 1964 | SA240341 | 1 | ½ |
| FC, AFC Tigathoe's Magic Marker | 1971 | SA916015 | 67½ | 35 |
| Tigathoe's Misty Morning | 1971 | SB30200 | | 1½ |
| CFC Tigathoe's Pekoe Tea | 1962 | 538329CKC | | |
| Tigathoe's Teetotaler | 1962 | SA131935 | 1 | |
| Dual Ch. Tonkahof Esther Belle | 1944 | A793606 | | 10 |
| Woodland Quill | 1959 | SA203187 | ½ | 5 |

| Name | Date Birth | AKC Reg. Number | AKC Amateur Points | AKC Open Points |
|------|------|------|------|------|
| Yankee Fluff | 1974 | SB761655 | | 1/2 |
| Zipper of Laurentide | 1954 | S720184 | 1 | |
| Zulu Queen of Marianhill | 1950 | S407797 | | 3 |

## Irish Water Spaniel Dogs

| Name | Date Birth | AKC Reg. Number | AKC Amateur Points | AKC Open Points |
|------|------|------|------|------|
| Black Water Bog | 1934 | A314501 | | 1 |
| Bogg's Jiggs | 1936 | A314502 | | 3 |
| Duke | 1938a | | | 1 |
| Mike | 1935a | | | 1 |
| Sonny Sam O'Hart | 1936 | | | 5 |
| Step | 1936 | A128533 | | 6 |

## Labrador Retriever Dogs

| Name | Date Birth | AKC Reg. Number | AKC Amateur Points | AKC Open Points |
|------|------|------|------|------|
| Abe of Creek Road | 1957 | S878572 | 3 | |
| Abenaki's Sagamore | 1964 | SA267457 | 1 1/2 | |
| Ace V | 1954 | S722659 | 1/2 | |
| Ace Hi Indian Magic | 1960 | SA126374 | 3 1/2 | 1 1/2 |
| FC Ace Hi Lone Star | 1957 | S930834 | 1/2 | 13 |
| CFTC Ace Hi Royal Flush | 1957 | 400898CKC | | |
| FTC Ace Hi Scamp of Windsweep (1959 Co-Nat'l Derby Ch.) | 1957 | S975520 | | 101 |
| Ace of Balboa | 1953 | S730055 | 18 | 1 |
| CFTC Ace of Country Club | 1957 | 411749CKC | | 1/2 |
| FC Ace of Garfield | 1959 | SA8433 | 1 | 62 1/2 |
| Ace of Orchard Estates | 1956 | S849718 | 6 | 1 1/2 |
| CFTC Ace of Southwood | 1966 | SA398841 | 1/2 | 101 |
| FTC, AFTC Ace's Duke of Winniway | 1953 | S617772 | 40 1/2 | 28 1/2 |
| CFTC Ace's Duke of Ardyn | 1959 | SA20492 | | 2 1/2 |
| AFC Ace's Shed of Ardyn II | 1958 | S970878 | 7 | 23 1/2 |
| FTC AFTC Ace's Storm of Winniway | 1953 | S618774 | 34 1/2 | 27 1/2 |
| Acey's Uncle Woodys Weasel | 1975 | | 1 1/2 | |
| Acute Accent | 1965 | SA323175 | 8 1/2 | 3 1/2 |
| Admiral of Timbertown | 1950 | S390538 | 5 | 8 |
| Ahab's Emancipator | 1967 | SA524728 | 11 | 1/2 |
| CFTC Ainsville's Jet of Netley Creek | 1960 | 495605CKC | | |
| FC, AFC Air Express | 1968 | SA566263 | 25 1/2 | 10 1/2 |
| FC, AFC Alamo Black Jack | 1962 | SA185895 | 32 | 14 1/2 |
| CFTC Alberic of Avandale | 1964 | 607467CKC | | |
| Allah of Polor | 1955 | S767172 | 1 | |
| Allo Dere Louise | 1964 | SA301830 | 1 1/2 | |
| Alpaugh's Whistlin Jim | 1960 | SA73258 | 3 1/2 | |
| Alpine Black King | 1955 | S776343 | 5 1/2 | |
| Dual Ch., AFC Alpine Cherokee Rocket | 1955 | S776340 | 14 1/2 | 43 1/2 |
| Alvaleigh's Plenty of Pep | 1951 | S523113 | 1 | |
| Amber's Dandy Beau | 1965 | SA312737 | 6 1/2 | 3 |
| AFC Andy Black of Chestnut Hill | 1965 | SA3777663 | 25 | 1/2 |
| Andy of Upham | 1940 | A520630 | | 3 |
| Andy's King Smut | 1966 | | | 1/2 |

| Name | Date Birth | AKC Reg. Number | AKC Amateur Points | AKC Open Points |
|---|---|---|---|---|
| NAFC, FC Andy's Partner Pete (NARFC '70) | 1964 | SA400162 | 71½ | 55½ |
| FC Anzac of Zenith | 1963 | SA197088 | 5½ | 38 |
| Apostrophe And "S" | 1974 | | ½ | |
| April Fool's Yellow Jacket | 1960 | SA40128 | 4 | |
| AFC Aquarian's Der Bingo | 1971 | | 20 | 2½ |
| Archie the Cockroach | 1966 | SA4538832 | ½ | |
| FTC Ar-Dee's Smorgasbord | 1956 | S850126 | | 21½ |
| 1951 Can. Nat'l FTC, FTC, AFTC, CFTC Ardyn's Ace of Merwlfin | 1948 | S239617 | 33½ | 90 |
| Adryn's Black Bart | 1962 | SA146530 | 14 | |
| Arroyo Seco Rocket | 1963 | SA370193 | 3 | ½ |
| FC Attawa Pucka Sahib | 1960 | SA128617 | | 28 |
| AFC Arlab's Boomerang | 1958 | S998112 | 20 | 4 |
| Audobon Gold Chip | 1958 | S921144 | | 6½ |
| Autumn Moon's Bo Jang | 1974 | | 5½ | 5 |
| Autumn Moon's Sammy | 1972 | | 9½ | 6 |
| FC, AFC Autumn Moon's Comet | 1974 | | 15 | 12½ |
| FTC, AFTC Avalanche Burnt Sage | 1955 | S817671 | 39 | 44 |
| AFTC Aztec Chips | 1955 | S814193 | 25 | 4 |
| NFC, AFC Baird's Centerville Sam | 1966 | SA383706 | 28 | 85 |
| FC, AFC Baird's Sambo II | 1967 | SA578995 | 5½ | 5 |
| FTC, AFTC Baird's Bakelib Donder | 1951 | S595279 | 9½ | 25 |
| CFTC Baker's Black Jeff | 1953 | 336552CKC | | |
| Can. Dual Ch. Baker's Black Magic | 1951 | 312684CKC | | |
| Baker's Black Pathoe | 1952 | 323690CKC | 5 | |
| CFTC Baker's Jerry | 1951 | 323687CKC | | |
| FTC Bally Duff Jester | 1947 | S319947 | | 14½ |
| FC, AFC Balsom's Snooper Honker | 1967 | SA544131 | 26 | 10 |
| FTC Banchory Night Light of Wingan (*Field & Stream* Trophy, 1937) | 1932 | 893641 | | 21 |
| FTC Banchory Varnish of Wingan | 1933 | A61030 | | 15 |
| Bancstone Buck | 1936 | A173495 | | |
| Bancstone Turpentine | 1942 | A646119 | | 1 |
| CFTC Bandit of Carnmoney | 1959 | 464511CKC | | |
| Banks of Arden | 1937 | A159963 | | 6 |
| Bar Me None | 1965 | SA374778 | ½ | |
| Bard of Arden | 1944 | A793995 | | 3½ |
| Barrie Brown of Sugar Bay | 1957 | S912327 | 6½ | 1 |
| Bart's Jerry of Stonesthrow | 1952 | S580299 | 11½ | 3 |
| Bay City Little Steve | 1959 | SA4538 | | 4½ |
| CFTC Bayern | 1961 | SA192251 | ½ | |
| Bayou Beau | 1963 | SA229469 | 16½ | 6½ |
| Bayou Dubois | 1975 | | 3 | |
| Bayou Jimbeau | 1970 | | 3½ | 2 |
| Bayou Pirate | 1960 | SA225453 | 10 | |
| Beartooth's Bah-Humbug | 1975 | | | 4 |
| Bear Creek Java | 1950 | SA50451 | | 3 |
| Dual Ch. Beau Brummel of Wyndale | 1952 | S657661 | | 42 |
| AFC Beau Gentry | 1968 | SA600817 | 32 | |
| FC, AFC Beau of Blair House | 1965 | SA363311 | 17 | 33½ |

| Name | Date Birth | AKC Reg. Number | AKC Amateur Points | AKC Open Points |
|---|---|---|---|---|
| FTC, AFTC Beau of the Lark | 1950 | S483563 | 15 | 59½ |
| FTC Beau of Zenith | 1955 | S760925 | | 46½ |
| FTC Beau's Buzzsaw of Stonesthrow | 1956 | S878462 | 6 | 17½ |
| FTC Beautywood's Carbon Copy | 1952 | S552712 | | 28 |
| Beautywood's Licorice Kid | 1950 | S379835 | 3 | |
| FTC Beautywood's Rare Trouble | 1956 | S854387 | | 52 |
| Beautywood's Smoking Gun | 1949 | S304063 | 13 | |
| FTC, AFTC Beavercreek Bandit | 1947 | S293923 | 20½ | 21 |
| Beavercrest Black Tartan II | 1966 | SA395670 | 2½ | |
| Beavercrest Dirk | 1954 | S757904 | 10½ | ½ |
| Beavercrest Goin Gus | 1967 | SA485418 | ½ | |
| Beavercrest Kannonball Kidd | 1958 | S964636 | 3 | 4 |
| Beavercrest's Blade | 1955 | S744827 | 5½ | |
| AFC Beavercrest's Toreador | 1957 | S934653 | 19 | 9 |
| Beelzebub | 1973 | | 1 | 3 |
| FC Bel-Aire Lucky Boy | 1967 | SA604506 | 5½ | 22 |
| FC, AFC Bel Air's Black Duck | 1969 | | 27 | |
| Belle Shain's Steamboat Man | 1965 | SA421154 | 1 | ½ |
| AFC Bellota Cacahuete | 1965 | SA416532 | 28½ | 2 |
| Dual Ch., AFTC Bengal of Arden | 1944 | A998454 | 15 | 51 |
| Big Duke of Swampland | 1959 | SA42293 | | ½ |
| Big Gun of Ardwood | 1959 | SA21546 | 5 | 2 |
| Big Lost River Mike | 1971 | | 21 | 54½ |
| Big Mo of Audlon | 1956 | 400299CKC | 6 | |
| Big Oak's Black Rip | 1956 | S922525 | 5 | |
| Big River Dan | 1975 | | | 1 |
| Big Splash Pride of Georgia | 1958 | S993802 | | ½ |
| FTC, AFTC Bigstone Bandit | 1947 | S196133 | 15½ | 20½ |
| FTC, AFTC Bigstone Demon of Bruce | 1955 | S753363 | 38 | 16 |
| FC, AFC Bigstone Flint (1966 Nat'l Derby Ch.) | 1964 | SA329701 | 32½ | 74 |
| Bigstone Magnum Mike | 1955 | S847329 | | 3 |
| CFTC Bigstone Nig | 1958 | SA74270 | | 4 |
| FC Bigstone Scout | 1963 | SA281717 | 8 | 17 |
| Bigstone's Duke of Herber | 1960 | SA52588 | | 1 |
| CFTC Bigstone's Gaelic Pride | 1960 | 491433CKC | | |
| AFC Bigstone's Hard Happy | 1966 | SA456121 | 15½ | 5 |
| AFC Billy Pawlesta | 1962 | SA156685 | 39½ | 12½ |
| Bing of Penelope | 1955 | 368949CKC | 2 | |
| Bingol Bengal Bouncer | 1957 | S929040 | 6 | |
| FC, AFC Bingo's Ringo | 1957 | SA22423 | 44½ | 34½ |
| FTC, AFTC Bing's Tar Baby | 1956 | S836063 | 17 | 40 |
| Birchwood Yodel | 1944 | A897247 | 6 | 16½ |
| Bistineau Binx | 1974 | | | 4 |
| Bitterroot Bright Boy | 1956 | S827835 | 3 | |
| FTC, AFTC, CFTC Bitterroot Chink-ee | 1948 | S240308 | 40 | 71½ |
| Bitterroot's Taurus | 1970 | SA786114 | ½ | |
| Bitterroot's Triple | 1974 | | | 1 |
| Black Ace of Whitefish | 1951 | S449595 | | 1 |
| 1954 Can. Nat'l Ch., FTC, AFTC Black Bandit | 1952 | SA240168 | 38 | 6½ |
| Blackberry Brandy V | 1966 | SA544810 | 5½ | |

| Name | Date Birth | AKC Reg. Number | AKC Amateur Points | AKC Open Points |
|---|---|---|---|---|
| CFTC Black Boy XI[d] | 1950 | S403863 | 72½ | 104 |
| Black Boy O'Cedar | 1971 | | 1 | |
| AFC, CFTC Black Brook's Abenaki | 1958 | S961073 | 38 | 7 |
| FC, AFC Black Canyon Beauregard | 1956 | S805130 | 27 | 18 |
| CFTC Black Caesar of Birch | 1962 | 530519CKC | | |
| AFC Black Chief of Nakomis | 1962 | SA158423 | 26½ | ½ |
| Black Cloud of Whitmore | 1948 | S282835 | 3 | 7½ |
| Black Commanche of Whitmore | 1948 | S201835 | | 2 |
| FTC, AFTC Black Corsair of Whitmore | 1948 | S201854 | 7 | 62½ |
| FTC, AFTC Black Cougar | 1955 | S802085 | 43½ | 21½ |
| Black Dan of Dandy | 1954 | S715288 | 2½ | 3 |
| Black Deacon of Leyden | 1958 | S939154 | 1 | |
| Black Drake of Farley | 1949 | S318944 | | 9 |
| FC, AFTC Black Duke VIII | 1956 | S817074 | 15 | 10 |
| FC Black Duke of Sherwood | 1964 | SA292324 | 1 | 10 |
| AFTC Black Dusky | 1953 | S637097 | 16½ | 3 |
| AFC Black Foot Lobo | 1966 | SA478015 | 20½ | 12½ |
| Blackguard's Rasputin | 1974 | | ½ | 3 |
| Black Gum Gus | 1953 | S661480 | | 1 |
| Black Jack | 1934 | 938783 | | |
| FC, AFC Black Jack of Audlon | 1958 | S983720 | 25½ | 28½ |
| Black Jack of Woodland | 1975 | | ½ | |
| AFC Black Jake of Devon | 1958 | S960258 | 58½ | 9 |
| FTC, AFC Black Jet XVI | 1958 | S968754 | 38½ | 77 |
| Black King of Missoula | 1951 | S457051 | ½ | |
| AFTC Black Likie of White Bear | 1955 | S777564 | 8½ | 11½ |
| Black Major | 1944 | S884765 | | 5 |
| Black Market of Audlon | 1943 | S745195 | | 1 |
| FC, AFC Black Michael O'Shea | 1961 | SA137174 | 19½ | 15½ |
| AFC Black Mike of Lakewood | 1958 | SA4751 | 12 | 3 |
| FTC, AFTC Black Monk of Roeland | 1953 | S608275 | 26½ | 75½ |
| Black Nig Prince | 1967 | SA508402 | | 5 |
| Black of Burnham | 1948 | S286621 | | 4 |
| Black of Scottswood | 1945[a] | | | |
| FTC Black Panther | 1944 | A853111 | | 172½ |
| FTC Black Point Dark Destroyer | 1947 | S264003 | | 34½ |
| Black Point Dark Tiger (1950 Nat'l Derby Ch.) | 1949 | S363652 | 1 | 6½ |
| FTC, AFTC Black Point Rising Sun | 1950 | S408383 | 40½ | 28½ |
| FTC Black Point Sweep's Chance | 1945 | S363651 | 1 | 24½ |
| Black Point Trimmer | 1947 | S264001 | | 6½ |
| FTC, AFTC Black Prince of Sag Harbor | 1946 | S18395 | 16 | 58½ |
| AFC Black "R" of Birch | 1959 | SA96669 | 31½ | 6½ |
| Black Rambler | 1951 | S511990 | | 1½ |
| FTC, Can. Dual Ch. Black Rock's Beauty | 1956 | S993776 | | 19½ |
| AFC, FC Black Rocky | 1962 | SA199719 | 14 | 13 |
| Black Rogue of Random Lake | 1953 | S687996 | 2 | 6 |
| FTC Black Roland of Koshkonong | 1941 | A582260 | | 22 |
| FC, AFC Black Satin Surge | 1969 | | 30½ | 34½ |
| Black Smoke from J & L | 1956 | S972398 | ½ | |
| Black Sorcerer of Sunset | 1961 | SA114360 | 1 | |

| Name | Date Birth | AKC Reg. Number | AKC Amateur Points | AKC Open Points |
|---|---|---|---|---|
| CFTC Black Squeek of Netley Creek | 1956 | S853691 | | 6 |
| Black Viking of Gilberton | 1959 | SA11026 | 8 | |
| Blackwatch Sonic Boom | 1973 | | 8½ | 4 |
| Black Wind Super Rocket | 1974 | | | ½ |
| Blackfoot's Shadow | 1958 | S956237 | 1 | |
| Blackjack of Barrington | 1941 | A591103 | | 1 |
| FC Blitz Von Mobile | 1963 | SA238281 | 5½ | 15 |
| FTC Blind of Arden (*Field & Stream* Trophy, 1935) | 1933 | 965612 | | 47 |
| Blind of Wake | 1947 | S139969 | 4 | 5 |
| AFTC Blitzen II | 1951 | S503317 | 16 | |
| FC Blue Water Brigadier | 1972 | | | 30 |
| Can. Dual Ch. Blyth's Ace of Spades | 1951 | 303794CKC | | |
| FC Blyth's Baron of Cavendish | 1972 | | 9½ | 19 |
| Blyth's Black Joe of Marelvan | 1959 | SA1821 | 4 | |
| Can. Dual Ch. Blyth's Knave of Spades | 1955 | 358864CKC | | |
| Can. Dual Ch. Blyth's Pat | 1959 | 442576CKC | | |
| CFTC Blyth's Ranger | 1962 | 53668CKC | | |
| Bo-Fors Surge of Ornbaum | 1968 | | | 4 |
| FTC Boar Ranch Nip | 1941 | 320871FDSB | | 29½ |
| Boaz Borak | 1972 | | 9½ | |
| CFTC Boatswain's Stormy Spirit | 1966 | 700301CKC | 2 | 2 |
| FTC Bob's Speed | 1949 | S363647 | | 19½ |
| FC, AFC Bob's Black Rebel | 1965 | SA374921 | 48 | 10 |
| Bodoro's Coaley | 1963 | SA243992 | | 1 |
| Can. Dual Ch. Bogey Boy of Grainger's | 1947 | 248027CKC | | |
| FTC, AFTC Boise Buckeroo | 1952 | S588570 | 19 | 22½ |
| Boise's Black Bart | 1966 | SA438950 | 1 | |
| FTC, AFTC Boley's Cascade | 1954 | S74557 | 45 | 62 |
| 1958 Nat'l Am. Ch., Dual Ch., AFTC Boley's Tar Baby | 1951 | S543603 | 42 | 50½ |
| AFC Bomar's Blackfoot Wog | 1967 | SA604672 | 21 | 2½ |
| Bomar's Chris | 1965 | SA347340 | 9 | |
| Bomber II | 1966 | SA422670 | ½ | |
| FTC Boocindy's Renegade | 1958 | S986527 | | 16 |
| Borracho of Carmelina | 1956 | S812395 | 1½ | |
| AFC Bow-Mar Black Brandy | 1967 | SA481907 | 37½ | 15½ |
| AFTC Bracken's Flash | 1952 | S588678 | 18½ | |
| 1959 Nat'l Am. Ch. FTC, AFTC Bracken's High Flyer | 1952 | S539461 | 84½ | 56½ |
| 1947 Nat'l Ch., Dual Ch., CFTC, Bracken's Sweep (*Field & Stream* Trophy, 1947) | 1943 | A997169 | 9 | 111½ |
| AFC Brandy of Cortez | 1966 | SA467905 | 23 | 4½ |
| FC, AFC, CFTC Brandy Spirit of Netley | 1957 | SA83525 | 84½ | 58½ |
| CFTC Brant of Bardona | 1952 | 310757CKC | | |
| Brant of Blenheim | 1965 | SA747327 | | 1 |
| FC Brazil's Black Jaguar | 1961 | SA197211 | 7 | 59½ |
| FC, AFC Breckonhill's Sean O'Moore | 1960 | SA97685 | 23½ | 12 |
| Brette of West Park | 1960 | SA46772 | | 2 |
| FTC, AFTC Brignall's Fleet | 1951 | S501194 | 7½ | 20 |

| Name | Date Birth | AKC Reg. Number | AKC Amateur Points | AKC Open Points |
|------|-----------|-----------------|-------------------|-----------------|
| 1948 Nat'l Ch., FTC, 1953 Can. Nat'l Ch., CFTC | | | | |
| Brignall's Gringo (*Field & Stream* Trophy, 1948) | 1946 | S231197 | | 110 |
| FTC, AFTC Brignall's Nick | 1946 | S252026 | 14 | 12½ |
| Broadmoor Rex | 1961 | SA182696 | ½ | |
| Brother Lem of Upland Farm | 1963 | SA204811 | 4½ | |
| Bruce of Timbertown | 1951 | S469709 | ½ | 9½ |
| Bruce's Happy Warrior | 1967 | SA543771 | 1 | |
| Bry-Bry's Charger | 1975 | | 1½ | 9½ |
| B. S. Hooker | 1974 | | 2½ | |
| Buck of Bankhurst | 1957 | S896977 | ½ | |
| CFTC Buck of Ghent | 1963 | 584003CKC | | |
| Buck of Monona | 1938 | A398698 | | 4 |
| AFC Buck of Whittington | 1966 | SA440657 | 29 | |
| Buck of Woodlawn | 1963 | SA189549 | | 4 |
| FC, AFC Buckra of Ansonborough | 1974 | | 15½ | 16 |
| FC Buck's Hobo | 1964 | SA270807 | 8 | 33 |
| AFC Buckshot Jake | 1974 | | 21½ | 7 |
| Buckskin Bullet | 1966 | SA538575 | 3 | |
| Buckskin Torquin | 1968 | SA564672 | 6 | |
| Buddy Boy of Mckinney | 1973 | | | ½ |
| Buddy of Poverty Flats | 1955 | S762578 | 1½ | 3 |
| AFC Buffalo Charlie | 1961 | SA135524 | 19½ | |
| FTC Buffington of Yellowstone | 1952 | S588627 | | 34 |
| Bugla Brant | 1933 | 944816 | | 1 |
| Bullet of Parramore Island | 1972 | | | 6 |
| Bumble Buzz of Bee Sting | 1966 | SA451766 | | 6½ |
| Buster of Rocky Hill | 1961 | SA134332 | | 5 |
| FTC Butch's Bitterrot Smokey | 1951 | S528312 | 3 | 79½ |
| 1967 Nat'l Ch., FC, AFC Butte Blue Moon | 1963 | SA251930 | 93 | 131 |
| Butte King of the Road | 1965 | SA416535 | ½ | |
| AFC Button Boots | 1962 | SA150925 | 23 | 4 |
| Cable Car | 1974 | | | 5 |
| AFC Caesar of Swinomish | 1958 | SA68998 | 19 | |
| Cajan Smut | 1959 | SA72428 | 1 | |
| Calcutta of Sugar Bay | 1956 | S817211 | 14½ | |
| FC Caliph Obsidian Hobii | 1963 | SA225197 | ½ | 41 |
| Call Me Mister of Audlon | 1951 | S512903 | | 5½ |
| Calumet Rex-A-Ma-Tex | 1974 | | 1½ | 4 |
| Dual Ch. Calypso Clipper | 1957 | S969729 | 13½ | 21½ |
| FC, AFC Camliag Primero | 1960 | SA147565 | 36 | 19 |
| FC, AFC Candlewood's Beau of Beaumont | 1968 | SA578632 | 11½ | 13½ |
| FC, AFC Candlewood's Little Lou | 1967 | SA509496 | 20 | 13½ |
| FC, AFC Candlewood's Mad House | 1973 | | 31 | 21 |
| Candlewood's Super Deal | 1973 | | | 5 |
| Canuck Crest Fonthill Dell | 1958 | SA38196 | 1 | 3 |
| Canuck Crest Gallant | 1964 | 615489CKC | | 1 |
| CFTC Canuck Crest Gunner | 1959 | SA149951 | 6½ | ½ |
| Canuck Crest Silky Sullivan | 1959 | SA155351 | 3 | |
| FTC Canuck Stealer | 1957 | S932072 | | 13½ |
| Captain Ben of Lake Forest | 1962 | SA175959 | | 3 |

| Name | Date Birth | AKC Reg. Number | AKC Amateur Points | AKC Open Points |
|---|---|---|---|---|
| Captain Jiggs | 1941 | A605940 | | 1 |
| 1966 Nat'l Am. Ch., 1966 Can. Nat'! Ch., FC, AFC, CFTC, CAFTC Captain of Lomac | 1959 | SA176506 | 57 | 46 |
| Captain Tornado Cool | 1973 | | 2 | |
| Carbo Computer | 1966 | SA398899 | 10 | 16¼ |
| FC, AFC Carbon Maker | 1960 | SA62914 | 36 | 24½ |
| FTC Carbon of Barrington | 1943 | | | 10 |
| FTC Carity's Smodge | 1956 | S812082 | 8½ | 20½ |
| AFTC Carity's Timber of Black Wolf | 1954 | S674644 | 24 | 6 |
| Carl of Boghurst | 1929 | 799955 | | 8 |
| FC Carnation Butter Boy | 1964 | SA306298 | | 88 |
| FC Carnation Rainstar | 1967 | SA615367 | ½ | 19 |
| AFC, CAFTC Carnmoney Billy Jo | 1959 | SA151982 | 8½ | 12 |
| FC, AFC Carnmoney Brigadier | 1966 | SA537477 | 100 | 86½ |
| CFTC Carnmoney Carbon Copy | 1956 | 404514CKC | | |
| CFTC Carnmoney Dugal Dhu | 1963 | 583003CKC | | |
| Carnmoney Fancy Dhu | 1962 | SA406826 | | 5 |
| Carnmoney Magnum | 1964 | SA648328 | ½ | 4 |
| CFTC Carnmoney Sark | 1957 | 417968CKC | | |
| Carnmoney Spud | 1964 | SA429749 | 5 | 7 |
| Carr-Lab Challenger | 1972 | | | 1 |
| Carr-Lab Ditto's Dynamo | 1953 | S726093 | 1 | |
| 1962 Nat'l Am. Ch. FTC, AFTC, Carr-Lab Hilltop | 1955 | S787560 | 93½ | 81 |
| FC, AFC Carr-Lab Penrod | 1964 | SA270506 | | 51½ |
| AFC Carr-Lab Phantom Jet | 1973 | | 15½ | 4 |
| Carr-Lab Pond | 1971 | | 12 | ½ |
| AFC Carr-Lab Raider's Gain | 1974 | | 21½ | 6 |
| FC, AFC Carr-Lab Venture | 1969 | | 2½ | 23 |
| Carr-Lab Wild Bill | 1958 | SA10255 | 1½ | |
| Cascade's Rodney St. Clair | 1960 | SA189543 | 8 | |
| Castlebay's Chaptico Painter | 1974 | | | 3 |
| Cederhaven, J. B. | 1967 | SA608746 | 8½ | ½ |
| FTC Cedar Haven Matador | 1963 | SA288339 | | 23½ |
| CFTC Cedar Hill Lucky Black Banshee | 1957 | SA239725 | ½ | |
| Centennial Chukaluck | 1967 | S490194 | | 9 |
| Centennial Cric | 1964 | SA305926 | 1 | |
| Centerville Charley | 1970 | | 7 | 9 |
| AFC Cha Cha Dancer | 1964 | SA315713 | 23 | ½ |
| Champagne El Toro | 1968 | SA660314 | 4½ | |
| Chanbar Jigaboo | 1946 | S69675 | ½ | |
| Chanbar Shadow | 1948 | S233689 | 1 | |
| AFC Chap | 1960 | SA78967 | 32½ | 1 |
| Char Dust | 1959 | S975955 | 3 | 8 |
| Charcoal Smoke | 1961 | SA118242 | ½ | 6 |
| Chauncey of Ellenwood | 1964 | SA280068 | 1 | |
| Cherlin's Pride of Bangaway | 1971 | | | 1½ |
| Dual Ch. Cherokee Buck | 1947 | S198841 | 1 | 12 |
| AFC Cherokee Chief V | 1962 | SA180894 | 19 | 3 |
| FTC Cherokee Medicine Man | 1947 | S201994 | 1 | 17½ |

| Name | Date Birth | AKC Reg. Number | AKC Amateur Points | AKC Open Points |
|------|-----------|-----------------|--------------------|-----------------|
| Cherokee Peace Pipe | 1968 | SA425618 | ½ | |
| Cher-Te-Beau of Repman | 1961 | SA165920 | 5½ | 1½ |
| FC Cher-te-Neg | 1958 | SA84835 | 9½ | 27½ |
| FTC Chevrier's Golden Rod | 1944 | A803208 | | 22 |
| FC Chief Black Feather | 1964 | SA 300468 | | 21 |
| Chief Cody of Le-Mar | 1968 | SA568093 | 1 | ½ |
| Chief Consultation South Bay | 1968 | SA576436 | | 3 |
| Chief Half Moon | 1969 | | 1 | |
| FC Chief of Lakenham | 1958 | S989642 | ½ | 11 |
| Chief Little Big Man | 1970 | | 4½ | 5 |
| Chief New River Joe | 1972 | | | ½ |
| Chief of Nakomis | 1962 | SA158423 | 11½ | |
| Chief Sknikeb's Venture | 1954 | S727525 | | 8½ |
| Chief Storm Cloud | 1967 | SA55000 | | 5 |
| CFTC Chilliwack Tar | 1945 | 211226CKC | | |
| China Trip | 1972 | | | 5½ |
| Chino Ajax | 1958 | S965725 | | 5½ |
| FTC Chino Bacchus | 1953 | S703704 | | 20½ |
| Chino Lucifer | 1953 | S703705 | | 9 |
| Chip of Long Lake | 1956 | S865470 | 1 | |
| Chipper Spirit | 1958 | SA17650 | | 4 |
| Chips of Birchwood | 1962 | SA199109 | 6½ | |
| AFC Chipsal John Henry | 1964 | SA249618 | 37½ | ½ |
| Chipsdale Black Ack | 1955 | S739327 | | 9 |
| Chipsdale King Midas | 1958 | S909165 | 3 | |
| FC, CFTC Choc of San Juan | 1963 | SA191050 | 2 | 19½ |
| Choo-Choo Judd of Jolor | 1954 | S691247 | 5 | |
| CFTC Chuck of Bracken | 1950 | 295503CKC | | |
| Chuck of Craigend Rock | 1966 | SA553677 | 4 | |
| Chuck's Bitterroot Rascal | 1971 | | 3 | |
| Chuck's Mainliner Rascal | 1972 | | | ½ |
| Chuk-A-Long Chauncey | 1973 | | 4 | 1½ |
| FC, AFC Chukar's Big Jake | 1971 | | 53½ | 71½ |
| AFC Chukar Chuk | 1966 | SA450864 | 19½ | 5 |
| Chukar's Starshine | 1971 | | | 3 |
| Chum of Canton | 1940 | A586684 | | 1 |
| Cimaroc Coon Willie | 1966 | SA42833 | ½ | |
| FC, AFC Cimaroc Tang | 1963 | SA215192 | 30 | 64½ |
| FC Cinderfella of Stonethrow | 1962 | SA169898 | 8 | 36 |
| FTC, AFTC Cindy's Pride of Garfield | 1951 | S462235 | 80½ | 88½ |
| Cirrus Sea Serpent | 1968 | SA764762 | 1 | |
| Claymar's Academy Award | 1964 | SA305386 | 1 | ½ |
| Claymar's Crash Diver | 1966 | SA426774 | 1 | |
| FTC, AFTC Clear Weather | 1951 | S494792 | 33½ | 24½ |
| Clem's Midnight Toothache | 1959 | SA23539 | 4 | 7 |
| C.J.L.M. Cliff Hunt | 1972 | | 1 | |
| FTC Cliff's Patrick | 1944 | | 8 | 20 |
| Clipper 7 | 1974 | | 2 | |
| Cloud Burst | 1968 | SA586886 | 3 | |
| Coaldust Markwell Bully | 1962 | SA105135 | 1 | |

| Name | Date Birth | AKC Reg. Number | AKC Amateur Points | AKC Open Points |
|---|---|---|---|---|
| FC Cody of Wanapum | 1969 | SA690038 | 4 | 36 |
| Cokey | 1954 | listed | 3½ | |
| Coldshore Timber Trouble | 1976 | | 1 | 5 |
| FC, AFC Coldwater's Brendan | 1965 | SA478526 | 9½ | 12 |
| CFTC Colerain's Thunder Rock | 1959 | 499836CKC | | |
| Coley's Grand Clipper | 1964 | SA258859 | 4 | |
| FC, AFC Coll-A-Dene's Perky | 1968 | SA620587 | 24 | 24 |
| Coll-A-Dene's Squire | 1967 | SA496517 | ½ | |
| Col-Marsh of Blue Hayden | 1973 | | 5 | |
| Colmoor Bolo | 1946 | S217751 | | 1 |
| Colonel Smokey Squirrel | 1963 | SA205108 | 3 | |
| Colonel's Duke of Mansfield | 1955 | SA102448 | 5 | |
| FC, AFC Col-Tam of Craignook (1962 Nat'l Derby Ch.) | 1961 | SA114812 | 63½ | 19 |
| Columbine Copper | 1957 | S966773 | 6 | ½ |
| AFC Columbine Loran | 1961 | SA134008 | 25 | ½ |
| CFTC Comet of Molybru | 1965 | 635723CKC | | |
| Comus of Timber Town | 1951 | S503604 | 12 | |
| Coon Doctor | 1974 | | 7 | 7 |
| Coon's Oily Bear | 1973 | | | 5 |
| Coon's True Grit | 1974 | | 1½ | |
| Coot's Big Mac | 1970 | | | 5 |
| FC, AFC Copper City Buck | 1960 | SA111000 | 12 | 10 |
| Copper City's Colliery Cal | 1966 | SA411342 | 8 | ½ |
| 1955 Nat'l Ch. AFC Cork of Evergreen | 1953 | SA25583 | 36 | 4½ |
| FTC, AFTC, CFTC Cork of Oakwood Lane | 1951 | S499406 | 15½ | 75 |
| Corky's Pio Le Blanc | 1975 | | | ½ |
| FC, AFC Corky's Ramblin Riley | 1969 | | 29 | |
| AFC, CFC, CAFC Coronation Ebony Chips | 1968 | | 15½ | ½ |
| Cougar's Good Karma | 1973 | | 7 | 1 |
| Cougar's Handsome Dude | 1973 | | 5½ | 1 |
| Cougar's Kitch | 1970 | | 5½ | |
| Cougar's Lucas | 1974 | | ½ | 3 |
| FC, AFC Cougar's Rocket | 1961 | SA1455039 | 76½ | 80 |
| FC, CFC Coulee Crest Sure Shot | 1972 | | 5 | 15½ |
| Count of Frontier | 1958 | SA14822 | | 3 |
| FTC Count of Garfield | 1957 | S848754 | 5½ | 22 |
| FC Counter Smoke | 1960 | SA52831 | 1 | 21½ |
| FC Country Club El Cid | 1962 | SA253501 | | 10 |
| CFTC Country Club's High Torrs | 1959 | 479910CKC | | |
| FTC Country Club's Jet Pilot | 1957 | SA22605 | | 46½ |
| CFTC Country Club's Juneau | 1959 | 464302CKC | | |
| FC Country's Delight Caesar | 1967 | SA530474 | 1 | 9 |
| Cousin Jack of Upland Farm | 1964 | SA286763 | 15½ | ½ |
| CFTC, CAFTC Cowman's Black Atom | 1958 | SA151976 | ½ | 1 |
| CFTC Craigend Jock | 1950 | 291119CKC | | |
| CFTC Craigend Rock | 1953 | 334502CKC | | |
| CFTC Crailing Dan 2nd | 1947 | 239146CKC | | |
| CFTC Crailing Dick | 1947 | S494974 | | 3 |
| FC, AFC Cream City Sturdy Oak | 1956 | S793119 | | 10 |

| Name | Date Birth | AKC Reg. Number | AKC Amateur Points | AKC Open Points |
|------|-----------|-----------------|--------------------|-----------------|
| Creedy Park Simon | 1954 | S877386 | | ½ |
| FC, AFC Creole Carpetbagger | 1967 | SA471518 | 57 | 43½ |
| FC, AFC Creole Ducksoup | 1969 | | 42½ | 51 |
| CFTC Crevamoy Iron Duke | 1964 | 606385CKC | | |
| Crook's Happy Bear | 1957 | S9000073 | 5 | |
| Crook's Jolly Roger | 1963 | SA265756 | 1 | 4 |
| Crook's Pork and Beans | 1976 | | ½ | |
| FC, AFC Crook's Tahoe Pat | 1955 | S876084 | 7½ | 14 |
| FTC Crowder | 1955 | S857684 | | 19 |
| Crozier's Firebrand | 1968 | SA57684 | ½ | ½ |
| Cumshewa Sinbad | 1944 | S44905 | | 3½ |
| Curt's Lucky Ben | 1974 | | | 1 |
| CFTC Cutbank Boblink | 1950 | 293867CKC | | |
| Cy of Sugar Ray | 1954 | S697707 | ½ | |
| Dacity Shah of Offershire | 1960 | SA52320 | 14 | |
| FTC Dacity's Black Spider | 1951 | S511069 | | 19 |
| Dairy Hill's Mad Hatter | 1967 | SA277287 | 15½ | |
| FC, AFC Dairy Hill's Major Grey | 1970 | | 5 | 11 |
| FC, AFTC Dairy Hill's Mike | 1957 | S914668 | 97½ | 42½ |
| FTC, AFTC Dairy Hill's Night Cap | 1955 | S792027 | 96½ | 151 |
| FC, AFC Dairy Hill's Nightwatch | 1958 | S954552 | 58 | 47½ |
| Dairy Hill's Planter's Punch | 1964 | SA248674 | 14 | |
| Dairy Hill's Pokey | 1957 | S914667 | 6 | 10 |
| Dairy Hill's Top Banana | 1965 | SA396890 | 5 | |
| FC, AFC Dairy Hill's Wampum | 1968 | | 2 | 21 |
| Dajo's Black Velvet | 1959 | SA65774 | 11½ | |
| FC Dajo's Trouble | 1969 | | | 15½ |
| Ch. Dakota Jake | 1964 | SA277625 | 1 | |
| FC, AFC Dall-Chopper of Blackwatch | 1971 | | 18 | 49½ |
| FTC Dan McCrew of Wake | 1950 | S468440 | 4 | 14 |
| FTC, AFTC Dandy Dan of Repman | 1953 | S671760 | 11 | 18 |
| Dandy's Sandy | 1956 | S978847 | 1 | |
| Dangling Tar Baby | 1971 | | 3½ | |
| Danny's Cole Black Slate | 1963 | SA249836 | 1 | 17½ |
| Dark Hazard | 1955 | S809354 | | 4 |
| AFTC Dark Trouble | 1954 | S676603 | 14½ | 5 |
| Dart of Long Lake | 1960 | SA42180 | 10 | |
| Dat-So-La-Lee Painter | 1973 | | | 5 |
| FC Dave's Demetrius | 1961 | SA126073 | 5 | 11 |
| David's Idaho Pete | 1960 | SA62169 | 5 | |
| Deacon of Cochise | 1959 | SA32450 | 1 | |
| FTC Deacon's Crusader | 1953 | S650895 | 5 | 12 |
| Deadly Dudley's Deke | 1965 | SA312039 | 1 | |
| Deadly Dudley's Duxback Coot | 1965 | SA355145 | 3 | |
| Dee-Lites Mr. Bones | 1961 | SA172854 | | 1 |
| Deer Creek's Bargain Bachelor | 1949 | S371946 | 3½ | 9 |
| Deer Creek's Basic Issue | 1957 | S910271 | 6 | |
| Deer Creek's Busybody | 1957 | S880571 | 2 | |
| FTC Deer Creek's Cforcatl (1949 Nat'l Derby Ch.) | 1948 | S182302 | 1½ | 12 |

| Name | Date Birth | AKC Reg. Number | AKC Amateur Points | AKC Open Points |
|------|------------|-----------------|--------------------|------------------|
| Deer Creek's Do It Now | 1948 | S182303 | | 6 |
| Deer Creek's Little Peter | 1946 | S236608 | 5 | |
| Deer Creek's Swings Along | 1953 | S682581 | 1 | |
| FC, NARFC '71 Dee's Dandy Dude | 1967 | SA459172 | 230½ | 114½ |
| Dela-Winn's Disraeli | 1952 | S539992 | ½ | |
| Dual Ch., AFTC Dela-Winn's Tar of Craignook | 1953 | S598023 | 60½ | 30 |
| Dela-Winn's Tigh | 1944 | S157727 | | ½ |
| FC Deliverance | 1973 | | | 11½ |
| Dellfield's Black Jet | 1951 | S521693 | 4 | |
| Dell's Park Tag | 1942 | unreg. | | 2 |
| CFTC Delta's Black Mike | 1963 | 583296CKC | | |
| FC, CFTC Del-Tone Buck | 1961 | SA139689 | 2 | 45½ |
| 1961 & 1963 Nat'l Ch., 1966 Can. Nat'l Ch., FTC, AFC, AFTC Del-Tone Colvin | 1957 | S900483 | 66 | 114½ |
| Del-Tone Rex | 1962 | SA218179 | | 3½ |
| FTC, AFTC Del-Tone Ric | 1956 | S846614 | 18 | 36½ |
| FC, AFC, Denham's Delta Chief | 1970 | | 38 | |
| AFC Dent's Midnight Rick | 1964 | SA307745 | 15 | 9 |
| Deschute's Pat of Big Sticks | 1951 | S549099 | ½ | |
| Dessa's Black Angel | 1963 | SA227060 | 40 | 19 |
| FC, CFTC Dessa's Little Tar Baby | 1963 | SA227059 | 10½ | 57 |
| FC, AFC Dessa's Willie-B-Good | 1969 | | 78 | 74½ |
| Dewey Dew | 1961 | SA99831 | | 1 |
| Diablo Sobre La Asta | 1973 | | | 4 |
| FC, AFC Diade's Black Jet | 1970 | | 7 | 3 |
| Dick's Black Duke | 1964 | SA396834 | ½ | |
| FTC Di Mondi Danny | 1954 | S771423 | 11 | 20½ |
| Can. Dual Ch. Dirk of Avondale | 1953 | 339920CKC | | |
| Disaster of Audlon | 1970 | | | ½ |
| FTC, AFTC Discovery of Franklin | 1953 | S627583 | 25 | 36 |
| CFTC Diver of Trab | 1944 | S30665 | | 5 |
| Dixieland Coot's Tiger Baby | 1967 | SA560607 | 1 | |
| Dixieland Joe | 1963 | SA229455 | 9 | 8½ |
| Dixie's Midnight Raider | 1975 | | 10 | |
| FC Doc's Nodak Pistolario | 1969 | | | 18½ |
| AFC, FC Doctor Pepper of Le-Mar | 1965 | SA373818 | 20 | 12 |
| AFTC Dolobran's Angus | 1949 | S318951 | 17 | 3½ |
| C Dolobran's Little Ash | 1947 | S187971 | 5 | 21½ |
| 1960 Nat'l Ch., FTC, AFTC Dolobran's Smoke Trail | 1951 | S506106 | 158½ | 110½ |
| FTC Dolobran's Spook | 1948 | S253229 | | 28 |
| FTC Dolobran's Streak | 1948 | S407718 | 8 | 11 |
| CFTC Don Head Sugar Barley | 1959 | 444764CKC | | |
| Donald Grunt's Ray | 1967 | SA488874 | 13 | |
| Donald Dhu of Carnmoney | 1958 | SA54925 | | 7 |
| Don Ben's Rascal | 1972 | | | 3½ |
| Don-El's Key-Cee | 1956 | S830522 | 12 | 1 |
| Double Dare | 1972 | | | 7 |
| FC Double Play of Audlon | 1961 | SA110623 | 8 | 16½ |
| Drinkstone Pons of Wingan | 1931 | 905777 | | 6 |

| Name | Date Birth | AKC Reg. Number | AKC Amateur Points | AKC Open Points |
|------|-----------|-----------------|--------------------|-----------------|
| CFTC DuCap's Black Beauty | 1959 | SA75630 | 10 | 1 |
| Duck Wind Black Duck | 1951 | S494998 | | 1 |
| Duckmarsh Hot Flash | 1970 | | 11 | |
| CFTC Duckmaster's Ric-O-Dee | 1962 | 547060CKC | | |
| FC, AFC Dude's Double or Nothin' | 1972 | | 57½ | 72½ |
| 1974 Nat'l Derby Ch. Dude's Double or Nothin' | 1972 | | 73 Derby Points | |
| AFC Dude's Ditto of High Meadow | 1970 | | 22½ | 3 |
| AFTC Duke of Ashton | 1954 | | 39 | |
| FC, AFC Duke of Crookston | 1964 | SA136694 | 29½ | 28 |
| Duke of Groves | 1952 | S715908 | 6 | 2½ |
| Duke of Natator | 1947 | S195867 | | 5 |
| Duke of Oak-Aura | 1961 | SA322951 | 3 | 3½ |
| FC, AFC Duke of Teddy Bear | 1961 | S147529 | 32 | 16½ |
| Duke of Treasure State | 1947 | S117189 | | 4 |
| Duke of Tyrell | 1957 | S888096 | 10 | 1 |
| Duke of Whitmore II | 1947 | S173129 | | 1 |
| Dunc's Pierre of Jolor | 1962 | SA196297 | | 9 |
| FC, AFC Dusty's Dapper Danny | 1969 | | 18 | 25 |
| FC, AFC Dusty's Dingo Duke | 1973 | | 25½ | 13½ |
| Dunottar Plush | 1939 | A360928 | | 1 |
| FC, AFC Duster's Doctari | 1966 | SA440071 | 63½ | 118½ |
| FC Dutchmaster Supreme | 1971 | | | 15 |
| 1964 Nat'l Am. Ch., AFC Dutchmoor's Black Mood | 1960 | SA35121 | 62½ | 1 |
| Dutch's Black Lucifer | 1967 | SA722593 | ½ | |
| FC, AFC Dutch's Black Midnight | 1970 | | 19½ | 18 |
| Duxbak Black Oak | 1961 | 516597CKC | | 2 |
| FC, CFTC Duxbak Scooter | 1958 | SA137325 | 8½ | 132 |
| Dynamo's Trieven Travis | 1974 | | 1 | |
| Earlsmoor Moor of Arden | 1937 | A159966 | | |
| Easter Bunny of Audlon | 1955 | S770695 | 6½ | |
| FC, AFC Easter's Iron Mike of Rumsey | 1970 | | 17½ | 11 |
| Easy Does It of Valhalla | 1968 | SA694072 | 7 | |
| FC, AFC, CFTC Ebbanee's Ricochet | 1959 | SA140772 | 41 | 18½ |
| Can. Dual Ch. Ebb of Wetmore | 1948 | 258702CKC | | |
| FC, AFC Ebony Argonaut | 1972 | | 27 | 31 |
| Ebony Mood's Bingo | 1962 | SA157681 | | 8½ |
| AFTC Ebony's Jet Rebel | 1957 | S899490 | 21½ | 5 |
| FC Eezeegoen Samson of Audlon | 1973 | | | 16 |
| Egger's Royal Blue | 1963 | SA246744 | 4 | |
| El Duko Darry | 1957 | S914246 | ½ | |
| FTC El Jay's Ace Scenter | 1952 | S528512 | | 34 |
| AFTC El Jay's Smokey Willow War | 1952 | S528415 | 14½ | 12 |
| FC, AFC Elk Creek's Rebel | 1970 | | 18½ | 24½ |
| El Negro Sam | 1963 | SA217000 | 6 | ½ |
| AFC El Paso George | 1956 | S821088 | 17½ | |
| CFTC Elboya Bruno | 1956 | 385917CKC | | |
| Electricity of Audlon | 1960 | SA43337 | 13½ | 12½ |
| Eli's A Coming | 1970 | | 7½ | 1 |
| Elk Creek's Rebel | 1970 | | 1 | 6 |

| Name | Date Birth | AKC Reg. Number | AKC Amateur Points | AKC Open Points |
|---|---|---|---|---|
| FC, AFC E-Lynn's Super Strike Lucky | 1973 | | 29 | 23½ |
| Ern-Bar's Andy of Anzac | 1967 | SA530617 | | 2 |
| FC, AFC Evergreen Binx | 1968 | SA667591 | 54½ | 55½ |
| Expo's Super Tanker | 1974 | | 13 | |
| Express Charger | 1975 | | ½ | |
| Fair Oaks Ashanti | 1950 | S317680 | 1 | |
| Fair Oaks Samoli | 1950 | S371679 | | 1 |
| Fairie's Mark | 1951 | S524215 | ½ | |
| Falcon of Timbertown | 1955 | S741078 | ½ | 3 |
| FTC Farbee's Dugan | 1954 | S718318 | 1 | 12 |
| Faro's Mathew | 1963 | SA588427 | ½ | |
| Featherville Doc | 1950 | S412432 | 4 | 7 |
| Fenbroke's Belvoir | 1953 | S606186 | 6 | 6 |
| Fieldmarshal Heinz Guderian | 1965 | SA352815 | 5 | 1 |
| AFC Field Wood Mike | 1956 | S897831 | 26½ | ½ |
| FTC Firelei's Hornet | 1943 | A749743 | | 64 |
| FC, AFC Fisherman Bill of Delaware | 1960 | SA57901 | 55½ | 73 |
| Flair of Shedstone | 1943 | A709601 | | 4½ |
| CFTC Flapjack of Duckmaster | 1964 | 615237 | | |
| "Flash" of Sky | 1973 | | 6½ | |
| CFTC Flee Island's King Fish | 1955 | 353093CKC | | |
| FC, AFC Flint's Nifty Arrow | 1967 | SA562599 | 30 | 46 |
| Flip of Timbertown | 1955 | S741077 | 5½ | |
| FC, AFC Flood Bay's Baron O'Glengarven | 1962 | SA253706 | 45½ | 57½ |
| FC, AFC Flood Bay's Boomerang | 1962 | SA191300 | 47½ | 115½ |
| Floyd's Mr. Bang | 1951 | S499677 | | 1 |
| CFTC Flyway Bangor Mike | 1955 | 361022CKC | | |
| CFTC Flyway Tar | 1952 | 324552CKC | | |
| Fountain Valley's Dan | 1944 | S30707 | | 3 |
| Four Oh For Deer Creek | 1946 | S88947 | 1 | 7½ |
| Fox River Rebel | 1973 | | | ½ |
| Frankie of Rivernook | 1962 | SA179414 | | 6½ |
| FC, AFC Franklin's Tall Timber | 1965 | SA358903 | 32½ | 12½ |
| Frank's Bitterstreak Lucky | 1974 | | 12 | 6 |
| Fred's Ace of Spades | 1974 | | | 4 |
| FTC Freehaven Again | 1940 | A473727 | | 16 |
| Freehaven Bijiminy | 1949 | S372548 | | ½ |
| FTC Freehaven Jay | 1937 | A240811 | | 60 |
| FTC Freehaven Muscles | 1947 | S205695 | | 22 |
| Friar Tuck of Birchwood | 1960 | SA35642 | 3 | |
| Frosty Fortune of Flosum | 1962 | SA236466 | 3½ | |
| FTC Gabriel of Cram | 1940 | A508375 | | 10 |
| AFC, CFC, CAFC Gahonk's Mississauga Totem | 1973 | | 4½ | |
| Gahonk's Pow Wow | 1969 | | 13½ | 1 |
| FC, AFC Gahonk's Saygo | 1971 | | 21 | 33 |
| FC, AFC Gahonk's Traveller | 1969 | SA12002 | 4½ | ½ |
| Gayfeather's Domino | 1966 | SA447841 | | 1½ |
| Gaylab's Gabriel | 1967 | SA600628 | 3½ | ½ |
| FC, AFC Gaylab's Shamus | 1967 | SA573601 | 15½ | 26½ |
| FTC Gerba Adam of Paradise | 1952 | S595707 | | 13 |

| Name | Date Birth | AKC Reg. Number | AKC Amateur Points | AKC Open Points |
|------|-----------|-----------------|---------------------|------------------|
| Gee Baby | 1962 | SA147761 | 2 | |
| AFC Geechee | 1964 | SA307699 | 32 | 10 |
| Geechee's Buck | 1966 | SA429311 | 5 | |
| Geechee's Daniel Dexter | 1966 | SA460352 | 1/2 | 1 |
| Gemini Lucky Brandy | 1973 | | | 6 1/2 |
| CFTC Gene Joy's Gallant Rob | 1963 | 568875CKC | | |
| CFTC General Brock of Penfield | 1958 | 451878CKC | | |
| Gentleman Jiggs | 1968 | SA678855 | 3 | 3 |
| George of Poverty Flat | 1951 | S542888 | 1/2 | |
| George's Pennant of Glensprey | 1968 | | 4 | |
| AFC George's Second Try | 1972 | | 9 1/2 | |
| CFTC Gilherst's Gninnac Teco | 1961 | SA148875 | | 1 1/2 |
| AFC Gimp of Lakin | 1961 | SA182303 | 23 1/2 | 3 1/2 |
| Ginger Gold | 1959 | SA13966 | | 7 |
| CFC Ginger's Chocolate August | 1973 | | | 3 1/2 |
| Gin's Admiral Nemo | 1973 | | | 9 1/2 |
| Git'N Go Ace | 1958 | SA23105 | 5 1/2 | 1/2 |
| CFTC Glado's Cisco Kid | 1958 | 500272CKC | | |
| Glenairlie Blackjet | 1939 | A378726 | 1 | |
| FTC Glenairlie Rocket (1938 Nat'l Derby Ch.) | 1937 | A239815 | | 63 |
| FTC Glenairlie Rover | 1933 | A90631 | | 17 |
| FTC, AFC Glengarven's Kim | 1957 | SA19349 | 25 | 33 1/2 |
| FC, AFC Glengarven's Mik (All-Time highest score in amateur stakes through 1969) | 1959 | SA151980 | 233 | 120 |
| Glenmere Joe | 1929 | 768170 | | |
| Glenmere Monarch | 1927 | 7681169 | | 5 |
| CFTC Glenmore Jock | 1946 | S225233 | | 1/2 |
| Glenn's Black Jack | 1972 | | | 3 |
| Glen's Lady's Casper | 1964 | SA387316 | | 3 |
| Glor-Loral Tom Dooley | 1973 | | | 3 |
| FTC, AFC, Glor-Loral Watch My Smoke | 1958 | S952160 | 16 | 17 |
| Good Hope Angus | 1941 | A641461 | | 1 |
| FC, AFC Goodrich's Smokey Bear | 1963 | SA243588 | 10 | 12 |
| Goose Spooker | 1963 | SA293428 | | 1/2 |
| CFTC Goedon's Smokey | 1953 | 343677CKC | | |
| FTC, AFTC Gordy's Black Boy | 1950 | S723104 | 19 1/2 | 10 1/2 |
| Grace-Art's Black Diamond | 1960 | SA138289 | | 9 |
| Grand Admiral Reader | 1962 | SA242603 | 5 1/2 | |
| Grangemead Donder | 1947 | S164082 | | 1 |
| Dual Ch. Grangemead Precocious | 1946 | S127563 | | 30 |
| Grangemead Soloman | 1940 | A489250 | | 3 |
| Grangemead Stormy Petrel | 1948 | S281261 | | 1 |
| Great Smoke Cloud | 1967 | SA528026 | 5 1/2 | 1/2 |
| Grouse of Arden | 1934 | A7166 | | 2 |
| Grouse of Trabington | 1945 | S128563 | | 3 |
| Gueydan of Beaumark | 1964 | SA298348 | 3 1/2 | |
| Gumbo of South Bay | 1968 | | 6 | |
| FTC Gun of Arden | 1938 | A26828 | | 33 |
| FC Gun of Thunder Oly | 1961 | SA133017 | | 41 |
| Gunga Din of Lac Ouimet | 1952 | S711646 | 3 | |

| Name | Date Birth | AKC Reg. Number | AKC Amateur Points | AKC Open Points |
|------|------|------|------|------|
| AFC, CFTC Gung-Ho of Granton | 1958 | SA168850 | 29½ | 9 |
| Gunner | 1945 | A985572 | | ½ |
| Gunner of Gunthunder | 1965 | SA368042 | 1½ | |
| FC Gus Dhu | 1958 | S987855 | 13 | 14 |
| Guy of Geneva Woods | 1974 | | 6 | |
| 1969 Nat'l Am. Ch., FC, AFC Guy's Bitterroot Lucky | 1964 | SA308959 | 80½ | 82 |
| FC, AFC Hairspring Trigger | 1960 | SA150997 | 20 | 10 |
| Hall's Royal Flush | 1972 | | 5 | |
| Halroy's Black Cheer | 1954 | S748836 | 3 | |
| FTC, AFC Hal's Spywise Zeke (1952 Nat'l Derby Ch.) | 1951 | S483923 | 49 | 46 |
| Can. Nat'l Ch. Stake '72, FC Hal's Toba of Win-Toba | 1967 | | | 32½ |
| Hane's Black Sambo | 1943 | A749748 | | 5½ |
| FC Hank's Spook | 1967 | SA535525 | 9½ | 73½ |
| Dual Ch., Can. Dual Ch. Happy Playboy | 1963 | SA234174 | | 95½ |
| Happy Hollow's El Champo | 1970 | SA808251 | 1 | 5 |
| Harang's Grumpy Express | 1966 | SA439268 | 36½ | 15½ |
| AFC Hardrock Gem | 1970 | | 8 | 8 |
| Harrowby Dandy | 1964 | SA305633 | 22 | 3 |
| FC Harrowby Wheeler Dealer | 1963 | SA229269 | 5 | 10 |
| CFTC Harvey of Avondale | 1948 | 259859CKC | | |
| CFTC Harvey of Avondale II | 1950 | S571651 | | ½ |
| AFTC Havenhurst Cliff's Pride | 1949 | S400825 | 21 | 1½ |
| AFC Hawk Hill's Sam of Devon | 1961 | SA121897 | 58 | 9½ |
| Haze's Zipper Zap | 1972 | | | ½ |
| Hector Black | 1951 | S728973 | 4½ | |
| Hell Roaring Topper | 1954 | S659015 | 1 | |
| Dual Ch., AFTC Hello Joe of Rocheltree | 1949 | S426887 | 14½ | 39½ |
| FC Hermitage Hill Timberdoodle | 1966 | SA494751 | | ½ |
| Hey You of Lake View | 1963 | SA208142 | 1 | |
| Hielan Havoc | 1962 | SA234748 | 8 | |
| Highflight Solo | 1957 | S877135 | 9 | 5½ |
| CFTC Highlander's Bojangles | 1957 | SA151977 | 3 | |
| CFTC Highlander's Buccaneer | 1952 | S677801 | 1 | |
| Highland's Black Rebel | 1974 | | 5 | 1½ |
| Highlight Rockey | 1954 | S715071 | | 3½ |
| FC, AFC High Low Jick | 1966 | SA417011 | 47 | 26½ |
| High Thor | 1970 | | 5 | ½ |
| Hi-Go Niki | 1963 | SA200153 | 5 | |
| Hi-Jack Smoke | 1956 | S876861 | 10 | |
| Hi-Line King Pepper | 1964 | SA302101 | 1 | |
| FC, AFC Hi-M's Jake the Giant Killer | 1969 | SA839689 | 49 | 40 |
| Hi-On-Friskie | 1947 | S218555 | | 5 |
| FTC Hi-Tail of Wyandotte | 1944 | A885452 | | 13 |
| Hi-Water Pete | 1948[a] | | | ½ |
| FC, AFC Hi-Winds of South Bay | 1960 | SA40398 | 40½ | 33 |
| Hill's Tip Top Tye (1968 Nat'l Derby Ch.) | 1967 | SA531004 | | |
| Hiwood Don | 1951 | S649127 | | 4½ |

| Name | Date Birth | AKC Reg. Number | AKC Amateur Points | AKC Open Points |
|---|---|---|---|---|
| FTC Hiwood Fleet | 1946 | S319949 | | 44½ |
| FC Hiwood Larry | 1959 | SA55025 | 5 | 11 |
| FTC Hiwood Mike | 1935 | A382739 | | 41 |
| FTC, AFTC Hiwood My Delight | 1948 | S372406 | 39 | 41 |
| Hiwood Nero | 1938 | A386573 | | 3 |
| FC, AFC Hiwood Piper | 1970 | | 202 | 136 |
| FC, AFC Hiwood Piper's Kelly | 1974 | | 19½ | 35 |
| FTC Hiwood Storm | 1957 | S996026 | | 29 |
| Hiwood Stormy of Alaska | 1962 | SA176464 | 28 | 10½ |
| Hollybank Hurricane Robert | 1954 | S695667 | | 2½ |
| Holway Barty | 1971 | | 5 | |
| Holy Smoke Jumping Jack Flash | 1971 | | 1 | |
| Honor's Big Spender | 1973 | | 1½ | |
| FC, AFC Hoss of Palm Grove | 1963 | SA237031 | 46 | 20 |
| Hub's Nite Cap | 1973 | | 1 | |
| AFC Huck's Pride of Riverdale | 1963 | SA248640 | 22½ | 2½ |
| Hundred Proof Bourbon Ball | 1971 | | 7 | |
| FC, AFC Hundred Proof Tad | 1967 | SA533212 | 27 | 10½ |
| Hunter's Gunsmoke | 1973 | | 5 | 1 |
| Hunt's Nipper of Little Smokey | 1967 | SA478902 | | 1 |
| FTC, AFTC Hurricane's Bay | 1949 | S370339 | 15½ | 11 |
| FTC Hurricane's Don Juan | 1951 | S503203 | 1 | 27 |
| I Go Licorice-Split-To | 1966 | SA406596 | 1½ | 1½ |
| FC I Like Luke of Wyntuck | 1972 | | 5½ | 21 |
| Ike of Mira Monte | 1952 | S623852 | 4 | |
| AFTC Ila's Black Joe | 1947 | S226749 | 21½ | ½ |
| Inashotte Dee Chuggy | 1966 | SA467902 | | 1 |
| Inky of Enivar | 1947 | S229141 | 5½ | 2 |
| FC Invail's Cavalier Carom | 1963 | SA223571 | | 68½ |
| FC, AFC Invail's Gun Ho | 1969 | | 30½ | 45½ |
| Invail's Gunner | 1969 | SA77023 | ½ | |
| CFTC Invail's Medicine Man | 1961 | SA101099 | 3½ | 5 |
| FTC, AFTC Invail's Pennell | 1951 | S465533 | 64½ | 21½ |
| Invail's Western Chance | 1952 | S610676 | 5 | |
| AFT, CFTC Irwin's Toby | 1958 | SA167724 | 22½ | |
| Island Acres General Leecoy | 1955 | S775979 | | ½ |
| Island Acres Shoremeadow | 1958 | S907484 | 1 | |
| Istre's Digger of Anzac | 1974 | | | 8 |
| Istre's Loup-Garou De La Bayous | 1972 | | 2½ | |
| Itchin' To Go | 1976 | | 1 | |
| FC, AFC, CFTC Ivy Pat | 1961 | SA205581 | 16½ | 16 |
| AFC J & L's Spooky | 1963 | SA206561 | 32 | 11½ |
| J's Big Water Buck | 1961 | SA145521 | 4 | |
| Jack of Holly Lane | 1952 | S621177 | 5½ | 7½ |
| FTC, AFTC Jack Pot's Second Whirl | 1951 | S538354 | 46 | 16 |
| Jack's Ace | 1972 | | 5 | 4 |
| AFC Jackson's Blaze | 1959 | S984005 | 12½ | 3½ |
| Jackson's Ripsnorter | 1962 | SA172209 | 2½ | 4½ |
| Jac-Lor Blarney Stone | 1967 | SA488174 | 6 | 1½ |
| Jac-Lor Rebellion | 1967 | SA523788 | ½ | |

| Name | Date Birth | AKC Reg. Number | AKC Amateur Points | AKC Open Points |
|---|---|---|---|---|
| Jacques De Quick Start | 1975 | | 1/2 | |
| FC Jaffer's Blackie | 1974 | | 5 1/2 | 22 |
| Jake of Fall's Creek | 1974 | | 13 | 1 |
| FC Jamie's Little Tigger | 1965 | SA374518 | 1/2 | 15 |
| Ch. AFC Jason of the Golden Fleece | 1969 | | 10 1/2 | |
| Jerry of Grant's | 1944 | S268226 | | 1 1/2 |
| Jesse James Buck | 1971 | | | 1 |
| CFTC Jet 3rd | 1955 | 354890CKC | | |
| FTC Jet IV | 1948 | S291435 | 1 | 32 |
| Jet Black of Del-Tone | 1954 | S708948 | 8 1/2 | 5 1/2 |
| Jet Black Sin | 1948 | S207112 | 4 | 1 |
| Jet Captain of Whitmore | 1948 | S207723 | | 9 1/2 |
| CFTC Jet of Spook | 1954 | 339381CKC | | 7 1/2 |
| FTC Jet of Zenith (1960 Nat'l Derby Ch.) | 1959 | S997907 | 13 1/2 | 39 |
| Jet Propelled II | 1958 | S930065 | 6 1/2 | |
| Jet Skipper | 1958 | SA4555 | | 1 |
| CFTC Jet's Gai Jeff | 1962 | S24162CKC | | |
| FC, AFC Jet's Target of Claymar | 1962 | SA138869 | 22 1/2 | 29 1/2 |
| Jet's Victor | 1958 | S969395 | 1/2 | |
| FC, AFC Jetstone Muscles of Claymar | 1962 | SA133987 | 106 1/2 | 68 1/2 |
| Jibodad Beau | 1949 | S331134 | 1/2 | |
| Jibodad Blade | 1951 | S484595 | 3 | |
| FTC, AFTC Jibodad Dandy | 1951 | S484596 | 30 1/2 | 16 |
| Jibodad Rebel | 1957 | S891015 | 3 1/2 | |
| FTC, AFTC, CFTC Jibodad Topper | 1953 | S648116 | 23 1/2 | 15 1/2 |
| FTC, AFTC Jiggaboo of Mountaindale | 1956 | S817268 | 34 | 64 |
| Jiggaboo's Bandito | 1960 | SA83647 | 1 | 1 |
| AFC Jiggers Von Aaron | 1957 | S901682 | 14 | 4 1/2 |
| Jiggs of Random Lake | 1954 | S691957 | 1 | |
| AFC Jingo Jo's Duckmaster | 1962 | SA234276 | 31 1/2 | 9 |
| Jingos Black Rod's Rock | 1959 | S982093 | 1/2 | |
| J. J. Duckson of Cofield | 1975 | | 1 1/2 | |
| J. J. Mumbles | 1974 | | | 8 1/2 |
| Jo-Anne's Black Blade | 1966 | SA417076 | | 5 |
| Jock Dhu | 1935 | A196869 | | |
| CFTC Jock of Craigend | 1946 | 222801CKC | | |
| FC Jo-Do's Jet Fire | 1963 | SA237896 | | 38 1/2 |
| CFTC Joey of Country Club | 1959 | SA156576 | 8 1/2 | 6 |
| Joey of Long Lake | 1954 | S665142 | 1 | 1/2 |
| John Henry of Oakridge | 1963 | SA226720 | 1 | |
| John of Sandylands | 1946 | S74515 | 1 | 1/2 |
| John's Spike | 1965 | SA397129 | | 4 1/2 |
| AFC Joker of Cramer | 1955 | S7900801 | 21 1/2 | 7 1/2 |
| Joker of Powder River | 1949 | S388364 | 6 | 4 |
| Jolly Boy of Rocky Hill | 1961 | SA198714 | 1/2 | |
| FTC Jolor's Amigo | 1953 | S659422 | | 35 |
| FC Jolor's Compobosso | 1962 | SA179840 | | 16 1/2 |
| FTC Jolor's Snap Shot | 1955 | S865381 | 21 | 31 |
| FC, AFC Jonas Abraham Malarky | 1975 | | 6 1/2 | 17 |
| Jones Daddy Wags | 1964 | SA284331 | 1 | |

| Name | Date Birth | AKC Reg. Number | AKC Amateur Points | AKC Open Points |
|---|---|---|---|---|
| FC, AFTC Joy's Coal Dust | 1957 | S904776 | 49 | 33½ |
| Judy's Buttons | 1959 | SA70753 | 1 | |
| FTC Jug of Sheridan | 1948 | S248155 | 1 | 17½ |
| FC Ju Ju Jives | 1970 | | | 10 |
| AFTC Jupiter of Avondale | 1946 | S431028 | 25 | 2½ |
| FTC, AFC Jupiter's Hi-Laurel | 1962 | SA166518 | 53 | 36½ |
| Just A-While | 1968 | | | 1½ |
| Just Sampson | 1966 | SA459726 | | 3 |
| FC, AFC Kalispa's EE Kwie | 1970 | | 7 | 18 |
| CFTC Kangas of Mount-View-Farm | 1960 | 490980CKC | | |
| Kap's Kaptain Midnight | 1972 | | 6½ | 1 |
| FC, AFC Keg of Black Powder | 1961 | SA121307 | 16½ | 11 |
| FTC Keith's Black Atom | 1947 | S371961 | 5½ | 18 |
| Kennon's Jockeaux | 1965 | SA362721 | ½ | |
| Kentuckian | 1964 | SA303114 | 5½ | |
| Khandahar Major | 1955 | S868172 | | ½ |
| Kim of Klamath | 1946 | S270303 | | ½ |
| AFC Kim O'Sage | 1960 | SA75689 | 31½ | 4 |
| FTC, AFTC, CFTC Kimbrow General Ike Double Nat'l Ch. (1952, 1953), AFTC King Buck (*Field & Stream* Trophy, 1952 & 1953) | 1954 1948 | S932408 S307484 | 8½ 23 | 19½ 93½ |
| FC King Cole of Menomim | 1958 | S963619 | | 19½ |
| AFC King High Siam | 1958 | S944566 | 50½ | 4 |
| King Jet of Rock Bend | 1951 | S451963 | 3 | |
| King Kong II | 1964 | SA317329 | ½ | |
| King of Pleleu | 1947 | 422885FDSB | 3½ | 1 |
| King of Smokey Pines | 1951 | S536301 | 1 | 6 |
| King of Winwood | 1945 | S25333 | | ½ |
| Kingpin of Hennepin | 1956 | S836048 | 10 | 4 |
| AFC King Tut V | 1964 | SA292522 | 41 | 5 |
| CFTC Kingbird of Cutbank | 1954 | 352831CKC | | |
| Kingfish II | 1954 | S670859 | | 8 |
| Dual Ch., AFTC Kingwere Black Ebony | 1951 | S469714 | 35½ | 28 |
| Kingswere Black Sambo | 1948 | S315214 | 1 | |
| Kingswere Long Shot | 1948 | S329155 | 1½ | |
| Kip of Geneva | 1950 | S425107 | 2½ | 3½ |
| Kip's Front Page Banner | 1958 | S967632 | 7 | 1½ |
| Kip's Nic Nac | 1957 | S928964 | ½ | |
| Can. Dual Ch. Kiskadden's Little Squeak | 1960 | 469593CKC | | |
| Knight of Deer Creek | 1945 | A975809 | 3½ | ½ |
| FTC Knight Rider | 1955 | S865381 | 5 | 12½ |
| CFTC Knight Rider's Deuce | 1958 | 493355CKC | | |
| CFTC Knightwood Range | 1963 | 573959CKC | | |
| Knight Train | 1964 | SA330216 | 1½ | 1 |
| Knots | 1968 | SA600372 | 3 | |
| KOKO Clipper Dipper | 1956 | S816530 | | 13½ |
| Kootenai Buck | 1968 | SA642789 | 1 | |
| CFTC Koskinen's Colonel | 1959 | 458506CKC | | |
| CFTC Koskinen's Cork | 1959 | 458507CKC | | |
| Koskinen's Dirk | 1960 | SA128600 | | 5 |

| Name | Date Birth | AKC Reg. Number | AKC Amateur Points | AKC Open Points |
|---|---|---|---|---|
| CFTC Koskinen's Geronimo | 1965 | 633700CKC | | |
| Koskinen's Pyewacket | 1970 | SA885830 | | 5 |
| Kracken of Timbertown | 1965 | SA375816 | 3 | 1 |
| Kristi's Black Sambo | 1958 | S972980 | 6 | |
| CFTC Kromm's Go of Skoal | 1959 | 439023CKC | | |
| FTC Krooked Kreek Jupiter J | 1953 | S731056 | 3 | 17 |
| FC Krooked Kreek's Knight | 1958 | SA90800 | 1/2 | 12 |
| Lab-Kingdom's Son-of-a-Gun | 1970 | | 8 | |
| Laddie of Rockingell (1940 Nat'l Derby Ch.) | 1938 | A431662 | | 5 |
| Lady's Brazos Pete | 1966 | SA370441 | 15 | 2 |
| Lad's Crowders Ranger | 1965 | SA367617 | | 8 1/2 |
| AFC Lakeland Tiger of Bruce | 1965 | SA393093 | 11 1/2 | 5 |
| FC Lakenham Paha Sun Dance | 1961 | SA119516 | 3 | 10 |
| Lakeshore Cowie | 1966 | SA542211 | | 3 |
| Lakeside Dean's Shadow | 1963 | SA202783 | 1 | |
| CFTC Lakeside Lancaster Lad | 1960 | 487681CKC | | |
| Lallinden Beaver | 1961 | SA160700 | | 1 |
| Lallinden Bengay | 1951 | S517732 | 3 | 1 |
| Lallinden Starben | 1952 | S538572 | 11 | |
| Land-O-Lakes Sunburst | 1962 | SA342451 | 16 1/2 | 1 |
| FC Larry's Lasser | 1965 | SA345068 | | 44 1/2 |
| FTC, AFTC, CFTC La Sage's Smokey | 1951 | S467476 | 23 1/2 | 16 1/2 |
| FTC, AFTC La Sage's Neb | 1956 | S797907 | 52 | 56 1/2 |
| FC Lasser's Captain Hook | 1968 | SA582404 | 4 | 15 1/2 |
| FC, AFC Lawhorn's Cadillac Mack | 1974 | | 16 | 14 1/2 |
| Lea's Beau Shot | 1953 | S685971 | 1 | |
| Ledgeland's Donne | 1934 | 977680 | | 3 |
| Ledgeland's Sambo | 1938 | A330485 | | 4 |
| Lefty Bicuspid | 1975 | | 2 1/2 | 2 1/2 |
| Le Sauk Roxy | 1949 | S43581 | | 1/2 |
| CFTC Leecoy's Biff | 1949 | 274639CKC | | |
| CFTC Leecoy's Bob | 1949 | S607789 | 3 | 8 1/2 |
| FC, AFC Leroy III | 1969 | SA797218 | 29 1/2 | 60 1/2 |
| FC, AFC Les Coup De Grace | 1970 | | 29 1/2 | 22 |
| FC Lignite's Red Boy | 1960 | SA80376 | | 25 |
| CFTC Li'le Bert | 1950 | S713797 | 1/2 | |
| Li'le Black Sambo IV | 1948 | S293503 | 5 | |
| Can. Dual Ch. Li'le Larry | 1943 | 207155CKC | | |
| Li'le Nick of Brignall | 1954 | S719134 | 1 | |
| Lil' Luke of Gypsy Glen | 1973 | | 1 | |
| Lincoln of Bel Air | 1967 | SA559134 | 1 | |
| Little Boy Boo | 1960 | SA83646 | 6 1/2 | 1/2 |
| Dual Ch., CFTC Little Pierre of Deer Creek | 1943 | A776978 | | 79 1/2 |
| FTC, AFTC Lone Star Blackie | 1953 | S615575 | 21 | 20 |
| Lomac's Telum | 1968 | | 4 1/2 | |
| Lo-Mer's Tor | 1972 | | 8 1/2 | 2 |
| Lone Rhoads of Fortune | 1973 | | | 8 |
| Look Judge Look | 1952 | S634451 | | 12 1/2 |
| Can. Dual Ch. Loonscall Tony's Mr. Jay | 1969 | | | 1 |
| FC Lord Beaver of Cork | 1958 | S939231 | | 60 1/2 |

| Name | Date Birth | AKC Reg. Number | AKC Amateur Points | AKC Open Points |
|------|------------|-----------------|--------------------|-----------------|
| FTC, AFC Lord Black Berry of Hyatte | 1957 | S895302 | 4 | 18½ |
| FC, AFC Lord Bomar | 1961 | SA73516 | 74½ | 98½ |
| Lord Sauron of Mordor | 1973 | | 5 | 4½ |
| Lorrendon's Lulu Duke | 1943 | A953782 | | 5 |
| Lorre's Mick of the Corkies | 1952 | S564952 | ½ | |
| CFTC Love's Black George | 1955 | 352069CKC | | |
| Love's Black Juno's Duke II | 1959 | SA126371 | | 6 |
| CFTC Love's Black Rock | 1956 | 371159CKC | | |
| Luck of Big Ben | 1955 | S858119 | 4 | |
| Lucky Star Duke | 1959 | SA136046 | 3 | |
| Lucky's Arrow Jet | 1972 | | 3 | |
| FC, AFC Lucky's Bitterroot Shasta | 1968 | SA638135 | 18 | 19½ |
| Lucky's Crafty Critter | 1974 | | 3 | 3 |
| AFC Lucky's Shasta Beau | 1969 | SA858483 | 18 | 14 |
| Lucky Tuxedo Imp | 1972 | | 1 | |
| Luke of Patty Jimsue | 1967 | SA546968 | | 3 |
| Lulake's Rickie | 1966 | SA439800 | 4 | 3½ |
| Lu-zak's Lone Ranger | 1974 | | 3 | 6 |
| Lynn's Black Magic | 1947 | S362804 | ½ | 3 |
| Mac Gene's Fall Guy (1964 Nat'l Derby Ch.) | 1962 | SA188240 | 10½ | 2½ |
| MacKenzie's Black Buck | 1952 | S578142 | ½ | |
| FC, AFTC MacKensie's Clear Pitch | 1956 | S823377 | 26½ | 14 |
| FC, AFTC MacKensie's Ripco Mac | 1960 | SA77461 | 22 | 20½ |
| FC, AFTC MacKensie's Ripco Tar | 1961 | SA144119 | 19 | 15½ |
| FC, AFC McGuffy | 1973 | | 48½ | 25 |
| McTarnahan of Tartan | 1959 | SA27125 | 1 | 4½ |
| Macadoo of Innis Arden | 1973 | | | 10 |
| Macaroni II | 1974 | | | 12½ |
| AFC Macho De Nopal | 1970 | | 15½ | 6½ |
| AFC Macopian Cadet | 1957 | S890251 | 18½ | |
| Macopian Duplicate | 1959 | SA22437 | | 9 |
| Mac's Dandy Danny | 1956 | S831781 | 3 | |
| Mac's Jet II | 1950 | S527333 | 1 | |
| FC, AFC Magic Marker of Timber Town | 1967 | SA532713 | 23½ | 16½ |
| Magnificent Royal Black Ash | 1969 | | 1 | 6 |
| Magnum's Jetstream of Anzac | 1974 | | | 6½ |
| CFTC Mah's Golden Sandy | 1946 | 223821CKC | | |
| CFTC Mah's Rocky Mountain Boy | 1947 | 240625CKC | | |
| FTC Maidscorner Paul | 1954 | S872481 | | 45½ |
| FTC, AFTC Mainliner Mike | 1952 | S620186 | 33½ | 19½ |
| 1954 Nat'l Ch., 1957 Nat'l Am. Ch., FTC, AFTC Major VI | 1948 | S229142 | 36½ | 145½ |
| Major of Stonegate | 1944 | A884971 | | 1 |
| FTC Major Tobin of Island Acres | 1955 | S775985 | | 34 |
| Majoray's Ace of Spades | 1950 | S438527 | | 1 |
| FTC, CFTC Malarkey's Okanagan Pat | 1944 | A876934 | | 44 |
| FC, AFC Mallard of Devil's Garden | 1958 | S964100 | 33 | 13½ |
| Malone's Duke | 1946 | S307422 | 7½ | |
| Mamba's Random Chance | 1955 | S737109 | | 26½ |
| Mann's Valiant Jet | 1959 | listed | ½ | |

| Name | Date Birth | AKC Reg. Number | AKC Amateur Points | AKC Open Points |
|------|------------|-----------------|---------------------|-----------------|
| Mandlewood's Romulus | 1970 | | 1/2 | |
| Manzanal Curlew | 1951 | S474585 | 31/2 | |
| Manzanal Diver | 1953 | S624311 | 1/2 | 1 |
| FTC, AFTC Manzanal Nimbus | 1949 | S393243 | 20 | 22 |
| FC, AFC Marelvan Mike of Twin Oaks | 1963 | SA209663 | 70 | 28 |
| Marian's Herbert Sherbert | 1954 | S695144 | 51/2 | 3 |
| FTC, AFTC Marian's Timothy | 1950 | S541069 | 40 | 531/2 |
| CFTC Mark | 1952 | 317544CKC | | |
| Mark Duck Dago | 1961 | SA138019 | 41/2 | |
| Mark of Gloster | 1962 | SA149449 | 41/2 | |
| CFTC Mark of Greymar II | 1947 | S377451 | | 1/2 |
| Mark's Honeygold Tug | 1970 | | 3 | |
| FTC Markwell's Ramblin Rebel | 1956 | S8995561 | 71/2 | 221/2 |
| Marmac Chip of Round Valley | 1971 | | 1 | |
| Marshland's Cooley | 1955 | S844900 | | 5 |
| Marten's Black Beau | 1971 | | 1 | 5 |
| FC, AFC Marten's Castaway | 1967 | SA529326 | 77 | 20 |
| Marten's Hi-Buttons | 1971 | | | 31/2 |
| 1965 Nat'l Ch., FTC Marten's Little Smokey | 1959 | S986861 | | 69 |
| Marten's Lord Fletcher | 1971 | | 2 | 1 |
| Marten's Mr. Lucky | 1963 | SA228764 | 1 | 3 |
| FC Marten's Mr. Nifty | 1959 | SA15087 | | 38 |
| Marten's Mr. Runaway | 1973 | | 1 | 61/2 |
| Marten's Mr. Stubbs | 1968 | SA608577 | 1 | |
| Marten's Moneymaker | 1966 | | 1 | |
| AFC Marten's Rebel Scamp | 1971 | | 27 | 21/2 |
| Marten's Scokim | 1963 | SA201700 | | 4 |
| FC Marten's Scrubby Giant | 1960 | SA119789 | 181/2 | 101/2 |
| FC Marten's Stormy | 1959 | SA123324 | | 43 |
| 1949 Nat'l Ch., FTC, AFTC Marvadel Black Gum (1946 Nat'l Derby Ch., *Field & Stream* Trophy, 1949) | 1945 | A975648 | 41 | 63 |
| Marvadel Huron | 1948 | S214501 | | 1/2 |
| Marvadel Thorn's Rambler | 1950 | S405863 | 13 | 81/2 |
| Masai of Aberdeen | 1966 | SA418810 | 4 | |
| Masai's Bounty Hunter | 1961 | SA204001 | 1/2 | |
| 1956 Nat'l Ch., FTC Massai's Sassy Boots | 1948 | S262528 | | 147 |
| Dual Ch., AFTC Matchmaker for Deer Creek | 1946 | S45265 | 16 | 461/2 |
| FTC Meadow Farm Night | 1936 | A169876 | | 27 |
| FC Medlin's Otto of Toothache | 1962 | SA185383 | 1/2 | 121/2 |
| Medlin's Texas Jack Tar | 1958 | S955449 | 14 | 2 |
| FTC AFTC Medlin's Texas Right | 1956 | S834503 | 481/: | 17 |
| FC Medlin's Texas Ruff | 1960 | SA71978 | 8 | 10 |
| Medlin's Texas Trooper | 1961 | SA118531 | | 1 |
| FC Medlin's Tiny Boom | 1961 | SA151315 | 21/2 | 151/2 |
| "Meto" of Devil's Garden | 1961 | SA118444 | 7 | 1/2 |
| Me Too Rowdy Bupane | 1950 | S493241 | | 1/2 |
| Michael Duke | 1961 | SA98576 | | 2 |
| Dual Ch. Michael of Glenmere | 1935 | A150354 | | 14 |
| 1968 Can. Nat'l Ch. Mi-Cris Drambuie | 1963 | 592688CKC | 9 | |
| NRFC Mi-Cris Sailor | 1966 | SA470951 | | 93 |

| Name | Date Birth | AKC Reg. Number | AKC Amateur Points | AKC Open Points |
|---|---|---|---|---|
| Middles Punk Scamper | 1959 | SA31927 | 4½ | |
| CFC, CAFC Midnight IV | 1967 | | ½ | |
| Midnight in the Bighorn | 1960 | SA29757 | 5½ | |
| FC Mike of Burrview Acres | 1969 | SA786465 | | 13 |
| AFTC Mike of Lakeview | 1956 | S894254 | 40 | 12 |
| Mike of Swinomish | 1955 | S762409 | 4 | 3 |
| Mill Creek Buddy | 1954 | S799782 | 3 | |
| Miller's Bo-Jack | 1949 | S383096 | 3 | |
| FTC Ming | 1933 | A285385 | | 21 |
| FC Minot's Magic Marker | 1965 | SA356251 | | 10½ |
| Mint of Barrington | 1941 | A509320 | | |
| Mintartar | 1954 | S676655 | ½ | |
| FC, AFC Mirk of Daingerfield (1963 Nat'l Derby Ch.) | 1961 | SA151925 | 7 | 36½ |
| Miss Jan's Dobie | 1962 | SA188381 | | 6½ |
| Mister Bones | 1947 | S236636 | 5 | 1 |
| FTC Mister Jic of Maryglo | 1957 | S855245 | | 17 |
| FTC Mr. Jones of Mishayuna | 1955 | S732935 | | 27 |
| Mr. Lucky of Oak Hill | 1964 | SA373938 | 4½ | 15½ |
| FC Mr. Mac's Billy Boy | 1963 | SA239806 | 3 | 78 |
| Mr. Misty of San Juan | 1961 | SA128315 | 5 | 9½ |
| FC, AFC Mitch of Bitterroot | 1964 | SA370647 | 51 | 16 |
| FC Mitch's Dandy Bouncer | 1967 | SA54126 | | 24½ |
| AFTC Mitzee's Chipper | 1953 | S630251 | 27½ | 8 |
| CFTC Mixed Up Mortie of Hi-Noon | 1961 | 526494CKC | | |
| FC Moby Dick | 1966 | SA471823 | | 16 |
| Moki Bear of Devil's Garden | 1970 | | | 1 |
| Moltar Mike | 1953 | S628469 | | 3 |
| CFTC, FC, AFC Molybru Butch of Barmond | 1965 | SA515776 | 9 | 17½ |
| FTC Mom's Mink-Corky | 1956 | S896029 | | 31½ |
| Mondor's Jet | 1961 | SA119840 | 4½ | |
| FC, AFC Monster Mike | 1964 | SA304816 | 16½ | 17 |
| FC, AFC Mon Tour De Force | 1972 | | | 10½ |
| FC, AFC Moon Rocket of Zenith | 1969 | SA710568 | 17½ | 19½ |
| AFC Moon's Star Trek | 1968 | | 17 | 3 |
| FC, AFC Moon Tang | 1970 | | | 23½ |
| Moose | 1927 | | | |
| CFTC, CAFTC Moose of Lomac | 1957 | SA175423 | 3 | |
| Moose's Royal Goose | 1970 | | 5 | ½ |
| Morty's Ebony Magic | 1968 | SA93609 | | 1 |
| CFTC Massbank's Black Viking 2nd | 1957 | 412161CKC | | |
| FTC Mott Place Captain | 1944 | A853503 | | 13½ |
| Mountain View's Buff | 1959 | SA26847 | ½ | 3 |
| Mr. Bigshot | 1975 | | | 1 |
| Mucho Dinero | 1949 | S461812 | ½ | 1½ |
| FC, AFC Muktar of Offenshire | 1966 | SA440989 | 17½ | 15 |
| FTC Mully Gully Goo | 1944 | A963683 | | 35½ |
| Muscles Jet Rocket | 1967 | SA472914 | 5 | ½ |
| FC, AFC My Boy Bubba | 1971 | | 6 | 12 |
| FC, AFC My Man Shiner | 1974 | | 27 | 29 |
| FC My Rebel | 1963 | SA223985 | 11 | 63 |

| Name | Date Birth | AKC Reg. Number | AKC Amateur Points | AKC Open Points |
|---|---|---|---|---|
| AFC Mysacks Major Buck | 1964 | SA291489 | 20 |  |
| Mystery Ichabod | 1962 | SA219828 | 1 |  |
| Namahbin of Oakridge | 1959 | SA46443 | 6 |  |
| Namakgon Dan | 1957 | S907980 | 4½ |  |
| Nancy's Beau of Cheyenne | 1960 | SA63897 | 3 | 1 |
| Nan-Ger's Gad Zeus Blazo | 1974 |  |  | ½ |
| FC Nassau | 1963 | SA243717 | 3 | 11½ |
| FC Nassau's Nar of Minnewaska | 1965 | SA358399 |  | 35½ |
| Navajo Tar of Sunnymede | 1955 | S725458 | 5½ |  |
| Neb's Midnight Rebel | 1962 | SA157594 | 3 |  |
| CFTC Nelson's Black Prince | 1944 | A789610 |  | 7½ |
| FC, AFC Nemo's Spyder of Round Valley | 1967 | SA537146 | 44½ | 14 |
| Nenoki Judd | 1970 |  |  | ½ |
| Nero of Manzanita | 1947 | S184591 | ½ |  |
| FC Nethercroft Nemo of Nacopie | 1962 | SA281150 |  | 69½ |
| FC Netley Creek's Black Brute | 1968 | SA974304 | 8½ | 12 |
| FC Nicholas of Niles | 1968 |  |  | 10½ |
| Nicoll's Comeback | 1966 | SA508528 | 7 | ½ |
| FTC Nigger of Barrington (*Field & Stream* Trophy, 1938) | 1931 | 252208 |  | 43 |
| FTC Nigger of Swinomish | 1945 | S282876 | 1 | 12½ |
| Nigger of Upham (1945 Nat'l Derby Ch.) | 1944 | SA840377 |  |  |
| Nightrider of Audubon | 1958 | S921146 | 1½ | 1 |
| AFTC Nig's Black Phantom | 1954 | S490862 | 15 | ½ |
| CFTC Nilo Black Tail Buck | 1953 | S618094 | 23 |  |
| AFC Nilo Brandy Cork | 1968 | SA554527 | 18½ |  |
| Nilo Brian Boru | 1966 | SA384483 | 1½ | 11 |
| Nilo Dean | 1956 | S866188 | ½ |  |
| AFTC Nilo Linkboy | 1957 | S880521 | 20½ | 8½ |
| Nilo Mark's Gunsmoke | 1956 | S844108 | 6½ | 1½ |
| Nilo Mr. President | 1952 | S6000026 | 3½ |  |
| Nilo Muscle's Chief | 1959 | SA25448 | 1 | 4 |
| 1958 Nat'l Ch., Dual Ch., AFTC Nilo Possibility | 1952 | S565173 | 27½ | 51 |
| Nilo Pre-Don Jeff | 1957 | S886616 | 11 | 5½ |
| FTC, AFTC Nilo Senator | 1952 | S600028 | 24½ | 23 |
| FC Nilo Staindrop Charger | 1966 | SA406766 |  | 55½ |
| Nilo Tarzan | 1953 | S618408 | 1½ |  |
| Nith's Double | 1926 | 757643 |  |  |
| FTC Noah of Swinomish | 1949 | S391565 |  | 39½ |
| AFTC Nodak Ar-Dee (1956 Nat'l Derby Ch.) | 1955 | S749887 | 18½ | 8 |
| Nodak Black Target | 1953 | S610289 | 10 |  |
| FTC Nodak Boots | 1957 | S863338 | 3 | 53 |
| Nodak Haldon of Craignook | 1957 | S863336 | 3½ |  |
| FTC Nodak Hawkeye | 1957 | S875602 |  | 10½ |
| Nodak Kim | 1957 | S888990 | 9 |  |
| AFC Nodak Playboy | 1955 | S765954 | 27½ | 21 |
| Sh. Ch. Nodak Royal Knight | 1953 | S648077 |  | 1½ |
| Nodak Uncle Tom | 1949 | S344380 |  | 1 |
| Nodak's Top Sergeant | 1950 | S437716 | 1 | 1 |
| FC, CFTC Nodrog Nike | 1960 | SA94361 | 8½ | 18½ |

| Name | Date Birth | AKC Reg. Number | AKC Amateur Points | AKC Open Points |
|---|---|---|---|---|
| FC, AFC Nodrog Punkie | 1967 | SA504005 | 10 | 26½ |
| Northolt Daniel | 1955 | 361260CKC | ½ | |
| Nylic Ned | 1973 | | 1 | |
| FC, AFC Nyx's Rascal Tobias | 1974 | | | 21 |
| Oakwood Jack | 1945 | listed | 1 | |
| Odds On | 1928 | 811077 | | 3 |
| FC Ojibway Buck's Black Cloud | 1959 | SA93916 | | 16½ |
| Old VAV | 1964 | SA272594 | 63 | 8 |
| AFC Oklahoma's Redpath Smith | 1973 | | 16 | 5½ |
| Old North Shore's Korkki | 1973 | | | ½ |
| CFTC, CAFTC Olrega's North Arm Rip | 1958 | 418132CKC | | |
| CFTC Ilrega's Siwash Rocko | 1960 | 493721CKC | | |
| Ol' Yeller | 1967 | SA490179 | 9 | 6 |
| CFTC Onnie of Grainger's | 1954 | 340937CKC | | |
| Onyx King of Rice | 1946 | S138324 | | 3 |
| FTC Orchardton Dale | 1938 | A440958 | | 17 |
| FTC Orchardton Dorando | 1938 | A440957 | | 23 |
| Ore Hill's Sunday Punch | 1956 | S856949 | ½ | |
| Orion of River Park | 1963 | SA224863 | 6 | |
| FC, AFC Orion's Sirius | 1965 | SA348410 | 86 | 49½ |
| Otter O'Vyrnwy | 1958 | SA98611 | ½ | 2 |
| FC, AFC Ottley's Jazzbo | 1966 | SA485575 | 37 | 17 |
| Paddler of Wintergreen | 1965 | SA341035 | | 3½ |
| 1969 Can. Nat'l Ch. P.C.D.'s Black Stormy FTC, AFTC Paha Sapa Chief II | 1955 | S759971 | 59½ | 53 |
| AFC Paha Sapa Hardcase | 1965 | SA324662 | 16 | 6½ |
| FC Paha Sapa Jack | 1961 | SA133542 | 1 | 13 |
| Paha Sapa Jay | 1964 | SA300599 | | ½ |
| Paha Sapa Medicine Man | 1960 | SA75259 | 8½ | 6½ |
| Paha Sapa Pride of Casey | 1968 | SA599941 | ½ | ½ |
| Paha Sapa Renegade | 1962 | SA155903 | ½ | |
| FTC Paha Sapa War Cloud | 1957 | S867565 | 25½ | 88½ |
| FC, AFC Paha Sapa Warpaint | 1966 | SA484616 | 54 | 32 |
| FC, AFC Paha's Pow on Tap | 1970 | SA922931 | 15½ | 20 |
| FC, AFC Paha's Pow Wow | 1966 | SA455896 | 12 | 18 |
| FC, AFC Paha Sapa War Path | 1960 | SA88862 | 24½ | 25½ |
| AFC Paha Sapa War Path II | 1963 | SA205730 | 21½ | 22 |
| Paha Tucker of Le-Mar | 1973 | | | 1 |
| FC, AFC Paladin VII | 1970 | | 38 | 46 |
| Pam's Black Spark | 1967 | | 19½ | |
| Pam's Black Splash | 1967 | SA482099 | 4 | |
| Pancho's Little Trigger | 1959 | SA69648 | 1 | |
| Panther Baby | 1963 | SA222729 | 2 | 17 |
| Panther of Coeur d'Alene | 1962 | SA183348 | 4½ | 3 |
| AFC Parky | 1961 | SA203028 | 16½ | ½ |
| Pat of Orchard Glen | 1964 | SA262776 | 6 | 3 |
| Patrolman of Timber Town | 1941 | A539683 | | 3 |
| FC, AFC Patsy's Thunderchief | 1968 | SA563940 | 1 | 42½ |
| Paupermer's Triplicate | 1960 | SA37343 | 7 | 9½ |
| 1969 Can. Nat'l Ch. Pee-Cee-Dee's Black Stormy | 1962 | S37796CKC | | |

| Name | Date Birth | AKC Reg. Number | AKC Amateur Points | AKC Open Points |
|------|------------|-----------------|--------------------|-----------------|
| FTC Peconic Pyn of Arden | 1935 | A43615 | | 12 |
| Pelican Lake Boo Boo | 1966 | SA469218 | | 4 |
| AFC, CNFC, CAFC Pelican Lake Petey Two | 1973 | | 20 | 5½ |
| Penney's Nifty Bouncer | 1973 | | | ½ |
| Dual-AFC Penny Oaks Corky | 1972 | | 17½ | 20 |
| FC, AFC Penny Oaks Flint | 1971 | | 22 | 18½ |
| 1963 Nat'l Am. Ch., FTC, AFTC Pepper's Jiggs | 1955 | S817045 | 16 | 119 |
| Pepper's Omega | 1961 | SA124174 | | 6½ |
| Peter of Gaymark | 1961 | SA126453 | 7 | 1½ |
| Pete's Compari | 1954 | S659317 | | 3 |
| Dual Ch., AFC Petite Rouge | 1960 | SA85985 | 51½ | 56 |
| Phantomshire's St. Lucie Luke | 1974 | | | ½ |
| FC Phinney Pharms Brazen Brutus | 1973 | | | 18 |
| FTC Pickpocket for Deer Creek | 1946 | S104594 | | 35 |
| Picolino of Dairy Hill | 1951 | S518697 | 10 | |
| Pierrot of Stonegate | 1948 | S381982 | | 1 |
| Pin Oaks Little Otter | 1962 | SA188687 | 6½ | 3 |
| AFTC Pinehawk Black Tarquin of Glaven | 1948 | SA72677 | 21½ | 7 |
| FTC Pinehawk Nigger | 1948 | S511225 | 4 | 12½ |
| FTC, AFTC Pinocchio of Maryglo | 1953 | S639610 | 11 | 34½ |
| Piper's Black Diamond | 1975 | | | 5 |
| Piper's Super Jet | 1974 | | 1 | |
| Piper's Tsar of Penny | 1974 | | 7 | 1½ |
| Pirate's Gold | 1966 | SA438442 | 5 | |
| FTC, AFTC, CFTC Pitch of Timber Trouble | 1946 | S120875 | 20½ | 50½ |
| Pitch-O-Mastic | 1960 | SA49997 | 5½ | |
| Platte Valley Bart | 1951 | S541101 | | 3 |
| Plowboy of Western World | 1951 | S537481 | 3 | 1 |
| Pocatello Chief | 1969 | SA793536 | | 1 |
| Pocket of Sourdough | 1974 | | 5½ | 1 |
| AFC Polaris Luke | 1964 | SA319489 | 31 | 8 |
| FC, AFC Polaris Peter | 1968 | SA646602 | 3 | 6½ |
| FTC Pomme de Terre Pete | 1956 | S914033 | | 24½ |
| AFC Poncho Villa III | 1971 | | 12 | 8½ |
| Pons Jr. of Wingan | 1934 | 960063 | | 2 |
| AFC Pookie's Rebel | 1971 | | 29½ | ½ |
| Porter's Cognac | 1974 | | 4 | |
| AFT Portneuf Valley Duke | 1963 | SA248523 | | 1 |
| AFC Potomac Buddy | 1965 | SA361769 | 15½ | 3½ |
| FC Powhaten Painter | 1971 | | | 20 |
| Pow Wow's Royal Mountee | 1974 | | | 6 |
| FTC, AFTC Prairie Smoke | 1955 | S833261 | 45 | 50 |
| Pride of Highland | 1955 | S781018 | 6½ | |
| CFTC Prince of Lowestoft | 1945 | 212179CKC | | |
| Prince William of Erie | 1955 | S814073 | 6½ | |
| Dual Ch., AFT Problem Boy Duke of Wake | 1957 | S918421 | 16 | 57 |
| Problem Boy's Dinny | 1961 | SA119874 | 6 | |
| Pytchley Big Jug | 1956 | S897433 | | ½ |
| FC Quien Sabe | 1957 | S893934 | | 12 |
| Quien Sabe's Black Ace | 1961 | SA107987 | | 2 |

| Name | Date Birth | AKC Reg. Number | AKC Amateur Points | AKC Open Points |
|---|---|---|---|---|
| Rabel's Rouser's Commander | 1972 | | | 4 |
| FC, AFC Radar Rip | 1965 | SA332586 | 14 | 17 |
| Rag's Rippled Rascal | 1974 | | | 8½ |
| AFC Ralston Valley Dandy Jake | 1964 | SA314035 | 27½ | 8½ |
| Raffles of Earlsmoor | 1931 | 957536 | | 1 |
| FC Randy Dandy of Holly Hill | 1963 | SA268426 | | 17½ |
| FC, AFC Randy Mayhall of Tina | 1966 | SA393816 | 46½ | 30 |
| CFTC Ranger of Graingers | 1955 | 35987CKC | | |
| Rangeland Hardcash | 1956 | S837764 | 1 | 5½ |
| Rascal's Double Trouble | 1976 | | 3 | |
| Rascal's Medicine Man | 1975 | | 5 | 5 |
| CFTC Rathrippen's Black Star | 1956 | S380747 | 3 | ½ |
| CFTC Rathrippen's Rogue | 1957 | 396636CKC | 1 | |
| Rattler | 1955 | S874894 | ½ | 31½ |
| NAFC, FC Ray's Rascal (1969 Derby Ch.) | 1967 | SA558031 | 151 | 160 |
| Ray's Super Express | 1973 | | 2 | 6½ |
| Double Nat'l Am. Ch., 1965 & 1968 FC, AFC Rebel Chief of Herber | 1960 | SA82627 | 85 | 88 |
| Rebellion at Deer Creek | 1946 | S1765 | | ½ |
| AFC Rebellion's Pride of Woodland | 1959 | S982646 | 23½ | 9 |
| Rebel's Ace | 1958 | S959793 | 6 | 1½ |
| Red River Blackie | 1956 | S927381 | ½ | |
| Red River's Black Hawk | 1955 | S789558 | 5½ | |
| Red River's Rock and Roll | 1955 | S772359 | 13 | 1 |
| FC, AFC Reimrock's Duke of Orleans | 1965 | SA359030 | 18½ | 16½ |
| Relam Pago Blanco | 1969 | | 3½ | |
| Re-Mar's Black Buck | 1963 | SA228224 | | ½ |
| Remoch's Apollo Rocket | 1973 | | 1½ | |
| Remoch's Lejo Juderi | 1974 | | | 9 |
| Remoch's Rye on the Rocks | 1974 | | | 1 |
| Remoch's Ebony Ace | 1966 | SA408311 | ½ | 5 |
| AFC Renegade Pepe | 1961 | SA101589 | 22 | 16½ |
| Repman's Gentleman Jim | 1968 | | | 6 |
| CFTC Retaliation of Carnmoney | 1959 | 484467CKC | | |
| Double Can. Nat'l Ch. FTC 1959, 1962 CFTC Rhett of Coldwater II | 1954 | 344262CKC | | |
| AFTC Rick of Craignook | 1954 | S684127 | 24½ | 1 |
| Rick of Vredar | 1959 | SA13245 | 8 | |
| FTC, AFTC Rich of Charlemagne | 1950 | S432919 | 38 | 89½ |
| CFTC Richdale's Big Jeff | 1957 | 401362CKC | | |
| Dual Ch., AFC, CFTC Ridgewood Playboy | 1960 | SA55202 | 14 | 51½ |
| FTC, AFTC Riefler's Dutch | 1956 | S871313 | 47 | 24½ |
| Rille Ann's Burr | 1968 | SA612171 | 12 | 1 |
| Rille Ann's Cole Black Blazer | 1967 | SA527167 | 5 | |
| FC, AFC Rille Ann's Mickey | 1967 | | 25 | 25½ |
| Rimrock Roscoe | 1962 | SA179515 | 11½ | 3 |
| Rincon Valley Jet | 1961 | SA127235 | 2 | 1½ |
| Ring the Bell for Jack Pot | 1954 | S737745 | 5 | |
| Ringo From Happy Hollow | 1964 | SA273235 | | ½ |
| AFTC, Sh. Ch. Rinney's Cumulo Nimbus | 1952 | S660211 | 38½ | |

| Name | Date Birth | AKC Reg. Number | AKC Amateur Points | AKC Open Points |
|---|---|---|---|---|
| Rinney's Sage Sunday | 1957 | S944817 | 1 | |
| FC Rip of Chateaurox | 1958 | S937226 | | 41 |
| 1950 Can. Nat'l Ch., FTC, CFTC Rip of Holly Hill | 1946 | S187918 | | 107 |
| FTC Rip of Wake | 1946 | S73709 | | 20½ |
| Rip Van Winkle III | 1956 | S856091 | 7½ | |
| Rip Von Black Winkle | 1963 | SA215191 | ½ | 5 |
| FTC, AFC Ripco's Peter Pan | 1955 | S760834 | 33½ | 53½ |
| Ripco's Repeater | 1965 | SA317676 | 3½ | |
| Ripper of Rattlesnake | 1956 | S910622 | ½ | |
| CFTC Rippettal's Socrates | 1962 | SA269726 | 3 | |
| FC, AFC Ripple River | 1969 | SA722186 | 16½ | 14 |
| FTC, AFTC Rip's Bingo | 1947 | S270430 | 24½ | 51½ |
| Ripshin Booster | 1967 | SA510059 | | ½ |
| Riptide II | 1952 | S549069 | 1½ | 1 |
| FC Riskin | 1962 | SA291125 | | 25 |
| FC, AFC River Oaks Black Bingo | 1970 | | 66½ | 44½ |
| FC River Oaks Black Frost | 1968 | | | 42 |
| 1972-75 NAFC, FC, CNFC River Oaks Corky | 1966 | SA399497 | 174 | 289½ |
| AFC River Oaks Pali | 1970 | | 18 | 1 |
| FC River Oaks Ram of Simmer's Shot | 1970 | | 1½ | 25½ |
| NAFC, FC River Oaks Rascal | 1969 | SA603599 | 120½ | 56 |
| River Oaks Roscoe | 1973 | | 6½ | ½ |
| River Oaks Rowdy Bear | 1969 | SA721676 | | 15 |
| FC River Road Bippy | 1969 | SA773461 | | 54½ |
| River Road Reho | 1965 | SA402099 | | ½ |
| River Rock of Zenith | 1973 | | 4 | 5 |
| CFTC Robber of Carnmoney | 1954 | 352123CKC | | |
| FC, AFC Robbet's Black Hope | 1957 | S901588 | 38 | 26 |
| Robinhood's Geechee Junior | 1967 | SA523961 | | 3 |
| Robinson's Blackbird | 1959 | S988636 | 4 | |
| Rockbend's Kamakura | 1967 | SA503359 | 1 | 3 |
| Rockbend's Magic Marker | 1966 | SA440171 | ½ | 3 |
| Rocket of Frontier | 1968 | SA818965 | | 3 |
| Rock River Jack | 1945 | A859748 | | ½ |
| FC, AFC Rocky Road of Zenith | 1966 | SA384628 | 125½ | 97½ |
| Rocky Von Aaron | 1959 | SA3430 | | 1 |
| Rocky's Dartega | 1964 | SA317225 | 12 | 11 |
| Rocky's Shadee Plaything | 1975 | | | ½ |
| Rodarbal Black Magic | 1943 | A852992 | | 3 |
| FC, AFC Rodney's Mr. M. L. Coon | 1968 | SA570862 | 9 | 28 |
| Roger's Gun Bearer | 1973 | | | 8 |
| Rogue River Devilkin | 1953 | S721463 | 1 | 4 |
| Roland of Wood Cliffe | 1970 | | | 4 |
| Rolida's Stubby Bandit | 1963 | SA232512 | 1 | 4 |
| Rosedale Riptide | 1970 | | | 1 |
| AFC Round Trip Traveler | 1969 | | 16½ | 9½ |
| AFC Round Valley's Luck Pooh Bear | 1972 | | 12 | 8 |
| FC, AFC Round Valley's Lucky Tigger | 1969 | | | 39½ |
| FC, AFC Rover of Ramsey Place | 1963 | SA192706 | 25½ | 39½ |

| Name | Date Birth | AKC Reg. Number | AKC Amateur Points | AKC Open Points |
|---|---|---|---|---|
| Rowdy's Sean of Corkies | 1963 | SA223988 | 10½ | 9 |
| Royal Oaks Rebel of Dartmoor | N.A. | | | 9 |
| FC, AFC Royal Oaks Something Super | 1973 | | 27 | 13½ |
| FC Royal Oaks Super Sleuth | 1972 | | | 34½ |
| Royal Oaks Super Stuff | 1973 | | 13 | 6 |
| Royal Oaks Trent of Emil | 1973 | | 1 | |
| Royal of Garfield | 1957 | S848751 | | 3 |
| NRFC '72, AFC Royal Moose's Moe | 1963 | SA246647 | 97½ | 98½ |
| FC Royal Jay | 1964 | SA281614 | | 10½ |
| FC, AFC Roy's Revenge | 1968 | | 10 | 10½ |
| FTC Roy's Rowdy | 1955 | S762362 | | 22½ |
| AFTC Rubie's Sputnik | 1957 | S934025 | 11 | 9 |
| Ruffian of Mcgaffey Lake | 1974 | | 6½ | 2 |
| Ruffy's Loco Express | 1969 | | 10½ | |
| Can. Dual Ch. Rufus of Graingers | 1955 | 359792CKC | | |
| FC, AFC Rumba Dancer | 1971 | | 33 | 33½ |
| FC Run-N-Rock | 1974 | | ½ | 19½ |
| FC, AFC Rus-Lau's Mohave Valley Luck | 1971 | | 22 | 33 |
| Rusty of Bonny | 1952 | S530834 | 3 | |
| Sab of Tulliallan | 1922 | 757642 | | 1 |
| Saber Jet's Maverick | 1959 | SA35986 | ½ | |
| Sad Sam Jones | 1958 | S978961 | 2 | |
| FC, AFC Sage Joker | 1960 | SA81788 | 21 | 19 |
| Sage Rambler | 1960 | SA82503 | 5 | |
| Sage Rider | 1953 | S613259 | | 3 |
| FC Sage's Saskeram Pete | 1961 | SA129205 | | 26½ |
| Saglek | 1935 | | | 5 |
| St. Hubert of Tewkesbury Knob | 1968 | SA544926 | ½ | |
| St. Jones Blackie | 1947 | S164023 | 12½ | 5½ |
| CFTC Salt Valley Epamindondas | 1960 | SA127197 | 9 | 13 |
| Salt Valley Espresso | 1968 | SA734140 | | ½ |
| FTC, AFTC Salt Valley Ottie | 1957 | S896547 | 64 | 55½ |
| FTC, AFTC Salty of Sugar Valley | 1953 | S655174 | 30 | 26 |
| FTC, AFC Sam Frizel of Glenspey, C.D.X. | 1956 | S829932 | 61 | 80 |
| AFTC Sam of Alaska | 1954 | S658183 | 23 | |
| Sam of Arden | 1929 | 981723 | | 4 |
| Sam of Arrowhead Lake | 1967 | SA464812 | | ½ |
| FC Sam of Dixie Rapids | 1967 | SA527728 | 1½ | 10½ |
| Sam of Marlboro Country | 1963 | SA268155 | 7 | |
| Sam of Pickwick | 1973 | | | 4 |
| Sam of Woodend | 1942 | A698809 | | 1 |
| Sambo of Klamath | 1949 | S270235 | | 5½ |
| Sam's Thunder Cloud | 1963 | SA225806 | 5 | 5 |
| FC, AFC Samson's George of Glenspey | 1963 | SA223731 | 20½ | 67½ |
| Sanctuary Chase | 1974 | | | 4½ |
| NFC, AFC San Joaquin Honcho | 1973 | | 62½ | 63 |
| San Juan Coldwater | 1973 | | 4 | |
| FTC, AFTC Sandburr Pete | 1955 | S742946 | 10 | 25½ |
| FTC Sand Gold Terry | 1939 | A432378 | | 20 |
| FC, AFC Sandy of Sourdough | 1963 | SA212126 | 54½ | 32½ |

| Name | Date Birth | AKC Reg. Number | AKC Amateur Points | AKC Open Points |
|---|---|---|---|---|
| Sanka | 1959 | SA30471 | 1 | |
| FC, AFC Sasse-Ville Casper | 1970 | | | 19½ |
| Sassy of Swinomish | 1955 | S758320 | 5½ | 1 |
| Satan III | 1948 | S334887 | | 6½ |
| Satan of Yellowstone | 1955 | S871179 | 11½ | |
| Sauk Trail Black Mouse | 1965 | SA338536 | | 3½ |
| FC, AFC Sauk Trail Deepwell "Doc" | 1967 | SA490968 | 35 | 27½ |
| FC, AFC Sauk Trail Senator | 1968 | | 30½ | 52 |
| FC, AFC Sazerac Mac | 1958 | S965869 | 34 | 44½ |
| Schmidt's Okanagon Joe | 1944 | A876930 | | 3 |
| FTC Scoronine of Deer Creek (1943 Nat'l Derby Ch.) | 1942 | A607057 | | 11 |
| Sea Raider of Audlon | 1959 | SA72979 | 6 | ½ |
| Seaborne's Black Prince | 1938 | A322164 | | 13 |
| Seafield Chief | 1964 | SA269826 | 1 | |
| FC Sea Tac's General Mills | 1974 | | | 24½ |
| FC, AFC Sea Tac's Kee Man | 1973 | | 12½ | 14½ |
| AFC Sebastion St. George | 1958 | S980497 | 20 | 6½ |
| Selamat's Preacherman | 1972 | | 1 | |
| Semloh Tom Thumb | 1953 | S632076 | ½ | 6½ |
| Semloh's Rogue | 1947 | S221045 | | 3½ |
| FTC, AFTC Sentinel of Whitmore | 1951 | S493770 | 32 | 31 |
| AFC Shadow of Aspen | 1973 | | 8½ | 6½ |
| NFC, AFC Shadow of Otter Creek | 1971 | | 69½ | 40 |
| FC, AFC Shadow of Provincetown | 1968 | SA564529 | 35½ | 30½ |
| FC, AFC Shadow of Rocky Lane | 1966 | SA372771 | 28½ | 41½ |
| FTC Shadow's Ebony Bob | 1939 | A390827 | | 12 |
| Shag of Shanty Bay | 1966 | SA387762 | 1½ | |
| Shamrock Acres Black Bomb | 1971 | | | 1½ |
| FC, AFC Shamrock Acres Drake | 1966 | SA389721 | 65½ | 35 |
| FC, AFC Shamrock Acres Flint's Chance | 1972 | | | 10½ |
| AFC Shamrock Acres Gun Away | 1961 | SA150157 | 24½ | 6 |
| AFC Shamrock Acres Modac Painter | 1969 | SA646899 | 33 | |
| Shamrock Acres Nautilius | 1969 | | 11 | |
| Shamrock Acres NYLIC Ned | 1967 | SA519944 | ½ | |
| Shamrock Acres Painted Pony | 1972 | | | 1 |
| FC, AFC Shamrock Acres Rocky McCool | 1972 | | 38½ | 19 |
| Shamrock Acres Super Drive | 1967 | SA466881 | | 9½ |
| Shamrock Acres Superstition | 1967 | SA470518 | 14 | 9 |
| FC Shamrock Acres Super Value | 1968 | SA649586 | 6 | 118 |
| FC, AFC Shamrock Acres Waunakee Duke | 1971 | | 11 | 2 |
| AFC Shamrock Acres Wooglin | 1970 | | 14 | 1 |
| Shantoo Tar Buck | 1965 | SA317643 | | 2 |
| Shasta Dandy | 1954 | S708880 | 3½ | 1 |
| AFTC Shauna Buck | 1955 | S793847 | 90½ | 7½ |
| FC, AFC Shawnee Ace of Spades Triple Nat'l Ch. 1942, 1943 & 1946, Dual Ch., CFTC Shed of Arden (*Field & Stream* Trophy, 1942, 1943 & 1946) | 1939 | A330767 | | 59 |
| FTC, AFTC Shed's Prince of Garfeld | 1949 | S315174 | 22½ | 11 |

| Name | Date Birth | AKC Reg. Number | AKC Amateur Points | AKC Open Points |
|---|---|---|---|---|
| Shenandoah's Storming Chief | 1973 | | 4½ | 2 |
| Shoe Shine Boy of Audlon | 1956 | S875008 | 1 | |
| Shoremeadow Barnacle Bill | 1951 | S711090 | 5½ | 6½ |
| Shoremeadow Challenge | 1961 | SA117891 | 1 | 3 |
| FTC Shoremeadow Tidewater | 1954 | S711089 | | 105½ |
| FC, AFC Shyster of Le-Mar | 1973 | | 17½ | |
| FC, AFC Sill's Black Bandit | 1969 | SA786889 | 107½ | 80½ |
| Silver Squire | 1965 | SA381525 | 5 | |
| FC Sinbad IV | 1965 | SA349762 | 1½ | 10 |
| Sining Woods Explorer | 1959 | S964165 | 1½ | 3 |
| FTC, 1958 Can. Nat'l Ch., CFTC Sinser's Bulldozer of Crevamoy | 1954 | S997867 | | 12 |
| Sir Anthony of Cork | 1956 | S815905 | 3 | |
| FC, AFC Sir Caleb of Audlon | 1968 | SA601060 | 32½ | 5 |
| Sir Hobey Maverick Fetch | 1959 | S992061 | | ½ |
| FTC Sir Jock | 1941 | A511359 | | 34 |
| FC, AFC Sir Knight Falcon | 1959 | S979796 | 51 | 30 |
| FC, AFC Sir Mike of Orchardview | 1959 | SA46220 | 129½ | 49 |
| FC, AFC Skeeter Luck | 1972 | | 13½ | 11½ |
| AFC Skeeter of Upland Farm | 1959 | SA12417 | 54½ | 8½ |
| Skookum Bingo | 1966 | SA476150 | 13 | 1 |
| Skookum Dale's Nike Mark X | 1966 | SA595928 | | 13½ |
| CFTC Skookum Target | 1965 | 636576CKC | | |
| Slip of Grunt's Ray | 1970 | | 10 | 10 |
| FTC, AFTC Slow-poke Smokey of Dairy Hill | 1947 | SA427360 | 34 | 58½ |
| Smackwater Jack | 1974 | | | 6 |
| AFC Smoke Tail's Chico | 1960 | SA46197 | 31 | 9½ |
| AFC Smoke Tail's Cricket | 1960 | SA96343 | 18½ | 7 |
| CFTC Smokey of Jetcin | 1962 | 540617CKC | 13½ | |
| Smokey's Black Jet (FC) | 1965 | SA386598 | | 26½ |
| Smokey's Mot | 1969 | | 9½ | 5 |
| Smudge of Allen Winden | 1930 | 814009 | | 1 |
| Smudge of Prairie Creek Farm | 1944 | A843249 | ½ | |
| FTC Smudge's Bingo | 1951 | S513701 | | 11 |
| 1960 Can. Nat'l Ch., CFTC Smudge's Pitch | 1955 | 363401CKC | | |
| AFC Snake Eyes-Double or Nothin' | 1975 | | 29½ | 3 |
| Sneaky Pete III | 1975 | | 3½ | |
| Snikeb's Chief Joseph | 1954 | S718245 | | 2 |
| Snikeb's Cochise | 1954 | S720222 | | 8 |
| Snikeb's Ding Ding Ding | 1947 | S152940 | 1 | 6 |
| Snoopy of Dickinson | 1965 | SA376353 | | 1 |
| Solo of Gaymark | 1961 | SA114197 | | 4 |
| CFTC Sommers Rusty Boy | 1950 | 286216CKC | | |
| Son | 1939 | A434553 | | |
| Sondar's Song Bo | 1962 | SA142870 | 5 | |
| FC, AFC Sourdough's Quick Start | 1971 | | 26½ | 18 |
| South Bay Shazaam | 1975 | | | 1 |
| Sowega's Bojangles | 1974 | | 3½ | |
| FTC, AFTC Speed of Lancaster | 1953 | S628814 | 32½ | 24½ |
| FTC Spirit Lake Bay | 1953 | S609518 | 3½ | 14 |

| Name | Date Birth | AKC Reg. Number | AKC Amateur Points | AKC Open Points |
|---|---|---|---|---|
| Double Nat'l Ch. 1957 & 1959, FTC Spirit Lake Duke (Record total of open points through 1969) | 1953 | S609516 | ½ | 181 |
| FTC Spirit Lake Phanton | 1953 | S609520 | | 36½ |
| Spirit's Black Pepper | 1962 | SA190899 | | ½ |
| Splash | 1951 | S540577 | | 1½ |
| CFTC Spook of Jetcin | 1962 | 540618CKC | | ½ |
| Spook of Marian's Tim | 1958 | S986489 | 6 | 3 |
| Sport of Upland Farm | 1966 | SA437645 | | ½ |
| FTC Sprig of Swinomish | 1949 | S392026 | 6 | 7½ |
| AFC Sprigs Tule Rooter | 1969 | | 14½ | |
| Spring Farm's Luck | 1966 | SA411762 | 3 | 3 |
| FC, AFC Spring Farm's Smokey | 1968 | SA553356 | 42 | 30½ |
| CFTC Sprucelane's Chippewa Chief | 1960 | 485871CKC | | |
| Spunky of Belle Isle | 1954 | S808663 | | 2 |
| AFC Squire of Reo Raj | 1963 | SA261820 | 20 | 10 |
| Stampfli's Amos Moses | 1972 | | 3 | |
| Staindrop Ben | 1951 | S579626 | | 2½ |
| Staindrop Black Cock | 1954 | S804253 | 1½ | |
| FTC, AFTC Eng. FTC Staindrop Murton Marksman | 1952 | S649126 | 32 | 63½ |
| FTC, AFTC Staindrop Ringleader | 1953 | S781303 | 43½ | 33½ |
| FTC Staindrop Spanker | 1952 | S618416 | 1 | 28 |
| FTC Staindrop Striker | 1953 | S872419 | | 24 |
| Staindrop Trigger | 1953 | S716770 | 12½ | |
| Staindrop Whitewood Tim | 1950 | S605368 | | ½ |
| Stanton's Lucky Dice | 1972 | | 1 | 1 |
| FC, AFC St. Croix River Rascal | 1970 | | 16½ | 13½ |
| FTC Stan's Curly Boy | 1955 | S807995 | | 11½ |
| FTC Stemwinder of Audlon | 1954 | S790491 | | 13½ |
| Stilwater's Carry Back | 1964 | SA288918 | | ½ |
| Stilwater's Royal Rick | 1961 | SA88334 | 5 | |
| Stonecastle Yellow Jacket | 1965 | SA374692 | ½ | |
| FTC Stonegate's Ace of Spades (1955 Nat'l Derby Ch.) | 1954 | S700873 | 1 | 47½ |
| FC, AFC Stonegate's Arrow | 1959 | SA15715 | 50½ | 64½ |
| FTC Stonegate's Black Diamond | 1954 | S672376 | | 14½ |
| CFTC Stonegate's Pluto | 1956 | 393642CKC | | |
| Stonewall Jack | 1953 | S728457 | 1 | |
| Storm at West Newton | 1961 | SA116633 | 1 | |
| Stompin Satchmo | 1976 | | ½ | |
| Storm's Ebony Echo | 1963 | SA244739 | 1½ | |
| AFC Stormy of Southwood | 1971 | | | 8 |
| 1967 Can. Nat'l Ch., Can. Dual Ch. AFC Stormy Spirit Lake Gal | 1958 | S940420 | | 16 |
| AFTC, CFTC Strawberry Hill Regent | 1954 | S665648 | 19½ | 1 |
| Straw Hollow's Rowdy Crusader | 1964 | SA253640 | 1 | |
| Striper of Ramapo Valley | 1963 | SA210682 | | 3 |
| Suey Gee Dough | 1959 | S995043 | 6½ | |
| AFTC Sumpawams Tide Rip | 1951 | S457944 | 19½ | |

| Name | Date Birth | AKC Reg. Number | AKC Amateur Points | AKC Open Points |
|------|------------|-----------------|--------------------|-----------------|
| AFC Suncrest Nike Zeus | 1969 | | 12 | 4½ |
| AFTC Sungo | 1946 | S88849 | 13½ | 14½ |
| AFC Suncrest Super Streak | 1974 | | 22 | ½ |
| FC, AFC Sunshine Rockabye Mickie | 1971 | | | 45½ |
| 1967 & 1968 Nat'l Am. Ch., 1968 NFC, FC, AFC Super Chief | 1962 | SA153347 | 242 | 212½ |
| FC Super Duper Snooper | 1972 | | | 10½ |
| Super Powder | 1971 | | 2½ | |
| Supersonic Hot Rod | 1950 | S365007 | 5 | |
| 1963 & 1965 Can. Nat'l Ch., FC, AFC, CFTC, CAFTC Sweet Stuff | 1957 | S875268 | 57 | 102½ |
| FC Sweet William II | 1968 | SA688152 | | 11½ |
| FTC, AFTC Swifty of Sugar Valley | 1953 | S664978 | 23½ | 51 |
| FC Swing Tarzan Swing | 1966 | SA413002 | 9 | 29 |
| Syldonnel's Captain Jack | 1966 | SA455275 | 2½ | |
| Tab | 1956 | S907916 | ½ | |
| AFTC Taco of Honey Lake | 1955 | S751904 | 36½ | 11 |
| Tagalong II | 1950 | S398018 | 1 | |
| Taliaferro's Tracer | 1962 | SA144780 | 13½ | 6 |
| Tally-Ho Tar of Village Green | 1971 | | 3 | |
| FTC, CFTC Tanaca's Rocky of Random Lake (1954 Nat'l Derby Ch.) | 1952 | S594348 | | 13½ |
| FTC, AFTC Tar Baby of Holly Hill | 1948 | S239248 | 8 | 18½ |
| Tar Baby's Rascal | 1971 | | 1 | |
| FC Tar Dessa Venture | 1963 | SA246855 | ½ | 85 |
| FC, AFC Dessa's Comanche Mike | 1962 | SA613145 | 10 | 10½ |
| AFC Tar Ghee Sam | 1963 | SA208308 | 18 | 6 |
| Tar Heel Zak | 1969 | | 5 | |
| Tar Reed of Whitmore | 1953 | S678238 | ½ | |
| Tarblook Black Beaver | 1959 | S311052 | | 1 |
| FTC, AFTC Tarblood of Absaraka | 1957 | S898245 | 67½ | 165 |
| Tarblood Rimrocker | 1948 | S198408 | | ½ |
| Tarblood Spidercreek King | 1951 | S503085 | 9½ | 5 |
| Tark | 1956 | S829933 | ½ | |
| Tarnoff of V & C Chip | 1969 | SA646025 | | 6 |
| AFC Tar of Gogi Girl | 1972 | | 18 | 4½ |
| Tarpot of Abilena | 1969 | | 1 | |
| Tarsus of the Ages | 1953 | S918551 | | ½ |
| Tarsus the Bull | 1971 | | 3 | |
| FTC, AFC Teal Timmy of Glado | 1956 | S862023 | 39 | 42½ |
| Teal of Laurenwood | 1958 | S923450 | | ½ |
| FTC Techako's Ranger | 1957 | S885181 | | 127½ |
| Teddy Bear | 1957 | S815850 | 5 | |
| Telstar of Zenith | 1967 | SA540688 | | 1 |
| Terry's Golden Rex | 1952 | S72063 | 1½ | |
| AFC The Ballad of Tealbrook | 1963 | SA210659 | 23½ | 4 |
| The Bamboo Bandit | 1964 | SA361242 | 2 | |
| The Big Payoff of Audlon | 1955 | S843138 | 11 | 6½ |
| The Big Showoff of Audlon | 1955 | S857828 | 5 | 6½ |
| The Earl of Sussex | 1959 | SA7147 | 7½ | 13 |

| Name | Date Birth | AKC Reg. Number | AKC Amateur Points | AKC Open Points |
|---|---|---|---|---|
| The Early Worm | 1971 | | 1/2 | 9 |
| The Great Mistake of Audlon | 1951 | S571003 | | 1 |
| FC, AFC The Hustler | 1969 | | 24 1/2 | 10 1/2 |
| FTC, AFTC The Spider of Kingswere | 1946 | S61672 | 23 | 62 |
| FC, AFC The Sundance Kid | 1971 | | 12 1/2 | 10 |
| FC, AFTC The Web of Kingswere | 1949 | S377662 | 20 1/2 | 7 1/2 |
| Thor of Thunder Hollow | 1958 | S928881 | 1 | |
| Thorsmiolnir | 1969 | | 1/2 | |
| Thunder of Rebel's Gypsy | 1969 | SA663159 | 3 1/2 | |
| FC, AFC Thunder of Audlon | 1957 | S913456 | 21 1/2 | 29 |
| Tidewater Max Pak | 1974 | | 1/2 | |
| Tiger's Lucky Buck | 1969 | SA718792 | | 15 |
| Tiger's Texas Tiger | 1967 | SA536928 | | 3 1/2 |
| Tigre del Rio | 1969 | | | 3 1/2 |
| Timber Fire of Dairy Hill | 1951 | S461776 | 3 1/2 | 3 |
| FTC Timber Stone Trigger | 1946 | S88092 | 6 | 25 1/2 |
| FTC Timber Town Clansman | 1936 | A128842 | | 21 |
| CFTC Timbershet Toten of Mascopie 2nd | 1956 | 377395CKC | | |
| AFC Timcin's Black Domino | 1963 | SA231115 | 16 1/2 | 5 1/2 |
| Time of Frontier (1965 Nat'l Derby Ch.) | 1964 | SA278640 | 8 | 9 |
| Timewaster's Black Pepper | 1953 | S657647 | 1 | |
| Timewaster's Shadow | 1953 | S650781 | 3 1/2 | |
| Timfree Rebel | 1949 | S390769 | 3 | |
| Tina's Black Chip | 1966 | SA386845 | 1/2 | |
| Ti-Son Flint | 1971 | | | 8 |
| Todd's Tartar | 1940 | S230799 | | 8 |
| FC, AFC Togam's Tiger of Abilena | 1968 | SA607026 | 74 | 30 1/2 |
| Tomarven Skean of Birsemohr | 1954 | S750523 | 4 | 5 1/2 |
| Tom's Thadius | 1968 | SA568715 | 1 | |
| Tongue River's Rascal | 1976 | | 5 | |
| FC Toni's Blaine Child | 1969 | SA700112 | 11 1/2 | 64 |
| AFC Toni's Star | 1962 | SA157123 | 18 | 1 |
| AFC Tonka Sahdon M'Nee | 1972 | | 21 | 6 |
| Toots of Dunecht | 1946 | S193508 | | 1/2 |
| FC, AFC Torque of Daingerfield | 1962 | SA238006 | 71 | 57 1/2 |
| Touchstone Trotter | 1974 | | 1 | |
| Townsend of Vigloma | 1947 | S293480 | 1 | |
| T. R. Trucker | 1973 | | 1/2 | 1 |
| FC Trappers Paha Cork | 1960 | SA78491 | | 10 |
| FC, AFC Traveler of Audlon | 1958 | SA934494 | 27 | 11 |
| AFC Trebor's Nodrog Gise | 1971 | | 10 | |
| Tremendo of Quesnel Lake | 1952 | SA580261 | 5 1/2 | |
| Dual Ch. Eng. FTC, CFTC Treveilyr Swift | 1946 | SA335201 | 5 1/2 | 36 |
| Trevrchamp Minyok | 1952 | SA628416 | 12 | |
| Trevrchamp Radar | 1948 | SA181228 | | 4 |
| Trevrchamp Spider | 1956 | SA869706 | 1 1/2 | |
| Tri Stada Binx | 1958 | SA950431 | 6 1/2 | 7 |
| FC, AFC Trieven Canvasback Zip Zac | 1973 | | 1/2 | 22 |
| FC, AFC Trieven Thunderhead | 1972 | | 45 1/2 | 49 |
| Trigger II | 1947 | SA162370 | | 3 1/2 |

| Name | Date Birth | AKC Reg. Number | AKC Amateur Points | AKC Open Points |
|---|---|---|---|---|
| FC Triple Echo | 1971 | | 3½ | 33½ |
| Triple M Charcoal | 1958 | SA982155 | 8½ | |
| Trollgaard Abenaki | 1971 | | 4 | |
| Trollgaard's Davy Crockett | 1955 | S761819 | 14 | |
| FC Troublemaker of Audlon II | 1964 | SA313146 | 4 | 12½ |
| Trowbridge Topper | 1943 | SA740474 | | 5 |
| Troy's Preto Noite | 1955 | SA723033 | 1½ | |
| FC, AFC T. R. Tucker | 1973 | | 29½ | 37 |
| FC Truckee's Nitro Chief | 1973 | | 10 | 42½ |
| FC Truckee Water-Gator Sam | 1973 | | | 52 |
| Trumarc's AWOL | 1975 | | 3 | |
| FC, AFC Trumarc's Raider | 1970 | | 25½ | 16½ |
| Dual Ch. AFC Trumarc's Triple Threat | 1970 | | 98½ | 64 |
| FC, AFC Trumarc's Triple Treat | 1971 | | 81½ | 41 |
| Tsaile Taylor Hurst | 1973 | | 7 | 5 |
| Tuck's Irish Mick | 1951 | SA510684 | ½ | |
| Tugney of Oakview | 1953 | SA686915 | ½ | |
| CFTC Turner's Smokey Boy | 1955 | 358971CKC | | |
| Tuxedo of Chagrin | 1954 | SA720147 | 3 | ½ |
| FC, AFC Tweet's Bebe | 1966 | SA525090 | 42 | 33 |
| Tycoon of Ralston Valley | 1963 | SA219685 | | ½ |
| Tyke of Barrington | 1935 | | | 11 |
| Tyke of Woodend | 1938ᵃ | | | |
| Tyker Baby | 1963 | SA222730 | 4 | |
| Tyker's Fleck of Cork | 1968 | SA584122 | 1 | 8 |
| CFTC Valentine's Luke | 1953 | 346912CKC | | 5 |
| Valhalla Bonefish Sam | 1969 | SA660966 | | ½ |
| AFC Valhalla Fairhaired Viking | 1971 | | 23 | |
| AFC Valhalla Misfire | 1970 | | 18½ | 1 |
| FC V and C Chip | 1967 | SA523993 | 5½ | 34 |
| V Day for Deer Creek | 1944 | SA975104 | | 4½ |
| CFTC Van Wagner's Kernel | 1955 | 368950CKC | ½ | |
| Van's Bomber | 1965 | SA358225 | ½ | |
| CFTC Vern's Prize | 1956 | 371555CKC | | |
| Vestal's Norge | 1937 | unreg. | | 10 |
| CFTC Vic's Winsome Timberland Boy | 1945 | 209283CKC | | |
| Vicki's Mister Kelley | 1969 | | 5½ | |
| Victor of Little Pierre | 1952 | S531762 | 4 | |
| Vigor of Springfield | 1956 | S813958 | | 1½ |
| FC V-Jay's Black Paddle | 1960 | SA70891 | | 37 |
| AFC Waccamaw's Tinker | 1964 | SA274302 | 24½ | 8½ |
| Waldi Jaeger Von Haden | 1973 | | 1 | 4 |
| Wallace's Playboy's Topsy Tar | 1965 | SA304348 | 1 | 1½ |
| Walla Walla Supercoot | 1973 | | 8 | 4 |
| AFC Waluke Moonshine | 1972 | | 18½ | 9 |
| 1975 NFC, AFC Wanapum Dart's Dandy | 1970 | | 65 | 62 |
| Wanapum Lucky YoYo | 1969 | SA769753 | 25 | 12½ |
| FC Wanapum Pow Wow Punch | 1972 | | | 23 |
| Wanapum Sky Shooter | 1975 | | ½ | |
| Wandarin Heights Venture | 1965 | SA389901 | 1 | 2 |

| Name | Date Birth | AKC Reg. Number | AKC Amateur Points | AKC Open Points |
|---|---|---|---|---|
| Warcon's Carbon Copy | 1970 | | | 2 |
| Warpath Cowboy Joe | 1966 | SA417753 | 6 | 1/2 |
| Warpath Just in Case | 1968 | SA631769 | 1 1/2 | |
| Warpath Macho | 1974 | | 6 | 5 |
| FC, AFC Warpath Rip | 1964 | SA390594 | 33 | 58 1/2 |
| FC, AFC Warpath Tuff | 1964 | SA272597 | 40 | 33 1/2 |
| Wasatch Renegade | 1959 | SA9308 | 5 | |
| AFC Washington's Shi Shi Bens | 1974 | | | 9 |
| Wascott's Tomahawk | 1948 | SA294019 | 3 | 7 |
| FC, AFC Watchim Sneak | 1969 | | 76 1/2 | 65 |
| FC, AFC Watergate Gambler | 1973 | | 34 | 10 1/2 |
| Wayside Black Cluster | 1965 | SA366371 | 3 | 5 |
| FTC, AFTC Webway's Crusader | 1953 | SA333525 | 13 1/2 | 27 1/2 |
| Wellzenheim's Okaboji Jet | 1953 | SA668121 | 1 1/2 | 1 1/2 |
| CFTC Wendigo Beau Jet | 1959 | 451912CKC | | |
| CFTC Wes' Black Pete | 1952 | 311683CKC | | |
| West Island Chief | 1953 | SA637686 | 7 | 1 1/2 |
| AFTC, CFTC West Island Comet | 1950 | SA419685 | 24 | |
| West Island Easter Parade | 1950 | SA450820 | 5 1/2 | 1/2 |
| West Island Hobo | 1950 | SA444662 | | 3 |
| FTC West Island Tramp | 1950 | SA420214 | | 12 |
| FTC West Island Whiz | 1950 | SA382329 | | 24 1/2 |
| Westwind's Lucky Bounce | 1974 | | 10 1/2 | |
| Whiskey Creek War Chief | 1969 | | | 7 |
| Whiskey Creek's Blue Sahib | 1964 | SA172101 | | 1/2 |
| White Rajah Mahomet | 1957 | SA937526 | 10 | 8 |
| AFC White River Duke | 1966 | SA410334 | 17 | 3 |
| FC, AFC White's Mar-Ke-Tam Nerro | 1966 | SA461391 | 8 1/2 | 10 |
| NRFC '66 & '69 Whygin Cork's Coot | 1962 | SA157920 | | 137 |
| FC Whygin High Doctor | 1969 | | | 13 1/2 |
| AFC Whygin Wellmet Angus | 1967 | SA504268 | 23 1/2 | 3 |
| Wichita Tex | 1962 | SA163039 | | 1/2 |
| Wig of Kregness | 1952 | SA570799 | 5 | 3 |
| FC Wildflower's Nitro Express | 1969 | | | 21 |
| Wild Fowler Nitro Express | 1969 | | | 6 |
| AFC Wildfowler's Superman | 1971 | | 34 1/2 | |
| FC, AFC Wild Joker of Napi | 1970 | SA866789 | 77 | 37 |
| Willamette River Buck | 1953 | SA669031 | | 2 |
| CFTC Williwaw of Trab | 1948 | SA425347 | 10 | 7 |
| FC, AFC Willowmount El Diablo | 1968 | SA804280 | 24 1/2 | 123 |
| Willowmount Smoke Screen | 1971 | | 5 | |
| Willow's Boe Longshot | 1965 | SA333664 | 6 | 1/2 |
| Wind Alley Gobbler | 1975 | | 6 1/2 | |
| Windy of Hellgate | 1952 | SA542411 | 1/2 | |
| Wingford's Big Flintstone | 1967 | SA490799 | 8 | 1 |
| Wingover Cherokee Chief | 1965 | SA364671 | 8 | |
| Winroc Chaos | 1968 | | | 8 1/2 |
| AFC Winroc's Ripper | 1968 | SA550579 | 11 1/2 | 8 1/2 |
| FC Winston Hill's Bull Durham | 1970 | | 7 1/2 | 10 |
| FC Win-Toba's Black High Point | 1964 | SA365050 | | 13 1/2 |

| Name | Date Birth | AKC Reg. Number | AKC Amateur Points | AKC Open Points |
|------|------------|-----------------|--------------------|-----------------|
| FC Win-Toba's Majestic Lad | 1970 | | | 49 |
| AFC Wolf River Nigger | 1959 | SA33945 | 21 | 8 |
| FC, AFC Woody's Black Baby | 1971 | | 19 | 34½ |
| Wraith's Gelt | 1971 | | ½ | |
| Yahara River Duke | 1958 | SA956533 | 1 | |
| Yankee Black Power | 1967 | SA542085 | 3½ | 2 |
| 1957 Can. Nat'l Ch., FTC, AFTC, CFTC Yankee Clipper of Reo Raj | 1953 | S653240 | 30 | 42½ |
| Yankee Minute Man | 1970 | | | ½ |
| Yaz Razzmatazz | 1963 | SA197896 | | 8½ |
| Yellowstone Joe Louis | 1954 | S657646 | 3 | 3 |
| Yellowstone Ninety Proof | 1959 | SA14407 | ½ | |
| Dual Ch. Yodel of Morexpense | 1940 | A473730 | | 14 |
| Yogi II | 1967 | SA636382 | | 3 |
| Yogi Bear's Angel | | | | 1 |
| FTC Young Mint of Catawba (1951 Nat'l Derby Ch.) | 1950 | SA4551177 | | 18 |
| Your Shot on the Rocks | 1971 | | | ½ |
| FC Your Shot Minnesota Fats | 1967 | SA486728 | 1½ | 23½ |
| Zarr-Tam Penrod | 1972 | | | 3 |
| Zelstone Pepper | 1962 | SA172432 | 4 | |
| CFTC Zephyr's Ebony Sambo | 1955 | SA788089 | 4 | 1 |
| Zip of Geneva Lake | 1963 | SA200328 | 3 | |
| FC Zipper Dee Do | 1967 | SA464617 | | 132 |
| FC, AFC Zipper of Clear Lake | 1958 | S972032 | 6 | 14 |
| FC Zipper's Dapper Sapper | 1972 | | 2 | 36½ |
| FC Zipper's Jumping Jake | 1973 | | | 16 |

*Retriever point summaries after 1973 did not include AKC Registration numbers.

## Labrador Retriever Bitches

| Name | Date Birth | AKC Reg. Number | AKC Amateur Points | AKC Open Points |
|------|------------|-----------------|--------------------|-----------------|
| FC Acadiana Dixie | 1973 | | | 12 |
| 1961 Nat'l Am. Ch., FTC, AFTC, CFTC Ace's Sheba of Ardyn (1959 Co-Nat'l Ch.) | 1957 | S905428 | 66 | 75½ |
| AFC Cute Accent | 1965 | SA323175 | 11½ | 3½ |
| Adac's Little Gypsy Doll | 1970 | | 8½ | |
| Aerco's Bit O'Honey | 1965 | SA398226 | 5 | 3½ |
| FC, AFC Alaska's Fall Blizzard | 1970 | | 21½ | 43 |
| Allo Dere Louise | 1964 | SA310830 | 2½ | 1 |
| FC, AFC Angelique | 1969 | SA699633 | 32½ | 90 |
| FC Anzac's Topa Topa Misty | 1972 | | | 10 |
| 05757FC, Aquarium Lady O'The Autumn Moon | 1969 | SA731579 | 20½ | 11 |
| Ardyn's Mercy Bound | 1959 | SA37855 | | 1 |
| FC, AFC Babbs Hollow Pooka Rue | 1972 | | 19½ | 12½ |
| Baby Doll | 1958 | SA200006 | 7½ | |
| FC, AFC Balsom's Mandy | 1958 | S971964 | 23½ | 26½ |
| AFC Barb's Mighty Mouse | 1973 | | 7 | 8½ |
| FTC, AFTC Bay City Zany Jane | 1956 | S819669 | 76 | 39½ |
| FC, AFC Bean Ball | 1960 | SA72441 | 32½ | 10 |

| Name | Date Birth | AKC Reg. Number | AKC Amateur Points | AKC Open Points |
|---|---|---|---|---|
| Beaumark of Lomac | 1960 | SA177999 | ½ | |
| Beautywood's Peggydidit | 1952 | S552717 | | 8 |
| FTC, AFTC Beautywood's Sooty Scamp | 1950 | S444654 | 21½ | 12½ |
| FC Beautywood's Tingler | 1960 | SA38571 | 14 | 18½ |
| AFC Beavercrest Sassy Sioux | 1961 | SA154932 | 12 | 4 |
| Bel-Aire Pam | 1962 | SA192814 | 3 | |
| Bellatrix of Hickory Glen | 1967 | SA527564 | 6 | 3 |
| Belle of Newport | 1950 | S475521 | ½ | |
| Belle Ringer | 1968 | SA657442 | 5½ | |
| 1955 Can. Nat'l Ch., FTC, AFTC, CFTC Belle of Zenith | 1952 | S565402 | 36½ | 35½ |
| Bigstone Black Longshot II | 1964 | SA311146 | 11 | 1½ |
| 1962 Nat'l Ch., FTC, AFTC Bigstone Hope | 1955 | S778945 | 67½ | 71 |
| Bigstone Prairie Wind | 1963 | SA231365 | 3 | 7 |
| FC, AFTC Bigstone Shady Lile | 1958 | SA74269 | 48½ | 32½ |
| CFTC Bill's Bell from Penfield | 1958 | 640504CKC | | |
| Birdie of Audlon | 1959 | S987703 | 1 | |
| FC, AFC Black Angel's Valiant Lady | 1969 | | 24 | 33 |
| FTC, AFTC Black Brook's Lady Bimba | 1951 | S52405 | 66 | 23 |
| AFTC Black Brook's Miss Chief | 1955 | S790748 | 45½ | |
| Black Brook's Pride of January | 1958 | S961072 | 21½ | 1 |
| Black Brook's Midnight Marauder | 1974 | | 1 | |
| Blackguard's Ms Paha Sapa | 1974 | | 5½ | 4 |
| Black Irish Kelly | 1966 | SA399234 | 10 | 6½ |
| 1945 Nat'l Ch., FTC Black Magic of Audlon (1944 Nat'l Derby Ch., *Field & Stream* Trophy, 1945) | 1943 | A745194 | | 26 |
| Black Minx of Franklin | 1958 | S928010 | 3 | |
| Black Point Black Gnat | 1949 | S363655 | 4 | |
| Black Point Interlude | 1947 | S264002 | 3 | 2 |
| Black Point Sweep and Span | 1946 | S103030 | | ½ |
| Black Susan of Pothemus | 1964 | SA255118 | 3½ | |
| Black Witch of Random Lake | 1955 | S76744 | ½ | 21½ |
| AFC Blanchard's Queen | 1958 | S950776 | 18 | 5 |
| Can. Dual Ch. Blue Jay of Upland Farm | 1957 | 418243CKC | | |
| Blue Water Gypsy | 1971 | | | 7½ |
| Blyth's Flash | 1955 | 358862CKC | 3 | |
| Can. Dual Ch. Blyth's Queen of Spades | 1951 | 303795CKC | | |
| Bob's Miss Zipper | 1958 | S924274 | 5 | |
| Boo's Black Molly | 1956 | S823992 | 3 | |
| CFTC Bracken of Timber Town (First Retriever Field Champion recorded by CKC, 1942) | 1940 | 160245CKC | | |
| Bracken's Jill | 1945 | 185007CKC | | 1 |
| CFTC Bracken's Dynamite | 1945 | 212315CKC | | |
| CFTC Bracken's Peggy of Lynnmoor | 1943 | S40038 | | 1 |
| Dual Ch. Braes of Arden | 1937 | A159960 | | 14 |
| Bramble of Timber Town | 1940 | A416362 | | 1 |
| Brandi of Cayne | 1966 | SA406484 | 1 | |
| Brandywine Star | 1961 | SA97577 | 5½ | 2½ |

| Name | Date Birth | AKC Reg. Number | AKC Amateur Points | AKC Open Points |
|---|---|---|---|---|
| Breckonhill Erin's Kelli | 1964 | SA295745 | 7½ | |
| Bridget VIII | 1971 | | ½ | |
| Bridget's Black Cargo | 1965 | SA331822 | 1 | |
| Brock's Lively Lark | 1966 | SA516161 | ½ | |
| Buck's Delta Clipper | | | 11½ | 1 |
| Budda of Arden | 1941 | A557014 | | 3 |
| FTC, AFTC Buenger's Niki of Pawlesta | 1955 | S729780 | 7 | 14 |
| CFTC Burndale's Cedar Lass | 1955 | 364128CKC | | |
| Dual Ch., AFC Burnham Buff | 1956 | S862613 | 17½ | 40 |
| Burnham Chanda | 1957 | S878483 | ½ | |
| Burrill's Black Sheba | 1949 | S369520 | 5 | 9 |
| Busta Monte Brandy | 1952 | S556437 | ½ | |
| Button's Spook | 1951 | S475958 | | 10 |
| Calamity Jane of Rockmount | 1965 | SA397711 | 3 | |
| AFC Calcutta of Sugar Bay | 1956 | S817211 | 4½ | |
| Camliag's Jill | 1960 | SA69215 | 8 | 1 |
| FC, AFC Candlewood's Nellie B Good | 1973 | | 19 | 12½ |
| Canuck Crest Cutty Sark | 1961 | SA187048 | | 109 |
| CFTC Canuck Crest Sally | 1961 | SA178825 | ½ | ½ |
| Captain's Miss | 1967 | SA548811 | ½ | |
| AFC Carnmoney's Samantha | 1973 | | 9 | 6½ |
| Carr-Lab Babe | 1956 | S903587 | 1 | |
| Carr-Lab Spirit | 1965 | SA351217 | | 1 |
| AFC Carr-Lab Washington's Weeko | 1974 | | 36 | 6 |
| Carryback's Callback | 1972 | | ½ | |
| FC Cascade Charade | 1965 | SA328791 | 2½ | 41 |
| Cha-Cha-Cha of District Ten | 1960 | SA85858 | 7 | 7½ |
| Chain's Princess Pet | 1960 | SA101858 | 1 | |
| AFC Charcoal Brandy Briquette | 1973 | | 20 | |
| Chief 's Duchess of Shenandoah | 1970 | | 7 | 7½ |
| Chonna's Black Diamond | 1959 | S987371 | | ½ |
| AFC Choppy Babe | 1965 | SA395018 | 13 | |
| Chukar's Starshine | 1971 | | | 3 |
| Cinar's Tulle | 1939 | A350469 | | |
| Cinder of Cole | 1964 | SA300366 | 1 | |
| FTC, AFTC Cindie of Salomonsen | 1950 | S385476 | 16½ | 41½ |
| Cindy Lou of Blue Wing | 1962 | SA236162 | ½ | |
| Coal Cinder | 1974 | | 1 | |
| Coaltown's Bridget | 1959 | A445686 | 5 | |
| Coffee of Bohland Hill | 1947 | S187990 | | ½ |
| CFTC Cola of Duck Land | 1957 | 403246CKC | | |
| Coldstream's Sugar Suzie | 1973 | | 1 | 4 |
| Coll-a Dene's Kelly | 1967 | SA506870 | 3 | |
| Confusion at Deer Creek | 1943 | A776977 | | 9 |
| FC Copy Cat del Norte | 1967 | SA532168 | 1 | 30½ |
| FC Copy of Ace | 1971 | | | 17 |
| Cougar's Little Tara Baby | 1970 | | 6 | 1 |
| Cougar's Midnight Lace | 1968 | | 9½ | 5 |
| FC Cream City Coed (1961 Nat'l Derby Ch.) | 1959 | SA406 | 13 | 59 |
| NRFC '70 Creole Sister | 1961 | SA124799 | 130 | 88 |

| Name | Date Birth | AKC Reg. Number | AKC Amateur Points | AKC Open Points |
|---|---|---|---|---|
| CFTC Crevamoy Pride<sup>c</sup> | 1943 | 178136CKC | | ½ |
| Cute Cover Girl | 1972 | | | 7½ |
| CFTC Cyndi Sue | 1947 | 249015CKC | | |
| FC, AFC Dairy Hill's Michikiniquia | 1968 | SA626535 | 17½ | 13 |
| FTC, AFTC Dairy Hill's Tart | 1953 | S599588 | 14½ | 11½ |
| Dairy Hill's Toddy Tot | 1960 | SA122318 | 12½ | 1 |
| FC, AFC Dairy Hill's Wampum | 1967 | SA569645 | 2 | 21 |
| CFTC Dark Galaxie | 1959 | 465283CKC | | |
| CFTC Dart of Netley Creek | 1961 | 493814CKC | | |
| FTC, AFTC Das Gluck Von Yonder | 1956 | S909858 | 18 | 16 |
| AFC Dawn of Audlon | 1963 | SA228129 | 25 | 8½ |
| FTC Decoy of Arden | 1933 | 965611 | | 17 |
| FTC Deer Creek's Vewsie | 1948 | S182307 | | 10½ |
| Deer Creek's Toddy Time II | 1948 | S182310 | 1 | |
| Deer Creek's Winning Ways | 1948 | S235755 | 6 | |
| FC, AFC Deerwood Shantoo | 1964 | SA295377 | 30½ | 26½ |
| AFC Delta Waters Moondoggie | 1974 | | 15½ | 1 |
| Del-Tone Mac's Belle | 1965 | SA390155 | | ½ |
| Den Mel's Cheer Chaser | 1975 | | 1 | |
| Desert Gypsy II | 1967 | SA545202 | | 4½ |
| Desert Queen | 1957 | S85876 | 3 | |
| FC, AFC Dessa Rae, C. D. | 1960 | SA34521 | 29½ | 59 |
| Dessa Sweet | 1963 | SA233505 | ½ | 2 |
| Diamond Lil of Bali Machree | 1952 | S580579 | ½ | |
| Dilly Be Wise | 1962 | SA182047 | 1 | |
| FC Dink's Ginger Guiness Stout | 1967 | SA481043 | ½ | 11 |
| FC Doc's Dynamite | 1971 | | | 49½ |
| FC, AFC Dobe's Desdemona | 1960 | SA78083 | 32 | 30 |
| Dolly of Cram | 1955 | S899855 | 5 | |
| Donnybrooks St. Jude (1975 Derby Ch.) | 1973 | | 81 Derby Points | |
| FC, AFC Donnybrooks St. Jude | 1973 | | 25 | 23½ |
| Dotty of Raven's Roost | 1956 | S872237 | 9 | 1 |
| Dove of Little Dutch Boots | 1964 | SA288080 | 6 | |
| Duchess XI | 1949 | S385720 | 5 | |
| Duchess of Rosehill | 1958 | S961566 | | 1 |
| FTC Duckblind Snowball | 1949 | S390385 | | 11 |
| CFTC Duckeye's Penny | 1948 | 265818CKC | ½ | |
| Ducky O'Cedar | 1967 | SA547972 | ½ | 7 |
| Dukertu Buff | 1957 | S977503 | 5½ | 5 |
| Dukertu Gidget | 1962 | SA262993 | 1 | |
| Duke-Trax Mandehgo | 1962 | SA190162 | 1 | |
| Dusang's Muffins of Vondalia | 1974 | | 1½ | |
| CFTC Duxbax Vronce | 1962 | 526724CKC | | |
| Dyna-Mite-Win | 1963 | SA219412 | 1 | |
| Sh. Ch. Earlsmoor Marlin of Arden | 1939 | A330770 | | 6 |
| FTC Earlyanna of Countrywood | 1953 | S601679 | | 27½ |
| AFTC Ebony Babe of Jolor | 1951 | S585333 | 14½ | 3 |
| Ebony Major Sassy Miss | 1962 | SAi57860 | ½ | 3 |
| Echo of Arden | 1934 | A7165 | | 1 |
| FC, AFC Ern-Bars Twinkle Boots | 1967 | SA530618 | 66 | 40 |

| Name | Date Birth | AKC Reg. Number | AKC Amateur Points | AKC Open Points |
|---|---|---|---|---|
| Esskay's Lou Lou From LSU | 1975 | | | 6 |
| NFC, AFC Euroclydon | 1973 | | 75½ | 71 |
| Fancy Cat Dancing | 1974 | | 3 | 1 |
| FTC Firelei of Deer Creek | 1940 | A509058 | | 17 |
| FTC, AFTC Frances Fishtail | 1956 | S8220403 | 82½ | 64 |
| Freehaven Darkie | 1940 | A460413 | | 5 |
| Freehaven India | 1946 | S133027 | | 3 |
| Freehaven Molly | 1939 | A367504 | | 4 |
| Friday My Gal by Nimbus | 1958 | S944816 | 10 | |
| Gabriel's Diana | 1947 | S135724 | | 1½ |
| Gahonk's Sassy Sioux | 1972 | | 1 | 13½ |
| FC, AFC Gahonk's Tyendinaga Totom | 1968 | SB33653 | 59 | 82½ |
| Garscube Meg | 1928 | | | 5 |
| CFTC Gerwin's Petite Viking, Can. C.D. | 1960 | 470401CKC | | |
| Giljo's Nikki of Bowmar | 1967 | SA499350 | 6½ | ½ |
| Giljo's Sky Anchors Aweigh | 1970 | | 7½ | 1 |
| FTC Gilmore's Peggy | 1945 | A947741 | | 55 |
| AFC Ginny | 1958 | S959172 | 17 | |
| Girl of Reelfoot | 1953 | S741293 | | ½ |
| Glenairlie Eve | 1939 | A448267 | | 8 |
| Glen's Lady of the Mountains | 1957 | S862272 | | 1 |
| FC Glenspey's Evergreen Cricket | 1972 | | | 14½ |
| FTC, AFTC Go-Kit's Gypsy | 1953 | S985876 | 28½ | 19½ |
| Goldie of Goldieland | 1939 | A675679 | | 8 |
| Goldshores Clearice Breaker | 1972 | | 3 | |
| Dual Ch. Gorse of Arden | 1937 | A159961 | | 13 |
| FC Grace Arts Classy Boots | 1957 | S880343 | | 12 |
| FC, AFC, CFTC Grady's Shadee Ladee | 1963 | SA235270 | 47½ | 60 |
| Grant's Lady Bird | 1965 | SA498443 | 1 | |
| Grangemead Watsnext | 1952 | S530863 | 1 | |
| CFTC Greatford Churchfield Jet | 1952 | 320825CKC | | |
| CFTC Green Timber Jewell | 1958 | 437852CKC | 1 | |
| Greenlief's Black Imp | 1963 | SA220740 | ½ | ½ |
| CFTC Grevamoy Pride (see Crevamoy Pride)[c] | 1948 | | | |
| Grilse of Kidwell | 1948 | S239208 | ½ | |
| Guy's Bitterrot Lou | 1950 | S446601 | 5½ | 1 |
| AFC Gwen's Ringtail Velvet | 1962 | SA190997 | 18 | |
| AFC Gwen's Trouble | 1962 | SA191291 | 25½ | 3 |
| Gypsy IV | 1953 | S625328 | | 1 |
| Gypsy Queen of Random Lake | 1951 | S405727 | | 3 |
| FC, AFC Gypsy Rose XII | 1973 | | 35 | 15 |
| Hal's Chula Prieta | 1967 | SA475914 | 3 | |
| Happy Hunter of Craignook | 1959 | SA48997 | 8½ | 1 |
| NFC, AFC Happy Playboy's Pearl | 1969 | SA700534 | 49½ | 54½ |
| Happy's Lucky Lass | 1974 | | ½ | |
| Happy's Twinkle | 1965 | SA325114 | 3 | ½ |
| Haze's Panikinki | 1972 | | | 3½ |
| Highlander's Dame Sally | 1967 | SA567433 | 1 | |
| High Brass Sassy | 1965 | SA437653 | ½ | |
| CFTC Hillside Ebony Lassie | 1956 | 372866CKC | | |

| Name | Date Birth | AKC Reg. Number | AKC Amateur Points | AKC Open Points |
|---|---|---|---|---|
| Hi-Ya Cindie | 1961 | SA126476 | 7 | |
| Holly Bridd | 1953 | S607180 | 1 | |
| Holly's Wake of Ardyn | 1955 | S796833 | | 9½ |
| FTC Honey Chile Trixie | 1944 | A977320 | | 10½ |
| FTC Hot Coffee of Random Lake | 1949 | S342690 | | 17½ |
| Howard's Lady Lou | 1953 | S639640 | 3 | |
| CFTC How-Hi Curlew | 1946 | S59119 | | |
| FC Howie's Happy Hunter | 1957 | S967930 | | 72½ |
| Hullabaloo of Audlon | 1950 | S417937 | | 3 |
| AFC Hunt's Cloud of Smoke | 1967 | SA476047 | 13½ | 5 |
| Hunt's Digger of Little Smokey | 1965 | SA397873 | 11 | |
| I'd Rather Be Lucky | 1974 | | 8½ | |
| FC I Love Lucy of Audlon | 1950 | S417937 | | 3 |
| Imperial Crest Maggy | 1964 | SA249858 | 4 | 3 |
| Invail's Vicki of Sugar Valley | 1955 | S772374 | | 4 |
| J.A.M.'s Steamin' Deamon | 1965 | SA387713 | 1 | 4½ |
| J. J.'s Lady Ebony | 1968 | SA593789 | ½ | |
| Jac-Lor's Laja | 1964 | SA301339 | 3 | |
| Jac-Lor's Miss Cindy | 1960 | SA120308 | 1 | |
| Jade of Sandylands | 1936 | A125387 | | 4 |
| FC Jeaux-Jeaux Binee' of Adalar | 1971 | | | 10 |
| Jenny Lind | 1970 | | | 3 |
| Jersey's Secret Queen | 1974 | | 1 | |
| Jet Flash of Windy Acres | 1954 | S762874 | 8 | |
| Jet Noir La Petite | 1960 | SA158370 | | 3½ |
| FC, AFC Jet of Hart | 1958 | S976152 | 9½ | 10½ |
| Jet of Sugar Valley | 1953 | S665175 | 15 | 4 |
| Jet's Tammy | 1958 | S969538 | 5 | 6 |
| Jewel of Sandylands | 1936 | A123299 | | |
| FTC, AFTC, CFTC Jibodad Gypsy | 1947 | S172358 | 1 | 26½ |
| Jibodad Jalopy | 1947 | S174366 | 3 | |
| FC Jibodad Moxie | 1954 | S648115 | | 14 |
| FTC, AFTC Jibodad Velvet | 1955 | S751950 | 61½ | 51 |
| AFC Jilly Girl | 1960 | SA128986 | 16 | 8½ |
| Jingle's Bitter Trace | 1969 | SA687477 | 7 | |
| Jodi of Twin Pines | 1970 | | 1½ | |
| CFTC Jo-Ker's Lady 2nd | 1958 | 483088CKC | | |
| FC John's Minnie | 1964 | SA314419 | ½ | 16½ |
| Jonny's High Yellow | 1966 | SA461039 | ½ | |
| Joy of Arden | 1936 | A82221 | | 12 |
| FC Julie Cole of Menomin | 1963 | SA187349 | | 20½ |
| Jumper | 1960 | SA175735 | 1 | 10 |
| NAFC, FC Kannonball Kate | 1972 | | 120 | 107 |
| Katy of Avondale | 1960 | SA103903 | 5 | |
| FC, AFC Keg of Black Powder | 1961 | SA121307 | 16½ | 11 |
| FTC Keith's Black Magic | 1944 | S3052 | ½ | 71 |
| Keno's Ebony Deuce | 1973 | | 2 | 5 |
| Can. Dual Ch. Kilarney Sheba | 1949 | 265600CKC | | |
| FTC Kilsyth Cleo | 1947 | S265087 | | 16 |
| Kilsyth Goldie | 1937 | A251342 | | 3 |

| Name | Date Birth | AKC Reg. Number | AKC Amateur Points | AKC Open Points |
|---|---|---|---|---|
| Kingdale's Ink Spot | 1947 | S51248 | | 1½ |
| FC Knight's Noel | 1961 | SA191865 | | 14½ |
| Krystolida's Dynamite | 1943 | A780075 | | ½ |
| FTC, AFTC Ladies' Day at Deer Creek | 1946 | S45266 | 15½ | 14½ |
| Lady VI | 1965 | SA314138 | | 1 |
| Lady Banji | 1976 | | | 3 |
| Lady Be Good at Deer Creek | 1946 | S1766 | | 3½ |
| Lady of Wake | 1966 | SA443371 | | 8½ |
| Lady Red's Lucky Rascal | 1972 | | | 5½ |
| Lake Ripley Pooka | 1965 | SA348609 | 3 | |
| Lake Ripley Smudge | 1954 | S751475 | 12½ | 4½ |
| FC, AFC Layla Puna Raider | 1972 | | 48½ | 13 |
| FTC Ledgeland's Dora | 1934 | 995266 | | 10 |
| Ledgeview's Classic Beauty | 1968 | | 6 | |
| CFTC Leecoy's Judy | 1952 | 319398CKC | | |
| CFTC Lee's Dixie | 1944 | 208260CKC | | |
| Le-Mar's Pinewood Kochy | 1972 | | 1½ | |
| Lilli of Corfu | 1956 | S902550 | 1 | |
| Lil's Lucky Linda | 1967 | SA560303 | 3 | 10 |
| Limestone Tinker Belle | 1959 | SA5526 | | 3 |
| CFTC Lisa's Pet | 1962 | SA352850 | | 7½ |
| Little Billie Jo | 1966 | SA465207 | 8½ | 2½ |
| AFTC, Sh. Ch. Little Magic Lady | 1955 | S761847 | 20½ | |
| FC, AFC Little Miss Samantha | 1966 | SA430697 | 35 | 10½ |
| Dual Ch. Little Miss Timber | 1950 | S440049 | | 17 |
| Little Trouble of Audlon | 1947 | S173112 | 10 | 20 |
| FC, AFC Littlewood's Country Slicker | 1972 | | 31 | 12 |
| Lokate of High Point | 1955 | S752921 | 1½ | |
| 1961 Can. Nat'l Ch., CFTC Long Point Belle | 1958 | 411476CKC | | |
| FC, AFC Longshot Waterloo | 1972 | | 54 | 44 |
| Lorrendons Nylon | 1945 | S31061 | | 4 |
| FC, AFTC Lucifer's Lady | 1958 | S944958 | 37 | 51 |
| FTC, AFTC Lucinda of Crater Lake | 1954 | S799625 | 56 | 28½ |
| Lucky Kelly Girl | 1974 | | 1 | |
| FC, AFC Lucky's Lady in Red | 1968 | SA671729 | 46 | ½ |
| FC, AFC Luka of Casey's Rocket | 1963 | SA221876 | 9½ | 31 |
| Lulake's Tracy | 1970 | | 1 | |
| CFTC Luther's Black Juno | 1957 | 410996CKC | | |
| FC, AFC Macariolyn's Feather Tiger | 1971 | | 59½ | 38 |
| FC Madam Queen | 1972 | | | 10 |
| McClintock's Ebony Belle | 1963 | SA251804 | 1 | |
| McKemie's Pola | 1963 | SA217535 | 9 | |
| FTC, AFTC Manzanal Clover | 1953 | S598961 | 35½ | 45½ |
| FC Marten's Black Powder Katy | 1965 | SA342479 | | 23½ |
| Marten's Hi-Buttons | 1971 | | | 3½ |
| FTC Marten's Little Bullet | 1951 | S512928 | | 27½ |
| Marvadel Cinders | 1939 | A351115 | | |
| FTC Mary-Go-Round Deer Creek | 1946 | S1767 | | 21 |
| May Millard | 1927 | 703064 | | |
| Medlin's Gay Teal of Castawac | 1964 | SA287780 | 3½ | ½ |

| Name | Date Birth | AKC Reg. Number | AKC Amateur Points | AKC Open Points |
|------|------------|-----------------|---------------------|------------------|
| Mel's Yuletide Honey | 1965 | SA372588 | 4 | 3 |
| Melissa Princess of Arcadia | 1969 | | | ½ |
| FC Michelle | 1963 | SA246304 | | 152½ |
| CFTC Mi-Chris Black Lady | 1958 | 444185CKC | | |
| FC Mi-Chris of Hayden | 1963 | SA272601 | | 11½ |
| FC, AFC Midge of Greenwood | 1966 | SA439323 | 28½ | 17½ |
| Midge of Ravenhue | 1949 | S392058 | 1 | |
| Mike's Lizzie Odom | 1964 | SA286084 | 6 | |
| Miss Debit of Shady Valley | 1953 | S689252 | 5 | |
| Miss Fortune | 1967 | SA482195 | | ½ |
| FTC Miss Madison | 1938 | A400964 | | 11 |
| Miss NYX | 1969 | SA687124 | ½ | |
| Misty Morning Teal | 1974 | | 9 | 5 |
| FC, AFC Misty of Otter Creek | 1964 | SA249760 | 14 | 33 |
| Miz Scamp of Landfall | 1974 | | | 3 |
| Montgomery's Rough and Ready | 1973 | | | 3 |
| Montina Lady | 1963 | SA213644 | 3 | |
| Moor's Toots of Brewster | 1946 | S62394 | ½ | 5 |
| Moose's Louise | 1967 | SA556389 | 5½ | 5 |
| Moose's Ridgewood Tar Baby | 1969 | | 6 | |
| Muffet's Tuffet | 1969 | SA744877 | 5 | 1½ |
| Muse's Bonnie Girl | 1963 | SA224383 | 1 | |
| My Lady Castlemaine | 1954 | S692132 | ½ | |
| FC, AFC Nakai Anny | 1970 | | 15 | 21 |
| CFTC Nascopie Cinder of Lucifer | 1965 | 639805CKC | 9½ | 8 |
| Neb's Katy | 1961 | SA113895 | 6 | |
| Nefertite | 1964 | SA287608 | ½ | 5 |
| CFTC Neil's Tia Marie | 1964 | 618185CKC | | |
| FTC Nelgard's Counter Point (1953 Nat'l Derby Ch.) | 1952 | S562753 | | 23 |
| Nemo's Dell-Gin | 1967 | SA551395 | ½ | |
| Netley Creek's Chickadee | 1963 | SA338527 | | 3 |
| New Policy | 1973 | | ½ | |
| FTC Nic-O-Bet's Black Candy | 1951 | S502690 | 5 | 44 |
| Nilo Gypsy | 1966 | SA406761 | 4 | 9 |
| AFTC Nilo Solo's Margie | 1956 | S817260 | 19½ | |
| FTC Nodak Cindy (1957 Nat'l Derby Ch.) | 1955 | S787526 | 5 | 17½ |
| CFTC Nodak Tar Pride | 1954 | 441389CKC | | |
| Nodak Trixie | 1951 | S465544 | 13 | |
| FC, AFC Nodrog Penny | 1960 | SA94360 | 72½ | 52½ |
| Nodrog Pixie | 1966 | SA442553 | ½ | ½ |
| Oakwood Jane's Delilah | 1955 | S886181 | | 3 |
| Orchardton Doris | 1930 | 905779 | | 3 |
| FC, AFC Orlon's Lady Dart | 1968 | SA567867 | 40 | 22 |
| AFC Ornbaum's Black Candy | 1962 | SA163899 | 15½ | 7½ |
| FC Ornbaum's Diamond Lil | 1972 | | | 31½ |
| AFC Oscar's Petite Lightning, C. D. | 1962 | SA311676 | 33½ | |
| Oxbow Cinderella | 1959 | SA33615 | 5 | |
| FC, AFC Paha Sapa Belle | 1957 | S919047 | 34½ | 27½ |
| Paha Sapa Little Sioux | 1960 | SA84769 | | 1 |

| Name | Date Birth | AKC Reg. Number | AKC Amateur Points | AKC Open Points |
|------|------------|-----------------|--------------------|-----------------|
| Pat of Orchard Glen | 1964 | SA262776 | 6 | 3 |
| FC, AFC Pat's Penny Jo | 1967 | SA471112 | 27 | 9 |
| Pawlesta's Boomtown Bet | 1955 | S729783 | 7½ | 5 |
| Pawlesta's Little Toto | 1962 | SA171260 | ½ | |
| FC Peg of Turkey Run | 1961 | SA92531 | | 44 |
| Peggy of Woodend | 1937 | A210293 | | |
| Can. Dual Ch., CAFTC, FC Pelican Lake Peggy (All-time highest scoring retriever in Canada through 1969) | 1964 | 597233CKC | 12 | 10 |
| Penelope Jane | 1940 | 305654FDSB | | |
| AFTC Penny Girl | 1956 | S863327 | 36 | ½ |
| FC, AFC Penny of Evergreen | 1965 | SA352451 | 34 | 17 |
| Peppers Maggie | 1950 | S491265 | 6 | 4½ |
| Pheasant Lawn's Lady Grace | 1960 | SA60561 | 3½ | |
| FC, AFC Piegan's Cryseyde | 1969 | SA652932 | 23½ | 5½ |
| Pixie IV | 1967 | SA498805 | 2½ | 6½ |
| Pow on Tap's Pacific Pearl | 1974 | | | ½ |
| FTC Princess Black Belle | 1952 | S536435 | 1 | 18 |
| Princess Pat of the Corkies | 1948 | S199982 | ½ | |
| FTC, AFTC Princess Patricia Stieg | 1954 | S669572 | 58½ | 17½ |
| Purty Sure Judy | 1958 | SA23106 | 7 | |
| Queen VII | 1947 | S244051 | | 8 |
| Queenie Mayflower | 1959 | SA170197 | ½ | |
| 1960 Nat'l Am. Ch., FTC, AFTC Queenie of Redding | 1954 | S711600 | 52 | 31½ |
| FC, AFC Raider's Torrid Lady | 1973 | | 36 | 18 |
| Ravenhill's Lucky Lady | 1968 | SA730753 | 1 | |
| Raven's Gingerbread Girl | 1966 | SA379507 | 1 | |
| Red Cedar Hershey | 1974 | | 1 | |
| Red Jacket | 1974 | | | 7½ |
| Regina Di Campi | 1961 | SA93721 | 14½ | |
| Rehl Shadee Playgirl | 1973 | | ½ | ½ |
| FC, AFC Rill Shannon's Dark Dell | 1960 | SA148551 | 118½ | 49½ |
| Rinney's Desedo | 1954 | S660209 | 14 | |
| FC, AFC Ripco's Lady Pam | 1959 | SA76523 | 25½ | 21 |
| 1964 Nat'l Ch., FC, AFC Ripco's V. C. Morgan | 1959 | SA37521 | 41 | 42½ |
| Ripple's Raven | 1958 | S932042 | 9 | 6 |
| AFC Risky Business Ruby | 1976 | | 13½ | 4 |
| River Oaks Black Frost | 1968 | SA603598 | | 2 |
| River Oaks Call Girl | 1971 | | 3 | |
| River Oaks Cream Cadet | 1968 | SA603597 | 5½ | 1 |
| Rocky's Pat | 1951 | S597824 | | ½ |
| Roffey Gay Time | 1951 | S719417 | | 1 |
| FC, AFC Rosehill's Little Dutch Boots | 1961 | SA122448 | 70½ | 14½ |
| Rosie's Black Magic | 1973 | | | 8½ |
| Roxie of Mercer Lake | 1961 | SA173420 | 4 | 1 |
| Royal Oaks Ginny | 1972 | | 1 | |
| Royal Oaks Havoc Haze | 1968 | SA605040 | 6½ | |
| Dual AFC Royal Oaks Jill of Burgundy | 1968 | SA601255 | 53½ | 65 |
| Royal Oaks Magic Rose | 1974 | | | 3 |

| Name | Date Birth | AKC Reg. Number | AKC Amateur Points | AKC Open Points |
|------|------------|-----------------|--------------------|-----------------|
| Royal Oaks Sasse-Ville Genie | 1972 | | 10 | 3 |
| AFC Royal Oaks Share of Burgundy | 1971 | | 3 | 9 |
| AFC Royal Oaks Soup's On | 1971 | | 18½ | |
| FC Rus-Lau's Lucky Penny | 1971 | | | 13½ |
| Sage Brandy of Sunny Slope | 1966 | SA447609 | 8 | ½ |
| FC, AFC Sailor's Echo | 1974 | | 18 | 15 |
| FC, AFC Sand Gold Kim | 1960 | SA52832 | 60 | 57 |
| Sand Gold Venus | 1959 | SA530 | 9½ | ½ |
| FC Sandhill's Happy Hooker | 1973 | | 10 | 11½ |
| Sandlake Hornet | 1946 | S104480 | | 1 |
| FC Sandy's Cindy | 1970 | | | 36½ |
| Sapphire's Ruby Begonia | 1971 | | 1 | |
| FC Sassy Sioux of Tukwila | 1968 | SA567865 | 10 | 81 |
| FC Sassy Sioux of Willow Creek | 1964 | SA294094 | | 10 |
| Satan's Black Magic | 1973 | | 3 | |
| Sauk Trail Black Pepper | 1965 | SA305899 | | ½ |
| Scioto Black Libby | 1962 | SA180465 | | 7 |
| CFTC Sebasticook Duxcross | 1956 | 453569CKC | | |
| Semloh's Peggy | 1951 | S550724 | 5½ | 1 |
| FC, AFC Serrana of Genessee | 1963 | SA192717 | 38½ | 50 |
| Seymour's Black Diamond | 1965 | SA451756 | | ½ |
| Seymour's Hot Line Pepper | 1967 | SA519949 | 3 | 4 |
| AFC Shamrock Acres Columbine | 1968 | | 19 | |
| Shamrock Acres Domino Queen, C. D. X. | 1957 | S855932 | 8 | |
| Shamrock Acres Lucky Lady | 1969 | SA640266 | | 3 |
| Shamrock Acres Sassy Rascal | 1974 | | 6 | 9½ |
| Ch. AFC Shamrock Acres Simmer Down | 1961 | SA99844 | 54½ | 9½ |
| FC, AFC Shamrock Acres Wine Country | 1970 | | 26½ | 18 |
| Shamrock Acres Winnie Pooh | 1969 | SA771320 | 8½ | 1 |
| Sha-Na-Lae | 1974 | | 8 | |
| Shannon's Terror | 1966 | SA481451 | ½ | |
| Shar-Loy's Miss Midnight | 1965 | SA307503 | ½ | |
| FC Sheba's Westmoor Cleopatra | 1964 | SA285108 | 9½ | 10 |
| FC Sheba's Westmoor Contessa | 1963 | SA221476 | 2½ | 25½ |
| FTC, AFTC Shed's Dinah of Whitefish | 1949 | S339362 | 14½ | 16½ |
| FC, Ch. Sherwood's Maid Marion | 1963 | SA320722 | | 13 |
| Simmerdown Black Widow | 1976 | | | 3 |
| AFC Simmer's Shot of Brandy | 1963 | SA266820 | 24 | 1½ |
| Skookum Redwing | 1967 | SA531776 | 8½ | |
| CFTC Skyhill's Lady Evelyn | 1956 | 375549CKC | | |
| Sky Pilot's Judy | 1939 | | | 1 |
| FC, AFC Smokey of Park Avenue | 1964 | SA245034 | 53 | 28½ |
| Smokey's Bonnie Gay | 1956 | S814024 | 8 | |
| Smudge's Little Monster | 1957 | S924986 | 9 | |
| FTC, AFTC Snake River Dilly | 1948 | S311424 | 12 | 28½ |
| Southdowns Roulette | 1973 | | | 1 |
| Sparkle Didit | 1971 | | ½ | 1½ |
| Spider Gal | 1961 | SA147087 | 10 | |
| Spirit Lake Jet | 1953 | S609512 | 3½ | |
| AFC Spring Farms Cup of Wild Honey | 1972 | | 12 | 5½ |

| Name | Date Birth | AKC Reg. Number | AKC Amateur Points | AKC Open Points |
|------|------------|-----------------|--------------------|-----------------|
| Star Girl | 1941 | A568530 | | |
| FTC, AFC Star of Fate | 1955 | S787622 | 12 | 24 |
| CFTC Spruceland's Jody | 1961 | 513845CKC | | |
| Sunburst Dawn Breeze | 1971 | | 1/2 | |
| AFC Suncrest Zuni | 1971 | | 20 1/2 | 5 1/2 |
| Super Value Dolly | 1973 | | | 8 |
| Susie Wild Fire | 1975 | | 5 | |
| Sweep's Pippin | 1947 | S299457 | | 3 |
| CFTC Syldonnell's Duxie | 1959 | 596971CKC | | |
| Taffy of Janie Lane | 1968 | SA614223 | 4 | |
| FC, AFC Tally Ho the Vixen | 1970 | | 17 1/2 | 40 1/2 |
| FTC, AFTC Tam O'Shanter of Craignook | 1955 | S733010 | 52 1/2 | 33 |
| FTC Tar of Arden (*Field & Stream* Trophy, 1941) | 1937 | A210256 | | 53 |
| Tattler of Timber Town | 1951 | S469710 | | 3 |
| Tealwood Tammy | 1967 | SA553422 | | 1/2 |
| Tepee Tea | 1974 | | 1/2 | 1 1/2 |
| CFTC The Bay Lady Narda | 1957 | 412726CKC | | |
| The Contesse | 1956 | S881469 | 9 1/2 | 3 |
| FC, AFC, CFTC The Dutchess of Rosehill | 1958 | S961566 | 23 | 54 |
| AFC Tidewater Mallard | 1969 | | 35 1/2 | 6 |
| FC, AFC Tigathoe's Mainliner Marish | 1965 | SA370868 | 175 | 79 |
| Tiger's Texas Tiger | 1967 | SA536928 | | 3 1/2 |
| AFC Timberlake Flying Muffin | 1962 | SA149204 | 15 1/2 | 1 |
| Timewaster's Miss Chief | 1960 | SA45577 | 1/2 | |
| FC, AFC Tintinnabulum Obsidian Tyna | 1970 | | | 37 1/2 |
| Tirie 'Tiang | 1969 | | 3 | |
| FTC, AFTC Toto of Audlon | 1953 | S606362 | 8 1/2 | 10 |
| FTC, AFTC Trabington's Black Witch | 1945 | S255453 | | 11 |
| Treasure State Bewise | 1951 | S487393 | 1 | |
| Trevrchamp Marsey | 1944 | S4014 | | 4 1/2 |
| FC, AFC Trieven Classic | 1971 | | 27 | 35 |
| Trieven Jumping Jenny | 1973 | | 8 | |
| Trieven Thunder's Mug | 1974 | | 2 1/2 | 6 |
| Triever Point Missy | 1959 | SA68264 | | 1/2 |
| FTC, CFTC Tri Stada Gun Moll | 1943 | A806669 | | 13 |
| FC, AFC Truckee's Little Crackerjack | 1974 | | 25 | 22 1/2 |
| FTC, AFTC Truly Yours of Garfield | 1950 | S414236 | 34 | 72 1/2 |
| FC, AFC Trumarc's Billy Jean | 1975 | | 17 1/2 | 20 1/2 |
| AFC Trumarc's Lucky Streak | 1972 | | 19 1/2 | 7 |
| FC, AFC Trumarc's Raider | 1970 | | | 29 |
| AFC Trumarc's Shindana | 1970 | | 9 | 7 1/2 |
| Tussy of Mark (1947 Nat'l Derby Ch.) | 1946 | S35781 | | |
| Twiggy's Holiday Express | 1974 | | 6 | 1 |
| FC, AFC Twinkle's Mandy | 1968 | SA628860 | 22 | 32 |
| Twink's Tinker Belle | 1967 | SA531197 | 5 | |
| Tyker's Lucky Penny | 1966 | SA457562 | 5 | |
| Ursa Minor | 1958 | S947163 | | 3 1/2 |
| AFC Valhalla Lujah | 1972 | | 20 1/2 | 5 |
| AFC Valhalla Misfire | 1970 | | 39 1/2 | 7 1/2 |
| Valhalla's Valkyrie | 1972 | | 5 | |

| Name | Date Birth | AKC Reg. Number | AKC Amateur Points | AKC Open Points |
|---|---|---|---|---|
| FC Vans Pride Ebony Shadow | 1962 | SA152054 | | 84½ |
| FC, AFC Velvet's Jezebel | 1961 | SA130191 | 27½ | 12 |
| Victory Joy | 1945 | A980567 | | 5 |
| Vince's Sassafras | 1974 | | 1 | ½ |
| Can. FTC Virginia Lady | 1956 | S861972 | | 6 |
| Volwood's Abby | 1976 | | ½ | 6 |
| Wacap's Windy | 1967 | SA661895 | 3 | |
| Walla Walla Wheatie | 1974 | | 1 | |
| Wanapum Chuska Yazzie | 1975 | | | 4 |
| NFC, NAFC, CNFC Wanapum Dart's Dandy | 1970 | SA827919 | 107½ | 106½ |
| FC, CNFC Wanapum Dart's Garbo | 1970 | | | 56½ |
| Wanapum Sheba | 1968 | SA565263 | 5 | 5 |
| Wanapum Sheba's Lil Come Back | 1972 | | 3½ | 1 |
| Warcon's Carbon Copy | 1970 | | | 2 |
| Wardwyn Bonny Boots | 1947 | S131689 | ½ | |
| Wardwyn Welcome | 1944 | A816283 | | ½ |
| Warpath Just In Case | 1968 | | 11 | |
| Warpath Kitty | 1966 | SA411130 | 3 | |
| Warpath's Black Powder Shama | 1970 | | 5½ | |
| Washington's Lucky Minerva | 1972 | | 1 | 2 |
| FC Washington's Tizzy Lizzy | 1969 | SA662472 | 12½ | 23½ |
| Webway's Dolphin (1948 Nat'l Derby Ch.) | 1947 | S330517 | | |
| CFTC Westhaven Pride | 1940 | 164147CKC | | |
| FTC West Island Raven | 1950 | S480800 | | 35 |
| West Wind Blue Lady | 1974 | | | 7½ |
| Whitecairn Wendy of Wingan | 1932 | 934280 | | 9 |
| Whitmore's Rowdy Lady | 1951 | S526186 | 1 | 6 |
| Whittaker Firefly | 1963 | SA229940 | 11½ | |
| FC, AFC Wildhearted Dinah | 1968 | SA625632 | 57½ | 14½ |
| CFC Willowmount Gemina 2nd | 1968 | | | 1 |
| CFTC Willowmount Honey Bunny | 1965 | 639498CKC | | |
| AFC Willow's Boe Longshot | 1965 | SA333664 | 16 | ½ |
| Wingan's Daily Double | 1936 | A104408 | | |
| FTC Woodcroft Inga's Bonus | 1947 | S241309 | | 13 |
| FC, AFC Woody's Black Baby | 1971 | | 19 | |
| AFC World Famous Sweet Pea | 1973 | | 21½ | |
| Yogi Bear's Angel | 1971 | | | 1 |
| Your Shot Annie Fanny | 1973 | | | ½ |
| FTC, AFTC Zipper of Sugar Valley | 1947 | S289941 | 31 | 42½ |
| FC Zoe | 1973 | | 2 | 16½ |
| Zoe of Sandy Port | 1966 | SA392795 | 1½ | |
| Zoe of Sleight | 1970 | | 18½ | |

(a) Date given is date of first placement. The whelping date is not known.

(b) Died shortly after derby year.

(c) Not eligible for AKC registration.

(d) Title recorded but not recognized by the Canadian Kennel Club because this dog is not registered in its stud book.

(e) CFTC Crevamony Pride erroneously recorded in *Canadian Kennel Club Stud Book* as "Grevamoy Pride."

# Appendix III

RETRIEVER CLUBS

## NATIONAL CLUBS

American Amateur Retriever Club, Leonard La Bud, 17 W315, Tioga Tr., Bensenville, IL 60106

American Chesapeake Club, Miss Deborah Reaves, 506 N.W. 39th Road, Gainesville, FL 32607

Labrador Retriever Club, John W. McAssey, 2608 Harrison Hills Drive, Boise, ID 87302

## LOCAL CLUBS

*Alabama*

Mobile Amateur Retriever Club, E. Rob Leatherbury, 5800 Fairfax Rd., Mobile, AL 33608

*Alaska*

Alaska Retriever Club, Ms. Linda Chase, 5000 Lake Otis, Anchorage, AK 99507

Fairbanks Retriever Club, Ken Ulz, Box 845, Fairbanks, AK 99701

*Arizona*

Phoenix Retriever Club, Mrs. Jo Zimmerman, 7743 N. 17th Dr., Phoenix, AZ 85021

Southern Arizona Retriever Club, Miss Lucy E. Austin, P.O. Box 5527, Mohave Valley, AZ 86440

*California*

California South Coast Retriever Club, Ms. Kathy Bulicz, 12502 Camus Lane, Garden Grove, CA 92641

Lassen Retriever Club, Peter F. Lane, P.O. Box 2125, Redding, CA 96001

Northern California Retriever Trial Club, Harold Mack, Jr., 617 Matsonia, Foster City, CA 94044

Redwood Empire Retriever Club, Nancy Clemenza, 2475 Ridgewood Dr., Eureka, CA 95501

Sacramento Valley Retriever Club, Ms. Claudia Fenner, 2649 Orchid St., Fairfield, CA 94533

Sagehen's Retriever Club, Mrs. William Sabbag, 3679 Evergreen Dr., Palo Alto, CA 94303

San Diego Retriever Field Trial Club, Ginger Cope, 9735 Vomac Road, Santee, CA 92071

San Jose Retriever Club, George Coughran, 6935 Burning Tree Court, San Jose, CA 95119

Southern California Retriever Club, Mrs. Barbara Smith, 1430 Fairway Drive, Camarillo, CA 93010

*Colorado*

Arkansas Valley Retriever Field Trial Club, William D. Connor, 7025 Grashio Dr., Colorado Springs, CO 80918

Ft. Collins Retriever Club, Mrs. Clarice Rutherford, 631 No. Overland Trail, Ft. Collins, CO 80521

Mile-Hi Golden Retriever Club, Anne Couttet, Box 561, Georgetown, CO 80444

Pikes Peak Retriever Club, A. R. Kistenbroker, 1008 Mars Dr., Colorado Springs, CO 80906

Rocky Mountain Retriever Club, Ms. Joyce Olinger, 5945 Ward Rd., Arvada, CO 80004

*Connecticut*

Shoreline Retriever Club, Mrs. Iveaux Andersen, 50 Northwestern Dr., Bristol, CT 06010

*Delaware*

Del Bay Retriever Club, Jay T. Chandler, 5401 Lancaster Pike, Wilmington, DE 19807

*Florida*

Jacksonville Retriever Club, James R. Rentz, 5806 Lake Lucina Dr. So., Jacksonville, FL 32211

North Florida Amateur Retriever Club, Mrs. Neal D. Sapp, 1906 High Road, Tallahassee, FL 32303

*Georgia*

Atlanta Retriever Club, Joseph Cooper, III, 1837 Colland Dr. NW, Atlanta, GA 30318

*Idaho*

Eastern Idaho Retriever Club, Ms. Carolyn. L. McRoberts, 885

Clair View Lane, Idaho Falls, ID 83401

Idaho Retriever Club, Russell L. Worthan, 1089 Cruser Dr., Boise, ID 83705

Snake River Retriever Club, Donald L. Burnett, 701 S. 19th Ave., Pocatello, ID 83201

Wood River Retriever Club, Mrs. Betty Shanaman, P.O. Box 1556, Sun Valley, ID 83353

*Illinois*

Golden Retriever Club of Illinois, Paul Roseman, 1969 Prairie St., Glenview, IL 60025

Mid-Illinois Retriever Club, Ms. Norma Dawson, R.R. 2, Brinfield, IL 61517

Midwest Field Trial Club, Mrs. James T. Venerable, 10425 Woodbine Lane, Huntley, IL 60142

River King Retriever Club, Mrs. Jackie Stroh, 21 Fenwood, Belleville, IL 62220

*Indiana*

Central Indiana Amateur Retriever Club, Ms. Gretchen Seeburger, R.R. 3, Box 88, Zionsville, IN 46077

Lincoln Trail Amateur Retriever Club, Charles Schreiber, Jr., 441 Tenth St., Tell City, IN 47586

Michiana Retriever Club, Ken Urgonski, 63722 SR #23, North Liberty, IN 46554

Southwestern Indiana Retriever Club, Mrs. Freddie King, 400 W. 7th Street, Mt. Vernon, IN 47620

White River Golden Retriever, Barbara Rollins, R.R. 1, Box 400, Zionsville, IN 46077

*Iowa*

Mid-Iowa Retriever Club, Robert W. Mann, 800 E. 24th St., Des Moines, IA 50317

Missouri Valley Hunt Club, Donald R. Feekin, 400 Carson Ave., Council Bluffs, IA 51501

Northwest Iowa Retriever Club, Dale Lundstrom, Box 311, Spirit Lake, IA 51360

*Kansas*

Jayhawk Retriever Club, John R. Blair, 15629 E. 45th St., North Wichita, KS 67228

Kansas City Retriever Club, Mrs. Roberta Ryan, 8821 Catalina, Prairie Village, KS 66207

Topeka Retriever Club, Joseph Dusang, 4501 W. 62nd, Fairway, KS 66205

*Kentucky*

Western Kentucky Retriever Club, Louis Igert, III, Rt. 11, Box 699A, Paducah, KY 42001

*Louisiana*

Calcasieu Retriever Club, Jack Hicks, 1100 Beach St., Westlake, LA 70669

North Louisiana Retriever Club, Donald P. Weiss, 411 Commercial National Bank Building, Shreveport, LA 71101

South Louisiana Retriever Club, Harold T. Buckley, Jr., 826 St. Louis St., Suite 200, New Orleans, LA 70~~130~~

*Maine*

Maine Retriever Club, Mrs. Zelma C. Clark, 13 Wildwood Drive, Saco, ME 04072

*Maryland*

Maryland Retriever Club, August Belmont, Rt. #1, Box 564, Easton, MD 21601

Talbot Retriever Club, Don Gearheart, Cedar Point, Royal Oak, MD 21662

*Massachusetts*

Colonial Retriever Field Trial Club, Dudley L. Millikin, Jr., 109 Holt Rd., Andover, MA 01810

Yankee Golden Retriever Club, Arlee Recktenwald, Nashua Rd., Bedford, MA 01730

*Michigan*

Flat River Retriever Club of Michigan, Ms. Sue Bailey, 2300 Van Wormer Rd., Saginaw, MI 48603

Wolverine Retriever Club, S.C. Shea, 919 Sunningdale Dr., Grosse Pointe Woods, MI 48236

*Minnesota*

Central Minnesota Retriever Club, Dennis J. Cahill, RFD 2, Box 69A Monticello, MN 55362

Duluth Retriever Club, Mrs. Elizabeth Lotti, 9875 Old North Shore Rd., Duluth, MN 55804

Minnesota Valley Retriever Club, Gary Dallmann, Box 23, New Ulm, MN 56073

Tri State Hunting Dog Association, Ronald Maul, 4690 Ninth St., Winona, MN 55987

*Missouri*
Mississippi Valley Retriever Club, Richard D. Schultz, 425 Breeze-wood Dr., Ballwin, MO 63011
*Montana*
Montana Retriever Club, Glenn P. Scheihing, 2807 Lyndale Lane, Billings, MT 59102
Treasure State Retriever Club, Mrs. Beryl Zbitnoff, 2040 Utah Ave., Butte, MT 59701
Western Montana Retriever Club, Ms. Sally Hoffman, 2522 Strand, Missoula, MT 59801
*Nebraska*
Central Nebraska Retriever Club, Bob McAuliff, 444 Sunset Dr., Hastings, NE 68901
Nebraska Dog & Hunt Club, Ed Schulenberg, 7832 Broadview Dr., Lincoln, NE 68505
Western Nebraska Retriever Club, Tom Southard, North Star Rt., Kimball, NE 69145
*Nevada*
Sierra Nevada Retriever Club, Ms. Sharon Featham, 100 Eleanor Avenue, Reno, NV 89523
*New Jersey*
Garden State Golden Retriever Club, Mrs. Ann Johnson, 1040 Mercer Rd., Princeton, NJ 08540
Shrewsbury River Retriever Club, Dr. Frank S. Moran, Jr., 120 Fair Haven Rd., Fair Haven, NJ 07701
South Jersey Retriever Club, Mrs. Paulette Booth, 920 Coach Rd., Turnersville, NJ 08012
Swamp Dog Club for Training & Trials, Ms. Shirley Racquet, R.D. #1, Box 478, Mohnton, PA 19540
*New Mexico*
Albuquerque Retriever Club, Jim Fanning, 813 Salamanca NW, Albuquerque, NM 87107
*New York*
Black Creek Retriever Club, William C. Royer, Ashdown Rd., R.D. #3, Ballston Lake, NY 12019
Central New York Retriever Club, Robert Orzelek, 49 Adams St., Binghamton, NY 13905
Finger Lakes Retriever Club, Mrs. Archangel Letta, 849 Rt. #21, Shortsville, NY 14548

Long Island Golden Retriever Club, Mrs. Gloria Affattao, 11 Fairway Drive, Rocky Point, NY 11778

Long Island Retriever Trial Club, Ms. Peggy Pendzick, 28 Union Ave., Center Moriches, NY 11934

Westchester Retriever Club, John J. Cassidy, 1123 Cox Crow Rd., R.D. #1, Toms River, NJ 08753

Western New York Retriever Club, Ms. Mary Parker, 101 Rounds Ave., Buffalo, NY 14215

*North Carolina*

Tal Heel Retriever Club, H. M. Dalton, M.D., Doctors Dr., Kinston Clinic North, Kinston, NC 28501

*North Dakota*

Minot Retriever Club, D. B. Whitson, 56 Valley Circle, Minot, ND 58701

North Dakota Retriever Club, Roy Martinson, Rt. #1, Moorhead, MN 56560

*Ohio*

Buckeye Retriever Club, Robert G. Woolham, 2500 Stratford Rd., Cleveland Heights, OH 44118

Ohio Valley Retriever Club, David Maurice, 11715 Smith Road Canal, Winchester, OH 43110

*Oklahoma*

Sooner Retriever Club, Inc., Gay Faulker, Rt. #1, Box 41, Washington, OK 73093

*Oregon*

Oregon Retriever Trial Club, John Poer, 18805 NW Lapine, Portland, OR 97229

Rogue Valley Retriever Club, Ms. Francine Bailey, 3072 Delta Waters Rd., Medford, OR 97501

Shasta Cascade Retriever Club, Rich Hampson, 1117 Laurel St., Klamath Falls, OR 97601

Willamette Valley Retriever Club, Ms. Marge Browning, 28794 Hillaire, Eugene, OR 97402

*Pennsylvania*

Fort Pitt Retriever Club, Mrs. Edwin H. Gott, Jr., 56 Beaver St., Wewickley, PA 15143

Waterland Retriever Club, Meg Evangalist, 317 Waverly Rd., Glenside, PA 15143

*South Carolina*
Palmetto Retriever Club, Waddy W. Chapman, Jr., Rt. #1, Box
261–A, Wedgefield, SC 29168
*South Dakota*
Mount Rushmore Retriever Club, Howard A. Jacobs, 321 Cleve-
land, Rapid City, SC 57701
Sioux Valley Retriever Club, Ken Smail, 423 W. Okabena St.,
Worthington, MN 56187
*Tennessee*
Memphis Amateur Retriever Club, Mrs. Robert R. Milner, Jr., P.O.
Box 281, Grand Junction, TN 38039
Middle Tennessee Amateur Retriever Club, Dr. Edward H. Martin,
1900 Hayes Street, Nashville, TN 37203
*Texas*
Alamo Retriever Club, Mrs. June Varner, 127 Teakwood Lane, San
Antonio, TX 78216
East Texas Retriever Club, Inc., John D. Parker, 1407 Woodland,
Lufkin, TX 75901
Lone Star Retriever Club, Ms. Ellen McCrory, 5457 Holly Spring,
Houston, TX 77023
North Texas Retriever Club, Mrs. Mickey Thompson, 3522 Rankin,
Dallas, TX 75205
Port Arthur Retriever Club, Nolan Montondon, 901 12th Ave., Port
Arthur, TX 77640
South Texas Retriever Club, Paul Provenzano, 121 Poesta, Portland,
TX 78374
*Utah*
Great Salt Lake Retriever Club, Mrs. Hazel Mathews, 340 W. 2650
N. Layton, UT 84041
Northern Utah Retriever Club, Larry McKenzie, 5029 Doren Dr.,
Ogden, UT 84403
*Virginia*
James River Retriever Club, H. Wayne Overton, Jr., 1301 Wilkin-
son Rd., Richmond, VA 23227
*Washington*
Evergreen Golden Retriever Club, Charlotte Davis, P.O. Box 3429
Mid Way Sta., Kent, WA 98031

Northwest Retriever Trial Club, Charles L. Hills, 16718 SE 300 Bellevue, WA 98008

Puget Sound Retriever Club, Chester E. McRorie, 5720 Kaster Dr., Bremerton, WA 98310

Samish Retriever Club, Mrs. Hal Loop, 4796 NW Road, Bellingham, WA 98225

Spokane Retriever Club, Ms. Isabelle Haggarty, 3220 E. 16th, Spokane, WA 99203

Tacoma Retriever Club, Don Hutt, 7604 52nd Ave. West, Tacoma, WA 98467

*Wisconsin*

Badger Golden Retriever Club, Mrs. Mary Newell, 157 N. Dries St., Saukville, WI 53080

Madison Retriever Club, Ken Birkholz, Rt. 1, Nelson Rd., Sun Prairie, WI 53590

Manitowoc County Kennel Club, Mrs. Olga Hoyer, 3054 S. 10th St. Manitowoc, WI 54220

Ozaukee Retriever Club of Wisconsin, Mrs. Nora Larson, N. 28, W 24358, Hwy. SS, Pewaukee, WI 53072

Peaks Lake Retriever Club, Robert L. von Haden, Jr., 1935 Hillview Dr., Green Bay, WI 54302

West Allis Training Club, Lorraine Hill, Rt. 1, Box 607, Waterford, WI 53085

Wisconsin Amateur Field Trial Club, Vern Weber, 5632 County Hwy. MM, Larsen, WI 54947

*Wyoming*

Big Horn Basin Club, Mrs. Norma Young, 876 Riverside Dr., Powell, WY 82435

Central Wyoming Retriever Club, Mrs. F. L. "Dusty" Bacus, 421 Fitzhugh Rd., Casper, WY 82601

Cheyenne Retriever Club, Mrs. Mary McCartney, 216 W. 3rd Ave., Cheyenne, WY 82001

Sheridan Retriever Club, Ms. Paula Hosking, Box 291, Dayton, WY 82836

# A Bibliography for Further Reading

## ABOUT RETRIEVERS

### Compiled and Evaluated by Herm David
#### Updated 1979 by Arthur Liebers

Although this bibliography does not attempt to be all-inclusive, it is probably the most complete ever published on the subject of retrievers. The publications it lists can lead the reader into the furthest realms of our knowledge of retrieverdom. Those few volumes and periodicals which are especially recommended are shown in boldface type. Readers who wish to suggest further entries for use in future editions of *Training Your Retriever* are invited to address the compiler in care of the publisher.

H.D.

## Periodicals

*American Chesapeake Club, Inc. Official Club Bulletin.* Bimonthly. Available to members only. Secretary, Miss Deborah Reaves, 507 N.W. 39th Road, Apt. 157, Gainesville, Fla. 32607.

*American Field.* Weekly. American Field Publishing Company, 222 West Adams Street, Chicago, Ill. 60606. Carries registrations of *Field Dog Stud Book.* Mainly concerned with bird dog field trials. The *FDSB* is a highly respected all-breed registry. Subscription rates: $12.00 per year, $7.00 for 6 months. Single copies 60 cents.

**American Kennel Club,** *List of Judges who have judged stakes carrying championship points during the past five years.* **Twenty stapled letter-size sheets printed both sides for the compiler's copy dated January, 1979. Presumably issued annually, and available to clubs on request.**

*American Kennel Club Stud Book and Register.* Monthly from Vol. I. (1878) to date. American Kennel Club, 51 Madison Avenue, New York, N.Y. 10010. Listing of AKC registrations. Currently, registrations are published only when get are offered for registration. Subscription rates: $18.00 per year (12 issues), Single issues $2.00.

*Canadian Kennel Club Stud Book.* **First published in 1892. Issued annually in spring.** Canadian Kennel Club, 1173 Bay Street, Toronto 5, Ont., Canada. **Contains Canadian registrations and records.**

*Dogs in Canada.* Monthly. Official publication of Canadian Kennel Club. Apex Publishers and Publicity, Ltd., 200 Davenport Road, Toronto, Ont., Canada. Contains schedules and results of trials and shows, proceedings of the CKC.

*Field Trial News. See Retriever Field Trial News.*

*Golden Retriever News.* Publication of the Golden Retriever Club of America. Subscription through annual membership. Editor Susan Fisher, 27140 Irwin Road, Armada, Mich. 48005. News of breed in show, field and obedience activity.

*Kennel Club Calendar and Stud Book.* Published annually since 1874 by the Kennel Club (England). The Kennel Club, 1–4 Clarges Street, Piccadilly, London W.1, England. Contains registrations and results of English trials and shows.

*Kennel Gazette.* Monthly. The Kennel Club, 1–4 Clarges Street, Piccadilly, London, W.1, England. Contains schedules of English trials and shows, proceedings of the Kennel Club.

*Kennel Review.* Monthly. Kennel Review, 3625 Potosi Road, North Hollywood, Calif. 91604. Almost exclusively concerned with dog shows.

*Official Dogs.* Bimonthly. Published by Countrywide Publications, Inc., 257 Park Avenue South, New York, N.Y. 10010. Offers itself as the magazine "for everyone who enjoys dogs." Annual Subscription $6.75. Newsstand price $1.50.

*Pure-Bred Dogs American Kennel Gazette.* Monthly. The American Kennel Club, 51 Madison Avenue, New York, N.Y. 10010. Contains schedules and results of field trials, lists new champions, carries AKC proceedings and rule changes, in addition to articles and breed columns. Yearly subscription $15.00. Single copy $2.50.

*Retriever Field Trial News.* Published by the National Retriever Field Trial Club and the National Amateur Retriever Club 10 times yearly. Robert N. Wolfe, Editor-in-Chief, Mrs. Toni Reynolds, Editor. 4213 South Howell Ave., Milwaukee, Wis. 53207. Subscription $20.00 annually, U.S. Single copies current issues $2.10, back issues $2.20. Higher rates for foreign, Canadian subscriptions. This is the news center and the marketplace for retriever activity afield in the United States and Canada.

### Books and Pamphlets

Alington, Charles, *Field Trials and Judging.* The Kennel Gazette, London 1929, 109 pp. A look at English retriever and spaniel training, trials, and judging.

American Kennel Club, *Complete Dog Book.* Howell Book House, Inc., N.Y. Official descriptions and standards of breeds as recognized by the AKC. Covers breedings, training, care and management. Revised periodically. Purchasers should make certain to get the latest edition.

*American Kennel Club Rules Applying to Registration and Dog Shows.* American Kennel Club, 51 Madison Avenue, New York, N.Y. 10010. Pamphlet. Single copies free upon request. Amended as required.

*American Kennel Club Rules Applying to Registration and Field Trials.* American Kennel Club, 51 Madison Avenue, New York, N.Y. 10010. Pamphlet. Single copies free upon request. Amended as required.

American Kennel Club, *Standing Recommendations of the Retriever Advisory Committee.* American Kennel Club, 51 Madison Avenue, New York, N.Y. 10010. Revised annually or as necessary. Single copies free upon request. Pamphlet offering consensus on the conduct of retriever trials of delegates from all member retriever clubs.

Antuñano, J. A. Sanchez, *Practical Education of the Bird Dog*. American Field Publishing Co., 222 West Adams Street, Chicago, Ill. 60606, 1944, 164 pp. Penetrating insight into psychology of hunting dogs. Much of training described is adaptable to retrievers, although some methods employed are not recommended to the novice by Mr. Free.

Ash, Edward C., *Dogs: Their History and Development*. Two volumes. Houghton Mifflin, Boston and N.Y., nd, circa 1926. Indexed, 27 appendices. This is the classic work on the dog to date. Ash was a careful researcher who, unfortunately, did not always cite his sources of information. If anything, this work is overinclusive.

——, *The New Book of the Dog*. Cassel & Co., London, 1938, 556 pp. Contains British breed standards, general historical information.

——, *The Practical Dog Book*. The Derrydale Press, N.Y., 1931, 375 pp. Includes useful history of retrievers and British breed standards.

——, *This Doggie Business*. Hutchinson & Co., London, 1934, 215 pp. Ash relates many anecdotes of sagacious dogs and their foolish owners and promoters.

Badock, Lt. Col. G. H., *The Early Life and Training of a Gundog*. Watmoughs, Ltd., Idle Bradford, England, 1931, 111 pp. Includes "reclaiming spoiled dog to discipline," English field trials.

Barton, Frank Townend, M.R.C.V.S., *Gun Dogs*. John Long, London, 1913, 318 pp. Brief chapter and photo of each retrieving breed (except Chesapeakes).

Becker, Bob, editor, *Bob Becker's Dog Digest*. Paul, Richmond & Co., Chicago, 1947. Sections on Curly-Coated and Flat-Coated Retrievers by E. D. Knight.

Benson, Frank W., *Modern Masters of Etching, Number Six*. The Studio, London, 1925. Tipped-in litho reproductions of 12 of Benson's etchings. Anything the wildfowl fancier can find of Benson's work is to be treasured.

Bliss, Anthony A., *The Chesapeake Bay Retriever*. American Chesapeake Club, rev. ed., 1936, 63 pp. Includes history, club matters, field rules, standard, list of champions, article on "Speed in Retrievers," numerous illustrations. (*See also A History of the Chesapeake Bay Retriever*, edited by Eloise Heller.)

Bogardus, Capt. Adam H., *Field, Cover and Trap Shooting*. J. B. Ford & Co., N.Y., 1874, 343 pp. True, though boastful, stories of fabulous shooting by a market hunter-marksman.

*Book of Sports, British and Foreign*. Walter Spires, London, 1843. Two volumes in one. Some text, but delightful because of numerous engraved plates.

Brackett, Lloyd, *Planned Breeding*. Dog World, 469 East Ohio Street, Chicago, Ill. 60611. Understandable explanation of canine genetics.

Brice, Major Mitford, *The King's Dogs*. A. & G. Black, London, 1935, 108 pp. George V was a fancier of Labradors. This volume contains many fine photos of his dogs.

Brown, William F., *How to Train Hunting Dogs*. A. S. Barnes & Co., N.Y., 1942, 288 pp. Sound principles of training. Chapter on retriever training.

——, *Retriever Gun Dogs*. A. S. Barnes & Co., N.Y., 1945, 155 pp. The first modern American treatise on retriever training. Chapter on Chesapeakes by Dr. George V. I. Brown.

Bruette, Dr. William A., *Modern Breaking*. Published by author, Newburgh, N.Y., 1906, 169 pp. Training methods for bird dogs, but some fine approaches to the psychology of all hunting dogs.

Buckingham, Nash, *Blood Lines* (1938), *De Shootingest Gentman* (1934), *Game Bag* (1943), *Mark Right!* (1936), *Ole Miss'* (1937), *Tattered Coat* (1939), all pub. by G. P. Putnam's Sons. N.Y., and *Hallowed Years*, Stackpole Co., Harrisburg, 1953. Semifiction. Many appreciative readers consider Buckingham the equal of Mark Twain and Bret Harte. All of these works are treasure chests of delight for wildfowlers and lovers of hunting dogs and/or the gentle life.

Burges, Arnold, *The American Kennel and Sporting Field*, first edition. J. B. Ford & Co., N.Y., 1876, 201 pp., errata slip. Contains first published American kennel registry. Accounts in detail of first shows and field trials in America. Has useful glimpse of Chesapeake history in quote from O. D. Foulks.

——, *The American Kennel and Sporting Field*, second edition. D. S. Holmes, Brooklyn, N.Y., 1882–83, 243 pp. Much changed from the first edition. Burges offers second thoughts on several subjects.

Burtis, Edwin, editor and collector, *All the Best Dog Poems*. Thomas Y. Crowell Co., N.Y., 1946, 252 pp.

Butler, Francis, *Breeding, Training, Management, Diseases, etc., of Dogs*. Pub. by author, N.Y., 1857, 224 pp. Appeared in several editions. One of the earliest American dog books. Butler campaigned for a less fearsome attitude toward rabies, died of the disease from the bite of one of his own dogs.

Buytendijk, F. J. J., *The Mind of the Dog*. Houghton Mifflin Co., Boston and N.Y., 1936, 213 pp. Translation by Lillian A. Clare. A serious and useful study by an outstanding researcher.

Caius, Dr. Johannes, *De Canibus Britannicis*. England, 1570. Separate publication of Caius contribution on dogs to Conrad Gesner's work on natural history. Since republished in several editions. *See also* Fleming, Abraham.

Camp, Raymond R., editor, *Hunter's Encyclopedia*. Stackpole & Heck, Telegraph Press, Harrisburg, Pa., 1948.

Cane, R. Claude. *See* Phillips, C. A.

Carhart, Arthur H., and Young, Stanley P., *The Last Stand of the Pack*. J. H. Sears & Co., N.Y., 1929, 315 pp. The compiler of this bibliography believes there is much to be learned of our domestic dogs from a study of the wild canines. Here are accounts of the elimination of the last of the gray wolves of Colorado by U.S. Biological Survey trappers.

Carlton, H. W., *Spaniels: Their Breaking for Sport and Field Trials*. The Field & Queen (Horace Cox), London, 1915, 115 pp. Insofar as retriever and spaniel training are similar, this work can be a useful look at World War I methods in England.

Carman, E. S., *Ahaodah Society's Views Respecting the Setter and Pointer*. D. Appleton & Co., N.Y., 1872, 135 pp. Penetrating insight into psychology of dog training.

Chapin, Howard M., *The Peter Chapin Collection of Books on Dogs*. The

College of William and Mary Bulletin, Vol. 32, No. 7, Nov., 1938, Williamsburg, Va., 131 pp. Short list of 1,993 titles, probably the longest cynological list ever compiled.

Charlesworth, W. M., *The Book of the Golden Retriever*. The Field, London, nd, circa 1933, 131 pp. Plates historically illuminating, but disregard the breed history as offered in the text.

Colfield, Thomas R., *Training the Hunting Retriever*. Van Nostrand, Princeton, N.J., 1959, 148 pp.

Compton, Herbert, compiler, *The Twentieth Century Dog*. Grand Richards, London, 1904, two volumes.

Connett, Eugene E., editor, *American Sporting Dogs*. D. Van Nostrand, N.Y., 1948, 549 pp. A fine contemporary review by qualified breed authorities including such retriever luminaries as Paul Bakewell, III, Thomas W. Merritt, Walter Roesler, J. Gould Remick, Prentice Talmage, Muriel W. Jarvis and Theodore A. Rehm. A "must" for the complete retriever library.

Corbett, T. M., compiler, *The Dog Owners' Guide and Who's Who in Dogdom*. Watmoughs, Ltd., London, nd, circa 1937, 272 pp. A close look at England's dogdom of the mid-thirties.

Cousté, Col. H., *Mechanics Applied to the Race Horse*. Pub. and translated by E. B. Cassat, N.Y., 1916. Two editions, the second of which is a continuation of the first, which was first published in Paris in 1909, 80 pp. For serious students of animal locomotion, of which, unhappily, there are too few.

Davis, C. T., Henry P., and Marcellus L., *Stranger*. J. B. Lippincott Co., Phila., 1938, 59 pp. Three great dog stories.

Davis, Henry P., editor, *Modern Dog Encyclopedia*. Stackpole & Heck, Harrisburg, Pa., 1949, 626 pp. Authoritative and complete as of the date of publication. A new edition in preparation.

——, *Training Your Own Bird Dog*.

Day, J. Wentworth, *The Dog in Sport*, George C. Harrap & Co., London. Chapter on Chesapeakes.

"Dinks." *See* Peel, Jonathan.

Duffey, David Michael, *Hunting Dog Know How*. Winchester Press, Tulsa, Oklahoma, 1972, 192 pp. Revised Edition. Written by the Dog Editor of Outdoor Life Magazine; practical and easy to apply, readable and down to earth. A book worthy of any sportsman's shelf.

——, *Hunting Hounds: How to Choose, Train and Handle America's Trail and Tree Hounds*. Winchester Press, Tulsa, Oklahoma, 1972, 192 pp. Reference for sportsmen seeking authentic information about origin, development, selection, care and usage of every breed and strain, as well as entertaining reading; full of amusing anecdotes and practical training tips.

Dufresne, Frank. *See* Godfrey, Joe, Jr.

Edward, Second Duke of York, *The Master of Game*, edited by William A. and F. Baillie-Grohman. First edition pub. by Ballantyne & Co., London, 1904. Second edition pub. by Chatto & Windus, London, 1909, 332 pp. This was the first English manuscript on hunting and was, to a degree, an adaptation and translation of Gaston de Foix's *Miroir de Phébus*. *Master* was written between 1406 and 1413. It was not published for nearly 500 years.

Eley, Charles C., *The History of Retrievers*. The Field Press, London, 1921, 206 pp.

Elliott, David D., *The Labrador Retriever*. Privately published by Wingan Kennels, East Islip, Long Island, N.Y., 1936, 29 pp.

Falk, John R., *The Practical Hunter's Dog Book*. Winchester Press, Tulsa, Oklahoma, 1971, 320 pp. Expert advice on everything from selecting the puppy, through training tools and conditioning to advanced field training.

Fischer, Gertrude, *The Complete Golden Retriever*. Howell Book House, Inc., N.Y., 1974, 288 pp. How retrievers began; The Golden Retriever in the U.S. and in Canada; Field Trials; Great Obedience Dogs; Show Ring Competition, and a most informative appendix.

Fleming, Abraham. *See* Caius, John.

Foix, Comte Gaston de. *See* Edward, Second Duke of York.

Frothingham, Robert, compiler. *Songs of Dogs—An Anthology*, Houghton Mifflin Co., Cambridge, Mass., 1920, 175 pp.

Gayot, Eugène, *Le Chien, Histoire Naturelle*. Librairie de Firmin Didot Frères et Cie, Paris, 1867. Two volumes, the second of which contains the illustrations.

"A Gentleman" (Charles Bell?), *The Sportsman's Companion; or an Essay on Shooting*. Robbins, Mills and Hicks, N.Y., 1783. Reprinted by Stackpole & Heck, Harrisburg, Pa., 1948, 209 pp. Annotated and illustrated by Jan Thornton. America's first sporting book.

Gipson, Fred, *Hound Dog Man*. Harper & Bros., N.Y., 1949, 247 pp. Absorbing fiction.

Godfrey, Joe, Jr., and Dufresne, Frank, editors, *Lure of the Open*. Brown and Bigelow, St. Paul, Minn., 1949, 449 pp. An outdoors encyclopedia.

Golden Retriever Club of America, *Golden Retriever, 1950*. Pub. by the author, 1950, Reinhard M. Bischoff, editor-in-chief. Bound in loose-leaf form.

Golden Retriever Club of America, *The Golden Retriever, 1957*. Pub. by the author, Mr. and Mrs. Sam R. Gay, editors. Supplement to the above.

Goodall, Charles, *How to Train Your Own Gun Dog*. Howell Book House, Inc., N.Y., 160 pp. Topics include yard breaking, quartering, response to signals, working in water, retrieving bucks, handling game, with photographs to illustrate the points.

Goodman, Jack, editor, *Fireside Book of Dog Stories*. Simon and Schuster, N.Y., 1943, 607 pp. Anthology of fiction and nonfiction.

Graham, Joseph A., *The Sporting Dog*. Macmillan & Co., N.Y., 1904, 327 pp. Brief chapter on Chesapeakes and Water Spaniels. An outstanding survey of the American sporting dog at the time. Appendix contains interesting Chesapeake standard used at the turn of the century.

Griffith, Beatrice Fox, *Historic Dogs*. Clarence L. Mellor, Inc., Haverford, Pa., 1952, 90 pp. Fugitive publication, useful to cynological students and those interested in dogs in art.

Grinnell, George Bird, *American Game Bird Shooting*. Forest & Stream, N.Y., 1910, 576 pp. Interesting in that this otherwise complete book, in its chapter on dogs, does not mention retrievers.

H. H. (probably Holland Hibbert), *Scientific Education of Dogs for the Gun*. Sampson, Low, Marston & Co., London, nd (circa 1890), 217 pp.

Probably because the name of the author is nowhere officially recorded, this book has been pretty much ignored by retriever historians. It is all but certain that Hibbert was the author—and he was a very early pioneer in the Labrador breed. The first third of this book is devoted to retrievers and wildfowling. Hibbert had some odd ideas about training, including confidence in communication with his dogs by mental telepathy, but his anecdotes are interesting and salted with bits of retriever history.

Haag, William G., *An Ostreometric Analysis of Some Aboriginal Dogs.* Univ. of Kentucky, Reports in Anthropology, Vol. VII, No. 3, Dec., 1948, Lexington, Ky., 160 pp. For the cynologist interested in prehistoric American dogs.

Hallock, Charles, editor, *Sportsman's Gazatteer and Guide.* Forest & Stream, N.Y., 1877, 896 pp. Minute picture of outdoor American sports of the time. Interesting sections on Chesapeakes and Irish Water Spaniels. For a water retriever, a cross of "the smaller kind of Newfoundland, sometimes called the Labrador dog" and a setter is recommended.

Hammond, S. T., *Dog Training.* Forest & Stream, N.Y., 164 pp. Unsung, probably only because they are buried in the back of this training book, are two of the best hunting dog stories in American literature.

Hardy, Capt. H. F. H., *Good Gun Dogs.* Country Life, London, 1930, 92 pp. Sixteen dry point etchings by G. Vernon Stokes beautifully reproduced, including those of Labradors, Irish Water Spaniel and, probably the best, a Golden Retriever.

Hartley, Oliver, *Hunting Dogs.* A. R. Harding Publishing Co., Columbus, O., 1909, 251 pp. Pretty "country," but, since we can learn about our own breeds by studying other breeds, this can offer a welcome glimpse at how some other kinds of hunting dogs operate.

Hayes, Capt. M. H., *Points of the Horse.* Hurst & Blackett, London, 1906, 764 pp. Third edition. There is so little published about canine locomotion, students of this subject are advised to pursue studies of the horse, such as this classic. Third edition is greatly enlarged and corrected, and recommended over earlier editions.

Hazelton, William C., compiler, *Wildfowling Tales.* Pub. by the compiler, Chicago, 1921, 125 pp.

Heller, Mrs. Eloise, editor, *A History of the Chesapeake Bay Retriever.* Pub. by the American Chesapeake Club, San Rafael, Calif., 1959. Edition limited to 500 copies. Available from the editor, 19770 Eighth Street, Sonoma, Calif. 95476.

——, *Retriever Trial Handbook.* Published by author, Sonoma, Calif. Available from author, see address above. An extremely useful booklet for those interested in retriever trials. Contains many records. Recommended for the novice. $3.25.

Herbert, Henry William (Frank Forester), *American Game in Its Seasons.* Charles Scribner, N.Y., 1853, 343 pp., illus. by author.

——, *Frank Forester's Complete Manual for Young Sportsmen.* Stringer and Townsend, N.Y., 1856, 480 pp., illus. by author.

——, *Frank Forester's Field Sports of the U.S.* George Woodward, N.Y., 1848, two volumes. Vol. I, 382 pp., Vol. II, 389 pp. These and other outdoor works by Herbert should delight on armchair evenings. Herbert was an outright genius who excelled when writing of hunting, shooting and nature. In his time his influence was tremendous and it was Herbert who established the pattern for American sportsmanship.

Hibbert, Holland. *See* H. H.

Hildebrand, Milton, "How Animals Run," *Scientific American* magazine, May, 1960, pp. 148–160. Again, for the serious student of canine locomotion.

Hill, Lewis Webb, M.D. *See* Phillips, John C.

Holland, Ray P., *Bird Dogs.* A. S. Barnes & Co., N.Y., 1948, 204 pp. Brief chapters on each of the retrieving breeds.

Hubbard, Clifford L. B., *Literature of British Dogs.* Pub. by the author at Ponterwyd, Wales, 1949, 56 pp. Intended as a predecessor piece for a cynological bibliography which has not, as yet, been completed by Hubbard. Highly useful for its evaluations and information from a scholarly researcher.

——, *Observer's Book of Dogs.* Frederick Warne & Co., London, 1945, 224 pp. A roundup of most of the world's breeds of dogs in a handy form.

Hutchinson, Gen. W. N., *Dog Breaking.* John Murray, London. Appeared in at least ten editions, the first of which was published in 1848. A true classic, this work revolutionized dog training methods and has been much borrowed from since it first appeared. Most editions include excellent woodcuts of various retrievers and retriever crosses.

Hutchinson, Walter, editor, *Hutchinson's Dog Encyclopedia.* Hutchinson & Co., London, nd, circa 1935. Three volumes, 2,034 pp., 2,953 illus. More comprehensive than scholarly, fantastic collection of pictures.

"Idestone." *See* Pierce, Rev. Thomas.

Irish Water Spaniel Association (England), *Year Books, 1927–37.* Pub. by author, Essex, England. Include lists of officers, members, awards, etc.

Kersley, J. A., *Training the Retriever.* Howell Book House, Inc., N.Y., 1971, 183 pp. Firm and original guidelines on the subject, from early principles to advanced training. Fundamental understanding of the dog, scent and training. An invaluable book.

"Killbird, Kit." *See* Percy, W. C.

Klapp, H. Milnor, and Kreider, John, *Kreider's Sporting Anecdotes.* A. Hart, Phila., 1853, 292 pp. Classic hunting stories of early Pennsylvania.

Kreider, John. *See* Klapp, H. Milnor.

Labrador Retriever Club, Inc., *The Labrador Retriever Club, 1931–1961.* Pub. by the author, N.Y., 1962. Contains U.S. field trial records in detail for all AKC-reconized retrieving breeds since the first trials in America; many other valuable lists and statistics. Invaluable to the retriever trialer. Available from the club secretary, addressed in care of the American Kennel Club.

Larson, May, *Kennel, Show and Field.* Charles Scribner's Sons, N.Y., 1948, 258 pp. Useful advice for those who would know more about showing and kennel management.

Latrobe, Ferdinand C., *Iron Men and Their Dogs.* Bartlett Hayward Division, Koppers Co., Baltimore, 1941, 229 pp. History of an industrial firm which includes one chapter on Chesapeakes and another on "Canvasback and Diamondback."

Leach, Maria, *God Had a Dog.* Rutgers University Press, New Brunswick,

N.J., 1961, 560 pp. Exhaustive study of the dog in folklore and religion.

LeClerc, Maurice J., *The Retriever Trainer's Manual*. Ronald Press, N.Y., 1962, 210 pp.

Lee, Rawdon B., *Modern Dogs of Great Britain and Ireland (Sporting Division)*. Horace Cox, London, 1894, 428 pp. Some exceedingly useful historical notes on the retrieving breeds. Some mention of first retriever trials in 1871–72. Also various later editions.

Leedham, Charles, *Care of the Dog*. Charles Scribner's Sons, N.Y., 1961, 257 pp. Rather complete and sensible on its subject.

——, *See also* Pearsall, Milo.

Leighton, Robert, *Dogs and All About Them*. Cassel & Co., London, 1910, 352 pp. Some brief historical notes about the retrieving breeds.

——, *The New Book of the Dog*, Cassel & Co., London, nd, circa 1908. Two volumes, 648 pp. Chapters on retrievers, another on Irish Water Spaniel.

Leonard, R. Maynard, editor, *The Dog in British Poetry*. David Nutt, London, 1893, 350 pp. The best of the cynological poetry collections.

Lewis, E. J., M.D. *See* Youatt, William.

Little, Dr. Clarence C., *Inheritance of Coat Color in Dogs*. Comstock Pub. Division of Cornell Univ. Press, Ithaca, N.Y., 1957, 194 pp. Highly recommended for serious students of canine color genetics.

Lorenz, Dr. Konrad Z., *Man Meets Dog*. Houghton Mifflin Co., Boston, 1955, 233 pp. Pleasurable reading leading to a better understanding of canine psychology and the man-dog relationship.

——, *King Solomon's Ring*. Thomas Y. Crowell, N.Y., 1952, 202 pp. An outstanding naturalist takes a warm look at animals and men. Highly recommended for those who would better understand their own dogs.

Lyon, McDowell, *The Dog in Action*. Orange Judd, N.Y., 1950, 288 pp. The pioneer and still the premier work on canine locomotion. Lyon had wanted to revise and expand this work, but died before he could get the project under way.

Lytle, Horace, *Simple Secrets of Dog Discipline*. D. Appleton & Co., N.Y., 1946, 63 pp. A great deal of insight and useful knowledge in a small package. Lytle wrote several books on hunting dogs, all of which are entertaining, most of which are informative—but this is his most useful.

Maxwell, Bede C., *The Truth About Sporting Dogs*. Howell Book House, Inc., N.Y. 1972. A spectacular study of all the sporting breeds. Now out of print. May be available at your public library.

Miller, Harry, Editor, *Who's Who in Dogdom*. National Research Bureau, Chicago, 1958, 343 pp. Lists many prominent persons, dogs, clubs, records, trials, shows, races, service organizations, etc. Many, many key omissions.

Moffit, Ella B., *Elias Vail Trains Gun Dogs*. Orange Judd, N.Y., 1937, 219 pp. Recommended by Mr. Free for those who want instruction in force training.

Morgan, Charles, *Charles Morgan on Retrievers*. Edited by Ann Fowler and D. L. Walters. October House, N. Y., 1968, 178 pp. One of the important works on retrievers. Excellent on forced retrieving.

Muybridge, E. J. *See* Stillman, Dr. J. B. D.

National Amateur Retriever Club, *Handbook of Amateur Retriever Trials,* published by the author, 1962, 197 pp. Records of Amateur All-Age stakes and National Amateur Retriever Championship stakes. *The Handbook of Amateur Retriever Trials,* 1967 Supplement, 1962–1966. Prepared by the Double Headers and published by the NARC. 8 vols., 177 pp. Compiled by Richard H. Hecker and John W. McAssey.

*The National Retriever Field Trial Club,* 1941–1960. Published by the author, 1961, 147 pp. Detailed records of the National Retriever Championships from the first through 1960. Includes a club history and roster of member clubs.

Norris, Dr. Charles C., *Eastern Upland Game Shooting.* J. B. Lippincott Co., Phila., 1946, 408 pp. Not a retriever book—but a delight to the shooting man and the dog fancier. Has excellent bibliography.

"Old Gamekeeper," *Shooting on the Wing.* Industrial Publication Co., N.Y., 1873, 88 pp.

Onstott, Kyle, *The Art of Breeding Better Dogs.* Denlinger's, Washington, D.C., 1946, 247 pp. A thorough treatise.

Papashvily, George and Helen, *Dogs and People.* J. B. Lippincott, Phila., 1954, 283 pp. Several cuts above the usual run of cynological literature.

Pearsall, Milo, and Leedham, Charles G., *Dog Obedience Training.* Charles Scribner's Sons, N.Y., 1958, 384 pp. Excellent for those interested in obedience training.

Peel, Jonathan, *Dinks on Dogs.* Stringer and Townsend, N.Y., 1850, 74 pp. Second American dog book. A lot of good sense—and a brief mention of retrievers.

Percy, W. C. ("Kit Killbird"), *Principles of Dog Training* (pub. earlier under title *Dog Paths to Success*). Edited by J. Frank Perry, M.D. ("Ashmont"). J. Loring Thayer, Boston, 1886, 61 pp. Considered by some authorities to be a true gem among training books.

Phillips, C. A., and Cane, R. Claude, *The Sporting Spaniel.* Our Dogs, Manchester, Eng., 1906. Also second edition, circa 1927, 159 pp. Chapter on the Irish Water Spaniel and another on the history of water retrievers.

Phillips, John C., and Hill, Lewis Webb, M.D., editors, *Classics of the American Shooting Field, 1783–1926.* Houghton Mifflin Co., Boston, 1930, 214 pp. Reprints of some of the best sporting literature which has appeared in the English language.

Pierce, Rev. Thomas ("Idestone"), *The Dog.* Cassel & Co., London, 1872, 258 pp. Pierce was a controversial, promotion-minded figure of his time. Chapters on retrievers.

Pond, Fred ("Will Wildwood"), editor, *Fugitive Sporting Sketches of Frank Forester.* Pub. by the editor, Westfield, Wis., 1879, 147 pp. *See also* Herbert, Henry William. Pond rescued some treasures.

Redlich, Anna, *The Dogs of Ireland.* Dundalgan Press, Dundalk, Ireland, 1949, 200 pp. Chapter on the Irish Water Spaniel.

Richardson, H. D., *Dogs: Their Origins and Varieties.* Dublin, 1847. (Compiler's American edition copy was pub. by Orange Judd, N.Y., 1865, has 127 pp.) Historical notes pertaining to all the retrieving breeds.

Ross, Estelle, *The Book of Noble Dogs*. Century Co., N.Y., 1922, 298 pp. Dogs in legend, folklore and heroic action.

Sanderson, C. C., editor, *Pedigree Dogs*. G. Howard Watt, N.Y., 1927, 362 pp. Section on retriever breeds with brief accounts by active English breeders of the day, English bench standards.

Sanderson, C. Mackay, *The Practical Breaking and Training of Gundogs*. Our Dogs Pub. Co., Manchester, Eng., nd, circa (second edition) 1942, 147 pp.

Sands, Ledyard, *The Bird, the Gun and the Dog*. Carlyle House, N.Y., 1939.

Saunders, Blanche, *Training You to Train Your Dog*. Second edition. Doubleday & Co., Garden City, 1952, 313 pp. The classic work on obedience training, particularly for competition.

Schley, Frank, *American Partridge and Pheasant Shooting*. Baughman Bros., Frederick, Md., 1877, 222 pp.

Sharpe, R., *Dog Training by Amateurs*. Country Life, London, 1924, 137 pp.

Shaul, H. Edwin, *The Golden Retriever*. Indian Springs Press, Boston, 1954, 119 pp. Chapters on history, show and field trials, breeding, rearing, etc.

Shaw, Vero, and others, *Illustrated Book of the Dog*. Cassel, Petter, Gelpin & Co., London, 1879–1881, 664 pp. Many attractive early color lithographs of dogs, including one showing Flat- and Curly-Coated Retrievers. Chapter on retrievers.

Shelley, Er M., *Bird Dog Training Today and Tomorrow*. G. P. Putnam's Sons, N.Y., 1927, 140 pp. One of the great dog trainers imparts his secrets and his thinking. Shelley was one of the first of the bird dog trainers to appreciate and respect the retrievers. His chapter on force retrieving is especially recommended for those who wish to use this method.

Shields, G. O. ("Coquina"), *The American Book of the Dog*. Rand, McNally & Co., N.Y., 1891, 702 pp. Many articles written by historymakers in their breeds, a detailed insight into American dogdom of the time. Chapters on the Chesapeake Bay Retriever (by George W. Kierstaed) and the Irish Water Spaniel (by P. T. Madison).

Shoemaker, Paul E., *Training Retrievers for Field Trials and Hunting*. Superior Pub. Co., 708 Sixth Ave. N., Seattle, Wash. 98111. A most knowledgeable author.

Skinner, John Stuart, and others, *The Dog and the Sportsman*. Lee & Blanchard, Phila., 1845, 224 pp. The first American book devoted exclusively to dogs. Chapter on "The Newfoundland and Chesapeake Bay Water Dog," wherein was first published the story of "Canton" and "Sailor." Very rare, but required reading for all historians of the Chesapeakes. Skinner founded the *Turf Register* and edited the *American Farmer*. He also served as Assistant U.S. Postmaster General. The etchings are by August Kollner of the U.S. Bureau of Engraving. Unfortunately, they were copied from Smith's English work of a few years earlier—and therefore tell us nothing about the appearance of the American dogs of the time.

Smith, A. Croxton, *About Our Dogs*. Ward, Lock & Co., London, 1931, 448 pp. Chapter on retrievers, photos.

——, *British Dogs*. Collins, London, 1945, 48 pp. Offers a compelling color painting of a Labrador by G. Vernon Stokes.

——, *Gun Dogs: Their Training, Working, Management*. Seeley, Service & Co., London, 1932, 114 pp.

——, *Sporting Dogs*. Country Life, London, and Charles Scribner's Sons, N.Y., 1938, 167 pp. Chapter on retrievers contains useful historical notes. Drawings of a Labrador and a Golden by G. Vernon Stokes.

——, *Tail Waggers*. Country Life, London, 1925, 158 pp. Art edition has 26 tipped-in plates from etchings by Malcolm Nicholson, including a Labrador and a Golden. No publication offers more winning illustrations of dogs. The reproduction of the Golden should attract every devotee of that breed.

Smith, Lt. Col. Charles Hamilton, *Dogs, Vol. I, Vol. IV, Mammalia, Vol. XVIII, The Naturalist's Library*. Edited by Sir William Jardine. Pub. by W. H. Lizars, Edinburgh, nd (listed date, 1839), 267 pp., 33 hand-colored plates. Deals chiefly with the wild dogs of the world as they were then known.

——, *Natural History of Dogs, Vol. II, Mammalia, Vol. XX, The Naturalist's Library Vol. V*. Edited by Sir William Jardine. W. H. Lizars, Edinburgh, 1840, 299 pp., 38 hand-colored plates. Together with the above, this constitutes the first comprehensive treatise in the English language on the canines of the world. Only one work (St. George Mivart's *Monograph on the Canidae*) has since attempted to encompass the same area.

Smith, Lawrence B. (Lon), *Modern Gun Dogs*. Charles Scribner's Sons, N.Y., 1936, 173 pp.

Smythe, Dr. R. H., M.R.C.V.S., *Animal Vision*. Herbert Jenkins, London, 1961, 250 pp. Much here for the hunter who would better understand how his dog and his prey see—and the adaptations of their sight to their ways of eating and surviving. Especially useful to retriever fanciers since injury to and inflammation of the eyes of their dogs is more than ordinarily common.

——, *The Conformation of the Dog*. Popular Dogs, London, 1957, 159 pp. Offered as "A practical guide for judges, owners, breeders and exhibitors." There is much here that is useful, but this compiler shudders to think there may be a new generation of bench judges following the outdated and disproven concepts of canine locomotion which Smythe professes here.

*Sports Illustrated* Editors, *Sports Illustrated Book of Dog Training*. J. B. Lippincott, Phila., 1958, 88 pp. A glossy once-over.

Sprake, Leslie C., and others, *The Popular Retrievers*. Popular Dogs Publishing Co., London, nd, circa 1935, 105 pp. Training, management, field trials and ailments reviewed.

Stillman, J. B. D., M.D., and Muybridge, E. J., *Horse in Motion*. Pub. for Leland Stanford by James R. Osgood & Co., Boston, 1882, 127 pp. plus numerous plates and 11 colored anatomical drawings. Stillman did the text, Muybridge the revolutionary photography. This remains the subject's classic and is an essential for the student of animal locomotion.

Stokes, G. Vernon, R.B.A., *The Drawing and Painting of Dogs*. Vol. XVII, Second Series, The New Art Library. J. B. Lippincott, Phila., 1934, 112 pp. We can all learn from the artist's techniques of observation.

Stonehenge." *See* Walsh, Dr. J. H.

Stonex, Mrs. Elma, *Golden Retriever Handbook*. Nicholson & Watson, London, 1953, 134 pp.

Streever, Fred, *The American Trail Hound*. A. S. Barnes & Co., N.Y., 1948, 202 pp. An authentic work on a particularly American kind of dog. And it is by studying the other fellow's kind of dog that we can learn about our own.

Taplin. W. ("A Veteran Sportsman"), *Sportsman's Cabinet, or a Correct Delineation of the Canine Races*. J. Cundee, London, Vol. I. 1803; Vol. II, 1804. Vol. I 285 pp., Vol. II 312 pp. Fifty etchings from Rinagle, Bewick, Rysbrack and Pugin. most engraved by Scott. Includes one etching of what was called the "water dog."

Taylor, Maj. J. M., *Bench Show and Field Trial Records and Standards of Dogs in America, 1874–1891*. Rogers & Sherwood, N.Y., 1892, 519 pp. A fantastic storehouse of information compiled by a founder of the AKC who was also an early judge, breeder and exhibitor in the field and on the bench. Includes Chesapeake Bay Dog Club's roster and standard. Reprints Stonehenge's standard for Irish Water Spaniels, then used in this country.

——, *Field Trial Records of Dogs in America 1874–1907*. Pub. by the author at Pittsburgh, Pa., and Rutherford, N.J., 1908, 545 pp. Field trial portion of the above brought up to date.

Teasdale-Buckell, G. T., *The Complete English Wing Shot*. McClure, Phillips & Co., and Methuen & Co., London, 1907, 382 pp. A chapter on training retrievers and another chapter which comprises one of the earliest histories of the Labrador. Pictures of several turn-of-the-century English retrievers. The reader should challenge Teasdale-Buckell as he reads him. Buckell was, at least as often as not, grinding some personal ax, or serving the interests of some wealthy patron. For example, this book is dedicated to Holland Hibbert—and there are apologies for Hibbert's dogs when they did not win.

Thomas, Joseph B., M.F.H., *Hounds and Hunting Through the Ages*. Garden City Publishing Co., N.Y., 1937, 253 pp. An interesting look at formal fox hunting and the pleasures to be derived from it.

Thornton, Jan. *See* "A Gentleman."

Tossutti, Hans, *Companion Dog Training*. Orange Judd, N.Y., 1948, 268 pp.

Trapman, Capt. A. H., *Man's Best Friend—The Story of the Dog*. The Macauley Co., N.Y., 1928, 379 pp. Has depth and scholarship. One of the better cynological studies.

Trew Cecil G., *The Story of the Dog and His Uses to Mankind*. E. P. Dutton & Co., N.Y., nd, circa 1939, 207 pp. Well researched, interestingly written.

Underwood, Acil F. *See* Whitney, Leon F., D.V.M.

Vesey-Fitzgerald, Brian, editor, *The Book of the Dog*. Borden Publishing Co., Los Angeles, 1948, 1039 pp. (Compiled in England, printed in Holland.) An encyclopedic work on a generally high level. Chapter on retriever training by P. R. A. Moxon and another on "The Dog in the Shooting Field" by Eric Parker. Brief chapters on each of the retrieving breeds except the Chesapeake.

Wagner, Alice M., editor, *Visualizations of the Dog Standard*. Second edition. Popular Dogs, Phila., 1962, 556 pp. Pictures and bench standards of all AKC-recognized breeds.

Walsh, Dr. J. H. ("Stonehenge"), *British Rural Sports*. Frederick Warne & Co., London, 1855 (many subsequent editions), 892 pp. Walsh is generally viewed as a giant among cynological writers. In his time, and long after, he was the most influential of all men in dogdom. Some of his whims are still slavishly followed, as, for example, some coat color preferences.

——, *The Dog*. Condensed from *British Rural Sports* and other of Walsh's works. London, about 1878.

——, *The Dog in Health and Disease*. Longmans, Green, Reader & Dyers, London, 1859, 468 pp. Many later editions. Woodcuts largely borrowed from Youatt.

——, *Dogs of the British Islands*. Horace Cox, London, 1867. There were five editions, in all, of this work, the last in 1886, two years before Walsh's death. There was so much revision that each of these editions is cherished by those who hold them. Most consider this to have been Walsh's most significant work. It was certainly his most influential book—and probably the most influential dog book ever written by anyone. The compiler's copy is of the third edition, 1878. It has a chapter on retrievers which, oddly, includes the deerhound. There are full-page woodcuts of the Flat Coats "Paris" and "Melody" owned by G. Brewis, and another of Thorpe Bartram's Curly Coat "Nell" and Mr. Morris's "True."

——, *The Greyhound*. Longman, Brown, Green & Longmans, London, 1853 (and several later editions), 400 pp.

Wardle, Arthur, *Elements of Drawing: Dogs*. Stehli Bros., Zurich, nd, circa 1950. Twelve lithographs and artist's comments in a paper folder.

Waters, B., *Fetch and Carry, A Treatise on Retrieving*. Pub. by the author, N.Y., 1895, 124 pp. This little-known work was probably the first American book on retrievers and retrieving. Has a photograph of a Chesapeake and a brief chapter on the breed, another on the Irish Water Spaniel.

Waters, B. ("Kingrail"), *Training and Handling of the Dog*. Little, Brown & Co., Boston, 1894, 332 pp. Chapters on retrieving and quartering.

Watson, James, *The Dog Book*. Doubleday, Page & Co., Garden City, 1906, 750 pp. Reprinted many times, sometimes as one volume, sometimes as two volumes. There was only one edition of this classic work. Watson was an authentic authority and a careful scholar. Three chapters on the retrieving breeds. Photographs of Chesapeakes and Irish Water Spaniels.

Webb, Henry, editor, *Dogs: Their Points, Whims, Instincts and Peculiarities with a Retrospection of Dog Shows*. Dean & Son, London, 1872, 355 pp. First dog book to reproduce photographs. Chapter on retrievers, including a very emotional poem.

Weber, Joseph, *The Dog in Training*. Whittlesey House, N.Y., 1939, 243 pp.

Whitford, C. B., *Training the Bird Dog*. Macmillan Co., N.Y., 1928, 258 pp., revised and amended by Edward Cave. Good training psychology applies equally to bird dogs and to retrievers. Whitford's is one of the best of all of the training books.

Whitney, George D., D.V.M. *See* Whitney, Leon F., D.V.M.

Whitney, Leon F., D.V.M., *Feeding Our Dogs*. D. Van Nostrand, N.Y., 1949, 243 pp. Dr. Whitney's researches did much to revolutionize dog feeding. He writes directly and authoritatively.

——, *How to Breed Dogs*. Orange Judd, N.Y., 1949, revised edition, 441 pp. Whitney is one of the world's leading canine geneticists. Many genetic characteristics are defined and explained.

——, *Complete Book of Home Pet Care*. Doubleday & Co., Garden City, 1950, 522 pp. This work has been condensed into *The Complete Book of Home Dog Care*.

——, *The Truth About Dogs*. Thos. Nelson & Sons, N.Y., 1959, 184 pp. This book created a mild sensation when it first appeared since it attacked some "sacred" institutions. All of it is not worthy of Whitney. Some of his charges have been poorly researched and documented— and some even have a ring of vengeance. However, there is much that is useful and worthwhile in this book.

Whitney, Leon F., and Underwood, Acil F., *Coon Hunter's Handbook*. Henry Holt & Co., N.Y., 1952, 210 pp. Easy route to exploration of another kind of hunting dog pleasure.

Whitney, Leon F., D.V.M., and Whitney, George D., D.V.M., *The Distemper Complex*. Practical Science Pub. Co., Orange, Conn., 1953, 230 pp. For the professional man and the truly serious student.

Wildner, Clare, *Retriever Training*. Outdoorsman, Chicago, 1941, 25 pp. Booklet by a successful trainer.

"Wildwood, Will." *See* Pond, Fred.

Winge, Dr. O., *Inheritance in Dogs*. Comstock Publishing Co., Ithaca, N.Y., 1950, 162 pp. Translated from Danish by Catherine Roberts, Ph.D. Most useful to the student of canine genetics, a bit easier to absorb than Dr. Little's treatise on canine color genetics.

Youatt, William, and Lewis, E. J., M.D., *The Dog*. Leavitt and Allen, N.Y., 1846, 403 pp. Dr. Lewis "Americanized" this edition of Youatt's book, which was first published by Longman, Green in London in 1845. There were many subsequent editions. Has brief but very interesting reference to "small, black, muscular Newfoundlands" being used as sporting retrievers.

Young, Stanley Paul, *The Wolf in North American History*. Caxton Printers, Caldwell, Idaho, 1946, 149 pp. Again, we learn about our domestic dogs by studying the wild ones. And—the wolves have played an important role in North American history. No one has known our wolves and coyotes better than Young.

——, *The Clever Coyote*.

——, *The Wolves of North America*.

——. *See also* Carhart, Arthur H.

# Index

348